17th Workshop of the Australasian Language Technology Association (ALTA 2019)

Sydney, Australia
4 – 6 December 2019

ISBN: 978-1-7138-0074-3

ALTA 2019

**Proceedings of the 17th Workshop of the
Australasian Language Technology Association**

4–6 December, 2019
UTS
Sydney, Australia

Sponsors

ALTA is extremely grateful to the following sponsors who helped make ALTA as accessible to as many NLP researchers as possible

Platinum

Gold

Bronze

IBM **Research** AI

Introduction

Welcome to the 17th edition of the Annual Workshop of the Australasian Language Technology Association (ALTA 2019) in Sydney, Australia. The purpose of ALTA is to promote language technology research and development in Australia and New Zealand. Every year ALTA hosts a workshop which is the key local forum for socialising research results in natural language processing and computational linguistics, with presentations and posters from students, industry, and academic researchers. This year ALTA 2019 is being hosted by the University of Technology Sydney and we acknowledge and pay our respects to the Gadigal people of the Eora Nation, the Boorooberongal people of the Dharug Nation, the Bidiagal people and the Gamaygal people upon whose ancestral lands the university stands.

In total we received 36 paper submissions. We accepted 8 long papers (of 14 submissions), 7 short papers (of 22 submissions) to appear as oral presentations in the programme, giving a total of 15 paper presentations (42% of submissions). Of the 36 submissions 23 were first-authored by students, with submissions from 6 of the 8 states and territories of Australia. We are extremely grateful to the Programme Committee members for their time and their detailed and helpful comments and reviews, both locally and abroad. This year we had committee members from all over the globe including Sweden, Scotland, USA, UAE, and Germany, and 16% of the committee being made up of our near neighbours in New Zealand.

Overall, there are 6 sessions of oral presentations in the programme, two of which are jointly organised with the Australasian Document Computing Symposium (ADCS 2019), starting each day with an ALTA keynote talk. The main workshop follows a tutorial on *NLP for Healthcare in the Absence of a Healthcare Dataset* guided by Sarvnaz Karimi and Aditya Joshi (CSIRO Data61). To encourage a broader participation of the local NLP community we organised a poster session, jointly with ADCS, of which 10 papers were included. These papers have undergone the same double-blind review process as the oral presentations. In addition, this year we also ran a shared task on sarcasm detection organised by Diego Molla-Aliod (University of Macquarie) and Aditya Joshi (CSIRO Data61).

The talks from our keynote speakers reflect the main themes in our workshop as well as the direction in which our field is taking us. Nicholas Evans and Ben Foley present their work on the *New wings for the Library of Babel: The transcription challenge for the world's 7000+ languages*. We face the challenge of creating resources and adapting methodologies for the low-resource domain – which most of the worlds languages fit into – as well as the many tasks that we undertake in the field. Mark Johnson presents research in *Building new kinds of Natural Language Understanding and Conversational AI with Deep Learning*, which reflects the continuing trend towards neural and deep learning methods in natural language processing as well as the need to look beyond the sentence by taking into consideration context from the discourse and document level, to develop more naturalistic language interfaces with AI agents.

ALTA 2019 is very grateful for the financial support generously offered by our sponsors, without which the running of these events to bring together the NLP community of the Australasian region would be a challenge.

We very much hope that you will have an enjoyable and inspiring time at ALTA 2019!

Meladel Mistica, Andrew MacKinlay and Massimo Piccardi

Sydney, December 2019

Organisers:

Local Chair: Massimo Piccardi
Program Chairs: Meladel Mistica
General Chair: Andrew MacKinlay

Program Committee:

Abeed Sarker, Afshin Rahimi, Alistair Knott, Andrea Schalley, Antonio Jimeno, Ben Hachey, Benjamin Boerschinger, Brian Hur, Daniel Beck, David Martinez, Diego Molla, Dominique Estival, Gabriela Ferraro, Gholamreza Haffari, Hamed Hassanzadeh, Hanna Suominen, Hiyori Yoshikawa, Jennifer Biggs, Jeremy Nicholson, Jey-Han Lau, Jojo Wong, Karin Verspoor, Kristin Stock, Laurianne Sitbon, Lawrence Cavedon, Lizhen Qu, Mahsa Mohaghegh, Mariano Phielipp, Mark Dras, Markus Luczak-Roesch, Michael Witbrock, Myunghee Kim, Nitika Mathur, Nitin Indurkhya, Parma Nand, Rolf Schwitter, Sarvnaz Karimi, Scott Nowson, Sharon Gao, Shervin Malmasi, Spandana Gella, Stephen Wan, Sumithra Velupillai, Sunghwan Mac Kim, Timothy Baldwin, Trevor Cohn, Will Radford, Wray Lindsay Buntine, Xiang Dai, Xiuzhen Zhang, Yitong Li

Invited Speakers:

Mark Johnson, Oracle and Macquarie University
Nicholas Evans, ANU; with Ben Foley, University of Queensland

Invited Talks

Mark Johnson: Building new kinds of Natural Language Understanding and Conversational AI with Deep Learning

Deep learning provides new fundamental tools, such as contextualised word embeddings and seq2seq models, that let us build new kinds of Natural Language Understanding apps faster, better and cheaper than ever before. The advanced pattern-matching capabilities of deep learning enable a new approach to app development where the system's behaviour is learnt from training data, dramatically reducing the need for manual scripting. This talk describes how we are using this technology in the Oracle Digital Assistant, focusing especially on Conversational AI. The talk ends with a discussion of how research advances in areas such as explainability, few-shot learning, data augmentation and transfer learning can help this technology achieve its full potential.

Nicholas (Nick) Evans and Ben Foley: New wings for the Library of Babel: The transcription challenge for the world's 7000+ languages

There is increasing awareness that we stand on the brink of massive knowledge loss as perhaps half of the world's languages risk not being learnt by the next generation, and of the attendant urgency of recording them in some form. Yet our conceptions for just how much we should record of each language, if we are to do justice to the intellectual richness of the oral traditions they represent, remain tragically unambitious. How much of the knowledge of English or Chinese-speaking cultures would be captured in ten hours of text, a typical amount to be recorded in a language documentation project? Compare this to the 60 million words or so we have in corpora of Classical Greek or Sanskrit, equivalent to about 6,000 hours of recordings. Is it inconceivable for modern day speech communities, seeking a deep abiding record of their language, to record and transcribe that much data? After all, ten members of a speech community, each recording three hours per day, could gather this much in a year.

The real challenge, as linguists and language community members have come to realise, is the transcription bottleneck, the fact that writing down a transcription of one hour of recording typically takes from 40 to 100 hours (and in the early phases of work almost always at the upper end). The result of this bottleneck is that even if we record something like the above amount, current language documentation methods of a few people working together over three years cannot transcribe more than around 15 hours of primary material. This does not touch the levels needed to give a rich corpus for one language, nor does it reach the one hundred hours normally cited as a necessary minimum for a deep-learning training corpus.

In this talk we describe the TAP initiative – Transcription Acceleration Project – which is a joint enterprise of language documentation fieldworkers, community language users, computational linguists, software engineers and machine learning researchers, supported by the ARC-funded Centre of Excellence for the Dynamics of Language (CoEDL). This project aims to break the impasse posed by the transcription bottleneck while maintaining the language community members' social and cultural roles. TAP's semi-automated speech recognition workflow is designed as a user-in-the-loop architecture which involves critical stakeholders in the process of creating cultural and linguistic artefacts. The tools within TAP aim to improve the transcription experience, and support new ways of working to improve the state of language documentation globally. For Australia and its neighbours, we will be able to secure a much greater proportion of the region's rich but often ignored linguistic cultural heritage – around a quarter of the world's languages – for the generations to come.

PROGRAMME

4th December (Wednesday) Tutorial, Day 1

12:30 - 1:00	Registration
13:00 - 16:30	NLP for Healthcare in the Absence of a Healthcare Dataset Sarvnaz Karimi & Aditya Joshi (CSIRO Data61)

5th December (Thursday) Day 2

8:15 - 9:00	Registration
9:00 - 9:15	Welcome to ALTA 2019
9:15 - 10:15	Keynote: Nicholas Evans (ANU) and Ben Foley (UQ) *New wings for the Library of Babel: The transcription challenge for the world's 7000+ languages* (Session Chair: Tim Baldwin)
10:15 - 10:45	MORNING TEA
10:45 - 12:15	Session 1 – Linguistic Diversity in NLP (Session Chair: Mark Dras) Long papers are 20 minutes and short papers are 12 minutes.

Towards a Robust Morphological Analyser for Kunwinjku (**ALTA Best Student Paper Award**)
    William Lane and Steven Bird
From Shakespeare to Li-Bai: Adapting a Sonnet Model to Chinese Poetry (long)
    Zhuohan Xie, Jey Han Lau AND Trevor Cohn
Readability of Twitter Tweets for Second Language Learners (long)
    Patrick Jacob and Alexandra Uitdenbogerd
A neural joint model for Vietnamese word segmentation, POS tagging and dependency parsing (short)
    Dat Quoc Nguyen
Modelling Tibetan Morphology (short)
    Qianji Di, Ekaterina Vylomova and Timothy Baldwin

12:15 - 13:15	LUNCH
13:15 - 14:15	Keynote 2: Wilson Wong (GO1) *Findability and discoverability in learning and employment*
14:15 - 15:25	Session 2 – Language Use and Applications (Shared ADCS Session, Session Chair: Alistair Moffat) ADCS papers are 25/15 mins and ALTA papers are 20/12 mins for the long/short format

Differences in language use: Insights from job and talent search (ADCS short)
    Bahar Salehi, Borhan Kazimipour and Timothy Baldwin
Character profiling in low-resource language documents (ADCS short)
    Tak-Sum Wong and John Lee
Towards a model for spoken conversational search (ADCS long encore presentation)
    Johanne R. Trippas, Damiano Spina, Paul Thomas, Mark Sanderson, Hideo Joho and Lawrence Cavedon
A multi-constraint hinge loss for named-entity recognition (ALTA short)
    Hanieh Poostchi and Massimo Piccardi

15:25 - 16:00	AFTERNOON TEA

16:00 - 17:25   Session 3 – Application and Evaluation (Session Chair: Andy MacKinlay/Massimo Piccardi)

Grounding learning of modifier dynamics: an application to color naming (short abstract presentation)
    Xudong Han, Philip Shultz and Trevor Cohn
Feature-guided Neural Model Training for Supervised Document Representation Learning (short)
    Aili Shen, Bahar Salehi, Jianzhong Qi and Timothy Baldwin
Red-faced ROUGE: Examining the Suitability of ROUGE for Opinion Summary Evaluation
(ALTA 2nd Place Best Student Paper Award)
    Wenyi Tay, Aditya Joshi, Xiuzhen Zhang, Sarvnaz Karimi and Stephen Wan
Modeling Political Framing Across Policy Issues and Contexts (short)
    Shima Khanehzar, Andrew Turpin and Gosia Mikolajczak
Box Embeddings for Inferring Predicate Entailment (long abstract presentation)
    Ian Wood, Mark Johnson, Stephen Wan, Javad Housseini and Mark Steedman

19:00 - late   DINNER

6th December (Friday) Day 3

Keynote: Mark Johnson (Macquarie University and Oracle)
9:00 - 10:00   *Building new kinds of Natural Language Understanding and Conversational AI with Deep Learning*
(Session Chair: Diego Molla-Aliod)

10:00 - 11:00   MORNING TEA AND POSTER SESSION

11:00 - 12:05   Session 4 – Parsing and Sequential Modelling (Session Chair: Trevor Cohn)

Improved Document Modelling with a Neural Discourse Parser (long)
    Fajri Koto, Jey Han Lau and Timothy Baldwin
Does an LSTM forget more than a CNN? (long)
    Gaurav Arora, Afshin Rahimi and Timothy Baldwin
Domain Adaptation for Low-Resource Neural Semantic Parsing (short)
    Alvin Kennardi, Gabriela Ferraro and Qing Wang
A Pointer Network Architecture for Context Dependent Semantic Parsing (short)
    Xuanli He, Quan Tran and Gholamreza Haffari

12:05 - 13:00   LUNCH

13:00 - 14:00   ADCS Keynote: Guido Zuccon (QUT)
Better Search, Better Health? Search engines, their evaluation and the impact on health decisions

14:00 - 15:00   Session 5 – Science and Medicine (Shared ADCS Session, Session Chair: Sarvnaz Karimi)

Detecting Chemical Reactions in Patents (**ALTA 2019 Best Paper Award**)
    Hiyori Yoshikawa, Dat Quoc Nguyen, Zenan Zhai, Christian Druckenbrodt, Camilo Thorne,
    Saber A. Akhondi, Timothy Baldwin and Karin Verspoor
Identifying Patients with Pain in Emergency Departments
    Using Conventional Machine Learning and Deep Learning (**ALTA 2nd Place Best Paper Award**)
    Thanh Vu, Anthony Nguyen, Nathan Brown and James Hughes
Learning inter-sentence, disorder-centric, biomedical relationships from medical literature (ADCS encore)
    Anton van der Vegt, Guido Zuccon, Bevan Koopman

15:00 - 15:30   AFTERNOON TEA

Table of Contents

Long Papers

Short Papers

Long Papers (Posters)

Short Papers (Posters)

Shared Task (Not Peer Reviewed)

Towards A Robust Morphological Analyzer for Kunwinjku

William Lane and Steven Bird
Charles Darwin University
The Northern Institute

Abstract

Kunwinjku is a polysynthetic language spoken in northern Australia. Members of the community have expressed interest in co-developing language applications which could assist in the production of written language resources for education and language learning. Modelling Kunwinjku morphology is a step towards accomplishing these goals. We discuss some of the modeling challenges presented by Kunwinjku verbal morphology, and in polysynthetic languages more generally. We show that a model using standard features of the *Foma* toolkit can account for much of the verb structure. Our contributions include the first morphological analyzer for Kunwinjku, and a discussion of polysynthetic language features and how they affect modelling decisions. Continuing challenges include robustness in the face of variation and unseen vocabulary, as well as how to handle complex reduplicative processes.

1 Introduction

Kunwinjku is an Aboriginal language of the Gunwinyguan language family (ISO gup), spoken by about 2000 speakers in the West Arnhem region of northern Australia. Several Kunwinjku communities have shown interest in leveraging technology to support the production of literacy materials and language learning applications (Bird, 2018).

A major focus of our research group is to implement language technologies that have positive social impact, such as a morphologically-aware dictionary which lowers the barrier to entry for users who cannot reliably identify or spell citation forms (Hunt et al., 2019; Arppe et al., 2016), or a tool that generates linguistic structures which could help language learners master conjugation and verb structure (Kazantseva et al., 2018).

One thing that these applications have in common is the need to decompose and manipulate text at the level of morphology. In order to accomplish this, we must address polysynthesis, morphophonemic alternations, incorporation, reduplication, and long-distance dependencies. Which aspects of morphosyntax can we model? What are the limitations of computational approaches for modeling polysynthetic languages more generally?

In the sections that follow, we will first give an overview of those features of the language which affect how we approach the modelling task (sec 2). Next, we introduce our data sources and the metrics we use to evaluate performance (sec 3). This is followed in section 4 by a detailed description of our implementation and how we addressed the linguistic features described in section 2. Finally, we report accuracy and coverage on both a development data set and a blind test set, provide an error analysis and discussion, and conclude with some thoughts on future directions. To our knowledge, this is the first morphological analyzer for Kunwinjku.

2 Features of Kunwinjku Verbs

We model and evaluate the morphosyntax of Kunwinjku verbs according to Evans' *Pan-dialectal Grammar* (Evans, 2003). In this section we describe some of these features, and follow-up later with how we account for them in the model.

2.1 Polysynthesis and Agglutination

Kunwinjku is a polysynthetic language, with verb roots having 12 prefix slots including the subject/object/tense pronominal, directional, benefactive, incorporated nominals, and comitative affixes (Figure 1). There are 3 suffix slots for indicating reflexivity, tense/aspect/mood, and case. (In limited cases, embedding one verb in another is allowed between the -1 and 0 slots).

−12	−11	−10	(−9)	(−8)	(−7)	(−6)	(−5)	(−4)	(−3)	(−2)	(−1)	0	+1	+2
Tense	Subject	Object	Directional	Aspect	Misc1	Benefactive	Misc2	Gen.inc.nom	Bod.par.inc.nom	NumeroSpacial	Comitative	Verb Stem	RR	TAM

Figure 1: Verbal affix positions in Kunwinjku. Regions where indices share a cell ([−12,−10], [+1,+2]) indicate potentially fused segments. Slot indices in parentheses indicate optionality. Adapted from (Evans, 2003, Fig 8.1).

The morphology is described as agglutinative, almost "lego-like" (Evans, 2003; Baker and Harvey, 2003), though with some unusual morphophonemic alternations involving glottal stop, long distance dissimilation of peripheral nasals, and complex types of reduplication. Additional complexity can be found in the peripheral "fusion zones" spanning slots [−12, −10] and [0, +2].

2.2 Noun Incorporation

Figure 1 shows the optional slots −4 and −3, labeled for the general incorporated nominal (GIN), and the body part incorporated nominal (BPIN), respectively. The GIN class represents a closed set of nouns which, after losing their gender/class and case inflections, can be injected into the verb to satisfy valency. Consider the incorporable noun *kunrerrng* "wood", and the phrase *karrimang* "we would go get." To form the phrase "we would go get wood" using noun incorporation, *kunrerrng* loses its noun class inflection *kun-*, and is placed in slot −4:

(1)   a. karri-ma-ng kun-rerrng
         1pl-get-past IV-wood

      b. karri-rerrng-ma-ng
         1pl-GIN.wood-get-past
         'We would go and get wood' [E.145]

Nouns from the BPIN class perform a similar function, with the characteristic difference of being loosely associated with the human corporal form (an arm, a leg, your shadow, etc). Here we see the noun *kunkanj* "meat," loses its noun class inflection *kun-* and is placed in the verb slot at −3:

(2)   a. bi-ngu-neng   kun-kanj
         3sg.3Hsg.past-eat-past IV-meat

      b. bi-kanj-ngu-neng
         3sg.3Hsg.past-BPIN.meat-eat-past
         'He is eating meat' [E.687]

Additionally, BPIN is an *open* class.

2.3 Valency-affecting prefixes

As can be seen in Figure 1, Kunwinjku allows for 15 morph slots to complete a verb form. Transitivity of the verb is lexically defined, but there are three morph slots which signal valency change and affect the resulting semantic interpretation: the benefactive (BEN), comitative (COM), and reflexive (RR) (Evans, 2003; Ponsonnet, in press).

The following subsections describe the morphemes which affect the valency of the verb.

2.3.1 Benefactive marne-

The benefactive prefix indicates that one of the verb objects is the beneficiary of the action of the verb. For example, the English verb for *say* in Kunwinjku is translated as *yime*, and is designated by the grammar as intransitive. Consider the case where *yime* is paired with the benefactive *marne-* prefix:

(3)   ben-marne-yime-ng
      3sg.3pl.past-BEN-say-PastPerf
      'He told them' [E.637]

We see that this prefix opens up the intransitive verb, in this case *yime*, to the possibility of taking on the 3rd person plural object. That object can be present in the verb itself via the pronominal or an incorporated noun, or it could be located outside of the verb entirely.

2.3.2 Comitative yi-

The comitative slot is located at position −1. Its presence extends verb valency by 1. If the verb root is intransitive, the COM indicates that the additional object is "with" (accompaniment, not instrumental) the subject of the verb. For example:

(4)   ben-yi-yibme-ng
      3sg.3pl-COM-sink-PastPerf
      'He took them down under the water' [E.433]

If the verb root is transitive, then it conveys the meaning that the new argument accompanies the object of the transitive verb. For example:

(5)   nga-kole-yi-kurrme-ng
      1sg.3sg-GIN.spear-COM-put.down-PastPerf
      'I left the spear with him' [E.433]

2.3.3 Reflexive and Reciprocal -rre

Reflexivity and reciprocity are expressed using the morph *-rre* in slot +1. In either case, the result is that the valency of the verb is reduced by 1.

(6) bene-marne-kinjwe-rre-nj
    3ua.3sg-BEN-be.jealous-RR-PastPerf

    'They were jealous of each other over
    him.' [E.430]

In this example, *bene-* is the 3rd person dual
subject (those two) with a 3rd person singular object. The reflexivity occurring after the verb root
directs the action of *being jealous* back onto the
subject, with the indirect object (the 3sg "him")
remaining unaffected.

2.4 Morphophonemic Considerations

Where morphs combine, there are a few morphophonemic patterns to account for. The
most widespread is that of *d-flapping*, where
morpheme-initial *d* becomes *rr* after vowel-final
syllables. For example, the inflected form *nga-*
rranginj has the verb root *dangen*, but we see the
d has been changed to *rr* because it is preceded
by the syllable *nga* which contains a syllable-final
vowel. While this rule is fairly regular, Evans'
grammar also recognized cases where the pattern doesn't seem to apply and concludes that "a
fuller understanding of stress and prosody will be
needed before such examples can be accounted
for". Take the verb "dirri", "to play" for example:

(7) a. * nga-rrirri-$\emptyset$

     b. * nga-rridi-$\emptyset$

     c. nga-dirri-$\emptyset$
         1sg-play-nonpast
         'I play'

Another morphophonemic pattern is the deletion of morpheme-initial *r* following apical consonants *rr*, *l*, and *n*. In careful speech and written Kunwinjku, this pattern is not always obliga-
tory; Evans argues that it is not evident whether
these changes should be treated as "fast-speech
phenomena" and therefore not shown in the orthography. The most consistent example of this
alternation that we have seen is that of $r \rightarrow \emptyset \| rr\_$,
which manifests itself in the example of *ngarr-re*
which becomes *ngarre, we two go*.

There are other morphophonemic changes that
occur in Kunwinjku speech, but which do not appear to be reflected in the accepted orthography.
Evans posits that since the Kunwinjku dialect has
a longer tradition of literacy (relative to other dialects), these changes are not usually reflected in
the written medium. Some of the phenomena that
fall into this camp are specific cases of *nasal as-*
similation, and *peripheral dissimilation*. Since the
goal of our morphological analyzer is to recognize the inflected forms of written verbs, we avoid
giving a more complete description of morphophonemic processes which do not impact the standard written form. It is important to note however that these processes may cause variation in
how speakers of the language write. A truly robust analyzer intended for applications like spell-
checking would need to consider such processes
as they manifest themselves in human input.

2.4.1 Reduplication

Kunwinjku has three main types of partial verbal
reduplication signalling iterative, inceptive, and
extended meaning. Moreover, each type of reduplication can have more than one consonant (C)
and vowel (V) reduplicative pattern, depending on
which of the 11 verb form paradigms the verb belongs to. See Figure 2 for details.

Computational modeling of partial reduplication in human language using finite state transducers (FSTs) has been addressed in the past (Culy,
1985; Roark et al., 2007; Dras et al., 2012), with
the general consensus being that these kinds of
partially reduplicative processes explode the state
space of the model, and are therefore highly bur-
densome to develop. More recent work addresses
these challenges using 2-way FSTs (Dolatian and
Heinz, 2018, 2019), and offers a promising future
avenue of exploration for our work with Kunwinjku. We include reduplication in this paper for the
sake of completeness (see Figure 2), but acknowledge that a solution lies beyond the scope of this
work.

3 Data and Metrics

As mentioned previously, the grammar implementation is based on (Evans, 2003). The lexicon
was subsequently expanded using the resources
curated at kunwok.org, a website dedicated to
open sharing of content and teaching the Kunwinjku language (Bird and Marley, 2019), as well as
the verbs from the online Kunwinjku dictionary
at njamed.com (Garde et al., 2019). In terms of
written or digital language materials Kunwinjku is
firmly in the low-resource camp, though we are in
the favorable position of being supported by motivated native speakers who work with us to clarify
questions about language data.

Type of reduplication	Pattern(s)	Unreduplicated Verb	Reduplicated Verb	Semantic Effect on the verb (V)
Iterative	CVC	dadjke = cut	dadj-dadjke = cut to pieces	Doing V over and over again
	CV(C)CV(h)	bongu = drink	bongu-bongu = keep drinking	
	CVnV(h)	re = go	rengeh-re = go repeatedly	
Inceptive	CV(n)(h)	yame = spear (something)	yah-yame = try (and fail) to spear (something)	Failed attempt to do V
		durnde = return	durnh-durnde = start returning	Starting to do V
Extended	CVC(C) ‖ _ men	djordmen = grow	djordoh-djordmen = grow all over the place	Doing V all over the place
	CVC(C) ‖ _ me	wirrkme = scratch	wirri-wirrkme = scratch all over	

Figure 2: Reduplication in Kunwinjku has three forms, and each form has its own patterns defining how much of the verb is captured and copied. In the case where we've used the form X ‖ _ Y, we mean that pattern X is the reduplicated segment if found in the context of Y. Figure adapted from (Evans, 2003).

To construct our development corpus of inflected verbs, we extracted all of the Kunwinjku examples from the reference grammar; a total of 567 glossed verbs. We further refined the list to exclude cases of reduplication (cf 2.3.4) which left us with 530 verbs which we used to produce a data set to support the development of the FST.

Additionally, we glossed a small set of 114 verbs randomly sampled from the Kunwinjku translation of the Bible, for the purpose of judging how well the FST generalizes to another domain. The Bible translation was recently completed in 2018, and targets the modern vernacular.

We use accuracy and coverage to measure the effectiveness of the model on the development data set as well as the test set.

4 Implementation

Finite state transducers are viewed as an ideal framework to model morphology (Beesley and Karttunen, 2003; Chen and Schwartz, 2018; Lachler et al., 2018). Our FST was implemented using the *Foma* toolkit (Hulden, 2009) which is a popular framework for building morphological analyzers for polysynthetic languages (Chen and Schwartz, 2018; Moeller et al., 2018; Littell, 2018). The definition of an FST in *Foma* is comprised of a lexicon implemented in the *.lexc* format, and a *.foma* file for defining rules covering regular morphophonemic changes. The final FST is produced by composing the FSTs defined in both files.

4.1 The .lexc file

The *.lexc* file contains definitions of lexicon groups corresponding to morphological units of the language. Lexical entries of the group are listed below the group definition. Each entry in the lexicon is paired with its *continuation class* which defines legal paths through the FST, enforcing valid sequences of morphs. Figure 3 gives a

```
LEXICON TSOPreBase
[V][1sg.nonpast]:nga GINPreBase ;

LEXICON GINPreBase
[GIN]:0  IncNounBase  ;
0  PostNominal  ;

LEXICON IncNounBase
0:kanj PostNominal ;

LEXICON PostNominal
@R.TYPE.VERB@ IntransVerbs  ;

LEXICON IntransVerbs
ngu V3IrrPostBase ;

LEXICON V3IrrPostBase
[NonPst]:n  #;
```

Figure 3: Lexicon groups are defined in the *.lexc* file using the LEXICON keyword. Valid paths through lexicons are defined on an entry-by-entry basis. Here each lexicon only has one entry, and there is only one path through the graph. The accept state in the graph is signaled by the # character.

stripped-down example of this by implementing a *.lexc* file capable of mapping the inflected Kunwinjku verb *ngakanjngun*, "I am eating meat", to its analysis: *1sg.nonpast-GIN.meat-eat-nonpast*.

In general, slot positions in the grammar mapping to lexicons in the implementation have a one-to-many relationship, that is, one slot can be satisfied by an entry from one of many lexicon groups. In the example of Figure 3, we show only 4 lexicons filling 4 of the available 16 positions: *TSOPrebase* corresponding to the entry which fuses the morph positions spanning indices $[-12, -10]$, *GINPrebase* corresponding to the morph position at index -4, *IntransVerbs* corresponding to the verb root at index 0, and *V3IrrPostBase* corresponding to the suffix at index $+2$. Our complete implementation contains 63 lexicons, each of which map to one of the 16 slots defined in the grammar.

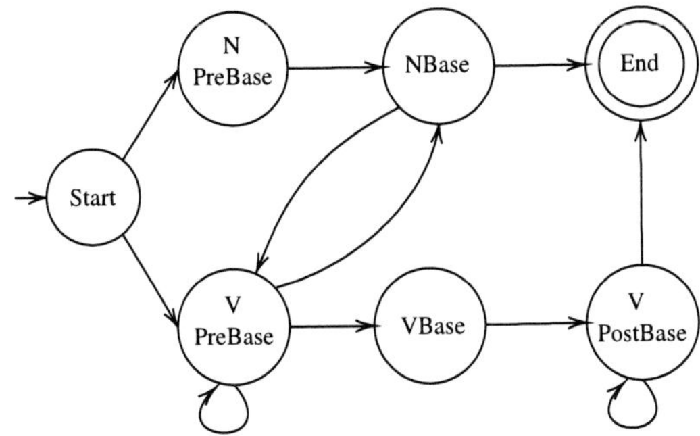

Figure 4: A high-level overview of the morphological analyzer. Verbal prefix lexicons are represented by *VPreBase*, verb root lexicons are represented by *VBase*, and verbal suffixes are represented by *VPostBase*.

4.1.1 Noun Incorporation

We handle noun incorporation similarly to Chen and Schwartz (2018): we allow transitions from states in the verbal pre-base lexicons (specifically, the GIN and BPIN slots) to the noun base lexicon (see Figure 4). We use flag diacritics to enforce constraints on word type: if the word begins with verbal morphology and crosses into the noun base via incorporation, it can only be recognized as a valid string if it also ends with verbal post-base morphology.

As described in Figure 3, we define *GINPre-Base* as a lexicon which points to the IncNoun-Base class, which enumerates the closed class of incorporable nouns. Similarly, we define a lexicon named *BPINPreBase* representing the open class of body part nouns which can be incorporated, and which fill the optional position at index -3.

4.1.2 Tense Agreement

The inflected Kunwinjku verb requires agreement between tense in the pronominal prefix and the TAM suffix. To address this we need to discriminate between ambiguous paths in the FST based on a feature value that is set at some node in the graph and persists to enforce agreement downstream. In Foma, we use flag diacritics to implement this. Flag diacritics take the form of *@FLAGTYPE.FEATURE.VALUE@* where *FLAGTYPE* defines the behavior of the flag, selected from the set of predefined flag types, and *FEATURE* and *VALUE* must be defined by the user (Hulden, 2011). We make use of flag types *P* and *R* in our implementation of tense agreement. *P* defines the action of setting *FEATURE* to *VALUE* and *R* defines the action of requiring

that *FEATURE* equal *VALUE* in order to remain a valid path.

We define the following tags to enforce tense agreement:

1. @P.TENSE.PAST@
2. @P.TENSE.NONPAST@
3. @R.TENSE.PAST@
4. @R.TENSE.NONPAST@

To see how this works in the *.lexc* format, we update the example in Figure 3 to reflect the enforcement of tense agreement between the pronominal and the tense inflection on the verb using flag diacritics (Figure 5). Notice how *@P.TENSE.PAST@* is present before the continuation class transitions in the new TSOPreBase lexicon: this effectively labels all paths proceeding from this point as having the attribute *TENSE* set to a value of *PAST*, indicating that this path will agree with any attempt to enforce agreement with a past tense. Indeed, at the bottom of Figure 5 we see the *@R.TENSE.PAST@* diacritic on both the up and down side of the transducer, indicating that in either direction[1] if we match the morphological entry, the path we've taken must also match the *TENSE* flag feature value in order for the analysis to be valid.

4.1.3 Valency Agreement

As described in 2.3, the valency of the verb is affected by the presence of certain prefixes: the benefactive *marne-*, the comitative *yi-* and the reflexive *rre-*. Our initial belief was that in order to analyze an inflected verb in Kunwinjku, it would be necessary to model these valency changes. We saw no reason to allow the FST to generate analyses which seemed to demonstrate valency imbalance in either the direction of over-saturation or under-saturation. For example, the following verbs seem to provide too many or too few arguments:

(8) bi-marne-bong-yo-y
     3sg.3Hsg.past-BEN-GIN.string-lie-PP
     +2   −1   +1   −1   0

‘He had the string lying there for her’ [E.429]

---

[1] If you label a continuation class with a flag diacritic, it has the same effect as if you explicitly label both sides of the FST up/down transitions inside that continuation class with a diacritic flag.

```
LEXICON Root
@P.TYPE.VERB@ TSOPreBase ;

LEXICON TSOPreBase
@P.TENSE.PAST@ SingleIntransPastTSO ;

LEXICON SingleIntransPastTSO
[V][1sg.past]:nga GINPreBase ;

LEXICON GINPreBase
[GIN]:0 IncNounBase ;
0 PostNominal ;

LEXICON IncNounBase
0:kanj PostNominal ;

LEXICON PostNominal
@R.TYPE.VERB@ IntransVerbs ;
@R.TYPE.NOUN@ # ;

LEXICON IntransitiveVerbs
ngu V3IrrPostBase ;

LEXICON V3IrrPostBase
@R.TENSE.PAST@[NonPst]:@R.TENSE.PAST@n #;
```

Figure 5: Updating our *.lexc* file to constrain possible paths through the FST based on the value of the TENSE feature. Shown also is a diacritic enforcement of word type in the PostNominal lexicon.

(9) Ø-djare-ni
3sg.past-want-PastImperf
+1   −2   0

'He was wanting _' [E.229]

However, both of the above examples are valid. In these glossed examples, we've added a row under the morpheme analysis to mark which morphemes satisfy valency (+1 if it represents 1 object, +2 if it represents 2 objects), morphs which increase the valency of the verb (−1 if it demands 1 object, etc), and morphs which have no effect on valency (0). This allows us to do the simple arithmetic to convince ourselves that (9) is over-saturated, while (10) is under-saturated.

In (9), we have a subject ("he") and two object candidates ("her" and "the string"). The verb root "yo" ("to lie") is inherently intransitive, and the presence of *marne-* opens up room for the verb to take an additional argument as the benefactor: "her". In this instance, the verb appears to be saturated, leaving "the string" to act rather as specification of the verb "yo". As this case shows, ambiguity around when an incorporated nominal is acting as an object rather than providing referential specification impedes the attempt to model valency based on surface form morphology alone.

In (10), the object of the transitive verb for *want* is not incorporated, but exists in the wider sentential context. This implies that valency cannot be disambiguated without reference to syntactic context. Indeed, a syntactic concept can be expected to have syntactic scope, and it is not uncommon for languages containing valence-altering morphs to provide valence-satisfying objects outside of the verb (Haspelmath and Müller-Bardey, 2004). In light of this, we decided to take a permissive stance, allowing valence-imbalanced analyses at the level of individual verbs.

4.2 The .Foma File

The *.Foma* file is the place to encode morphophonological rules in the form of $A \rightarrow B \| \Gamma \_ \Delta$, ie "A changes to B in the context $\Gamma \_ \Delta$", where A and B are orthographic symbols representing phonemes which alternate in the given context. These rules define an FST which can then be composed with the lexicon FST defined in the *.lexc* file, resulting in a final FST representing the complete grammar. Since Kunwinjku is largely agglutinative, with relatively little morphophonemic change to account for. This makes the content of our *.Foma* file a relatively simple composition of three parts: A list of special symbols we define to make our rules more compact, an enumeration of allophonic rules, and finally the composition of the lexicon with the rules to produce the final grammar.

In Figure 6 we give a Foma file that maps the intermediate from *karri^bim^bu^~om* to the correct final surface form, *karribimbom*. First, the *DeletePrecedingVowel* rule is activated by the observation of a vowel "u" followed by the morpheme boundary marker "^" and the "~", which is an arbitrary symbol we encode in the lexicon to indicate that the TAM inflection *om* tends to override any final vowel in the preceding morpheme. The context is recognized, and the vowel is deleted (changes to 0) followed by deletion of the "~" itself. Application of this first rule now yields *karri^bim^b^om*. But we aren't done yet: the cleanup step occurs with the *CleanMorphBoundaries* rule, which recognizes the "^" symbol in any context, and deletes it. We now have the final form *karribimbom*; "we painted".

```
read lexc kunwok.lexc
define Lexicon;

define V [ a | e | i | o | u ];

define CleanMorphBoundaries "^" -> 0;

define DeletePrecedingV V -> 0 || _ "^" "~" .o.
                        "~" -> 0 ;
    .
    .
    .
define FlapChange "(rr)" -> r r || V "^"_ .o.
                  "(rr)" -> d ;

define Grammar Lexicon                    .o.
               DeletePrecedingV           .o.
                      .                    .o.
                      .                    .o.
                      .                    .o.
               FlapChange                 .o.
               CleanMorphBoundaries ;

regex Grammar;
```

Figure 6: An example of our *.Foma* file. We define phonemic rules which are applied to the *Lexicon* FST by composition, which produces a new and final FST named *Grammar*

5 Evaluation

The final FST implements the rules required to produce verbs in Kunwinjku. This includes 157 pronominal entries (including variations reflecting combinations of tense and transitivity), 23 adverbial/aspective/quantitative modifiers of the verb, 77 general incorporable nouns (a closed class), 31 body part incorporable nouns (an open class), 541 verb roots, and 124 TAM inflection possibilities. As mentioned in section 3, we extracted 530 inflected verb forms from the Evans' grammar which we used to optimize coverage and accuracy. Accuracy in this context refers to the number of correct analyses out of the set of analysis the FST attempted. We calculate it this way to avoid double-counting information already captured in the coverage metric. Those numbers are shown in Figure 8, along with the reported performance over the test set.

6 Discussion

In order to better understand the performance of the FST, we analyzed the coverage and accuracy on the Bible dataset and identified four classes of error: missing verb root, missing incorporated nominal, irregular inflection patterns, and reduplication (see Fig 7).

The most common error type is *missing verb root*, which represents 47% of errors. Similarly,

missing incorporated noun, which accounts for another 29%, for a total of 76% of errors due to missing lexical entries. We posit that while it may be possible to infer unseen roots by recognizing the surrounding inflection and stripping it away, the presence of unseen incorporated nouns which attach directly to the verb root have the potential to complicate the matter. However, stemming like this would be sufficient for automatically discovering potential verb roots from unannotated text, which can then be verified by language experts prior to adding them to the lexicon.

Reduplication represents 18% of errors. As we discussed in 2.3.4, there are potential solutions including 2-way FSTs (Dolatian and Heinz, 2018, 2019), and the possibility that neural approaches to morphological analysis could learn to recognize reduplication through supervised learning (Micher, 2017; Moeller et al., 2018; Schwartz et al., 2019). It would be interesting to observe a similar error analysis on a much larger sample size to see if this rate of reduplicative structure holds, and to get an idea for the relative distribution of reduplicative structure in Kunwinjku.

The least common class of error contained a single instance: *Irregular inflection pattern*. Here, a path through the FST could not be found because we come across irregular variation of the TAM inflection. Whether this represents an entire class of error or is caused by simple orthographic variation is unknown: the question requires a larger sample size and consultation with language experts.

7 Conclusion

Kunwinjku is low-resource Australian language for which we would like to develop useful language learning applications. Being able to model the rich verbal morphology is an important step towards that goal. In this work, we identified several areas of Kunwinjku morphology which fit well within the framework of finite state transduction, and some for which a different approach may be better suited to the task. FSTs do well at handling the templatic structure of polysynthetic morphology. For languages which exhibit high rates of allomorphy and morphophonemic change, the ability to compose multiple FSTs into a final grammar has been shown to be quite effective (Chen and Schwartz, 2018; Littell, 2018).

The most significant shortcomings of our FST are expanding the lexicon, accounting for redupli-

	Verb Form	Meaning/Problem
	ngurrimirnde**mornnamer**ren	bear/place on the shoulders
	wobekkang	variation of *bekkan*; to hear about
	nga**kohbanjminj**	become an old person
Missing Verb Root - 47%	ngar**rukkendi**	variation of *dukkan*; tie up; put in handcuffs
	nga**djareni**wirrinj	variation of djare; to want
	yi**djareni**wirrinj	variation of djare; to want
	ka**menyime**	variation of menmenyime; to mean
	yiwernh**marnedjaren**in	variation of marnedjare; to love somebody
	yiben**kange**marnbom	heart
	kan**kange**murrngrayekwong	heart
Missing Inc. Noun - 29%	kan**njilng**marnbom	feelings
	yi**malng**darrkiddi	soul
	kan**kange**marnbom	heart
	burrbuhburrbun	keep thinking
Reduplication - 18%	**djawah**djawan	keep asking; plead
	djawahdjawani	keep asking; plead
Irreg. TAM Inflection - 8%	ngayimer**ranj**	expected past perfect *-inj* TAM suffix

Figure 7: The inflected verbs from the Bible test set for which the FST had no analysis, sorted into one of the four buckets for error analysis. The **bold substrings** are the morphs which the FST could not account for.

	Coverage	Accuracy
Kunwinjku Bible-Test	85.09	97.94
Evans Grammar-Dev	97.17	95.28

Figure 8: Coverage and accuracy of the FST model of verbs in Kunwinjku. The Evans Grammar represents the data we optimised our FST against. The Kunwinjku Bible data is a blind test set.

cation, and being robust in the face of variation in form and orthography.

Additionally, we could have benefitted from a much larger annotated test set. While the Bible set was sufficient to point out the issue of lexicon coverage in our FST, more data could help solidify the relative importance of the other much smaller error classes. It could also give us more insight into the distribution of other constructions in Kunwinjku, which may inform the pedagogical aspect of designing language learning applications in a low-resource setting.

In future work we hope to expand the lexicon of this tool in parallel with developing other approaches to morphosyntactic analysis. Specifically, recent work in bootstrapping recurrent neural models using an FST to generate training examples has showed significant increase in coverage and accuracy in other polysynthetic environments (Micher, 2017; Moeller et al., 2018; Schwartz et al., 2019).

Acknowledgments

We are grateful for the support of the Warddeken Rangers of West Arnhem. We thank Maïa Ponsonnet for her valuable insights into Gunwinyguan morphology, syntax and semantics. We also thank Alexandra Marley for contributing her expertise on Kunwinjku morphosyntax. This research has been supported by grants from the Australian Research Council and the Indigenous Languages and Arts Program of the Federal Department of Communication and the Arts. Finally, we would like to thank the three anonymous reviewers for their constructive feedback.

References

Antti Arppe, Jordan Lachler, Trond Trosterud, Lene Antonsen, and Sjur N Moshagen. 2016. Basic language resource kits for endangered languages: A case study of Plains Cree. *Collaboration and Computing for Under-Resourced Languages: Towards an Alliance for Digital Language Diversity*, pages 1–8.

Brett Baker and Mark Harvey. 2003. Word Structure in Australian Languages. *Australian Journal of Linguistics*, 23:3–33.

Kenneth R Beesley and Lauri Karttunen. 2003. Finite-state morphology: Xerox tools and techniques. *CSLI, Stanford*.

Steven Bird. 2018. Designing mobile applications for

endangered languages. In *The Oxford Handbook of Endangered Languages*. Oxford University Press.

Steven Bird and Alex Marley. 2019. Kunwok.org. `https://kunwok.org/`. Accessed: 2019-08-30.

Emily Chen and Lane Schwartz. 2018. A morphological analyzer for St. Lawrence Island / Central Siberian Yupik. In *Proceedings of the Eleventh International Conference on Language Resources and Evaluation*, Miyazaki, Japan. European Language Resources Association.

Christopher Culy. 1985. The complexity of the vocabulary of Bambara. In *The Formal Complexity of Natural Language*, pages 349–357. Springer.

Hossep Dolatian and Jeffrey Heinz. 2018. Modeling reduplication with 2-way finite-state transducers. In *Proceedings of the Fifteenth Workshop on Computational Research in Phonetics, Phonology, and Morphology*, pages 66–77, Brussels, Belgium. Association for Computational Linguistics.

Hossep Dolatian and Jeffrey Heinz. 2019. Learning reduplication with 2-way finite-state transducers. In *International Conference on Grammatical Inference*, pages 67–80. Proceedings of Machine Learning Research.

Mark Dras, François Lareau, Benjamin Börschinger, Robert Dale, Yasaman Motazedi, Owen Rambow, Myfany Turpin, and Morgan Ulinski. 2012. Complex predicates in Arrernte. In *Proceedings of the LFG12 Conference*, pages 177–197. CSLI Publications.

Nicholas Evans. 2003. A Pan-dialectal Grammar of Bininj Gun-Wok (Arnhem Land): Mayali, Kunwinjku and Kune. *Canberra: Pacific Linguistics*.

Murray Garde, Jill Nganjmirra, and Dan Kennedy. 2019. Bininj Kunwok Dictionary. `njamed.com`. Accessed: 2019-07-19.

Martin Haspelmath and Thomas Müller-Bardey. 2004. Valency change. In Geert Booij, Christian Lehmann, and Joachim Mugdan, editors, *Morphology: A Handbook on Inflection and Word Formation*, pages 1130–45. de Gruyter Berlin; New York.

Mans Hulden. 2009. Foma: a finite-state compiler and library. In *Proceedings of the 12th Conference of the European Chapter of the Association for Computational Linguistics*, pages 29–32. Association for Computational Linguistics.

Mans Hulden. 2011. Morphological analysis tutorial: A self-contained tutorial for building morphological analyzers. `https://fomafst.github.io/morphtut.html`. Accessed: 2019-09-30.

Benjamin Hunt, Emily Chen, Sylvia Schreiner, and Lane Schwartz. 2019. Community lexical access for an endangered polysynthetic language: An electronic dictionary for St. Lawrence Island Yupik. In *Proceedings of the 2019 Conference of the North American Chapter of the Association for Computational Linguistics*, pages 122–126, Minneapolis, Minnesota. Association for Computational Linguistics.

Anna Kazantseva, Owennatekha Brian Maracle, Ronkwe'tiyóhstha Josiah Maracle, and Aidan Pine. 2018. Kawennón:nis: the wordmaker for Kanyen'kéha. In *Proceedings of the Workshop on Computational Modeling of Polysynthetic Languages*, pages 53–64, Santa Fe, USA. Association for Computational Linguistics.

Jordan Lachler, Lene Antonsen, Trond Trosterud, Sjur Moshagen, and Antti Arppe. 2018. Modeling Northern Haida verb morphology. In *Proceedings of the Eleventh International Conference on Language Resources and Evaluation*, Miyazaki, Japan. European Language Resources Association.

Patrick Littell. 2018. Finite-state morphology for Kwak'wala: A phonological approach. In *Proceedings of the Workshop on Computational Modeling of Polysynthetic Languages*, pages 21–30, Santa Fe, USA. Association for Computational Linguistics.

Jeffrey Micher. 2017. Improving coverage of an Inuktitut morphological analyzer using a segmental recurrent neural network. In *Proceedings of the 2nd Workshop on the Use of Computational Methods in the Study of Endangered Languages*, pages 101–106, Honolulu. Association for Computational Linguistics.

Sarah Moeller, Ghazaleh Kazeminejad, Andrew Cowell, and Mans Hulden. 2018. A neural morphological analyzer for Arapaho verbs learned from a finite state transducer. In *Proceedings of the Workshop on Computational Modeling of Polysynthetic Languages*, pages 12–20, Santa Fe, USA. Association for Computational Linguistics.

Maïa Ponsonnet. in press. Comitative applicative constructions and their "transfer" extensions in Dalabon and other Gunwinyguan languages (non-Pamanyungan, Australia). In Myriam Bouveret, editor, *A Contrastive study of Give Constructionalization*. John Benjamins Publishing Company, Amsterdam.

Brian Roark, Richard Sproat, and Richard William Sproat. 2007. *Computational approaches to morphology and syntax*, volume 4. Oxford University Press.

Lane Schwartz, Emily Chen, Benjamin Hunt, and Sylvia Schreiner. 2019. Bootstrapping a neural morphological analyzer for St. Lawrence Island Yupik from a finite-state transducer. In *Proceedings of the 3rd Workshop on the Use of Computational Methods in the Study of Endangered Languages Volume 1*, pages 87–96, Honolulu. Association for Computational Linguistics.

From Shakespeare to Li-Bai:
Adapting a Sonnet Model to Chinese Poetry

Zhuohan Xie   **Jey Han Lau**   **Trevor Cohn**
The University of Melbourne
zhuohanx@student.unimelb.edu.au   jeyhan.lau@gmail.com   t.cohn@unimelb.edu.au

Abstract

In this paper, we adapt Deep-speare, a joint neural network model for English sonnets, to Chinese poetry. We illustrate the characteristics of Chinese quatrain and explain our architecture as well as training and generation procedure, which differs from Shakespeare sonnets in several aspects. We analyse the generated poetry and find that the adapted model works well for Chinese poetry, as it can: (1) generate coherent 4-line quatrains of different topics; and (2) capture rhyme automatically to a certain extent.

1   Introduction

Classical poetry is an important Chinese cultural heritage and holds great value. The most popular poetry type is quatrain. Table 1 shows a seven-character quatrain written by Li Bai, one of the most famous poets in Chinese history, which we will use to explain characteristics of Chinese quatrain.

First, a Chinese quatrain must contain four sentences where each sentence has the same number (five or seven) of characters. Usually, these sentences follow the "introduction, follow-up, transition and conclusion" mode, which means the first sentence starts a topic, the second continues it, then the third sentence extends it to a new realm and the last provides a summarisation (Wang, 2002). The rhythmic scheme in Chinese quatrain is simple: the last characters of the second and fourth sentences should rhyme. Optionally, the last character of the first sentence can also rhyme with them, as the quatrain shows in Table 1. As for tone, each character contains one single syllable and there are two tones for middle Chinese (Pulleyblank, 2011): "Ping" (level tone) or "Ze" (downward tone). Generally, tones at the same positions of two adjacent sentences are opposite and four common tonal patterns are illustrated in Wang (2002). Character

望庐山瀑布
【唐】李白

日照香炉生紫烟，	＊Z P P Z Z P
遥看瀑布挂前川。	＊P ＊Z Z P P
飞流直下三千尺，	＊P ＊Z P P Z
疑是银河落九天。	＊Z P P Z Z P

Waterfall on Mount Lu
Li Bai
The Sunlit Censer peak exhales
a wreath of cloud.
Like an unpended stream
the waterfall sounds loud.
Its torrent dashes down
three thousand feet from high.
As if the Silver River fell from azure sky.

Table 1: A 7-character Tang Quatrain by Li Bai.

tone is indicated in Table 1 where 'P' indicates "Ping", 'Z' refers to "Ze" and '＊' means this character can be either tone.

Following all these constraints, a well-written Chinese quatrain are full of rhythm while expressing abundant emotions.

1.1   Motivation

Inspired by Deep-speare (Lau et al., 2018), a joint neural network model that is trained on English sonnets to generate quatrains in iambic pentameter (Halle and Keyser, 1971), we seek to adapt this model to poetry in other languages. The abundance of Chinese quatrain and its important cultural status makes it a natural choice.

We analyse the similarity between characteristics of English sonnets and Chinese quatrains and found it is possible to adapt the model to Chinese as the language model can be modified to handle Chinese characters.

Lau et al. (2018) found that a vanilla language

model can learn meter automatically at human level performance after it was trained on 2K sonnets. Given this, we have the expectation that the adapted language model should learn to generate quatrains with reasonable rhythm after we train it with sufficient data.

1.2 Contribution

The main contributions of the paper are:

1. We adapt Deep-speare to generate Chinese quatrains; source code of our adapted model is available at: ANONYMISED.

2. We find that our model is able to learn rhyme patterns automatically and can generate coherent quatrains of various topics; native Chinese speakers are unable to distinguish the best machine generated quatrains from human-written ones.

3. Our model is able to maintain originality in that BLEU scores and longest matching substring demonstrate the quatrains are not too similar to the training corpus.

2 Related Work

Poetry generation is a challenging task in Natural Language Processing. Many approaches were proposed to solve such problem, among which, the earliest methods were based on templates and rules. It requires users to provide keywords or titles and a rhyming template so the system can expand words and fill them into the user-selected template. This method is used in several successful poetry generation services, for instance, the haiku generation system of Wu et al. (2009) extracts rules from corpus and expand keywords from users to generate haiku sentences based on rules.

Another influential approach for Chinese quatrain generation is statistical machine translation (SMT). It is first utilised to generate Chinese couplets, which can be regarded as a special quatrain comprised of two sentences (Jiang and Zhou, 2008). They take the first sentence as input from users and generate an N-best list of second sentence candidates via a phrase-based SMT decoder. This method is extended by He et al. (2012) to generate Chinese quatrains where users are asked to provide the first sentence as input and then the system "translates" three following sentences based on the previous sentences.

Recently, neural networks are the predominant technique in the literature. Zhang and Lapata (2014) propose using recurrent neural networks (RNN) to generate the poem sentence by sentence. However, the model they provide is rather complex as it has one CNN and two RNNs, and it still observes theme drift when generating long sequences. To solve these problems, Wang et al. (2016) propose a simpler neural model which treats the whole poem as a character sequence. This approach can be easily extended to generate other genres such as Song Iambics or Haiku and they utilise the attention mechanism (Bahdanau et al., 2014) to avoid theme drift.

The closest work to our study is Deep-speare, which is a joint neural model designed for English sonnets. Deep-speare has 3 components: a language model, a pentameter model and a rhyme model. The language model is an LSTM encoder-decoder with attention that generates word by word and the pentameter model is trained to learn the iambic pentameter, an alternating stress pattern that sonnets exhibit. The rhyme model is optimised to separate rhyming word pairs automatically from non-rhyming ones in quatrains, which can help to enforce rhyme when generating the quatrains. All models are trained together (as a multi-task model), and the authors found that the model can generate sonnet quatrains with good stress and rhyme patterns.

3 Dataset

We source our poem dataset from Zhang and Lapata (2014), and use a modern Chinese pinyin dictionary[1].

3.1 Overview

We choose to use Tang quatrains as the Tang dynasty is one of the most famous dynasties for Chinese quatrains. We filter out non-quatrains from the Tang poetry collection and keep $2,349$ five-character and $7,219$ seven-character quatrains for our experiments. We sample 80% of the quatrains for training, 10% for development and 10% for test. Dataset statistics for each partition is presented in Table 2. There are $4,484$ unique characters in the full quatrain dataset ($9,568$ quatrains in total) and our training partition has a coverage of $4,283$ characters.

---

[1]https://github.com/DevinZ1993/Chinese-Poetry-Generation

Partition	#Qs	#Chs	#UniChs
Train (5-ch)	1879	38k	2785
Train (7-ch)	5775	162k	4091
Dev (5-ch)	235	5k	1279
Dev (7-ch)	722	20k	2385
Test (5-ch)	235	5k	1277
Test (7-ch)	722	20k	2325
Total	9568	249k	4484

Table 2: Dataset statistics. "Qs" denotes quatrains, "Chs" characters and "UniChs" unique characters.

To pre-train the word embeddings, we use approximately 300k quatrains from the full collection (quatrains in the development and test partition are excluded). The word embedding is trained per character, where each line in the quatrain is treated as a sentence and each character is treated as a word. We also tried *jieba* (Sun, 2012), a Chinese segmentation tool to tokenise phrases according to *ShiXueHanYing* (Liu, 1735), a poetic phrase taxonomy. We found that in preliminary experiments that the approach did not work well, and we hypothesise that this may be because classical poets compose their poems in a succinct manner by using minimum characters, and so each character is meaningful and can be treated as a word.

3.2 Rhyme Analysis

In total, $4,484$ unique characters exist in the whole quatrain corpus, and only some of them are rhyming characters that appear at the end of sentences. We analyse the number of rhyme combinations (i.e. rhyme tuples and triples) for each partition in Table 3. $2,450$ unique rhyme tuples and $2,882$ unique rhyme triples exist for seven-character quatrains and $1,034$ unique rhyme tuples and 244 unique rhyme triples appear in the five-character quatrains. We take into account of the order of rhyme combinations, for instance, ('尘', '春', '人') and ('春', '尘', '人') are considered different.

One interesting observation is that although the proportion of rhyme tuples in both five-character and seven-character quatrains is about the same (80%), the proportion of triples in seven-character quatrains is nearly 60%, which is much higher than that of five-character quatrains (13%).

We show the 5 most common rhyme tuples and triples in Table 4. We find that seven-character quatrains largely limit their rhyming patterns to the same words such as '尘' (chen), '春' (chun), '人' (ren), '新' (xin), '身' (shen).[2] By contrast, five-character quatrains have more variations for rhyming patterns, e.g. '道' (dao), '老' (lao), '草' (cao) and '厄' (zi), '辞' (ci), '离' (li).

4 Architecture

The original Deep-speare contains language model, rhyme model and pentameter model (Lau et al., 2018), here we only extend vanilla language model to work on Chinese quatrains where we treat each Chinese character as an individual word.

4.1 Language Model

The language model is a variant of an LSTM encoder-decoder where the encoder encodes previous sentences and the decoder predicts the next character in the current sentence, while attending to the encodings of previous sentences. Figure 1 shows the process of predicting the second sentence from the example in Table 1 where the encoder encodes the first sentence (bottom characters of Figure 1) while the decoder predicts the second sentence per character and each character (top-right of Figure 1) is generated based on its previous one (top-left of Figure 1) beginning from <s>, the sentence starting symbol. The encoder encodes first two sentences when decoder predicts the third sentence.

The encoder first uses a shared character embedding matrix W_{char} to embed the first sentence S_i to character vectors X_i. Then X_i is fed into a single layer bidirectional LSTM (Gers et al., 1999) to yield a sequence of hidden states $h_i = [\overrightarrow{h_i}; \overleftarrow{h_i}]$. Then selective encoding (Zhou et al., 2017) is applied to each h_i to filter out less useful information. We use the last forward hidden state concatenated with the first backward hidden state to represent the whole sentence $\overline{h} = [\overrightarrow{h_{-1}}; \overleftarrow{h_1}]$ (h_{-1} here means the last hidden state). The selective encoding filters out information from each hidden state h_i using $\overline{h}$ by the following equation:

$$h_i' = h_i \odot \sigma(W_a h_i + U_a \overline{h} + b_a)$$

where $\odot$ indicates element-wise multiplication and W, U and b refer to model parameters.

---

[2] The pinyin of the characters largely follow '人辰韵' pattern ('en', 'in', 'ün').

Partition	#Quatrains	#Tuples	%Tuples	#Triples	%Triples
Train (5-ch)	1879	1491	79.35	258	13.73
Train (7-ch)	5775	4769	82.58	3440	59.57
Dev (5-ch)	235	186	79.15	24	10.21
Dev (7-ch)	722	597	82.67	427	59.14
Test (5-ch)	235	184	78.30	30	12.77
Test (7-ch)	722	604	83.66	438	60.66
Total	9568	7831	81.85	4617	48.25

Table 3: Rhyme proportion in human-written quatrains.

R	Tuple	F	Triple	F	R	Tuple	F	Triple	F
1	('春', '人')	31	('人', '氛', '云')	2	1	('春', '人')	95	('尘', '春', '人')	22
2	('深', '心')	18	('道', '老', '草')	2	2	('身', '人')	57	('春', '尘', '人')	16
3	('开', '来')	15	('草', '道', '老')	2	3	('尘', '人')	49	('春', '新', '人')	13
4	('人', '春')	12	('半', '远', '转')	2	4	('开', '来')	42	('春', '身', '人')	11
5	('来', '开')	9	('厄', '辞', '离')	2	5	('家', '花')	37	('新', '春', '人')	11

(a) 5-char	(b) 7-char

Table 4: Top-5 rhyme combinations in human-written quatrains. "R" denotes rank and "F" denotes frequency.

The decoder embeds the current sentence S_t with the same shared character embedding matrix W_{char} to generate character vectors X_t and feed them into a unidirectional LSTM to produce the decoding state s_t:

$$s_t = \text{LSTM}(X_i, s_{t-1})$$

To attend to the encodings of previous sentences (h'_i), we compute a weighted sum (h^*_t) as follows:

$$e^t_i = v^T_b \tanh(W_b h'_i + U_b s_t + b_b)$$
$$a^t = \text{softmax}(e^t)$$
$$h^*_t = \sum_i a^t_i h'_i$$

Finally, s_t and h^*_t are combined by a gating unit (Chung et al., 2014) to generate state s'_t and fed into the output layer where softmax activation is used to yield a probability distribution over the character vocabulary.

$$s'_t = \text{GRU}(s_t, h^*_t)$$
$$p = \text{softmax}(W_{out} s'_t + b_{out})$$

We use standard cross-entropy loss to optimise the model and dropout as regularisation.

To reduce the number of parameters, the output matrix W_{out} is obtained from W_{char} via a projection matrix W_{proj}:

$$W_{out} = \tanh(W_{char} W_{proj})$$

4.2 Training Procedure

We combine five-character and seven-character quatrains together for training. In preliminary experiments we found that the model works better if we train quatrains from right to left, i.e. instead of generating starting with <s> to predict the first character and so on, we generate from </s>, the ending symbol, to predict the last character and generate backwards terminating with <s>. The context from the encoder is modified accordingly, and it does not encode the first sentence as shown in Figure 1. It instead encodes the last two sentences in reverse order for the second sentence. We think this is better way because: (1) the rhyme characters appear at the end of sentences, and it would be better if the model produces them first; and (2) for noun compounds (e.g. adjective+noun),

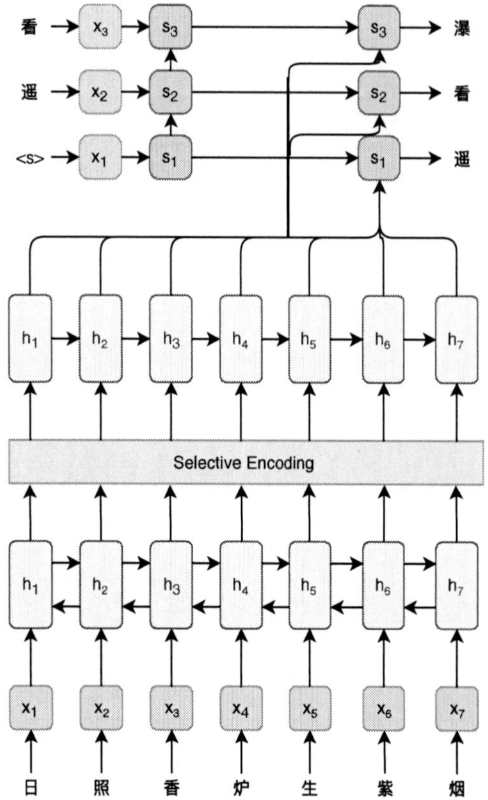

Figure 1: Architecture of the language Model

generating the last character first is a more sensible approach, as it limits the choices of adjective. For instance, 青山 (green mountain), 青龙 (green dragon), 青草 (green grass) are all frequent phrases in Chinese quatrains. The adjective would be 青 (green) if 草 (grass) is generated first. On the other hand, if 青 (green) is generated first, then there are many words that can appear after it, complicating the prediction.

We tune hyper-parameters of the model based on its performance on the development partition. We train the model for 30 epochs and use the Adagrad optimiser (Duchi et al., 2011). We pre-train CBOW (Mikolov et al., 2013a,b) embeddings on the full poetry collection, as described Section 3.1. The embeddings are updated during training. We set the learning rate to 0.2 and dropout probability to 0.4.

4.3 Generation Procedure

We use the same model to generate five-character and seven-character quatrains, by specifying the total length of quatrains (20 for five-character and 28 for seven-character). We generate one sentence

at a time (4 in total), and we sample characters one at a time and stop when we have a sufficient number of characters (5 or 7) for a sentence. We did not apply beam search to generate the quatrain since we found the topics of machine generated quatrains can be more diverse if we use sampling.

Since we train our data in reverse order, we generate quatrains in reverse order as well. We feed the hidden state of the previous character to the decoder of language model to compute the character distribution for the current character and sample from it using a temperature τ (Hinton et al., 2015) between 0.1 and 0.2.

$$\widetilde{p_i} = f_\tau(p)_i = \frac{p_i^{\frac{1}{\tau}}}{\sum_j p_j^{\frac{1}{\tau}}}$$

We resample if the sampled character is: (1) a character that has appeared more than once; (2) one of the preceding three characters; (3) the last character of any sentence; or (4) UNK or PAD special tokens. UNK tokens represent characters that are not in our vocabulary[3]; we also use UNK tokens to represent the previous context for the first sentence. PAD tokens are used to pad five-character quatrains so that they can be trained with seven-character quatrains together.

We find that setting temperature in the above range limits the possibility of generating more diverse poetry because the generated quatrains would usually end in frequent characters such as '人' (person), '来' (come) or '中' (in). As the rest of the quatrain will be generated based on these characters, it limits the topic and content for the poem, and there is little diversity in the generated quatrains. In light of this, we set temperature to 0.9 when generating the last character of the quatrain. We generate 100 quatrains under two different temperatures (0.2 and 0.9) to compare the differences between them; results are presented in Figure 2. The model produces 67 unique sentence-ending characters under temperature 0.9, but only 5 unique characters when we set temperature to 0.2. Also, the cumulative proportion of the top-9 characters is only 35% when temperature is 0.9. In contrast, the most frequent character '人' (person) alone occupies over 90% cumulative proportion at 0.2 temperature.

---

[3]Out-of-Vocabulary (OOV) Rate is 0.13% in our model.

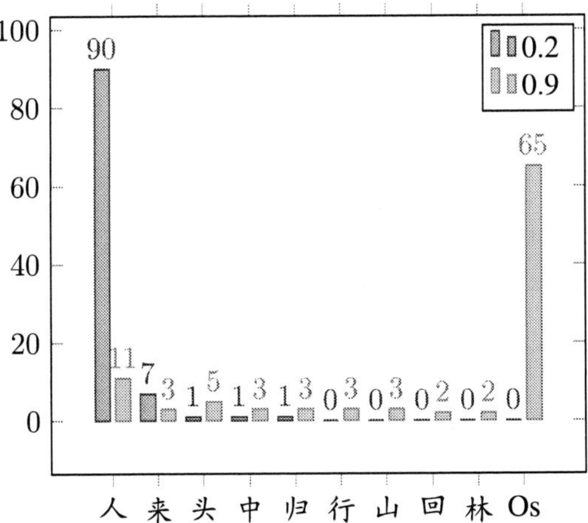

Figure 2: Relative frequency of sentence-ending characters under different temperatures. "Os" denotes Others.

桃花荷叶红，	孤舟行路不胜愁，
春水不成空。	万山云雨峡中幽。
花开绿窗下，	知君莫向荆州客，
何人入梦中。	不见青山湘水流。

Table 5: Quatrains generated by our model.

5 Evaluation

We select two representative quatrains (one five-word and one seven-word) generated by our system and present them in Table 5. We find that our system is able to: (1) capture rhyme patterns automatically; (2) generate quatrains of various topics; and (3) compose coherent poetry.

For the presented quatrains, the last characters of the first, second and last sentences rhyme. It demonstrates that the language model is able to learn rhyming pattern automatically, without requiring an additional rhyme model to enforce rhyming.

Various topics exist in Tang quatrains, such as "love" and "wanderer staying long in a foreign land" and our system is able to generate quatrains of various topics. The topic of the left quatrain is boudoir resentment, which is one of the major themes of love poems. Phrases that symbolise female appear in such quatrain, such as 桃花 (peach blossom) and 荷叶 (lotus leaf). The overall narrative depicts a love story. The topic of the right quatrain is about travelling, and it describes the scenery the poet observes when travelling alone on a boat, using phrases such as 万山 (thousands of mountains) and 云雨 (clouds and rain).

Our evaluation includes rhyme evaluation, similarity evaluation and human evaluation. We see various topics appear in the generated quatrains and they are coherent, therefore, we would like to perform diversity and coherence evaluation in the future work.

5.1 Automatic Evaluation

We generate 500 five-character quatrains and 500 seven-character using the hyper-parameter configuration discussed in Section 4.3, and analyse the number of rhyming quatrains and the variation of rhyming patterns. We also use BLEU and longest matching substring to check for similarity between our machine generated quatrains with the training corpus (so as to confirm that the model is not simply memorising and reciting quatrains from the training data).

Rhyme Evaluation We present the proportion of rhyming quatrains in Table 6. Our system works better with respect to rhyme when generating short sentences: 25% of the five-character quatrains rhyme, but only 8.4% of the seven-character quatrains rhyme. We hypothesise that this may be because shorter sentences are easier for the system to learn the rhyming patterns.

We also examine the number of unique rhyme combinations generated by our system for the 1,000 quatrains. 52 unique rhyme tuples and 22 triples appear in the five-character quatrains and 26 unique rhyme tuples and 8 triples appear in the seven-character quatrains. This again implies that it is more difficult for the system to learn the rhyming patterns for longer sentences. We show the top-5 rhyme combinations for the generated quatrains in Table 6. Comparing these to Table 4, we find that frequent combinations are learnt by the model.

The results show our system is able to capture rhyme pattern to some extent, but the generated quatrains do not rhyme as much as human written ones and rhyming combination is limited as well. This might suggest that we need a rhyming model to generate quatrains with better rhyme schemes.

Similarity Check We treat each generated quatrain as the hypothesis, and compute BLEU (Chen and Cherry, 2014) score against the training corpus (reference). The average BLEU score is 0.46 and 0.44 for five-character and seven-character quatrains respectively. Seven-character quatrains gen-

Partition	#Quatrains	#Tuples	%Tuples	#Triples	%Triples
5-ch	500	125	25	44	8.8
7-ch	500	42	8.4	11	2.2
Total	1000	167	16.7	55	5.5

Table 6: Rhyme proportion in machine generated quatrains.

(a) 5-char

R	Tuple	F	Triple	F
1	('空', '中')	12	('尘', '春', '人')	6
2	('开', '来')	12	('身', '春', '人')	6
3	('春', '人')	12	('开', '苔', '来')	5
4	('愁', '头')	10	('台', '开', '来')	4
5	('家', '花')	6	('愁', '秋', '头')	2

(b) 7-char

R	Tuple	F	Triple	F
1	('归', '飞')	6	('身', '春', '人')	3
2	('春', '人')	5	('尘', '春', '人')	2
3	('里', '西')	3	('尘', '尽', '春')	1
4	('尽', '春')	2	('台', '开', '来')	1
5	('开', '来')	2	('头', '首', '州')	1

Table 7: Top-5 rhyme combinations in machine generated quatrains. "R" denotes rank and "F" denotes frequency.

erally have lower BLEU scores, and they also have a bigger spread.

We also check the longest substring that can be matched in the training corpus for each of the generated quatrain. The average length of the longest substring is 3.70 for five-character quatrains (20 characters in total) and 4.05 for seven-character quatrains (28 characters in total). The length of the longest matching substring is 6 and 7 for five-character and seven-character quatrains respectively; for most quatrains this length ranges from 3 to 4, which is less than a quarter of the length of quatrain.

Taking the BLEU scores and longest matching substring results together, we see that our system can generate original poetry, i.e. it is not just memorising the quatrains from the training data and reciting them during generation.

5.2 Human Evaluation

For human evaluation, we pick 5 five-character and 5 seven-character machine generated quatrains with highest quality from our perspective. 4 out of the 5 quatrains contain rhyme tuples so as to mimic real rhyming patterns (as we saw in Section 3.2). We also sample 5 five-character and 5 seven-character human-written quatrains from the training data and mix the 20 quatrains in a questionnaire and ask native Chinese speakers to judge for each quatrain whether it is computer-generated or human-written.

We receive 171 valid responses from volunteers, where they are all native mandarin speakers and most of them hold a bachelor's degree. In general, the users found it very difficult to distinguish the machine-generated quatrains from the human-written ones. On average the accuracy is 45.15%, which is slightly worse than pure guessing at identifying the poems. The quatrain which is voted most (by 70% users) as being "human-written" is generated by our model (Table 5; right quatrain).

However, we acknowledge that our volunteers might not be the best at identifying quatrains, therefore, we would like to seek evaluations from experts in the future work.

6 Conclusion

In this paper, we extend Deep-speare, a joint neural network model for English sonnets, to generate Chinese quatrains. Chinese quatrain holds an important cultural status in China, and there is a large collection of these quatrains, making it a natural choice for adaptation. We analyse Chinese quatrains and detail how we adapt Deep-speare in terms of training and generation. We find the adapted model works well, as it can: (1) generate quatrains of different topics; (2) capture the rhyming scheme automatically; (3) compose coherent poetry. We also check the similarity of the generated quatrains with the training data, and find

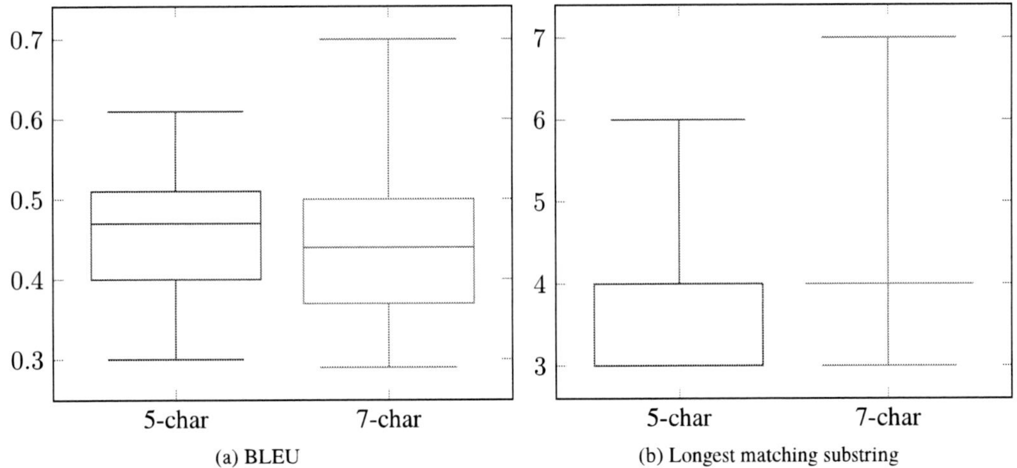

(a) BLEU   (b) Longest matching substring

Figure 3: Similarity Check.

that the generated poetry is original. Human evaluation demonstrates that our best machine generated quatrains are almost indistinguishable from human-written ones for native Chinese speakers.

For future work, we believe the following are promising directions:

1. There is potential to utilise data[4] that has tone labels to better understand the tonal patterns in Chinese quatrains.

2. Adapt the rhyme model of Deep-speare to produce rhyme more consistently in Chinese quatrains.

3. Train a reverse summarisation model on Chinese quatrains to generate a title given a quatrain.

References

Dzmitry Bahdanau, Kyunghyun Cho, and Yoshua Bengio. 2014. Neural machine translation by jointly learning to align and translate. *arXiv preprint arXiv:1409.0473*.

Boxing Chen and Colin Cherry. 2014. A systematic comparison of smoothing techniques for sentence-level bleu. In *Proceedings of the Ninth Workshop on Statistical Machine Translation*, pages 362–367.

Junyoung Chung, Caglar Gulcehre, KyungHyun Cho, and Yoshua Bengio. 2014. Empirical evaluation of gated recurrent neural networks on sequence modeling. *arXiv preprint arXiv:1412.3555*.

John Duchi, Elad Hazan, and Yoram Singer. 2011. Adaptive subgradient methods for online learning and stochastic optimization. *Journal of Machine Learning Research*, 12(Jul):2121–2159.

Felix A Gers, Jürgen Schmidhuber, and Fred Cummins. 1999. Learning to forget: Continual prediction with lstm.

Morris Halle and Samuel Jay Keyser. 1971. Illustration and defense of a theory of the iambic pentameter. *College English*, 33(2):154–176.

Jing He, Ming Zhou, and Long Jiang. 2012. Generating chinese classical poems with statistical machine translation models. In *Twenty-Sixth AAAI Conference on Artificial Intelligence*.

Geoffrey Hinton, Oriol Vinyals, and Jeff Dean. 2015. Distilling the knowledge in a neural network. *arXiv preprint arXiv:1503.02531*.

Long Jiang and Ming Zhou. 2008. Generating chinese couplets using a statistical mt approach. In *Proceedings of the 22nd International Conference on Computational Linguistics-Volume 1*, pages 377–384. Association for Computational Linguistics.

Jey Han Lau, Trevor Cohn, Timothy Baldwin, Julian Brooke, and Adam Hammond. 2018. Deep-speare: A joint neural model of poetic language, meter and rhyme. In *the 56th Annual Meeting of the Association for Computational Linguistics (ACL 2018)*, pages 1948–1958.

Wenwei Liu. 1735. Shixuehanying (诗学含英).

Tomas Mikolov, Kai Chen, Greg Corrado, and Jeffrey Dean. 2013a. Efficient estimation of word representations in vector space. *arXiv preprint arXiv:1301.3781*.

---

[4]https://github.com/jackeyGao/chinese-poetry

Tomas Mikolov, Ilya Sutskever, Kai Chen, Greg S Corrado, and Jeff Dean. 2013b. Distributed representations of words and phrases and their compositionality. In *Advances in Neural Information Processing Systems*, pages 3111–3119.

Edwin G Pulleyblank. 2011. *Middle Chinese: A study in historical phonology*. UBC Press.

J Sun. 2012. 'jieba' chinese word segmentation tool.

Li Wang. 2002. A summary of rhyming constraints of chinese poems (诗词格律概要). In *Beijing Press*.

Qixin Wang, Tianyi Luo, and Dong Wang. 2016. Can machine generate traditional chinese poetry? a feigenbaum test. In *International Conference on Brain Inspired Cognitive Systems*, pages 34–46. Springer.

Xiaofeng Wu, Naoko Tosa, and Ryohei Nakatsu. 2009. New hitch haiku: An interactive renku poem composition supporting tool applied for sightseeing navigation system. In *International Conference on Entertainment Computing*, pages 191–196. Springer.

Xingxing Zhang and Mirella Lapata. 2014. Chinese poetry generation with recurrent neural networks. In *Proceedings of the 2014 Conference on Empirical Methods in Natural Language Processing (EMNLP)*, pages 670–680.

Qingyu Zhou, Nan Yang, Furu Wei, and Ming Zhou. 2017. Selective encoding for abstractive sentence summarization. *arXiv preprint arXiv:1704.07073*.

Readability of Twitter Tweets for Second Language Learners

Patrick JACOB and Alexandra L. UITDENBOGERD
RMIT University - School of Science
124 La Trobe St
Melbourne VIC 3000
`patrick.jacob@rocketmail.com,sandra.uitdenbogerd@rmit.edu.au`

Abstract

Optimal language acquisition via reading requires the learners to read slightly above their current language skill level. Identifying material at the right level is the essential role of automatic readability measurement. Short message platforms such as Twitter offer the opportunity for language practice while reading about current topics and engaging in conversation in small doses, and can be filtered according to linguistic criteria to suit the learner. In this research, we explore how readable tweets are for English language learners and which factors contribute to their readability. With participants from six language groups, we collected 14,659 data points, each representing a tweet from a pool of 4100 tweets, and a judgement of perceived readability. Traditional readability measures and features failed on the data-set, but demographic data showed that judgements were largely genuine and reflected reported language skill, which is consistent with other recent studies. We report on the properties of the data set and implications for future research.

1 Credits

We thank Klerke et al. (2016) for the Twitter corpus from their unpublished research.

2 Introduction

Since the first half of the twentieth century researchers have analysed texts to determine their *readability*, that is, how easy the text is to read and comprehend, often expressed as levels of linguistic education, knowledge, age or experience. The findings around readability have been applied to education for selecting appropriate reading material for students, in communication with governmental bodies to reach a higher number of citizens (Temnikova et al., 2015) and in marketing/public relations of companies to increase the reach of their materials (Risius and Pape, 2016).

While there have been many studies on readability of regular text for students and foreign language learners, the same is not true for the microblog text genre. Twitter is a popular platform for reading current topics and engaging in social interaction, providing a cross-cultural, cross-interest, and cross-language platform for reading social media posts of up to 280 characters in length, and a filtered feed has potential as a source of regular reading material for learners. While the Flesch readability of English language tweets has been analysed to discover demographic trends and to compare them to other modern text genres (Davenport and DeLine, 2014), and judgements of tweet clarity for emergency communication has been researched (Temnikova et al., 2015), to our knowledge tweets have not been studied in relation to English as an Additional Language (EAL, a term that recognises that it may be a third language, for example).

Our aim was to extend readability research to tweets for EAL learners. Tweets are different from ordinary text due to their short length, hashtags, *mentions* (user identifiers preceded by an @ symbol), links, and other non-standard text tokens that they contain. This poses challenges for traditional readability formulae, which assume regular text, as found in books and periodicals. This study evaluates the applicability of readability formulae and the influence of the unique expressions used in tweets such as hashtags, mentions and links. The goal was to find predictors that increase accuracy in classifying Twitter tweets to language reading levels, which will assist users to find more appropriate material for their reading abilities and aid institutions to adjust their published tweets for foreign language reader target audiences.

3 Related Literature

3.1 Classic Studies

Text readability has been researched since early last century, and produced the widely used Flesch Reading Ease formula (Flesch, 1948).

$$206.835 - 1.015 \left(\frac{words}{sentences} \right) - 84.6 \left(\frac{syllables}{words} \right)$$

The Flesch formula shows an inverse relationship between readability and the number of syllables per word (lexical complexity) and the number of words per sentence (grammatical complexity). This simple measure has become a standard for text analysis in other fields of research, and is often used as a baseline for readability research, hence we include it in our study. Dale-Chall (1948) is another user-derived readability measure, based on children with English as a first language:

$$0.1579 \left(\frac{difficult\ words}{words} * 100 \right) + 0.0496 \left(\frac{words}{sentences} \right)$$

Dale and Chall's research determined that the percentage of difficult words in a given text and the number of words per sentence influence readability. This formula assumes every word not on a list of 3000 words a fourth-grade American student should be familiar with is difficult. It would be interesting to see the interaction between the Dale-Chall formula and research based on the findings of Uitdenbogerd (2005), which show that cognates (words that are same or very similar between the native language and the foreign language of study) influence the understanding of sentences for students of foreign languages.

Most readability measures and indexes are only considered valid for text samples with a minimum number of words or sentences (Collins-Thompson and Callan, 2004; Homan et al., 1994), and therefore not intended for typical tweet text. However, we include the above formulae and related classic readability features in this initial study.

3.2 Twitter-related Research

Davenport and DeLine (2014) studied the readability of a corpus of 17.4 Million tweets. They modified the Flesch formula by treating each tweet as a single sentence, due to their brevity and unconventional punctuation. This approach may no longer be adequate for a Twitter corpus, given the new character limit of 280 characters for tweets.

Temnikova et al. (2015) analysed the text difficulty of emergency messages on social media including Twitter. They used crowd-sourcing (CrowdFlower) to present a questionnaire of 500 tweets to participants, who rated them as one of *very clear*, *needs improvement*, or *very unclear*. Additionally, participants could suggest how to write a more understandable version of the tweet. Amongst the resulting recommendations are to use easy vocabulary and short complete sentences, exclude mentions, and minimise hashtag use. Even though the resulting recommendations appear to be valid, it is unclear what the background of the participants was, which can impact how text is perceived. In contrast, for our study, we selected and recorded the background of participants from specific populations.

4 Experiment Design

There are generally two types of research design for predicting readability. The first models reading difficulty using data collected from human participants. The readability measure by Kincaid et al. (1975) is one example of this. They invited 531 participants from two navy bases in the US to read from a set of eighteen passages of training manuals. The task was to answer questions about the manuals by filling in missing words (Cloze test). From the results, Kincaid et al. deduced the formula to predict the reading grade level for navy personnel. The advantage of this approach is that the collected data and resulting model represents the genuine user experience of text difficulty. The main challenge is obtaining sufficient data from the target user population for analysis.

The second research method, which has become prominent in NLP communities, uses large corpora of text samples that have been labelled by experts or publishers, to train machine learning models. One example is the research of François and Fairon (2012), who trained a machine learning algorithm with a text corpus labelled according to the levels of the Common European Framework of Reference for Languages (CEFR), to model the readability of French text for second language learners (François and Fairon, 2012). This approach allows modern classifiers to be trained on large data-sets of features. However, as has been confirmed by Vajjala and Lucic (2019), expert or publisher labels of text are a poor substitute for genuine user experience, and even the choice of method of measuring the reading experience can lead to large differences in results. This echoes the results found elsewhere in usability research (Jeffries and Desurvire, 1992).

There was no Twitter corpus annotated with difficulty levels available, hence our research design consisted of a user study of tweet readability, specifically for people with English as an additional language. Our approach has the added advantage of reflecting the user experience of language learners matching the demographics of the participants. Participants completed a questionnaire that collected demographic data and reading difficulty judgements of a set of tweets.

4.1 Participant Recruitment

Wilson VanVoorhis and Morgan (2007) recommends that with more than six predictors, to have at least ten participants per predictor. With 10-15 predictors from the survey (such as age groups, Twitter affinity, education levels) and text features from the tweets (such as the number of syllables, characters or Hashtags), we needed at least 150 participants per language. To account for contradicting, invalid or otherwise wrong responses that would need to be discarded from the corpus, we increased the target number of recruits to 200.

We tried to recruit 200 native speakers from each of the six target languages of our study (Spanish, Portuguese, German, Dutch, Cantonese, and Mandarin) via the crowd-sourcing platform Figure Eight[1]. The actual questionnaire was hosted on Qualtrics[2], a specialised website for conducting questionnaires. A participant would be forwarded to the Qualtrics questionnaire via a link once they accepted the survey questionnaire.

4.2 Twitter Corpus Collection

The Twitter corpus we used was merged from two Twitter corpora: one corpus from unpublished research by Klerke et al. (2016); and a larger corpus initially containing 6,000 randomly captured tweets using the Twitter Stream Application Developer Interface.

The second corpus was captured in August 2018 directly from the Twitter stream, utilising the `tweepy` python library[3], which allows searching

---

[1]`https://www.figure-eight.com`
[2]`https://www.qualtrics.com/au`
[3]`https://www.tweepy.org`

Original: *People Swea They KNOW E V E R Y T H I N G Bhou Me Bhuh They Dont Know NOTHING Bhuu my Name*
Corrected: *People swear they know everything about me, but they don't know nothing but my name*

Figure 1: An example of tweet simplification

for a specified number of tweets that contain defined keywords. We used both functions to search for about 400 English language tweets for each first language, containing at least one word from a list of cognates of that language. This ensured that the tweet corpus contained a minimum number of cognates from each language. Due to specific post-collection steps that lowered the final corpus of tweets, more tweets were collected than needed.

Tweets were filtered for offensive content, using an automatic profanity check, followed by a manual process by the researchers to filter any remaining offensive tweets. Lastly, we filtered and deleted duplicates (such as retweets) leaving the entire corpus at 4700 tweets, commencing with 873 from the Klerke corpus. The first 4000 were used for the survey.

Due to platform limitations we broke the survey up into five surveys for each language: four of 1000 tweets and one of 100 tweets used for further validity checking and analysis. The 100-tweet survey consisted of tweets originally containing colloquialisms and/or social media features, such as emojis, which were manually selected from the pool of 4000. The tweets were stripped of emojis, hashtags, mentions, and repetitious content; spelling corrected, and the text adjusted in other ways to standardise it (for example, see Figure 1). It was used to test the questionnaire setup prior to releasing the main surveys.

4.3 Questionnaire

To avoid reading fatigue and to stay within the budget, each person made 20 judgements. This approach should have resulted in six judgements per question for 4000 tweets. That is, for each tweet, we would have at least two human judgements from each language family group. Using the Qualtrics randomisation function, the tweet questions were selected randomly from the pool of 4100 tweets to minimise ordering effects. To ensure an even distribution of judgements, each tweet was presented to at least one participant before any were shown a second time.

Participants were asked for their age, gender, country, education and foreign language knowledge, to assist in providing context for the ground truth collected, as well as to capture potential confounding variables known to influence vocabulary knowledge. We then presented the participants with 20 tweets for them to judge according to reading difficulty. Participants were to position a slider on a scale from 1 (very difficult) to 10 (very easy) representing their perception of the tweet's readability, as shown in Figure 2.

The last task for the participant was to answer a short translation task to confirm the participant does indeed speak their stated first language. The translation question was based on common proverbs in the participant's native language, which they needed to translate from English to their native language. This had the advantage that it was a relatively easy task, since proverbs are usually widely known, but allowed us to evaluate if the participant speaks the claimed language.

Using the IP range of specific countries, we restricted the survey job to specific language speakers in countries where they predominately or officially spoke that language. This way we had another layer to ensure we would only recruit the right target participants.

4.4 Survey Execution and Outcome

For the 100-tweet test surveys we lowered the number of tweets per job from twenty to ten. After seeing that target participation was reached for three languages (Spanish, Portuguese and German) we released all other jobs, which were kept open for about a month. Table 1 shows that Spanish, Portuguese and German participants were most active, while Chinese and Dutch-speaking countries had much lower participation. In the case of Dutch-targeted jobs, someone hacked the survey and exhausted the available budget, leaving us with few judgements for Dutch speakers.

5 Data Restructuring and Cleansing

Data cleansing prior to analysis consisted of the following steps:

- Transposing the data columns into a format suitable for analysis
- Harmonising the contents of several columns such as country of origin or languages.
- Matching and unifying the columns about educations levels.

- Deleting rows with failed validation questions.

Table 1 shows the final data set size for each language after the data cleansing steps were finished,

Survey	Number of participants	Number of data points
Spanish	258	4188
Portuguese	233	4187
German	240	4179
Dutch	55	928
Mandarin	35	547
Cantonese	44	630
Total	865	14659

Table 1: Number of data points after cleaning

6 Descriptive Statistics

When visualising the judgement data as a histogram (see Figure 3) it shows an exponential distribution from very difficult to very easy perceived tweets. Fitting a line to the log of the number of judgements at each rating level has an R^2 of 0.97. Thus most tweets were evaluated as 10 (very easy to read and understand) by participants.

6.1 Twitter Use

When looking at the average ratings shown in Table 2, it can be seen that the more time someone spends with Twitter, the easier it is for participants to read tweets. Participants who used Twitter daily or weekly rated the tweets at 8.39 on average, while participants that never used Twitter averaged 7.99. Presumably frequent Twitter users are more accustomed to the linguistic conventions of Twitter and find it easier to understand tweets. This would partially explain why the majority of tweets are rated 10, as the majority of participants were heavy Twitter users.

Twitter usage	M	SD	Sample Size
Daily	8.39	1.85	6988
Weekly	8.39	1.96	3409
Occasionally	8.14	2.02	3156
Never	7.99	2.07	1109

Table 2: Mean and standard deviation of tweet readability judgements across Twitter usage groups

6.2 Education

Formal school and language education had a strong influence on the judgements in the data

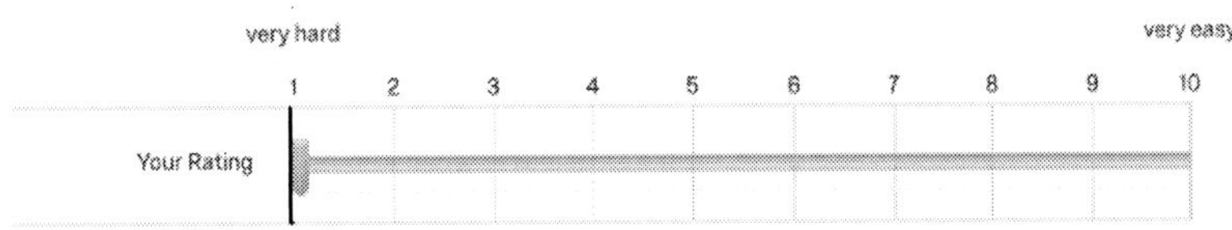

Figure 2: Example tweet question including slider.

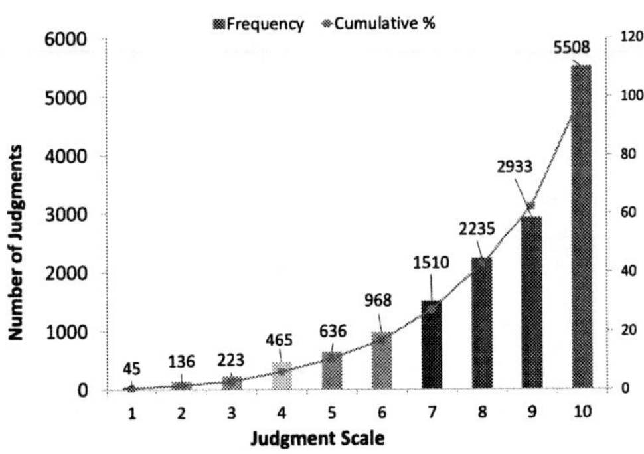

Figure 3: Histogram of judgements

(see Figure 4). Participants without any formal education didn't rate any tweets as 10, while the group of PhD graduates have the highest fraction of tweets rated 10. PhD graduates judged tweets as 9.07 on average, whereas participants without formal education rated their tweets on average at 7.25.

CEFR Level	M	SD	Sample Size
A1	9.35	1.0	160
A2	7.8	2.08	720
B1	8.46	1.77	1311
B2	8.52	1.66	1090
C1	8.64	1.62	547
C2	8.74	1.98	798

Table 3: Average judgement by CEFR Level

During data cleansing, we mapped all reported English education levels to the CEFR standard, which has levels in increasing order of skill, A1, A2, B1, B2, C1 and C2 respectively. This mapping was possible for 4523 data points, which represents 30% of all judgements. Our data shows that the higher the English education, the more likely the tweets are judged higher. The average of A2 participants is 7.8 (30% of tweets given a 10), while the average of the C2 group is 8.74 (65% of judgements being 10) and average ratings increase monotonically between those two levels. The exception is A1, which had an average of 9.35. This could be due to a Dunning-Kruger effect, in which those with minimal knowledge of a subject have a disproportionately high opinion of their knowledge, a problem with the CEFR mapping at the A1 end, or randomly assigned tweets coincidentally being easier to read. It should also be noted that there were only 160 A1-based judgements, whereas all other language groups had at least 547. Those with A1 level English or less are likely to have found the user interface itself challenging, let alone the tweets they were allocated, which may have impacted their participation, resulting in a high proportion of "false beginners" in the cohort.

No. of add. Lang.	M	SD	Sample Size
0	8.16	2.03	8105
1	8.43	1.84	5330
2	8.69	1.55	848
3	8.90	1.63	297
6	9.08	1.01	79

Table 4: Average judgement by additional languages spoken

We also captured any additional languages participants spoke besides their native language and English. Table 4 shows that the more languages a person spoke, the higher the average rating per tweet. The population of people speaking more than one additional language is relatively small, but so is the standard deviation. It is likely that

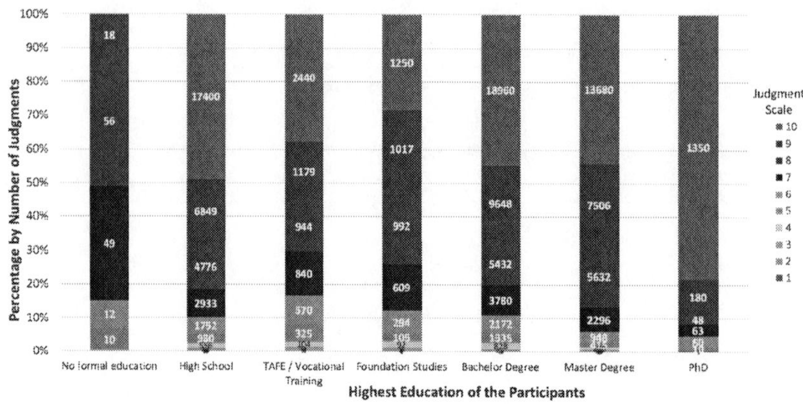

Figure 4: Chart of judgements by education level

broader language knowledge improves the reading capabilities of unusual text such as tweets.

6.3 Twitter-specific Text Features

Twitter is a social media platform, where additional features are used to graphically express emotions and other items (*emojis*); or connect with other users (*mentions*), tweets (*hashtags*) or websites in and outside of Twitter (*links*). We look at each of these features below.

Emojis Emojis are ideograms used in messaging, including stylised facial expressions for displaying emotions, places, animals, food, and flags, among other objects. For the large data set, tweets with 0, 1, 2, 3 and >3 emojis respectively all had ratings between 8.17 and 8.51 with no obvious trend, and standard deviations from 1.84 to 1.98. The emojis did not seem to influence the judgements.

We also analysed a subset (40) of the modified tweets from the small test set from which emojis had been stripped. The average judgements of tweets with emojis removed (8.18, $n = 246$) was lower than that of the original tweets ($M = 8.33$, $n = 93$) . Due to the universal understanding of emojis across languages, they *might* increase readability, or their removal from tweets may take essential semantic content away. However, the difference in means is small, the variability high, and the tweets themselves were not randomly selected, so strong conclusions cannot be drawn at this stage.

Hashtags Hashtags are used as metadata tags to reference themes or content and make them easily findable within and across social media platforms.

Hashtags per Tweet	Count	M	SD
>1	1215	8.14	2.01
1	1812	8.24	1.99
0	11632	8.33	1.92

Table 5: Mean and standard deviation of judgements according to number of hashtags

The question is if they influence the readability of tweets, since they are often composed of joined and abbreviated words, for example, *#muppetgovernment* or *#ImACeleb*. In our corpus the number of hashtags present ranged from zero to twenty, but with very few containing more than 3 hashtags, and no obvious trend was observed as hashtags increased without binning. As with emojis, the subset of 29 modified tweets stripped of hashtags was judged less readable on average (8.07, $n = 195$) than the original ones (8.43, $n = 61$). A reverse trend was found in the larger data-set (see Table 5), with minimal overlap of confidence intervals, indicating confidence in the estimate of the population mean. However, differences in the mean are much smaller than those of the standard deviation, so hashtags are not strong predictors of readability.

Mentions Mentions use the @-sign to refer to other users on Twitter, and like hashtags, are often used on social media, typically either at the beginning or end of tweets. Twitter does not count mentions in the character limit but only allows up to 50 mentions per tweet.

We used the test subset (22) to compare tweets that are stripped of mentions against those with mentions. On average, the judgement with modified tweets is 8.19 ($N = 156$), while the ones with mentions lie at 7.89 ($N = 72$). These numbers indicate that mentions decrease readability.

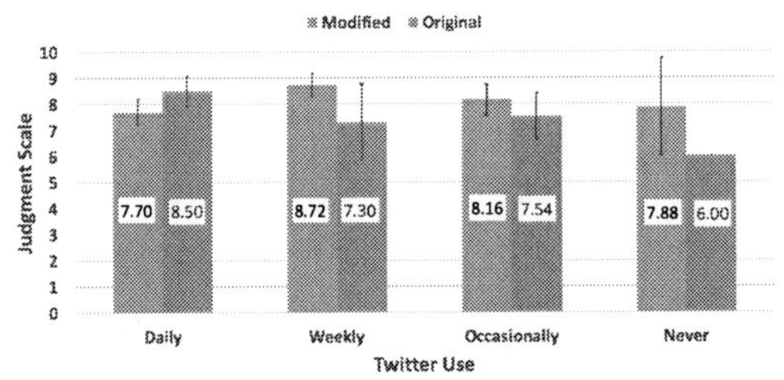

Figure 5: Chart of average judgements by mention broken down by Twitter use. Error bars are 95% confidence intervals.

Interestingly, when broken down by Twitter use, daily Twitter use led to tweets with mentions being rated higher than those without. The opposite was true for those who used Twitter weekly or less frequently. This behaviour could mean that frequent users are better able to filter or appropriately process mentions when reading.

Links   Links are often used on Twitter to refer to other resources on the internet, such as news articles or videos. The links are often abbreviated to save space (for example, *https://t.co/hle8l0AO1i*). We found no evidence that links influence judgements of tweets, whether we used the number of links or their length.

6.4   Readability Measures

We analysed the relationship between different text features and judgements, such as the number of characters per word, number of syllables per word, and sentence length. Most of them had negligible impact, except the total number of characters or words seems to show a trend on average that the more words, the lower the rating, but since they feed into readability measures, we would like to point out a few findings with traditional readability formulae.

Flesch Reading Ease   We compared judgements with Flesch scores, grouping scores into bins, which showed a peak at RE $\in$ [77,81], indicating most tweets were in the fairly easy to easy range. A slight upward trend was observed, indicating weak agreement between RE and judgements.

Some Flesch scores were extremely negative, due to the sentence length and frequent use of words with high syllable counts. For example the following tweet is one sentence long, with 30 Syllables and eight words with a Flesch Score of -118.53.

#FollowMikeaveli   #FollowMikeaveli   #FollowMikeaveli #FollowMikeaveli NO QUESTIONS JUST FOLLOW.

While this tweet had a very negative score, meaning very difficult, its three ratings were 10, 10 and 7. We also tried the Flesch-Kincaid formula, which had similar trends.

Dale-Chall   The feature that is unique to Dale Chall's formula is the number of difficult words, being all words not in a list of 3000 easy words. Our data shows that on average, tweets with a higher number of difficult words are judged more difficult. The Dale-Chall formula however, shows the opposite trend. That is, the harder the tweet according to the Dale-Chall score, the easier it was judged by participants. Additionally, we did an analysis and exchanged cognates for "easy words" in the formula to see if this would have any effect. The trend reversed to the expected direction, but was again weak. A more nuanced approach is probably needed, with high frequency words from the list retained and combined with cognates. This will be explored in future work.

6.5   Correlation

Using both Pearson and Spearman correlations, we calculated correlation matrices between all columns and features. We used both formulations, as Pearson calculates the linear relationship between two variables, while Spearman evaluates the monotonic relationship, which is more appropriate for ordinal data or not entirely linear data. (See Table 6.)

No single feature has a strong relationship to the judgements. The range is between negative and positive 9.6%, which is quite low. Correlation between native languages was also low, regardless of language similarity. This could mean that readability is different for each language. The highest positive Pearson correlation, and second highest Spearman, is the number of additional languages a participant speaks. Education and English level are also highly placed, confirming the previous finding that education or language skills have a stronger relationship with readability than the content itself. Twitter-specific features like the number of emojis and hashtags have little relationship with the judgements, the strongest being for mentions (Spearman -5.1%). In general, we find

Features	Pearson	Spearman
number_of_further_languages	9.6%	8.3%
english_level	7.2%	6.2%
twitter_usage	6.4%	4.8%
education	4.8%	4.4%
flesch_kincaid_twitter_adjusted	4.2%	5.3%
flesch_1948	3.2%	3.3%
percentage_cognates_per_Tweet	1.8%	0.2%
dale_chall	1.2%	-0.2%
number_of_Emojis	0.4%	0.9%
average_length_links	-0.5%	-1.3%
number_of_links	-0.6%	-1.4%
number_of_sentence	-1.6%	-3.3%
number_of_hashtags	-2.3%	-2.9%
number_of_cognates	-2.5%	-3.2%
number_of_mentions	-2.7%	-5.1%
cognates_dale_chall	-3.1%	-2.1%
flesch_kincaid	-4.5%	-5.0%
number_difficult_words	-5.3%	-8.2%
number_of_words	-5.5%	-8.5%
number_of_syllables	-5.8%	-8.6%
number_of_characters	-6.0%	-9.2%

Table 6: Pearson and Spearman rank correlation between judgements and features.

that demographic data are stronger predictors than text features.

6.6 Confidence in Results

Our correlation matrix showed that no feature has a strong correlation to the judgements. It made us question whether the results were trustworthy or whether the participants put in any effort. While we had a validation question for each participant to check if they spoke the native language they claim, we did not implement a similar question to measure sincerity in answering. However, we have some indication that participants answered thoughtfully. First, the slider for tweets was initially set to 1, representing very hard to read and understand, but most of the tweets were rated 10. It means the participants moved the bar to provide their response. Second, the test subset (17) we manipulated to more straightforward language (see, for example, Figure 1), had an average judgement of 8.35 ($n = 99$) compared to the original average of 7.55 ($n = 56$), meaning simplified ones were judged as easier to read. These results lower our doubts about the sincerity of the answers by the participants.

7 Future Work

The features we extracted have a low correlation to the judgements. However, these are not the only features that can be extracted. We saw that uncommon or incorrect words have an effect on readabil-

ity, therefore, constructing a measure of the severity of incorrectness might show stronger correlation than we currently have. Other possible features could be a percentile of non-lexical words, presence of particular grammatical terms or frequency of named entities to name a few. From the extracted features, emojis and mentions, while not showing high correlation themselves, may influence judgements when isolated and compared to tweets stripped of them. We are also yet to explore the use of features such as perplexity. Our machine learning results using further features will be reported elsewhere.

A difficulty with the current data set is that the majority of judgements are at the maximum of the scale, indicating a mismatch between participants and text. A new experiment that selects more homogeneous participant groups based on confounding variables such as age, Twitter usage, English levels and education may be more successful. Obtaining more judgements per tweet would allow more conclusions about user perceptions.

8 Conclusion

We started this research by asking what influences the readability of English tweets for foreign language speakers?

We designed and executed a survey on a crowd-sourcing platform where 865 participants made 10–20 readability judgements from a pool of 4100 tweets. It did not produce the results we expected, as all features showed a low correlation ($\leq 9.6\%$) to the judgements. These features included traditional readability formulae and their components, which in other studies correlate well with user judgements (for example, Uitdenbogerd (2005) achieved 9-85% correlation for traditional readability features and formulae). This study revealed that traditional readability formulae do not work well on tweets. Another observation we made is that some demographic data had stronger predictive power than the text features themselves. For example, English skill level, number of languages known besides English, and the native language showed the highest correlation out of the available features.

As for what makes it hard or easy to read tweets, we do not have a definitive answer, but our research points in the following directions. Slang, wrongly written and uncommon words seem to lower the readability. The number of words or characters and readability formulae have limited predictive value on the readability. From the Twitter-related features, emojis may improve readability, while using mentions and hashtags diminish it for those less familiar with tweets.

All these insights leave us to further investigate in future studies how strongly the observed effects influence the readability of tweets, and thereby build a useful model for filtering Twitter content for language learners.

References

Kevyn Collins-Thompson and James P Callan. 2004. A language modeling approach to predicting reading difficulty. In *Proceedings of the Human Language Technology Conference of the North American Chapter of the Association for Computational Linguistics: HLT-NAACL 2004*, pages 193–200. Association for Computational Linguistics.

Edgar Dale and Jeanne S. Chall. 1948. A formula for predicting readability: Instructions. *Educational Research Bulletin*, 27(2):37–54.

James R. A. Davenport and Robert DeLine. 2014. The readability of tweets and their geographic correlation with education. *Computing Research Repository*, abs/1401.6058.

Rudolf Flesch. 1948. A new readability yardstick. *Journal of Applied Psychology*, 32(3):221–233.

Thomas François and Cedrick Fairon. 2012. An AI readability formula for French as a foreign language. In *Proceedings of the 2012 Joint Conference on Empirical Methods in Natural Language Processing and Computational Natural Language Learning*, EMNLP-CoNLL '12, pages 466–477. Association for Computational Linguistics.

Susan Homan, Margaret Hewitt, and Jean Linder. 1994. The development and validation of a formula for measuring single-sentence test item readability. *Journal of Educational Measuremen*, 31(4):349–358.

Robin Jeffries and Heather Desurvire. 1992. Usability testing vs. heuristic evaluation: was there a contest? *ACM SIGCHI Bulletin*, 24(4):39–41.

J. Peter Kincaid, Robert P. Fishburne Jr., Richard L.Rogers, and Brad S. Chissom. 1975. *Derivation of New Readability Formulas (Automated Readability Index, Fog Count and Flesch Reading Ease Formula) for Navy Enlisted Personnel*. Naval Technical Training Command.

Sigrid Klerke, Alexandra L. Uitdenbogerd, Falk Scholer, and Tim Baldwin. 2016. Twitter corpus from eye gaze study. Twitter data-set from an unpublished paper.

Marten Risius and Theresia Pape. 2016. Developing and evaluating a readability measure for microblogging communication. In *E-Life: Web-Enabled Convergence of Commerce, Work, and Social Life*, pages 217–221. Springer International Publishing.

Irina Temnikova, Sarah Vieweg, and Carlos Castillo. 2015. The case for readability of crisis communications in social media. In *Proceedings of the 24th International Conference on World Wide Web*, WWW '15 Companion, pages 1245–1250. Association for Computing Machinery.

Alexandra L. Uitdenbogerd. 2005. Readability of French as a foreign language and its uses. In *ADCS 2005: Proceedings of the Tenth Australasian Document Computing Symposium*, pages 19–25.

Sowmya Vajjala and Ivana Lucic. 2019. On understanding the relation between expert annotations of text readability and target reader comprehension. In *Proceedings of the Fourteenth Workshop on Innovative Use of NLP for Building Educational Applications*, pages 349–359, Florence, Italy. Association for Computational Linguistics.

Carmen R. Wilson VanVoorhis and Betsy L. Morgan. 2007. Understanding power and rules of thumb for determining sample sizes. *Tutorials in Quantitative Methods for Psychology*, pages 43–50.

Red-faced ROUGE:
Examining the Suitability of ROUGE for Opinion Summary Evaluation

Wenyi Tay[1,2]**, Aditya Joshi**[2]**, Xiuzhen Zhang**[1]**, Sarvnaz Karimi**[2] **and Stephen Wan**[2]
[1]RMIT University, Australia
[2]CSIRO Data61, Australia
{wenyi.tay, xiuzhen.zhang}@rmit.edu.au
{Aditya.Joshi, Sarvnaz.Karimi, Stephen.Wan}@data61.csiro.au

Abstract

One of the most common metrics to automatically evaluate opinion summaries is ROUGE, a metric developed for text summarisation. ROUGE counts the overlap of word or word units between candidate summaries and reference summaries. This formulation treats all words in the reference summary equally. In opinion summaries, however, not all words in the reference are equally important. Opinion summarisation requires to correctly pair two types of semantic information: (1) opinion target, or aspect; and, (2) polarity of candidate and reference summaries. We investigate the suitability of ROUGE for evaluating opinion summaries of online reviews. We design three experiments to evaluate the behaviour of ROUGE for opinion summarisation on the ability to capture aspect and polarity. We show that ROUGE cannot distinguish opinion summaries of the same or opposite polarities for the same aspect. Moreover, ROUGE scores have significant variance under different configuration settings. As a result, we present three recommendations for future work on evaluating opinion summaries.

1 Introduction

Popular e-commerce websites allow users to express their opinion about products or services in the form of reviews. An opinion is formally defined as a combination of *aspect* (an attribute of the product or service as the opinion target, expressed through aspect words), and *sentiment polarity* (either positive or negative, expressed through opinion words) (Liu, 2012). The opinion expressed in online reviews potentially helps prospective buyers to make decisions. Given the large volume of reviews, it is time-consuming and often impractical for a user of these websites to read all reviews pertaining to the set of products that they are considering to purchase. This makes opinion summarisation important because it allows users to obtain aggregate key opinions about the product or service based on its reviews. Given the value of opinion summaries, automatic opinion summarisation is an active area of research with the focus of producing high-quality opinion summaries.

The quality of an opinion summary would ideally be evaluated by human annotators. For example, annotators may read a summary and rate it according to quality measures such as informativeness, ability to capture sentiment polarity, coherence and redundancy (Angelidis and Lapata, 2018). However, human evaluation is resource-intensive and not scalable. This motivates automatic evaluation. In the case of automatic evaluation, for a set of product reviews, reference summaries are written by human experts apriori. *Reference summaries* are the ground truth summaries against which *candidate summaries* to be evaluated.

Using reference and candidate summaries, automatic evaluation of opinion summaries adopts metrics from text summarisation (Lin, 2004) and machine translation (Papineni et al., 2002; Lavie and Denkowski, 2009). We focus on the most frequently reported metric for opinion summarisation, Recall-Oriented Understudy for Gisting Evaluation (ROUGE) (Lin, 2004) and leave the analysis of other evaluation metrics to future studies. ROUGE counts the overlap of word or word units between the candidate summary and reference summary with respect to the word units in the reference summary. A higher ROUGE score means a larger overlap of word units while a lower ROUGE score means a smaller overlap of word units. The ROUGE scores can then be used as a criterion to compare summaries and systems.

An opinion is a combination of aspect and sentiment, thus, the evaluation must assess both. ROUGE treats the contribution of all matched word units in the reference summary to the ROUGE score equally. This may not hold in the case of opinion summaries. For example, a lack of match to aspect terms in the reference summary may be due to the different ways people refer to the same aspect, or that it does not contain that aspect and thus the opinion is not present. The lack of a match to sentiment-bearing terms can mean there is no opinion present in the summary, the opinion is consistent but expressed differently or the opinion is opposite to the reference summary. That ROUGE does not differentiate the reasons for the lack of a word match or the reasons for mismatch has implications to evaluate opinions summaries. To date, opinion summarisation has been considered a special case of text summarisation. Therefore, the popularity of ROUGE for opinion summarisation seems intuitive. However, the distinction between opinion summarisation and text summarisation warrants a critical examination of the utility of ROUGE for opinion summarisation. Our research question is:

'Can ROUGE scores be used to correctly compare summaries to ensure that the candidate summary is accurate to the opinion aspect and polarity in the reference summary?'

This paper makes two-fold contributions: (1) Through experiments, we demonstrate that ROUGE is not able to accurately evaluate the opinions in the candidate summary against the reference summary[1]; and (2) Our discussion provides three recommendations for further research on opinion summary evaluation.

2 Related Work

Early work in opinion summarisation conducted their evaluation using metrics other than ROUGE. Pang and Lee (2004), an early work in extractive opinion summarisation, use sentence-level accuracy. Lerman et al. (2009) pre-date the existence of opinion summarisation datasets. Therefore, they use human evaluation for their systems. Pitler et al. (2010) propose an automatic metric for summarisation. This metric captures linguistic quality using a set of features. They conclude that syntactic features are the best indicators for linguistic quality of summaries. Following the availability of datasets with opinion summaries, ROUGE could be used for opinion summarisation. However, its value has been under-

stood to be limited for the evaluation of opinion summarisation. Jayanth et al. (2015) observe that ROUGE is influenced by topic terms more than sentiment terms. Therefore, they report two metrics: ROUGE scores and sentiment correlation. Mackie et al. (2014) show that, for microblog summarisation, ROUGE does not correlate with human judgment as well as a more naïve indicator: fraction of topic words. In addition, limitations of ROUGE to evaluate text summarisation have also been reported. Conroy and Schlesinger (2008) show that ROUGE may not correlate well with human evaluation for text summarisation, and needs to be combined with human scores. More recently, Graham (2015) present an extensive comparison of 192 variants of ROUGE, and show that the metrics have contrasting conclusions. Table 1 summarises key studies and the choice of automatic evaluation metrics used for opinion summarisation.

Despite the limitations, ROUGE is the most popular metric for opinion summarisation (Moussa et al., 2018). It continues to be used as an automatic evaluation in recent papers either on its own (Anchiêta et al., 2017) or in combination with other automatic metrics such as METEOR (Amplayo and Lapata, 2019). Angelidis and Lapata (2018) report ROUGE for multi-document opinion summarisation.

Alternatives to ROUGE have been proposed. Kabadjov et al. (2009) use sentiment intensity to measure sentiment summarisation. Kunneman et al. (2018) use gold standard summaries available in the forum as reference summaries, and report precision, recall and F_1 scores. Poddar et al. (2017) use a combination of lexical and sentiment similarity to capture sentiment-aware similarity between sentences.

We note that past work states the limitations of ROUGE as a part of the discussion of the results of their proposed systems, while examining these limitations is the focus of our work.

3 ROUGE

ROUGE measures content coverage of candidate summaries against reference summaries (Lin, 2004). Different variants of ROUGE have been proposed. For example, ROUGE-N, ROUGE-L and ROUGE-S count the number of overlapping units of n-gram, word sequences, and word pairs between the candidate summary and the reference

---

[1]Although the current analysis focuses on ROUGE for evaluating opinion summaries, the limitations of using word matching for evaluation is also a problem faced by text summarisation and text generation.

	Dataset	Task	ROUGE	Others
Ganesan et al. (2010)	Opinosis	Abstractive	R-1,R-2,R-SU4	No
Jayanth et al. (2015)	Movie	Abstractive	R-1,R-2	Senti Corr
Wang and Ling (2016)	RottenTomatoes	Abstractive	R-SU4	BLEU, METEOR
Angelidis and Lapata (2018)	Oposum	Extractive	R-1,R-2,R-L	No
Kunneman et al. (2018)	ProductReviews	Abstractive	No	Precision, Recall and F_1
Amplayo and Lapata (2019)	RottenTomatoes	Abstractive	R-1 R-2,R-L,R-SU4	METEOR

Table 1: Summary of automatic evaluation metrics used to evaluate opinion summaries.

Reference: The rooms were neat and clean.		**Summary1:** Clean room.				**Summary2:** The rooms were dirty.			
Configuration	**R-1**	**R-2**	**R-L**	**R-SU4**	**R-1**	**R-2**	**R-L**	**R-SU4**	
None	0.250	0.000	0.250	0.087	0.600	0.500	0.600	0.400	
Stemming	0.500	0.000	0.250	0.174	0.600	0.500	0.600	0.400	
StopWordRemoval	0.400	0.000	0.400	0.222	0.400	0.000	0.400	0.222	
StopWordRemoval+Stemming	0.800	0.000	0.400	0.444	0.400	0.000	0.400	0.222	

Table 2: F_1 score of ROUGE metrics under different configurations.

summaries respectively. The formula for ROUGE-N is shown in equation 1, where $gram_n$ is the choice of n-gram and S is the reference summary:

$$\text{ROUGE-N} = \frac{\sum_{gram_n \in S} Count_{match}(gram_n)}{\sum_{gram_n \in S} Count(gram_n)}.$$

$$(1)$$

The following considerations are important when using ROUGE:

1. **Multiple reference summaries**: A candidate summary with highest score for each pairwise evaluation of the candidate summary against each reference summary will be the ROUGE score for the summary. In this paper, we assume one reference summary.

2. **Pre-processing configurations**: Different pre-processing configurations can be taken into account. These typically include stemming and stop word removal. There are no recommended or commonly agreed pre-processing configurations. In this paper, we compare multiple combinations of these pre-processing configurations.

3. **Other configurations**: Although ROUGE is a recall-based metric, there is an option to report precision and F_1 scores with each ROUGE metric. The precision score takes the overlapping word units with reference to the word units of the Candidate summary. The F_1 score is the harmonic mean of the recall and precision score. In our work,

we investigate the different configurations of ROUGE for opinion summary evaluation.

4. **Comparing different systems**: ROUGE scores can be used to compare summarisation systems by taking the mean or median of all the summaries generated by the system. Should the ROUGE score at summary level be incorrect, the error propagates to the system level. We focus on the ROUGE scores at the summary level.

To demonstrate how ROUGE is computed, we consider the following hypothetical examples:
Reference summary: The rooms were neat and clean.
Candidate summary 1: Clean room.
Candidate summary 2: The rooms were dirty.

The opinion in Candidate summary 1 is consistent with the Reference summary since the two refer to clean rooms. Candidate summary 2 gives an opinion that is opposite to the Reference summary because it states that the rooms were dirty. Intuitively, Candidate summary 1 should be evaluated better as compared to Candidate summary 2.

We report the ROUGE scores of ROUGE-1 (R-1), ROUGE-2 (R-2), ROUGE-L (R-L) and ROUGE-SU4 (R-SU4) for these examples. Table 2 shows the ROUGE scores for various ROUGE metrics with different configurations for our example summaries. We see that for configurations "None" and "Stemming", all ROUGE metrics for Candidate summary 2 are higher than Candidate summary 1. In the case of "Stop-

No. of gold standard summaries	223
Min No. of Words in a summary	3
Max No. of Words in a summary	62
Average No. of Words in a summary	16.7
Median No. of Words in a summary	15

Table 3: Statistics of Opinosis Dataset.

WordRemoval", both summaries are the same. However, for "StopWordRemoval+Stemming", ROUGE metrics score Candidate summary 1 higher than Candidate summary 2. This demonstrates that the selection of the pre-processing configuration for ROUGE metrics may affect the scoring of summaries thus affecting the comparison of summaries.

The previous motivating example highlights that opinion summary evaluation requires a different notion of content coverage compared to text summarisation. Content coverage for opinion summaries is not just matching words. Opinion summary evaluation requires differential comparison of two groups of words, the aspect terms and sentiment-bearing words. We design three experiments that create summaries to reflect semantic and sentiment variability. They are described in the forthcoming section.

4 Experiment and Results

Opinosis is a opinion summary dataset by Ganesan et al. (2010). It contains 51 documents, where each document is a collection of opinions from online reviews on one aspect of hotels, cars and products. Examples of aspects are service for hotels, mileage of cars and size of netbooks (Note that aspects are called topics in the Opinosis dataset (Ganesan et al., 2010).) Each document is associated with three to five gold standard summaries. The gold standard summaries are created by human annotators by asking them to summarise the major opinions in the document. We observe duplicates in the gold standard summaries. After removing duplicates, there are 223 gold standard summaries left. Some key statistics of the dataset are listed in Table 3.

4.1 Summary Triplet Experiment

Our first experiment investigates a trivial case: "How does ROUGE respond when evaluating candidate summaries of similar or different aspects to the reference summary?"

We investigate this problem using summary triplets. Each triplet is made up of: (1) a reference summary (*Reference*); (2) a candidate summary of the same aspect (*Summ-SameAsp*); and (3) a candidate summary of a different aspect (*Summ-DiffAsp*). We begin by taking one gold standard summary as *Reference*. *Summ-SameAsp* is a randomly selected gold standard summary with the same aspect as *Reference*. For *Summ-DiffAsp*, we randomly select a summary with a different aspect from *Reference*. We repeat this process for every gold standard summary in the dataset. We have a total of 223 summary triplets.

Since the same aspect can be referred to by different words, we wish to avoid the bias from the same (different) aspect terms in the second (third) summary for the ROUGE metrics. Therefore, we mask the aspect terms in summaries[2]. Table 4 shows two examples of summary triplets. Observe that the terms in the *Summ-DiffAsp* are generally different from those in *Summ-SameAsp*.

Table 5 shows the proportion of triplets that *Summ-SameAsp* is scored higher than *Summ-DiffAsp*; higher values indicate better performance of ROUGE for ranking candidate summaries. The Recall score of ROUGE variants perform reasonably well with around 60% "accuracy" except for R-2. This result confirms our observation that there are few overlapping words between the candidate summary and reference summary when they are of different aspects.

We closely analyse the poor performance of R-2 and we found that it is due to the many ties in the scores of *Summ-SameAsp* and *Summ-DiffAsp*. In particular, many candidate summaries have a R-2 score of zero, as shown in Figure 1. When ROUGE scores are zero for both candidate summaries, scores are no longer meaningful for evaluation of candidate summaries.

We also observe that, with "Stemming", the proportion is higher than otherwise. One possible explanation is that "Stemming" relaxes the exact word match requirement to allow matching of different word forms.

We further examine how the choice of Recall, Precision or F_1 score affects the suitability of using ROUGE to compare summaries. In Table 5, we report the proportion of triplets that score

---

[2]For two aspects, summaries do not contain the given aspect terms. For the aspect "accuracy", we mask the word "accurate" and for aspect "eyesight-issues", we mask the word "eyes".

Reference	Summ-SameAsp	Summm-DiffAsp	R-1$_{\text{Summ-SameAsp}}$	R-1$_{\text{Summ-DiffAsp}}$
Great ⟨performance⟩ and handling. ⟨Performance⟩, styling and quality have good value for money.	Adequate ⟨performance⟩, nice looks, long distance cruiser. Overall ⟨performance⟩ good, poor engine ⟨performance⟩, gas mileage 22 highway and poor comfort level.	⟨Price⟩ was good. Best ⟨prices⟩ on other websites than Holiday Inn.	0.069	0.125
The ⟨rooms⟩ were very neat and clean.	The ⟨rooms⟩ are clean, large and comfortable. Not the most modern decor, however.	The Best Western in San Francisco is a decent, inexpensive option for one's stay in the city. It's ⟨location⟩ is terrific , being near many attractions, and the rooms, while small, are clean.	0.222	0.0.95

Table 4: Two examples of summary triplets. *Summ-SameAsp* is a randomly selected gold standard summary on the same aspect. whereas *Summ-DiffAsp* is on a different aspect. Words in angle bracket are the aspect terms we masked. We report the R-1 F_1 score with stemming and stop word removal.

	Recall				F_1 score			
Configuration	R-1	R-2	R-L	R-SU4	R-1	R-2	R-L	R-SU4
None	0.659	0.323	0.578	0.677	0.758	0.345	0.744	0.767
Stemming	0.682	0.341	0.596	0.695	0.771	0.359	0.744	0.776
StopWordRemoval	0.610	0.108	0.592	0.610	0.646	0.108	0.628	0.646
StopWordRemoval+Stemming	0.641	0.139	0.632	0.641	0.677	0.139	0.677	0.677

Table 5: Proportion of 223 summary triplets that *Summ-SameAsp* is scored higher than *Summ-DiffAsp*, by Recall and F_1 score, when the aspect terms are masked.

Summ-SameAsp higher than *Summ-DiffAsp*, using Recall and F_1 score. When using Recall score, the proportion of correctly assessed triplets is lower. Using F_1 score, the proportion is higher suggests that the Precision score plays a part in the comparison of candidate summaries of two different aspects and in a way controls for the different lengths in the candidate summaries.

There are three learning points to this experiment: (1) ROUGE gives a low score to candidate summary of a different aspect to the reference summary; (2) ROUGE-N score decreases as n-gram increases. It is possible that ROUGE-N scores are zero. Hence, is useful to plot the distribution of ROUGE scores; and, (3) Results suggest that "Stemming" increases ROUGE's ability to compare summaries.

4.2 Same Polarity Triplet Experiment

We had two annotators read all 223 gold standard summaries for 51 aspects and assign either a positive or negative sentiment polarity to each summary. When there is a conflict between the two assigned labels, a third annotator decides if the summary is positive or negative. Out of the 51 aspects, for 38 aspects (74.5%) the gold summaries of each aspect were consistent in their polarity whereas for 13 aspects (24.6%) the gold summaries were opposite.

Our second experiment is on the 38 aspects where all gold summaries have the same polarity. We design the experiment in a controlled way to study how ROUGE ranks candidate summaries containing same and opposite polarities compared to the same reference summary. Using the idea of a triplet summary as before, we create a triplet consisting of: (1) a reference summary (*Reference*); (2) a candidate summary that is consistent in aspect and sentiment polarity (*Summ-Syn*); and, (3) a candidate summary of the same aspect but opposite sentiment polarity (*Summ-Ant*). From the summary triplets we generated in the previous section, we use *Reference* and *Summ-SameAsp* summaries. By replacing the sentiment-bearing words of *Summ-SameAsp* with its synonym or antonym, we generate two versions of the same summary. We have a candidate summary that is consistent in aspect and sentiment polarity, *Summ-Syn*, and an-

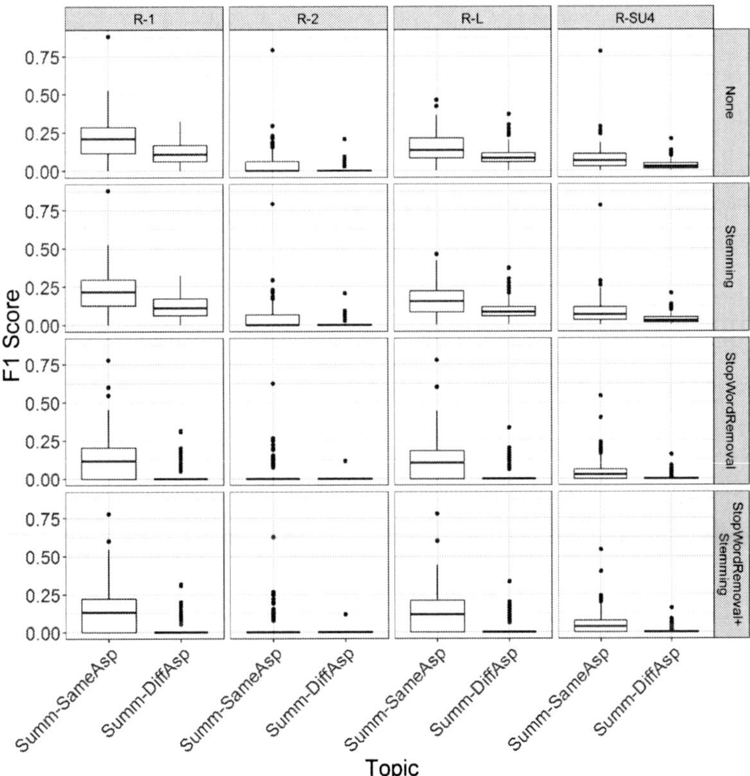

Figure 1: Boxplot of ROUGE scores show that scores for *Summ-DiffAsp* are generally lower than scores for *Summ-SameAsp*. Also, R-2 scores with "StopWordRemoval" are close to zero for candidate summaries which makes it less meaningful to be used to compare summaries.

other summary that is of same aspect but opposite polarity, *Summ-Ant*. This forms the second and third summaries of the triplet. This experiment controls for all the matching of the other words except for the sentiment-bearing words. Hence, we can study the impact of matching sentiment-bearing words in the reference summary.

To generate the synonym and antonym version of a summary, we first identify the sentiment-bearing words in the summary. A sentiment-bearing word is an adjective, adverb or verb and its lemmatised word form contains a sentiment score in SentiWordNet (Baccianella et al., 2010). The pre-processing steps of part-of-speech tagging, lemmatisation and looking it up in Senti-Wordnet was performed through python's NLTK package (Bird et al., 2009). We obtain synonyms and antonyms[3] from Wiktionary using the python package wiktionaryparser. Table 6 reports the pro-

portion of sentiment-bearing words present in the gold standard summaries and Table 7 shows examples of the synonyms and antonyms from Wiktionary.

Intuitively, *Summ-Syn* is accurate to *Reference* summary. As such, we expect *Summ-Syn* to be evaluated as a better summary over *Summ-Ant*. But, based on the ROUGE formula, we expect similar ROUGE scores for both candidate summaries.

Not all triplets have a synonym and antonym summary due to the nature of the synonym and antonym extraction method. We exclude triplets where there are no synonym and antonym summaries. We are left with 104 summary triplets with synonym and antonym summaries with at least one sentiment-bearing word replaced. On average, 0.124 of the summary is replaced by antonyms or synonyms. Table 8 shows two examples of summary triplet and Table 9 shows the proportion of triplets that ROUGE scored both summaries the same score.

From Table 9, most triplets have the same

---

[3]We also experimented with WordNet (Fellbaum, 1998) to get synonym and antonym of a sentiment-bearing word, however, the pairs we obtained from WordNet had lower coverage than Wiktionary.

	Proportion	Examples
Adjectives	0.122	easy, clean, friendly
Adverbs	0.050	not, very, too
Verbs	0.110	is, like, was

Table 6: Proportion of sentiment-bearing words of all words in gold standard summaries according to their part-of-speech tag.

Word	Synonym	Antonym
small	little	large
large	big	small
exceptional	excellent	ordinary
inferior	bad	superior
worse	unfavorable	good

Table 7: Five examples of sentiment-bearing words with its synonym and antonym.

score as expected from our understanding of the ROUGE formula. ROUGE scores cannot be used to differentiate summaries that are accurate to the reference summary in terms of sentiment polarity.

4.3 Opposite Polarity Triplet Experiment

Our third experiment is on the 13 aspects where gold summaries are not consistent in sentiment polarity. For example, for the topic "buttons_amazon_kindle", there are 1 negative summary and 3 positive summaries. We create a triplet consisting of: (1) a reference summary (*Reference*); (2) a candidate summary that is consistent in aspect and sentiment polarity (*Summ-SamePol*); and, (3) a candidate summary of the same aspect but opposite sentiment polarity (*Summ-DiffPol*). We took all possible combinations with the annotated gold standard summaries. We have a total of 142 summary triplets. An example of the triplet is shown in Table 10.

We report the proportion of the 142 summary triplets where *Summ-SamePol* is scored higher than *Summ-DiffPol* in Table 11. R-2 is excluded as the R-2 scores of both candidate summaries are mostly zero, which are not meaningful to compare summaries. We observe that in general, the proportion of triplets where ROUGE scores the second summary higher is lower than 50%. This suggests that ROUGE is not able to correctly rank candidate summaries of the same polarity with the reference summary. Also, we observe that configurations with "StopWordRemoval" is always lower than the configurations without.

From all experiments, the inclusion of "StopWordRemoval" often reduces the effectiveness of the the ability to use ROUGE scores to compare candidate summaries.

5 Discussion

Our empirical analysis for examining whether ROUGE is suitable for evaluating opinion summaries leads us to three suggestions for future studies for automatic evaluation in opinion summarisation:

1. The configurations for ROUGE can change or reverse the order of scores of summary. We observe that F_1 scores appear to compare summaries better than Recall. Also, "StopWordRemoval" seems to reduce the ability of ROUGE scores for comparing summaries for our dataset. Including "Stemming" often improve the ability to compare candidate summaries for our dataset. Hence, when reporting ROUGE scores, in addition to reporting ROUGE variants, we recommend reporting the configurations under which ROUGE was computed.

2. ROUGE scores will be low when candidate summary is of a different aspect from the reference summary. This is because opinions for different aspects are described by different sets of words. As such, there is little word overlap which leads to low ROUGE scores. Hence, for improvements to the opinion summary evaluation, we recommend checking for a match of the aspect in candidate and reference summary as a differentiating criteria.

3. It is not possible to infer from ROUGE scores if the candidate summary is accurate to the reference especially for sentiment polarity. ROUGE requires an exact match of the sentiment-bearing words in the reference summary. But reviewers express opinions differently which can result in the lack of match of sentiment-bearing words. We recommend sentiment agreement of candidate and reference summaries as another criteria for evaluation.

6 Conclusions

ROUGE is a popular metric for automatic evaluation of opinion summarisation. However, using ROUGE as a means to measure content coverage

Reference	Summ-Syn	Summ-Ant	R-1$_{\text{Summ-Syn}}$	R-1$_{\text{Summ-Ant}}$
Great ⟨performance⟩ and handling. ⟨Performance⟩, styling and quality have good value for money.	Adequate ⟨performance⟩, charming looks, long distance cruiser. Overall ⟨performance⟩ good, impoverished engine ⟨performance⟩, gas mileage 22 highway and impoverished comfort level.	Adequate ⟨performance⟩, horrible looks, long distance cruiser. Overall ⟨performance⟩ good, rich engine ⟨performance⟩, gas mileage 22 highway and rich comfort level.	0.069	0.069
The ⟨rooms⟩ were very neat and clean.	The ⟨rooms⟩ are clean, big and comforting. Not the most contemporary decor, however.	The ⟨rooms⟩ are clean, small and comfortless. Not the most ancient decor, however.	0.222	0.222

Table 8: Two examples of summary triplet. *Summ-Syn* is a synonym version of a gold standard summary. *Summary-Ant* is an antonym version of a gold standard summary. We report the R-1 F_1 score with stemming and stop word removal. The words that are replaced in the original summary are underlined.

Configuration	R-1	R-2	R-L	R-SU4
None	0.952	1.000	0.952	0.952
Stemming	0.933	1.000	0.942	0.933
StopWordRemoval	0.952	1.000	0.942	0.952
StopWordRemoval+Stemming	0.913	0.990	0.904	0.913

Table 9: Proportion of 104 summary triplets with same ROUGE scores for *Summ-Syn* and *Summ-Ant*.

Reference	Summ-SamePol	Summ-DiffPol	R-1$_{\text{Summ-SamePol}}$	R-1$_{\text{Summ-DiffPol}}$
New ⟨buttons⟩ are easy to use and effective. No more accidental ⟨button⟩ presses. ⟨Buttons⟩ make navigation easy.	Magical five way ⟨button⟩. Next page ⟨button⟩ on both side of kindle. No reset ⟨button⟩.	It is not user friendly and the ⟨buttons⟩ are not easily pressed.	0.000	0.118

Table 10: An examples of summary triplet. *Summ-SamePol* and *Summ-DiffPol* are gold standard summaries of the same aspect as *Reference* with same and different polarity respectively. We report the R-1 F_1 score with stemming and stop word removal.

Configuration	R-1	R-L	R-SU4
None	0.479	0.465	0.493
Stemming	0.479	0.465	0.500
StopWordRemoval	0.430	0.387	0.437
StopWordRemoval+Stemming	0.451	0.394	0.444

Table 11: Proportion of 142 summary triplets where *Summ-SamePol* is scored higher than *Summ-DiffPol*.

is not sufficient for the evaluation of opinion summaries. The word count overlap is not an indicator of accurate opinion summarisation. Our experiments simulate scenarios where inaccurate summaries are automatically generated. We observe that ROUGE is unable to differentiate summaries that are accurate and summaries that are inaccurate. For future work, we will investigate opinion summaries that contain multiple opinions. Based on the learning points from the investigation, we aim to propose a new metric that incorporates semantic similarity in terms of opinion target and opinion polarity.

Acknowledgments

We thank the anonymous reviewers for their thorough and insightful comments. Wenyi is supported by an Australian Government Research Training Program Scholarship and a CSIRO Data61 Top-up Scholarship.

References

Reinald Kim Amplayo and Mirella Lapata. 2019. Informative and controllable opinion summarization.

arXiv preprint arXiv:1909.02322.

Rafael Anchiêta, Rogerio Figueredo Sousa, Raimundo Moura, and Thiago Pardo. 2017. Improving opinion summarization by assessing sentence importance in on-line reviews. In *Proceedings of the Brazilian Symposium in Information and Human Language Technology*, pages 32–36, Uberlândia, Brazil.

Stefanos Angelidis and Mirella Lapata. 2018. Summarizing Opinions: Aspect Extraction Meets Sentiment Prediction and They Are Both Weakly Supervised. In *Proceedings of the Conference on Empirical Methods in Natural Language Processing*, pages 3675–3686, Brussels, Belgium.

Stefano Baccianella, Andrea Esuli, and Fabrizio Sebastiani. 2010. SentiWordNet 3.0: An enhanced lexical resource for sentiment analysis and opinion mining. In *Proceedings of the conference on International Language Resources and Evaluation*, Valletta, Malta.

Steven Bird, Ewan Klein, and Edward Loper. 2009. *Natural Language Processing with Python*, 1st edition. O'Reilly Media, Inc.

John M Conroy and Judith D Schlesinger. 2008. CLASSY and TAC 2008 Metrics. In *Proceedings of the Text Analysis Conference*, Gaithersburg, MD.

Christiane Fellbaum, editor. 1998. *WordNet: An Electronic Lexical Database*. MIT Press, Cambridge, MA.

Kavita Ganesan, ChengXiang Zhai, and Jiawei Han. 2010. Opinosis: A Graph Based Approach to Abstractive Summarization of Highly Redundant Opinions. In *Proceedings of the International Conference on Computational Linguistics*, pages 340–348, Beijing, China.

Yvette Graham. 2015. Re-evaluating Automatic Summarization with BLEU and 192 Shades of ROUGE. In *Proceedings of the Conference on Empirical Methods in Natural Language Processing*, pages 128–137, Lisbon, Portugal.

Jayanth Jayanth, Jayaprakash Sundararaj, and Pushpak Bhattacharyya. 2015. Monotone submodularity in opinion summaries. In *Proceedings of the Conference on Empirical Methods in Natural Language Processing*, pages 169–178, Lisbon, Portugal.

Mijail Kabadjov, Alexandra Balahur, and Ester Boldrini. 2009. Sentiment intensity: Is it a good summary indicator? In *Language and Technology Conference*, pages 203–212. Springer.

Florian Kunneman, Sander Wubben, Antal van den Bosch, and Emiel Krahmer. 2018. Aspect-based summarization of pros and cons in unstructured product reviews. In *Proceedings of the International Conference on Computational Linguistics*, pages 2219–2229, Santa Fe, NM.

Alon Lavie and Michael J. Denkowski. 2009. The meteor metric for automatic evaluation of machine translation. *Machine Translation*, 23(2-3):105–115.

Kevin Lerman, Sasha Blair-Goldensohn, and Ryan McDonald. 2009. Sentiment summarization: evaluating and learning user preferences. In *Proceedings of the Conference of the European Chapter of the Association for Computational Linguistics*, pages 514–522, Athens, Greece.

Chin-Yew Lin. 2004. ROUGE: A package for automatic evaluation of summaries. In *Text Summarization Branches Out*, pages 74–81, Barcelona, Spain.

Bing Liu. 2012. *Sentiment Analysis and Opinion Mining*. Morgan & Claypool Publishers.

Stuart Mackie, Richard McCreadie, Craig Macdonald, and Iadh Ounis. 2014. On choosing an effective automatic evaluation metric for microblog summarisation. In *Proceedings of the Information Interaction in Context Symposium*, pages 115–124.

Mohammed Elsaid Moussa, Ensaf Hussein Mohamed, and Mohamed Hassan Haggag. 2018. A survey on opinion summarization techniques for social media. *Future Computing and Informatics Journal*, 3(1):82–109.

Bo Pang and Lillian Lee. 2004. A sentimental education: Sentiment analysis using subjectivity summarization based on minimum cuts. In *Proceedings of the Annual Meeting on Association for Computational Linguistics*, page 271, Barcelona, Spain.

Kishore Papineni, Salim Roukos, Todd Ward, and Wei-Jing Zhu. 2002. Bleu: A method for automatic evaluation of machine translation. In *Proceedings of the Annual Meeting on Association for Computational Linguistics*, pages 311–318, Philadelphia, PA.

Emily Pitler, Annie Louis, and Ani Nenkova. 2010. Automatic evaluation of linguistic quality in multi-document summarization. In *Proceedings of the Annual Meeting of the Association for Computational Linguistics*, pages 544–554, Uppsala, Sweden.

Lahari Poddar, Wynne Hsu, and Mong Li Lee. 2017. Author-aware Aspect Topic Sentiment Model to Retrieve Supporting Opinions from Reviews. In *Proceedings of the Conference on Empirical Methods in Natural Language Processing*, pages 472–481, Copenhagen, Denmark.

Lu Wang and Wang Ling. 2016. Neural Network-Based Abstract Generation for Opinions and Arguments. In *Proceedings of the Conference of the North American Chapter of the Association for Computational Linguistics: Human Language Technologies*, pages 47–57, San Diego, CA.

Improved Document Modelling with a Neural Discourse Parser

Fajri Koto   **Jey Han Lau**   **Timothy Baldwin**
School of Computing and Information Systems
The University of Melbourne
`ffajri@student.unimelb.edu.au, jeyhan.lau@gmail.com, tbaldwin@unimelb.edu.au`

Abstract

Despite the success of attention-based neural models for natural language generation and classification tasks, they are unable to capture the discourse structure of larger documents. We hypothesize that explicit discourse representations have utility for NLP tasks over longer documents or document sequences, which sequence-to-sequence models are unable to capture. For abstractive summarization, for instance, conventional neural models simply match source documents and the summary in a latent space without explicit representation of text structure or relations. In this paper, we propose to use neural discourse representations obtained from a rhetorical structure theory (RST) parser to enhance document representations. Specifically, document representations are generated for discourse spans, known as the elementary discourse units (EDUs). We empirically investigate the benefit of the proposed approach on two different tasks: abstractive summarization and popularity prediction of online petitions. We find that the proposed approach leads to improvements in all cases.

1 Introduction

Natural language generation and document classification have been widely conducted using neural sequence models based on the encoder–decoder architecture. The underlying technique relies on the production of a context vector as the document representation, to estimate both tokens in natural language generation and labels in classification tasks. By combining recurrent neural networks with attention (Bahdanau et al., 2015), the model is able to learn contextualized representations of words at the sentence level. However, higher-level concepts, such as discourse structure beyond the sentence, are hard for an RNN to learn, especially for longer documents. We hypothesize that NLP tasks such as summarization and document classification can be improved through the incorporation of discourse information.

In this paper, we propose to incorporate latent representations of discourse units into neural training. A discourse parser can provide information about the document structure as well as the relationships between discourse units. In a summarization scenario, for example, this information may help to remove redundant information or discourse disfluencies. In the case of document classification, the structure of the text can provide valuable hints about the document category. For instance, a scientific paper follows a particular discourse narrative pattern, different from a short story. Similarly, we may be able to predict the societal influence of a document such as a petition document, in part, from its discourse structure and coherence.

Specifically, discourse analysis aims to identify the organization of a text by segmenting sentences into units with relations. One popular representation is Rhetorical Structure Theory (RST) proposed by Mann and Thompson (1988), where the document is parsed into a hierarchical tree, where leaf nodes are the segmented units, known as Entity Discourse Units (EDUs), and non-terminal nodes define the relations.

As an example, in Figure 1 the two-sentence text has been annotated with discourse structure based on RST, in the form of 4 EDUs connected with discourse labels `attr` and `elab`. Arrows in the tree capture the nuclearity of relations, wherein a "satellite" points to its "nucleus". The *Nucleus* unit is considered more prominent than the *Satellite*, indicating that the *Satellite* is a supporting sentence for the *Nucleus*. Nuclearity relationships between two EDUs can take the following three forms: Nucleus–Satellite, Satellite–Nucleus, and Nucleus–Nucleus. In this

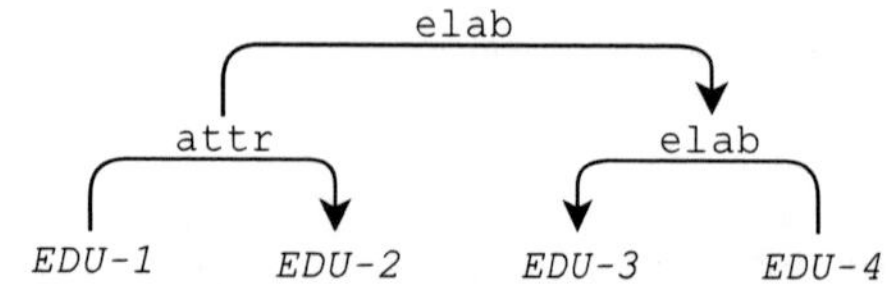

Figure 1: An example of a discourse tree, from (Yu et al., 2018); `elab` = elaboration; `attr` = attribute.

work, we use our reimplementation of the state of the art neural RST parser of Yu et al. (2018), which is based on eighteen relations: `purp, cont, attr, evid, comp, list, back, same, topic, mann, summ, cond, temp, eval, text, cause, prob, elab`.[1]

This research investigates the impact of discourse representations obtained from an RST parser on natural language generation and document classification. We primarily experiment with an abstractive summarization model in the form of a pointer–generator network (See et al., 2017), focusing on two factors: (1) whether summarization benefits from discourse parsing; and (2) how a pointer–generator network guides the summarization model when discourse information is provided. For document classification, we investigate the content-based popularity prediction of online petitions with a deep regression model (Subramanian et al., 2018). We argue that document structure is a key predictor of the societal influence (as measured by signatures to the petition) of a document such as a petition.

Our primary contributions are as follows: (1) we are the first to incorporate a neural discourse parser in sequence training; (2) we empirically demonstrate that a latent representation of discourse structure enhances the summaries generated by an abstractive summarizer; and (3) we show that discourse structure is an essential factor in modelling the popularity of online petitions.

2   Related Work

Discourse parsing, especially in the form of RST parsing, has been the target of research over a long period of time, including pre-neural feature engi-

neering approaches (Hernault et al., 2010; Feng and Hirst, 2012; Ji and Eisenstein, 2014). Two approaches have been proposed to construct discourse parses: (1) bottom-up construction, where EDU merge operations are applied to single units; and (2) transition parser approaches, where the discourse tree is constructed as a sequence of parser actions. Neural sequence models have also been proposed. In early work, Li et al. (2016a) applied attention in an encoder–decoder framework and slightly improved on a classical feature-engineering approach. The current state of the art is a neural transition-based discourse parser (Yu et al., 2018) which incorporates implicit syntax features obtained from a bi-affine dependency parser (Dozat and Manning, 2017). In this work, we employ this discourse parser to generate discourse representations.

2.1   Discourse and Summarization

Research has shown that discourse parsing is valuable for summarization. Via the RST tree, the salience of a given text can be determined from the nuclearity structure. In extractive summarization, Ono et al. (1994), O'Donnell (1997), and Marcu (1997) suggest introducing penalty scores for each EDU based on the nucleus–satellite structure. In recent work, Schrimpf (2018) utilizes the `topic` relation to divide documents into sentences with similar topics. Every chunk of sentences is then summarized in extractive fashion, resulting in a concise summary that covers all of the topics discussed in the passage.

Although the idea of using discourse information in summarization is not new, most work to date has focused on extractive summarization, where our focus is abstractive summarization. Gerani et al. (2014) used the parser of Joty et al. (2013) to RST-parse product reviews. By extracting graph-based features, important aspects are identified in the review and included in the summary based on a template-based generation framework. Although the experiment shows that the RST can be beneficial for content selection, the proposed feature is rule-based and highly tailored to review documents. Instead, in this work, we extract a latent representation of the discourse directly from the Yu et al. (2018) parser, and incorporate this into the abstractive summarizer.

---

[1]The details of each relation can be found on the RST website `http://www.sfu.ca/rst/index.html`

2.2 Discourse Analysis for Document Classification

Bhatia et al. (2015) show that discourse analyses produced by an RST parser can improve document-level sentiment analysis. Based on DPLP (Discourse Parsing from Linear Projection) — an RST parser by Ji and Eisenstein (2014) — they recursively propagate sentiment scores up to the root via a neural network.

A similar idea was proposed by Lee et al. (2018), where a recursive neural network is used to learn a discourse-aware representation. Here, DPLP is utilized to obtain discourse structures, and a recursive neural network is applied to the doc2vec (Le and Mikolov, 2014) representations for each EDU. The proposed approach is evaluated over sentiment analysis and sarcasm detection tasks, but found to not be competitive with benchmark methods.

Our work is different in that we use the latent representation (as distinct from the decoded discrete predictions) obtained from a neural RST parser. It is most closely related to the work of Bhatia et al. (2015) and Lee et al. (2018), but intuitively, our discourse representations contain richer information, and we evaluate over more tasks such as popularity prediction of online petitions.

3 Discourse Feature Extraction

To incorporate discourse information into our models (for summarization or document regression), we use the RST parser developed by Yu et al. (2018) to extract shallow and latent discourse features. The parser is competitive with other traditional parsers that use heuristic features (Feng and Hirst, 2012; Li et al., 2014; Ji and Eisenstein, 2014) and other neural network-based parsers (Li et al., 2016b).

3.1 Shallow Discourse Features

Given a discourse tree produced by the RST parser (Yu et al., 2018), we compute several shallow features for an EDU: (1) the nuclearity score; (2) the relation score for each relation; and (3) the node type and that of its sibling.

Intuitively, the nuclearity score measures how informative an EDU is, by calculating the (rela-

tive) number of ancestor nodes that are nuclei:[2]

$$\frac{\sum_{x \in \text{ancestor}(e)} \mathbb{1}_{\text{nucleus}}(x)}{h(\text{root})}$$

where e is an EDU; $h(x)$ gives the height from node x;[3] and $\mathbb{1}_{\text{nucleus}}(x)$ is an indicator function, i.e. it returns 1 when node x is a nucleus and 0 otherwise.

The relation score measures the importance of a discourse relation to an EDU, by computing the (relative) number of ancestor nodes that participate in the relation:

$$\frac{\sum_{x \in \text{ancestor}(e)} \mathbb{1}_{r_j}(x) h(x)}{\sum_{x \in \text{ancestor}(e)} h(x)}$$

where r_j is a discourse relation (one of 18 in total).

Note that we weigh each ancestor node here by its height; our rationale is that ancestor nodes that are closer to the root are more important. The formulation of these shallow features (nuclearity and relation scores) are inspired by Ono et al. (1994), who propose a number of ways to score an EDU based on the RST tree structure.

Lastly, we have 2 more features for the node type (nucleus or satellite) of the EDU and its sibling. In sum, our shallow feature representation for an EDU has 21 dimensions: 1 nuclearity score, 18 relation scores, and 2 node types.

3.2 Latent Discourse Features

In addition to the shallow features, we also extract latent features from the RST parser.

In the RST parser, each word and POS tag of an EDU span is first mapped to an embedding and concatenated to form the input sequence $\{x_1^w, ..., x_m^w\}$ (m is number of words in the EDU). Yu et al. (2018) also use syntax features ($\{x_1^s, ..., x_m^s\}$) from the bi-affine dependency parser (Dozat and Manning, 2017). The syntax features are the output of the multi-layer perceptron layer (see Dozat and Manning (2017) for full details).

The two sequences are then fed to two (separate) bi-directional LSTMs and average pooling is applied to learn the latent representation for an

---

[2]The ancestor nodes of an EDU are all the nodes traversed in its path to the root.

[3]Note that tree height is computed from the leaves, and so the *height* of the root node is equivalent to the *depth* of a leave node.

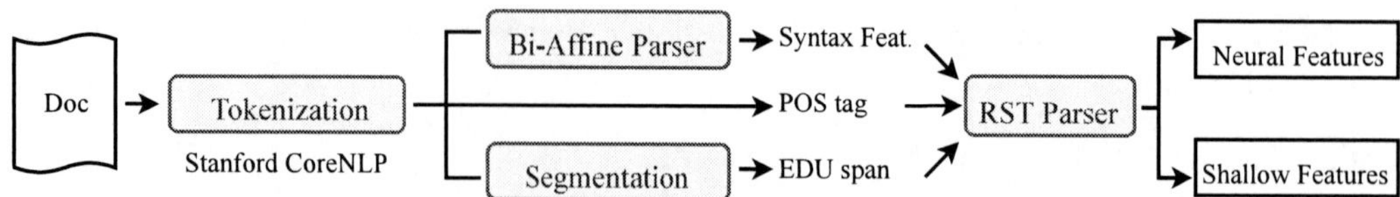

Figure 2: Pipeline of RST feature extraction

EDU:

$$\{h_1^w, .., h_m^w\} = \text{Bi-LSTM}_1(\{x_1^w, .., x_m^w\})$$
$$\{h_1^s, ..., h_m^s\} = \text{Bi-LSTM}_2(\{x_1^s, .., x_m^s\})$$
$$h^e = \text{Avg-Pool}(\{h_1^w, .., h_m^w\}) \oplus$$
$$\text{Avg-Pool}(\{h_1^s, ..., h_m^s\})$$

where $\oplus$ denotes the concatenate operation.

Lastly, Yu et al. (2018) apply another bi-directional LSTM over the EDUs to learn a contextualized representation:

$$\{f_1, ..., f_n\} = \text{Bi-LSTM}(\{h_1^e, .., h_n^e\})$$

We extract the contextualized EDU representations ($\{f_1, ..., f_n\}$) and use them as latent discourse features.

3.3 Feature Extraction Pipeline

In Figure 2, we present the feature extraction pipeline. Given an input document, we use Stanford CoreNLP to tokenize words and sentences, and obtain the POS tags.[4] We then parse the processed input with the bi-affine parser (Dozat and Manning, 2017) to get the syntax features.

The RST parser (Yu et al., 2018) requires EDU span information as input. Previous studies have generally assumed the input text has been pre-processed to obtain EDUs, as state-of-the-art EDU segmentation models are very close to human performance (Hernault et al., 2010; Ji and Eisenstein, 2014). For our experiments, we use the pre-trained EDU segmentation model of Ji and Eisenstein (2014) to segment the input text to produce the EDUs.

Given the syntax features (from the bi-affine parser), POS tags, EDU spans, and tokenized text, we feed them to the RST parser to extract the shallow and latent discourse features.

We re-implemented the RST Parser in *PyTorch* and were able to reproduce the results reported in the original paper. We train the parser on the same

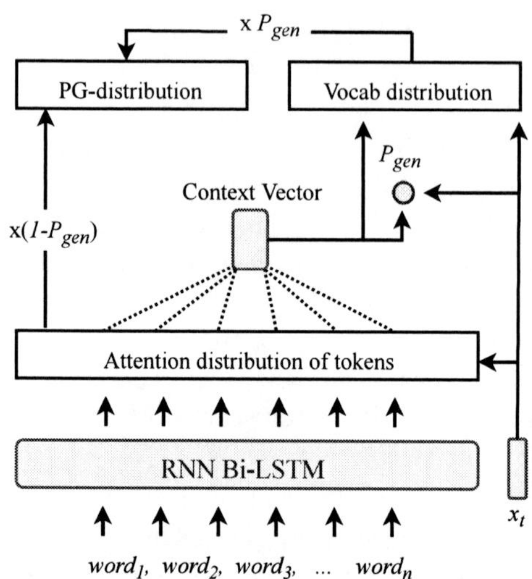

Figure 3: Architecture of the pointer–generator network (See et al., 2017).

data (385 documents from the Wall Street Journal), based on the configuration recommended in the paper.

To generate syntax features, we re-train an open-source bi-affine model, and achieve over 95% unlabelled and labelled attachment scores.[5] Source code used in our experiments is available at: `https://github.com/fajri91/RSTExtractor`.

4 Abstractive Summarization

Abstractive summarization is the task of creating a concise version of a document that encapsulates its core content. Unlike extractive summarization, abstractive summarization has the ability to create new sentences that are not in the original document; it is closer to how humans summarize, in that it generates paraphrases and blends multiple sentences in a coherent manner.

Current sequence-to-sequence models for abstractive summarization work like neural machine translation models, in largely eschewing symbolic

---

[4] `https://stanfordnlp.github.io/CoreNLP/`

[5] `https://github.com/XuezheMax/NeuroNLP2`

analysis and learning purely from training data. Pioneering work such as Rush et al. (2015), for instance, assumes the neural architecture is able to learn main sentence identification, discourse structure analysis, and paraphrasing all in one model. Studies such as Gehrmann et al. (2018); Hsu et al. (2018) attempt to incorporate additional supervision (e.g. content selection) to improve summarization. Although there are proposals that extend sequence-to-sequence models based on discourse structure — e.g. Cohan et al. (2018) include an additional attention layer for document sections — direct incorporation of discourse information is rarely explored.

Hare and Borchardt (1984) observe four core activities involved in creating a summary: (1) topic sentence identification; (2) deletion of unnecessary details; (3) paragraph collapsing; and (4) paraphrasing and insertion of connecting words. Current approaches (Nallapati et al., 2016; See et al., 2017) capture topic sentence identification by leveraging the pointer network to do content selection, but the model is left to largely figure out the rest by providing it with a large training set, in the form of document–summary pairs. Our study attempts to complement the black-box model by providing additional supervision signal related to the discourse structure of a document.

4.1 Summarization Model

Our summarization model is based on the pointer–generator network (See et al., 2017). We present the architecture in Figure 3, and summarize it as follows:

$$\{h_i\} = \text{Bi-LSTM}_1(\{w_i\}) \tag{1}$$
$$e_i^t = v^\intercal \tanh(W_h h_i + W_s s_t + b_e) \tag{2}$$
$$a^t = \text{softmax}(e^t)$$
$$h_t^* = \sum_i a_i^t h_i$$
$$P_{voc} = \text{softmax}(V'(V[s_t, h_t^*] + b_v) + b_v')$$
$$p_{gen} = \sigma(w_{h^*}^\intercal h_t^* + w_s^\intercal s_t + w_x^\intercal x_t + b_g)$$

where $\{h_i\}$ are the encoder hidden states, $\{w_i\}$ are the embedded encoder input words, s_t is the decoder hidden state, and x_t is the embedded decoder input word.

The pointer–generator network allows the model to either draw a word from its vocabulary (generator mode), or select a word from the input document (pointer mode). p_{gen} is a scalar denoting the probability of triggering the generator mode, and P_{voc} gives us the generator mode's vocabulary probability distribution. To get the final probability distribution over all words, we sum up the attention weights and P_{voc}:

$$P(w) = p_{gen}P_{voc}(w) + (1 - p_{gen}) \sum_{i:w_i=w} a_i^t$$

To discourage repetitive summaries, See et al. (2017) propose adding coverage loss in addition to the cross-entropy loss:

$$c^t = \sum_{t'=0}^{t-1} a^{t'}$$
$$e_i^t = v^\intercal \tanh(W_h h_i + W_s s_t + W_c c_i^t + b_e)$$
$$\text{covloss}_t = \sum_i \min(a_i^t, c_i^t)$$

Intuitively, the coverage loss works by first summing the attention weights over all words from previous decoding steps (c^t), using that information as part of the attention computation (e_i^t), and then penalising the model if previously attended words receive attention again (covloss_t). See et al. (2017) train the model for an additional 3K steps with the coverage penalty after it is trained with cross-entropy loss.

4.2 Incorporating the Discourse Features

We experiment with several simple methods to incorporate the discourse features into our summarization model. Recall that the discourse features (shallow or latent) are generated for each EDU, but the summarization model operates at the word level. To incorporate the features, we assume each word within an EDU span receives the same discourse feature representation. Henceforth we use g and f to denote shallow and latent discourse features.

Method-1 (M1): Incorporate the discourse features in the Bi-LSTM layer (Equation (1)) by concatenating them with the word embeddings:

$$\{h_i\} = \text{Bi-LSTM}_1(\{w_i \oplus f_i\}); \text{or}$$
$$\{h_i\} = \text{Bi-LSTM}_1(\{w_i \oplus g_i\})$$

Method-2 (M2): Incorporate the discourse features by adding another Bi-LSTM:

$$\{h_i'\} = \text{Bi-LSTM}_2(\{h_i \oplus f_i\}); \text{or}$$
$$\{h_i'\} = \text{Bi-LSTM}_2(\{h_i \oplus g_i\})$$

Method	F1			Recall			Precision		
	R-1	R-2	R-L	R-1	R-2	R-L	R-1	R-2	R-L
PG	36.82	15.92	33.57	37.36	16.10	34.05	38.72	16.86	35.32
+M1-latent	37.76	16.51	34.48	**40.15**	17.52	36.65	37.90	16.64	34.61
+M1-shallow	37.45	16.23	34.22	**40.15**	17.38	**36.68**	37.34	16.24	34.13
+M2-latent	**38.04**	**16.73**	**34.83**	38.92	17.05	35.62	**39.54**	**17.51**	**36.23**
+M2-shallow	37.15	16.13	33.96	38.52	16.68	35.21	38.19	16.67	34.91
+M3-latent	37.04	16.05	33.86	37.52	16.22	34.29	38.95	16.98	35.63
+M3-shallow	37.09	16.15	33.95	39.05	16.97	35.73	37.62	16.46	34.45
PG+Cov	39.32	17.22	36.02	40.33	17.61	36.93	**40.82**	**17.99**	**37.42**
+M1-latent	**40.06**	**17.63**	36.70	**44.44**	**19.53**	**40.69**	38.60	17.05	35.39
+M1-shallow	39.78	17.50	36.50	43.50	19.08	39.89	38.94	17.22	35.75
+M2-latent	40.00	17.62	**36.72**	43.53	19.17	39.94	39.28	17.37	36.09
+M2-shallow	39.58	17.30	36.36	44.00	19.19	40.38	38.40	16.87	35.31
+M3-latent	39.23	17.00	36.00	42.95	18.54	39.37	38.29	16.69	35.16
+M3-shallow	39.57	17.31	36.28	43.85	19.14	40.17	38.37	168.6	35.20

Table 1: Abstractive summarization results.

Method-3 (M3): Incorporate the discourse features in the attention layer (Equation (2)):

$$e_i^t = v^\mathsf{T} \tanh(W_h h_i + W_s s_t + W_f f_i + b_e); \text{ or}$$
$$e_i^t = v^\mathsf{T} \tanh(W_h h_i + W_s s_t + W_g g_i + b_e)$$

4.3 Data and Result

We conduct our summarization experiments using the anonymized CNN/DailyMail corpus (Nallapati et al., 2016). We follow the data preprocessing steps in See et al. (2017) to obtain 287K training examples, 13K validation examples, and 11K test examples.

All of our experiments use the default hyperparameter configuration of See et al. (2017). Every document and its summary pair are truncated to 400 and 100 tokens respectively (shorter texts are padded accordingly). The model has 256-dimensional hidden states and 128-dimensional word embeddings, and vocabulary is limited to the most frequent 50K tokens. During test inference, we similarly limit the length of the input document to 400 words and the length of the generated summary to 35–100 words for beam search.

Our experiment has two pointer–generator network baselines: (1) one without the coverage mechanism ("PG"); and (2) one with the coverage mechanism ("PG+Cov"; Section 4.1). For each baseline, we incorporate the latent and shallow discourse features separately in 3 ways (Section 4.2), giving us 6 additional results.

We train the models for approximately 240,000-270,000 iterations (13 epochs). When we include the coverage mechanism (second baseline), we train for an additional 3,000–3,500 iterations using the coverage penalty, following See et al. (2017).

We use ROUGE (Lin, 2004) as our evaluation metric, which is a standard measure based on overlapping n-grams between the generated summary and the reference summary. We assess unigram (R-1), bigram (R-2), and longest-common-subsequence (R-L) overlap, and present F1, recall and precision scores in Table 1.

For the first baseline (PG), we see that incorporating discourse features consistently improves recall and F1. This observation is consistent irrespective of how (e.g. M1 or M2) and what (e.g. shallow or latent features) we add. These improvements do come at the expense of precision, with the exception of M2-latent (which produces small improvements in precision). Ultimately however, the latent features are in general a little better, with M2-latent produing the best results based on F1.

We see similar observations for the second baseline (PG+Cov): recall is generally improved at the expense of precision. In terms of F1, the gap between the baseline and our models is a little closer, and M1-latent and M2-latent are the two best performers.

Example-1
Reference: nigel short said women should accept they 're ` hard-wired very differently ' made comments when explaining why there were so few women in chess . female chess players reacted angrily to mr short 's statements last night .
PG + Cov + M1-latent: nigel short , 49 , said women should accept they were ` hard-wired very differently ' and were n't as adept at playing chess as men . mr short , who was the first english player to play a world chess championship match , made the comments when explaining why there were few women in competitive chess .
PG + Cov: nigel short has controversially claimed women were not suited to playing chess because it required logical thinking . but critics immediately pointed out that he lost a high-profile game against a woman grandmaster . he told new in chess magazine : ` why should -lsb- men and women -rsb- function in the same way ? '
Example-2
Reference: deva joseph hit problems when she could n't fit handbag inside suitcase . 14-year-old left in floods of tears after flight to spain left without her . offered to pay for bag to go in hold but was told she needed a credit card . easyjet said it should have made an exception to policy of accepting cash .
PG + Cov + M1-latent: deva joseph , 14 , was left stranded at a busy airport after being told she would not be allowed to take her flight home to spain . the teenager offered to pay for the second item to be put in the hold but was told only credit cards would be accepted - even though she is too young to have one . a schoolgirl was left stranded at a busy airport after easyjet refused to let her board its plane - because she was carrying two pieces of hand luggage .
PG + Cov: deva joseph , 14 , was stranded at a busy airport after being told she would not be allowed to take her flight home to spain . teenager offered to pay for the second item to be put in the hold but she is too young to have one .

Figure 4: Comparison of summaries between our model and the baseline.

4.4 Analysis and Discussion

We saw previously that our models generally improve recall. To better understand this, we present 2 examples of generated summaries, one by the baseline ("PG+Cov") and another by our model ("M1-latent"), in Figure 4. The highlighted words are overlapping words in the reference. In the first example, we notice that the summary generated by our model is closer to the reference, while the baseline has other unimportant details (e.g. *he told new in chess magazine : ' why should -lsb- men and women -rsb- function in the same way ?*). In the second example, although there are more overlapping words in our model's summary, it is a little repetitive (e.g. first and third paragraph) and less concise.

Observing that our model generally has better recall (Table 1) and its summaries tend to be more verbose (e.g. second example in Figure 4), we calculated the average length of generated summaries for PG+Cov and M1-latent, and found that they are of length 55.2 and 64.4 words respectively. This suggests that although discourse information

helps the summarization model overall (based on consistent improvement in F1), the negative side effect is that the summaries tend to be longer and potentially more repetitive.

5 Petition Popularity Prediction

Online petitions are open letters to policy-makers or governments requesting change or action, based on the support of members of society at large. Understanding the factors that determine the popularity of a petition, i.e. the number of supporting signatures it will receive, provides valuable information for institutions or independent groups to communicate their goals (Proskurnia et al., 2017).

Subramanian et al. (2018) attempt to model petition popularity by utilizing the petition text. One novel contribution is that they incorporate an auxiliary ordinal regression objective that predicts the scale of signatures (e.g. 10K vs. 100K). Their results demonstrate that the incorporation of auxiliary loss and hand-engineered features boost performance over the baseline.

In terms of evaluation metric, Subramanian et al. (2018) use: (1) mean absolute error (MAE); and (2) mean absolute percentage error (MAPE), calculated as $\frac{100}{n} \sum_{i=1}^{n} \frac{\hat{y}_i - y_i}{y_i}$, where n is the number of examples and $\hat{y}_i$ (y_i) the predicted (true) value. Note that in both cases, lower numbers are better.

Similar to the abstractive summarization task, we experiment with incorporating the discourse features of the petition text to the petition regression model, under the hypothesis that discourse structure should benefit the model.

5.1 Deep Regression Model

As before, our model is based on the model of Subramanian et al. (2018). The input is a concatenation of the petition's title and content words, and the output is the log number of signatures. The input sequence is mapped to GloVe vectors (Pennington et al., 2014) and processed by several convolution filters with max-pooling to create a fixed-width hidden representation, which is then fed to fully connected layers and ultimately activated by an exponential linear unit to predict the output. The model is optimized with mean squared error (MSE). In addition to the MSE loss, the authors include an auxiliary ordinal regression objective that predicts the scale of signatures (e.g. $\{10, 100, 1000, 10000, 100000\}$), and found that it improves performance. Our model is based on the best model that utilizes both the MSE and ordinal regression loss.

5.2 Incorporating the Discourse Features

We once again use the methods of incorporation presented in Section 4.2. As the classification model uses convolution networks, only Method-1 is directly applicable.

We also explore replacing the convolution networks with a bidirectional LSTM ("Bi-LSTM w/ GloVe"), based on the idea that recurrent networks are better at capturing long range dependencies between words and EDUs. For this model, we test both Method-1 and Method-2 to incorporate the discourse features.[6]

Lastly, unlike the summarization model that needs word level input (as the pointer network requires words to attend to in the source document), we experiment with replacing the input words with EDUs, and embed the EDUs with either the latent ("Bi-LSTM w/ latent") or the shallow ("Bi-LSTM w/ shallow") features.

5.3 Data, Result, and Discussion

We use the US Petition dataset from (Subramanian et al., 2018).[7] In total we have 1K petitions with over 12M signatures after removing petitions that have less than 150 signatures. We use the same train/dev/test split of 80/10/10 as Subramanian et al. (2018).

We present the test results in Table 2. We tune the models based on the development set using MAE, and find that most converge after 8K–10K iterations of training. We are able to reproduce the performance of the baseline model ("CNN w/ GloVe"), and find that once again, adding the shallow discourse features improves results.

Next we look at the LSTM model ("Bi-LSTM w/ GloVe"). Interestingly, we found that replacing the CNN with an LSTM results in improved MAE, but worse MAPE. Adding discourse features to this model generally has marginal improvement in all cases.

When we replace the word sequence with EDUs ("Bi-LSTM w/ latent" and "Bi-LSTM w/ shallow"), we see that the latent features outperform the shallow features. This is perhaps unsurprising,

---

[6] Our LSTM has 200 hidden units, and uses a dropout rate of 0.3, and L2 regularization.

[7] The data is collected from `https://petitions.whitehouse.gov`.

Model	MAE	MAPE
CNN w/ GloVe	1.16	14.38
+ M1-latent	1.15	14.66
+ M1-shallow	**1.12**[1]	**14.19**
Bi-LSTM w/ GloVe	1.14	14.57
+ M1-latent	1.13	14.39
+ M1-shallow	1.13	14.25
+ M2-latent	1.12	14.02
+ M2-shallow	1.13	14.20
Bi-LSTM w/ latent	**1.11**[2]	**13.91**
Bi-LSTM w/ shallow	1.15	14.67

Table 2: Average petition regression performance over 3 runs (noting that lower is better for both MAE and MAPE). One-sided t-tests show that both (1) and (2) are significantly better than the baseline ($p < 0.05$ and $p < 0.005$, resp.).

given that the shallow discourse features have no information about the actual content, and are unlikely to be effective when used in isolation without the word features.

6 Conclusion and Future Work

In this paper, we explore incorporating discourse information into two tasks: abstractive summarization and popularity prediction of online petitions. We experiment with both hand-engineered shallow features and latent features extracted from a neural discourse parser, and found that adding them generally benefits both tasks. The caveat, however, is that the best method of incorporation and feature type (shallow or latent) appears to be task-dependent, and so it remains to be seen whether we can find a robust universal approach for incorporating discourse information into NLP tasks.

References

Dzmitry Bahdanau, Kyunghyun Cho, and Yoshua Bengio. 2015. Neural machine translation by jointly learning to align and translate. *International Conference on Learning Representations*.

Parminder Bhatia, Yangfeng Ji, and Jacob Eisenstein. 2015. Better document-level sentiment analysis from rst discourse parsing. In *Proceedings of the 2015 Conference on Empirical Methods in Natural Language Processing*, pages 2212–2218.

Arman Cohan, Franck Dernoncourt, Doo Soon Kim,

Trung Bui, Seokhwan Kim, Walter Chang, and Nazli Goharian. 2018. A discourse-aware attention model for abstractive summarization of long documents. In *Proceedings of the 2018 Conference of the North American Chapter of the Association for Computational Linguistics: Human Language Technologies, Volume 2 (Short Papers)*, pages 615–621, New Orleans, Louisiana.

Timothy Dozat and Christopher D. Manning. 2017. Deep biaffine attention for neural dependency parsing. In *Proceedings of the 2016 international conference on learning representations*, pages 1–8.

Vanessa Wei Feng and Graeme Hirst. 2012. Text-level discourse parsing with rich linguistic features. In *Proceedings of the 50th Annual Meeting of the Association for Computational Linguistics*, pages 60–68.

Sebastian Gehrmann, Yuntian Deng, and Alexander M Rush. 2018. Bottom-up abstractive summarization. In *Proceedings of Empirical Methods in Natural Language Processing*, pages 4098–4109.

Shima Gerani, Yashar Mehdad, Giuseppe Carenini, Raymond T. Ng, and Bita Nejat. 2014. Abstractive summarization of product reviews using discourse structure. In *Proceedings of the 2014 Conference on Empirical Methods in Natural Language Processing (EMNLP)*, pages 1602–1613.

Victoria C. Hare and Kathleen M. Borchardt. 1984. Direct instruction of summarization skills. *Journal Reading Research Quarterly, Wiley, International Reading Association*, pages 62–78.

Hugo Hernault, Helmut Prendinger, David A. duVerle, and Mitsuru Ishizuka. 2010. Hilda: A discourse parser using support vector machine classification. *Dialogue and Discourse*, 1(3):1–33.

Wan Ting Hsu, Chieh-Kai Lin, Ming-Ying Lee, Kerui Min, Jing Tang, and Min Sun. 2018. A unified model for extractive and abstractive summarization using inconsistency loss. In *Proceedings of the 56th Annual Meeting of the Association for Computational Linguistics*, pages 132–141.

Yangfeng Ji and Jacob Eisenstein. 2014. Representation learning for text-level discourse parsing. In *Proceedings of the 52nd Annual Meeting of the Association for Computational Linguistics*, pages 13–24.

Shafiq R. Joty, Giuseppe Carenini, Raymond T. Ng, and Yashar Mehdad. 2013. Combining intra- and multi-sentential rhetorical parsing for document-level discourse analysis. In *Proceedings of the 51st Annual Meeting of the Association for Computational Linguistics (Volume 1: Long Papers)*, volume 1, pages 486–496.

Quoc V. Le and Tomas Mikolov. 2014. Distributed representations of sentences and documents. In *Proceedings of The 31st International Conference on Machine Learning*, pages 1188–1196.

Kangwook Lee, Sanggyu Han, and Sung-Hyon Myaeng. 2018. A discourse-aware neural network-based text model for document-level text classification. *Journal of Information Science*, 44.

Jiwei Li, Rumeng Li, and Eduard H. Hovy. 2014. Recursive deep models for discourse parsing. In *Proceedings of the 2014 Conference on Empirical Methods in Natural Language Processing (EMNLP)*, pages 2061–2069.

Qi Li, Tianshi Li, and Baobao Chang. 2016a. Discourse parsing with attention-based hierarchical neural networks. In *Proceedings of the 2016 Conference on Empirical Methods in Natural Language Processing*, pages 362–371.

Qi Li, Tianshi Li, and Baobao Chang. 2016b. Discourse parsing with attention-based hierarchical neural networks. In *Proceedings of the 2016 Conference on Empirical Methods in Natural Language Processing*, pages 362–371.

Chin-Yew Lin. 2004. Rouge: A package for automatic evaluation of summaries. In *Text Summarization Branches Out: Proceedings of the ACL-04 Workshop*, pages 74–81.

William C. Mann and Sandra A. Thompson. 1988. Rhetorical structure theory: Toward a functional theory of text organization. *Text Interdisciplinary Journal for the Study of Discourse*, pages 243–281.

Daniel Marcu. 1997. From discourse structures to text summaries. In *Proceedings of of ACL Workshop on Intelligent Scalable Text Summarisation*, pages 82–88.

Ramesh Nallapati, Bowen Zhou, Cicero Nogueira dos santos, Caglar Gulcehre, and Bing Xiang. 2016. Abstractive text summarization using sequence-to-sequence rnns and beyond. In *Proceedings of The 20th SIGNLL Conference on Computational Natural Language Learning*, pages 280–290.

Michael O'Donnell. 1997. Variable-length on-line document generation. In *Proceedings of the 6th European Workshop on Natural Language Generation*, pages 82–91.

Kenji Ono, Kazuo Sumita, and Seiji Miike. 1994. Abstract generation based on rhetorical structure extraction. In *Proceedings of the 15th conference on Computational linguistics*, pages 344–348.

Jeffrey Pennington, Richard Socher, and Christopher D. Manning. 2014. Glove: Global vectors for word representation. In *Proceedings of the 2014 Conference on Empirical Methods in Natural Language Processing (EMNLP)*, pages 1532–1543.

Julia Proskurnia, Przemyslaw A. Grabowicz, Ryota Kobayashi, Carlos Castillo, Philippe Cudré-Mauroux, and Karl Aberer. 2017. Predicting the success of online petitions leveraging multidimensional time-series. In *WWW '17 Proceedings of the*

26th International Conference on World Wide Web, pages 755–764.

Alexander M. Rush, Sumit Chopra, and Jason Weston. 2015. A neural attention model for abstractive sentence summarization. In *Proceedings of Empirical Methods in Natural Language Processing*, pages 379–389.

Natalie M. Schrimpf. 2018. Using rhetorical topics for automatic summarization. *Proceedings of the Society for Computation in Linguistics*, 1(1):125–135.

Abigail See, Peter J. Liu, and Christopher D. Manning. 2017. Get to the point: Summarization with pointer-generator networks. In *Proceedings of the 55th Annual Meeting of the Association for Computational Linguistics*, pages 1073–1083.

Shivashankar Subramanian, Timothy Baldwin, and Trevor Cohn. 2018. Content-based popularity prediction of online petitions using a deep regression model. In *ACL 2018: 56th Annual Meeting of the Association for Computational Linguistics*, volume 2, pages 182–188.

Nan Yu, Meishan Zhang, and Guohong Fu. 2018. Transition-based neural RST parsing with implicit syntax features. In *roceedings of the 27th International Conference on Computational Linguistics*, pages 559–570.

Does an LSTM forget more than a CNN?
An empirical study of catastrophic forgetting in NLP

Gaurav Arora   **Afshin Rahimi**   **Timothy Baldwin**

School of Computing and Information Systems
The University of Melbourne
gaurava@student.unimelb.edu.au
{arahimi,tbaldwin}@unimelb.edu.au

Abstract

Catastrophic forgetting — whereby a model trained on one task is fine-tuned on a second, and in doing so, suffers a "catastrophic" drop in performance over the first task — is a hurdle in the development of better transfer learning techniques. Despite impressive progress in reducing catastrophic forgetting, we have limited understanding of how different architectures and hyper-parameters affect forgetting in a network. In this paper, we aim to understand factors which cause forgetting during sequential training. Our primary finding is that CNNs forget less than LSTMs. We show that max-pooling is the underlying operation which helps CNNs alleviate forgetting compared to LSTMs. We also found that curriculum learning (Bengio et al., 2009), placing a hard task towards the end of task sequence, reduces forgetting. We analysed the effect of fine-tuning contextual embeddings on catastrophic forgetting, and found that using fixed word embeddings is preferable to fine-tuning.[1]

1 Introduction

Transfer learning — transferring knowledge from a source task to a target task — has become an essential technique in both computer vision and NLP. Earlier attempts at transfer learning were limited in their applicability (Mou et al., 2016), as the transfer only worked for very similar tasks: if the source and target tasks were not very similar, training on the target task resulted in catastrophic forgetting (Ratcliff, 1990; McCloskey and Cohen, 1989), whereby the neural network abruptly forgets previously-acquired knowledge during training on a new task, limiting inductive transfer. ULMFit (Howard and Ruder, 2018) developed specialised techniques to reduce forgetting during the fine-tuning process, resulting in successful transfer learning. A general finding of this work was that uncovering underlying causes of catastrophic forgetting can result in improved architectures for transfer learning.

Previous studies found that using dropout (Goodfellow et al., 2014) and sharp activation functions (French, 1991) help reduce catastrophic forgetting. Sharp activation functions effectively distribute each task to different parts of the network. It is unknown if increasing the capacity of the network will also have a similar effect. Another study found that using a max operation (Srivastava et al., 2013) in the network reduces forgetting. There hasn't been a study comparing forgetting for different architectures to test if networks with the max operation have less forgetting. Task complexity (Nguyen et al., 2019) is positively correlated with total error observed, but it is unknown how we should arrange tasks in sequence to reduce forgetting. We conduct an empirical study to understand how factors like network architecture and capacity affect forgetting.

In this work, we design experiments to empirically address the following research questions:

RQ1: Do some neural architectures forget more than others?

RQ2 Should we fine-tune pre-trained embeddings in a continual learning setup?

RQ3 Do networks with more capacity forget less?

RQ4 Do networks forget more during/after training over a difficult task?

Our experimental setup consists of studying forgetting for various neural architectures and hyper-parameter configurations in a continual learning setup. We train the network without access to data from the previous tasks, and measure how much of the knowledge learned in previous tasks is forgotten. After performing initial experiments, we

---

[1]All code associated with this paper is available at https://github.com/gauravaror/catastrophic_forgetting

conduct further experiments to understand the underlying reason for the differences in forgetting.

We found that CNNs forget less than LSTMs, because of max pooling. Max-pooling decreases forgetting as the gradient doesn't update all the shared parameters. Further, adding contextual word embeddings such as ELMo (Peters et al., 2018a) with either an LSTM or a CNN as the top layer, reduces the forgetting for both architectures. Surprisingly, the LSTM forgets less when the ELMo embeddings are frozen, and fine-tuning performs worse than randomly initialised embeddings in a continual learning setup. We also found that, contrary to common wisdom, more network capacity doesn't always result in less forgetting. For CNNs, sequence forgetting increases as we increase the number of layers, whereas for the dimensionality of hidden layers, the degree of forgetting depends on the task sequence: the choice of which task to train first has more impact on forgetting than the number of hidden units in the network, and placing difficult tasks towards the end of the task sequence reduces overall forgetting.

2 Background

2.1 Catastrophic forgetting

Our work is similar to early work on catastrophic forgetting (Ratcliff, 1990; McCloskey and Cohen, 1989), which studied factors affecting forgetting like the width of the network or amount of training. The amount of new learning was found to be directly proportional to the amount of forgetting in previous tasks. They also found that lowering the learning rate decreases forgetting, but impairs the ability of the network to learn. Recent empirical work (Goodfellow et al., 2014) studied the effect of the activation function and different training algorithms. They found that training with dropout is always better, and the choice of activation is task-dependent and should be cross-validated.

Both earlier empirical studies focused on only two-task sequences, whereas we use four-task sequences, based on Nguyen et al. (2019) who studied the effect of total sequence complexity and sequential heterogeneity. They found that error rates do not correlate with the sequential heterogeneity of tasks.

Rebuffi et al. (2017) and Li and Hoiem (2018) found that training on a subsequent task doesn't update the classification layer of the previous task, and only updates the encoder layer, increasing

catastrophic forgetting. Knowledge distillation loss (Hinton et al., 2015) is a commonly used technique to avoid dramatic changes in the encoder layer, while adapting the classification layer for the new task.

Yogatama et al. (2019) found catastrophic forgetting while fine-tuning ELMo and BERT (Devlin et al., 2019) embeddings, similar to our findings. They also found that sampling examples from a different task (with uniform probability) enables a network to learn all tasks reasonably well; this requires access to all task simultaneously, which is different from our setup. We consider whether to fine-tune embeddings or not, which is similar to the question posed by Peters et al. (2019), who focused on various types of task. In contrast, we address the same question in a continual learning setup.

2.2 Transfer Learning

ULMFit (Howard and Ruder, 2018) was an effort to enable transfer learning in a pre-trained LSTM network. The authors utilised specialised techniques such as layer-wise fine-tuning, concat pooling (concatenation of final hidden state), and max and mean pooling of all hidden states to alleviate catastrophic forgetting during fine-tuning. In this work, we argue and empirically support the use of max pooling, as opposed to using only average pooling, as a means to reduce catastrophic forgetting. It would be interesting to further study the individual architectural design choices that enable successful transfer learning, which we leave to future work.

2.3 Evaluation metrics for Catastrophic forgetting

GEM (Lopez-Paz et al., 2017) proposed Average, Backward, and Forward Transfer to measure catastrophic forgetting. Backward Transfer measures the influence task t has on the previous task $k < t$, and Forward Transfer measures the influence on future task $k > t$. Since we are only concerned with forgetting in the network, we use Backward Transfer with a slight modification to measure catastrophic forgetting in a task sequence.

The amount of absolute drop in task performance is not a good measure of forgetting because tasks have different state-of-the-art (SOTA) performance and difficulty level (e.g. majority class performance). The forgetting ratio (Serra et al.,

2018) is a normalised measure of forgetting across multiple tasks which we also adapt in this work.

3 Method

We study catastrophic forgetting by training tasks sequentially. During sequential task training, networks suffer from forgetting knowledge acquired in previous tasks because of overfitting to new tasks, and also lack of access to the training data of the old tasks. Our setup is very similar to fine-tuning in transfer learning. Various tasks and task sequences used in our study are described in Section 4. Task sequences are trained using neural architectures with fixed hyper-parameters, as described in Section 6. We performed experiments to find how forgetting changes for different architectures (Section 7), ways to use embeddings (Section 8), network configurations (Section 9), and task sequences (Section 10). We compare the amount of forgetting of various architectural design choices using the evaluation metric proposed in Section 5.

4 Tasks

We selected four text classification tasks of different nature, each targeting different language learning tasks for English.

- **Stanford Sentiment Treebank ("SST"):** fine-grained sentiment classification over five classes (Socher et al., 2013).

- **Subjectivity ("SUBJ"):** binary classification of Subjectivity vs. Objectivity in IMDB reviews (Pang and Lee, 2004).

- **TREC Question classification ("TREC"):** coarse-grained classification of questions, based on 6 classes (Voorhees and Tice, 1999).

- **Corpus of Linguistic Acceptability ("CoLA"):** prediction of whether a sentence is grammatical or not (Warstadt et al., 2018).

Table 1 contains state-of-the-art (SOTA), majority class voting, and single-task performance using a CNN for all four tasks.

We consider a task difficult for our setup if we cannot attain performance close to SOTA with a simple architecture like an LSTM or CNN. SST is the most challenging task in our setup: achieving SOTA performance requires large pre-trained contextual embeddings like ELMo (Peters et al.,

2018a). Socher et al. (2013) proposed recursive neural networks for SST based on an explicit constituency parse tree, and results for standard LSTMs are well below SOTA. CoLA is a moderately difficult task as it also requires specialised techniques to perform reasonably well. For TREC and Subjectivity, on the other hand, it is possible to reach performance close to SOTA with simple architectures. We intentionally selected tasks of varying difficulty to see if forgetting increases with more complicated tasks.

4.1 Task Sequence

We formed various task sequences with length four using the tasks detailed in Table 1. We used all 24 task sequences possible. A selection of task sequences is listed in Table 6, wherein the code name indicates the order of the tasks during training (e.g. "TREC_SUBJ_CoLA_SST" = train on TREC first, then SUBJ, CoLA and SST).

5 Evaluation

We used accuracy as our metric for evaluation, except for CoLA where we used Mathews correlation (Matthews, 1975) as the dataset is unbalanced. All results are averaged over five runs with different random seeds.

After training a sequence, we calculate the performance score for each component task (over held-out test data). Because absolute metrics are not comparable between tasks, we normalise the raw performance score for each task to get a roughly uniform metric, disregarding task difficulty. Further, we use normalised performance scores to calculate forgetting for each task and the whole task sequence, as detailed below.

5.1 Normalisation

Direct comparison of forgetting between TREC and SST, e.g., is not ideal, as the absolute difference in accuracy could be up to 40%. Normalisation enables fairer comparison of forgetting, as it incorporates a measure of task difficulty based on SOTA and majority class performance. This normalisation is similar to the forgetting ratio proposed by Serra et al. (2018).

We normalise performance metric based on: (a) SOTA for the task PER_{SOTA}; and (b) majority class performance PER_{MAJ}. $\text{PER}_{i,j}$ refers to performance measured for the task at position i after training the task at position j (where $i \leq j$). $P_{i,j}$

Tasks	SOTA	Majority Class	CNN	#Training Instances	#Classes
TREC	0.98 Cer et al. (2018)	0.19	0.91	5452	6
SUBJ	0.96 Cer et al. (2018)	0.50	0.92	9000	2
CoLA	0.34 Warstadt et al. (2018)	0.00	0.25	8551	2
SST	0.55 Peters et al. (2018a)	0.25	0.38	8544	5

Table 1: The tasks targeted in this work, with state of the art (SOTA) performance, majority class performance, and performance when trained individually using a single-layer CNN. We used Mathew's Correlation Coefficient (Matthews, 1975) for CoLA, and accuracy as the performance measure for all other tasks.

refs to the normalised performance of the task at position i after training the task at position j. Negative values for $P_{i,i}$ indicate accuracy is below majority classifier accuracy.

$$P_{i,j} = \frac{\text{PER}_{i,j} - \text{PER}_{\text{MAJ}}}{\text{PER}_{\text{SOTA}} - \text{PER}_{\text{MAJ}}} \quad \forall i \leq j \quad (1)$$

5.2 Forgetting of a Sequence

We use this normalised performance to measure forgetting for an entire task sequence. Our forgetting metric is similar to Backward Transfer proposed by Lopez-Paz et al. (2017). We track forgetting of the task sequence, which is a scaled version of Backward Transfer.

Sequence forgetting (F_{Seq}) is the sum over the individual task forgetting values F_i. Individual task forgetting is the scaled performance drop for each task, indexed based on the position at which the task was trained. The difference between performance when the task was first trained and the end of the sequence, is considered to be performance drop:

$$F_i = \frac{P_{i,i} - P_{i,T}}{|P_{i,i}|} \quad (2)$$

$$F_{Seq} = \sum_{i=1}^{i=T} F_i \quad (3)$$

where T refers to the position of the last trained task. We also refer to F_i as F_{TASK} when TASK is trained at position i (e.g. when TREC is trained as the first task, $F_1 = F_{\text{TREC}}$). Lower forgetting is better.

6 Neural Models

Our network consists of an encoder and a classification layer. The encoder learns to extract useful

Optimiser	Adam
Learning Rate	0.001
Patience	10
Batch size	128
dropout	0.5
Embedding dimension	128
ELMo hidden size	1024

Table 2: Hyper-parameters used for training.

features for the task automatically. The classification layer uses the encoder output to label instances, which is dependent on the task and actual label set. We use the same encoder but different classifier layers for all tasks. Our architecture is similar to the one used by Li and Hoiem (2018). The AllenNLP library (Gardner et al., 2018) was used to build our neural models. We used Mathew's Correlation as the early stopping criteria for CoLA, and loss for the other tasks. Unless otherwise stated, we train networks with the hyper-parameters listed in Table 2.

7 RQ1: Do LSTMs forget more than CNNs?

CNN-based architectures (Krizhevsky et al., 2012) have been widely used for transfer learning, whereas LSTM-based architectures need specialised techniques to transfer successfully (Howard and Ruder, 2018). This difference motivated us to compare forgetting between LSTMs and CNNs.

We used the standard LSTM encoder implementation from AllenNLP. The CNN encoder in AllenNLP is single-layered, which we adapted to multi-layer with max-pooling applied after the final layer. We used a single n-gram filter with width two for the CNN. We ran experiments using LSTM and CNN encoders with all task sequences and network configurations.

7.1 Results: CNN vs. LSTM

Table 3 and Figure 1 compare the main results for forgetting between LSTMs and CNNs on task sequence TREC_SUBJ_SST_CoLA. Single-layered CNN networks forget considerably less than LSTM networks. The lowest Sequence Forgetting value of $F_{Seq} = 1.52$ for LSTMs is more than double the lowest F_{Seq} of 0.71 observed for CNNs. CNNs perform substantially better with single-layered networks, and forgetting starts increasing with higher numbers of layers. With higher numbers of CNN layers, forgetting is only slightly lower than LSTM networks. We also performed experiments with bi-directional LSTMs and observed very small-scale reductions in forgetting, which could be due to slightly better modelling of the task; because of the marginal difference in performance, we omit results for bi-directional LSTMs from the paper.

We conducted further experiments to understand what makes single-layered CNNs special in reducing forgetting. Convolution and pooling operations are two distinctive features of CNNs. We ran experiments replacing max-pooling with average pooling.

7.2 Results: max pooling vs. average pooling

Table 4 and Figure 2 compare the main results for forgetting between max pooling and average pooling on task sequence TREC_SUBJ_SST_CoLA. Replacing max pooling with average pooling resulted in a slight increase in F_{Seq}, indicating max-pooling helps in reducing forgetting.

A network with max pooling can train on different input distributions with less interference, as different sub-networks (paths created by max-pooling) can be used for each input distribution. Srivastava et al. (2013) also report less forgetting using a max operation in their proposed networks. We observe that even with average pooling, forgetting in CNNs is not as severe as in LSTMs.

8 RQ2: Should we fine-tune pre-trained embedding in continual learning setup?

Contextual embeddings like ELMo (Peters et al., 2018b) and BERT (Devlin et al., 2019) have became a standard component in recent NLP architectures. The embeddings used in these pre-trained architectures encode latent linguistic features from a large corpus, thus improving sample efficiency and generalisability of models, which could change the forgetting dynamics of the network. We used ELMo embeddings in a continual learning setup, and compared the model's forgetting in two scenarios: (a) embeddings are fine-tuned during each task's training; and (b) embeddings are fixed. Our experiments using fine-tuned and fixed ELMo embeddings are referred to as "CNN$_{Fix}$" and "CNN$_{FT}$" respectively, in the case of the CNN.

8.1 Results: fixed ELMo

Table 3 presents results with fixed ELMo. Freezing ELMo's parameters in continual learning reduces the forgetting, e.g. for a single-layered LSTM with 400 hidden dimensions, forgetting was reduced from 2.57 to 0.58, which is the least forgetting overall. The impact of fixed embeddings is similar for both LSTMs and CNNs. Surprisingly, LSTMs perform slightly better than CNN's, contrary to results when embeddings are not used. We hypothesise that this is due to the LSTM sharing a similar structure to the underlying model used by ELMo.

8.2 Results: ELMo with fine-tuning

Table 3 compares results using fixed and fine-tuned ELMo embeddings. While fixed ELMo helps the networks reduce forgetting, fine-tuning catastrophically degrades the networks' ability to retain previous knowledge. Most of the gain from using contextual embeddings is lost if we fine-tune the embeddings: our results show that fine-tuning increases forgetting from 0.58 to 2.57 in a single-layer LSTM network with 400 hidden dimensions. These results highlight the importance of specialised fine-tuning techniques like gradual unfreezing and discriminative fine-tuning in ULMFit (Howard and Ruder, 2018). Interestingly, the CNN performs better with fine-tuning, but the LSTM performs better with fixed ELMo embeddings.

#Layers	Hdim	CNN	LSTM	CNN$_R$	LSTM$_R$	CNN$_{Fix}$	LSTM$_{Fix}$	CNN$_{FT}$	LSTM$_{FT}$
1	100	**0.71**	**1.52**	**0.97**	**1.78**	0.77	0.71	1.90	2.63
1	400	0.76	2.24	0.98	2.57	**0.63**	**0.58**	**1.46**	**2.57**
2	100	1.51	2.23	1.94	1.92	1.02	0.85	2.28	2.81
2	400	1.74	2.11	1.95	2.30	1.01	0.95	2.08	2.19
3	100	2.03	2.04	2.02	2.13	1.83	1.53	2.16	2.33
3	400	2.04	1.81	2.45	1.79	1.18	1.47	2.28	2.33

Table 3: Sequence Forgetting (F_{Seq}) of TREC_SUBJ_SST_CoLA using CNN and LSTM for various network configurations. We denote the experiment with regularisation as "CNN$_R$", fixed ELMo as "CNN$_{Fix}$", and ELMo with fine-tuning as "CNN$_{FT}$". Similar notation is used for the LSTM, and "Hdim" denotes the dimensionality of the given hidden layer.

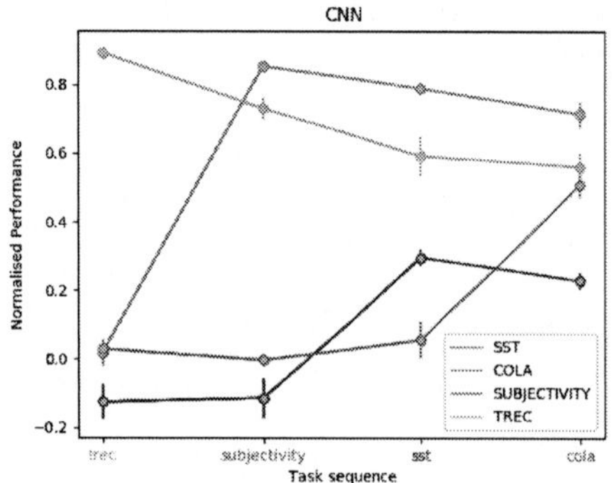
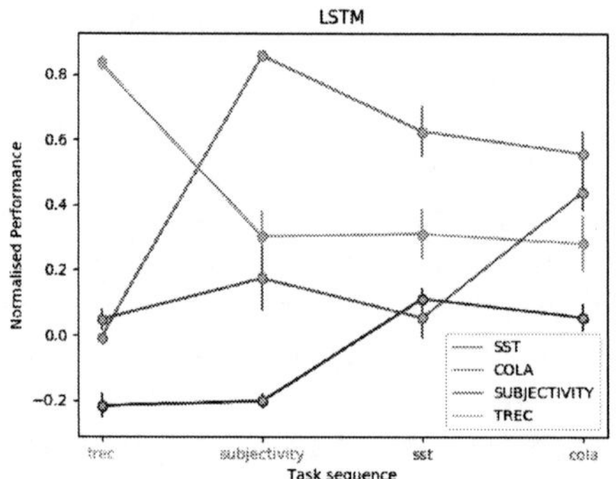

Figure 1: Performance of the LSTM and CNN on task sequence TREC_SUBJ_SST_COLA, with one layer and hidden dimensionality 100.

#Layers	Hdim	max pool	avg pool
1	100	**0.71**	0.97
1	400	0.75	0.97
1	900	0.72	**0.90**
2	100	1.66	1.61
2	400	1.72	1.83
2	900	1.58	2.18

Table 4: Sequence Forgetting (F_{Seq}) of TREC_SUBJ_SST_CoLA using max pooling and average pooling for a different configuration.

9 RQ3: Do networks with more capacity forget less?

A lot of work in the catastrophic forgetting literature has focused on freezing the weights of the network (Mallya and Lazebnik, 2018; Fernando et al., 2017). Here, we ask whether increasing the capacity of the network would encourage the network to use different sub-networks for different tasks. Another thought was that increasing capacity would drive the network to over-fit, which could further increase forgetting.

We considered neural networks up to four layers deep, with hidden dimensions of 100, 400, 900, and 1400. We trained each task sequence on sixteen different network configurations formed using four different layers and hidden dimensionalities. The hidden dimensionality refers to the number of features in the hidden state in an LSTM, or the number of output channels in a CNN.

Since networks with greater capacity are more vulnerable to over-fitting, we also studied the effect of regularising the network. We also ran all experiments using L2 regularisation by setting weight decay to 0.0001 during training. LSTM$_R$ and CNN$_R$ denote results for experiments with L2 regularisation.

9.1 Results: Layers

Table 3 lists results for different layers for both CNNs and LSTMs, and their regularised versions. Both CNNs and LSTMs have the least forgetting

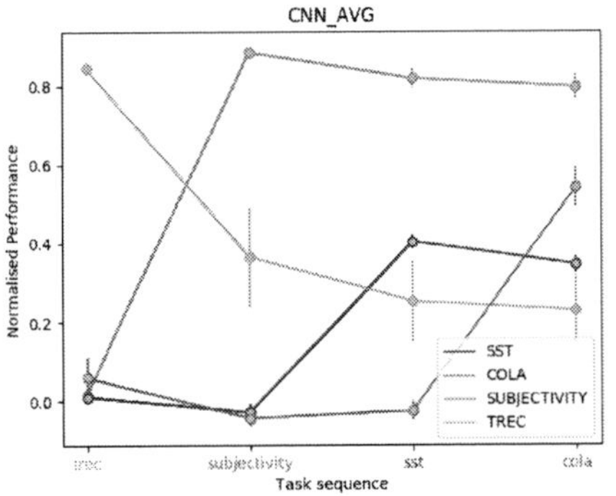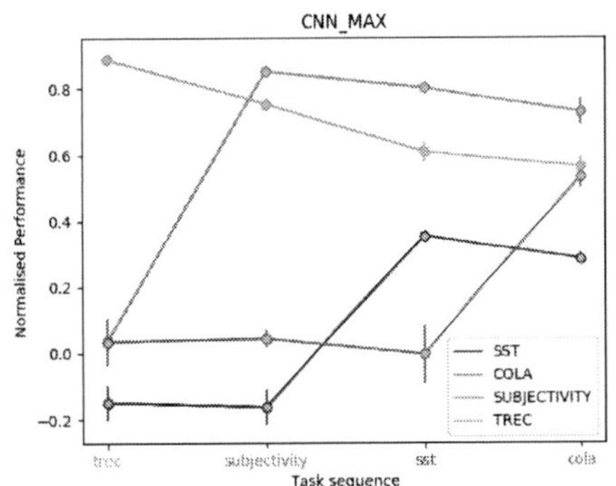

Figure 2: Performance of Max and Average pooling on task sequence: TREC_SUBJ_SST_CoLA, with Layer 1 and Hidden Dimension 100.

for the single-layered network. By increasing the number of layers in the network, forgetting also increases. For CNNs, there is a huge degradation when changing the network from one layer to two layers. This steep increase could be because we are using max-pooling only after the final layer. We might be able to reduce forgetting in a multi-layered CNN by having a pooling operation after every layer. We found that regularising using weight decay didn't help in reducing forgetting. Our finding differs that of previous work on dropout (Goodfellow et al., 2014), which found that it helps in reducing forgetting. However, the results are not comparable due to the different type of regularisation.

9.2 Results: Hidden Dimensionality

Table 5 shows forgetting for hidden dimensionalities 100 and 900 for four task sequences. We limit our analysis to single-layered CNNs without embeddings. We find that the hidden dimensionality with least forgetting is dependent on the arrangement of tasks in the task sequence. We observe that task sequences starting with TREC and CoLA have lower forgetting with $hdim = 100$ (the first and fourth task sequences in Table 5). In contrast, task sequences starting with SST and Subjectivity have less forgetting with $hdim = 900$ (the second and third task sequence in Table 5). Increasing the dimensionality reduces forgetting for some tasks, but increases forgetting for others. For task sequence CoLA_SST_TREC_SUBJ in Table 5, increasing the dimensionality from 100 to 900 increases forgetting for CoLA by 0.61, whereas forgetting for SST is reduced by 0.33. Out of the

24 tasks sequences considered, only four have $|F_{Seq}^{900} - F_{Seq}^{100}| > 0.3.$[2]

10 RQ4: Do networks forget more when training a difficult task?

From our experiments on task sequences of length four, we observed F_{Seq} varies from 0.63 to 1.81 on different task sequences. The task ordering has a substantial impact on F_{Seq}. To understand the forgetting behaviour for tasks individually, we ran an experiment with two tasks. We train two tasks sequentially, and report the forgetting observed on the first task after training the second task, averaged over five runs. We train all twelve possible configurations using four tasks.

10.1 Results: Two-task Sequence

Table 7 lists the results of forgetting on sequence lengths two with a single-layered network and hidden dimensionality of 100. We observed training a difficult task causes overall less forgetting for the previous task. Training TREC after Subjectivity results in forgetting of 0.46, whereas training hard tasks like SST only results in forgetting of 0.17. We also observe TREC suffers distinctively less forgetting by training SST and CoLA, which is also observable in our results for the four-task sequence.

To further understand why training a difficult task leads to less forgetting, we recorded the total number of epochs used in training each task. Table 8 shows the number of epochs used for the second task in training two-task sequences. TREC

---

[2]The superscript on F_{Seq} here indicates the dimensionality.

Code	Hdim	F_{TOTAL}	F_{TREC}	F_{CoLA}	F_{SST}	F_{SUBJ}
TREC_SUBJ_SST_CoLA	100	0.77	0.40	0.0	0.23	0.12
	900	+0.32	+0.215	0.0	+0.02	+0.08
SST_CoLA_TREC_SUBJ	100	1.36	0.12	0.58	0.65	0.0
	900	−0.41	−0.02	−0.22	−0.18	0.0
SUBJ_CoLA_SST_TREC	100	1.81	0.0	0.61	0.61	0.59
	900	−0.59	0.0	−0.35	−0.21	−0.03
CoLA_SST_TREC_SUBJ	100	0.99	0.15	0.31	0.54	0.0
	900	+0.23	−0.04	+0.61	−0.33	0.0
SST_TREC_SUBJ_COLA	100	0.93	0.19	0.0	0.61	0.12
	900	−0.10	+0.10	0.0	−0.16	−0.04

Table 5: F_{Seq} and individual task forgetting for four task sequences on a single-layered network with hidden dimensionality 100 and 900. The actual forgetting value is reported for dimensionality 100 and increment/decrement from reference value at 100 dimensionality is reported for 900 dimensionality, with red indicating an increase in forgetting and green indicating a decrease in forgetting from 100 dimensionality.

generally requires more epochs than other tasks, accounting for the large drop in performance when training TREC later in the sequence.

10.2 Results: Forgetting when training a difficult task

Table 6 lists the top and bottom task sequences based on minimum F_{Seq} across all considered dimensionalities. Results are in line with our observation from the two-task sequence, that training a difficult task causes less forgetting to tasks trained earlier. Having a difficult task like SST towards the end of a sequence reduces overall forgetting. In Table 6, all the top task sequences end with difficult task SST or CoLA, whereas all bottom tasks ends in TREC. This finding is similar to the findings from curriculum learning (Bengio et al., 2009): training a hard task later in a sequence has overall less error, and leads to better generalisation. Forgetting of a task is inversely proportional to its difficulty level, resulting in CoLA and SST having the least forgetting when added to the end of the sequence.

11 Discussion and Limitations

In our study, we used a very loose definition of what makes a task difficult, mainly comparing single-task performance on a simple CNN/LSTM model with SOTA. Our current analysis shows that task and task sequencing plays a pivotal role in forgetting observed in the network. To establish what quantifies a difficult task in a continual learning

Task Sequence	$\min(F_{Seq}^{100,400,900})$
TREC_SUBJ_CoLA_SST	0.63
TREC_SUBJ_SST_CoLA	0.78
SST_TREC_SUBJ_CoLA	0.81
CoLA_SUBJ_SST_TREC	1.3
SST_CoLA_SUBJ_TREC	1.4
CoLA_SST_SUBJ_TREC	1.4

Table 6: The top three (green) and bottom three (red) task sequences with F_{Seq} for Layer = 1. For each task sequence, minimum F_{Seq} was considered across dimensionalities $100, 400, 900$. Most of the top task sequences finish with SST or CoLA, and bottom ones with TREC.

setup would require extensive experiments with a large number of varied tasks.

For task sequence TREC_SUBJ_CoLA_SST, CoLA's performance improves after training on SST, resulting in negative F_{CoLA} and a slight drop in F_{Seq}. This task sequence and network with $hdim = 900$ is the only instance where we observed $F_i < 0$. Our two-task experiments saw forgetting of 0.16 when training SST after CoLA. This observation could be a consequence of training on TREC or SUBJ beforehand. It would be interesting to gain more insights on what enabled improvement on CoLA while training SST in this task sequence.

Our results with contextual ELMo embeddings are intriguing, as the amount of forgetting is vastly

Second Task → First Task ↓	CoLA	SST	SUBJ	TREC
CoLA	—	0.16	0.38	0.39
SST	0.36	—	0.40	0.57
SUBJ	0.35	0.17	—	0.46
TREC	0.09	0.08	0.15	—

Table 7: Forgetting on sequentially training two tasks; Layer= 1, Dimensionality = 100.

Second Task → First Task ↓	CoLA	SST	SUBJ	TREC
CoLA	—	10.6	11	16.4
SST	16.2	—	11.8	16.2
SUBJ	17.8	10.6	—	14.6
TREC	15.2	11.0	11.8	—

Table 8: Number of epochs used for training the **second task** in the sequence; Layer = 1, Dimensionality = 100.

different when ELMo's parameters are fixed, versus when they are fine-tuned for each task. Our experiments favour using fixed embeddings. This finding also points at the importance of developing new specialised fine-tuning approaches similar to the one introduced in ULMFit (Howard and Ruder, 2018). When fine-tuning ELMo embeddings, CNNs have less forgetting than LSTMs, and contrastingly LSTMs have less forgetting when ELMo embeddings are fixed.

12 Conclusion

We carried out an empirical study on catastrophic forgetting, observing that LSTMs forget more than CNNs. Further experimentation provided the insight that max-pooling helps CNNs alleviate abrupt forgetting. Our findings with pre-trained embeddings suggest one should avoid fine-tuning pre-trained embeddings in a continual learning setup. We also observed that more capacity doesn't help in reducing catastrophic forgetting, and that training a difficult task towards the end of a task sequence is beneficial.

Acknowledgement

We want to thank the anonymous reviewers for their insightful suggestions, which gave rise to the experiments with pre-trained embeddings.

References

Yoshua Bengio, Jérôme Louradour, Ronan Collobert, and Jason Weston. 2009. Curriculum learning. In *Proceedings of the 26th annual international conference on machine learning*, pages 41–48. ACM.

Daniel Cer, Yinfei Yang, Sheng-yi Kong, Nan Hua, Nicole Limtiaco, Rhomni St. John, Noah Constant, Mario Guajardo-Cespedes, Steve Yuan, Chris Tar, Brian Strope, and Ray Kurzweil. 2018. Universal sentence encoder for English. In *Proceedings of the 2018 Conference on Empirical Methods in Natural Language Processing: System Demonstrations*, pages 169–174, Brussels, Belgium. Association for Computational Linguistics.

Jacob Devlin, Ming-Wei Chang, Kenton Lee, and Kristina Toutanova. 2019. BERT: pre-training of deep bidirectional transformers for language understanding. In *Proceedings of the 2019 Conference of the North American Chapter of the Association for Computational Linguistics: Human Language Technologies, NAACL-HLT 2019, Minneapolis, MN, USA, June 2-7, 2019, Volume 1 (Long and Short Papers)*, pages 4171–4186.

Chrisantha Fernando, Dylan Banarse, Charles Blundell, Yori Zwols, David Ha, Andrei A Rusu, Alexander Pritzel, and Daan Wierstra. 2017. Pathnet: Evolution channels gradient descent in super neural networks. *arXiv preprint arXiv:1701.08734*.

Robert M French. 1991. Using semi-distributed representations to overcome catastrophic forgetting in connectionist networks. In *Proceedings of the 13th annual cognitive science society conference*, pages 173–178.

Matt Gardner, Joel Grus, Mark Neumann, Oyvind Tafjord, Pradeep Dasigi, Nelson F. Liu, Matthew E. Peters, Michael Schmitz, and Luke Zettlemoyer. 2018. Allennlp: A deep semantic natural language processing platform. *CoRR*, abs/1803.07640.

Ian J. Goodfellow, Mehdi Mirza, Xia Da, Aaron C. Courville, and Yoshua Bengio. 2014. An empirical investigation of catastrophic forgeting in gradient-based neural networks. In *2nd International Conference on Learning Representations, ICLR 2014, Banff, AB, Canada, April 14-16, 2014, Conference Track Proceedings*.

Geoffrey Hinton, Oriol Vinyals, and Jeff Dean. 2015. Distilling the knowledge in a neural network. *arXiv preprint arXiv:1503.02531*.

Jeremy Howard and Sebastian Ruder. 2018. Universal language model fine-tuning for text classification. In *Proceedings of the 56th Annual Meeting of the Association for Computational Linguistics (Volume 1: Long Papers)*, pages 328–339, Melbourne, Australia. Association for Computational Linguistics.

Alex Krizhevsky, Ilya Sutskever, and Geoffrey E Hinton. 2012. Imagenet classification with deep convolutional neural networks. In *Advances in neural information processing systems*, pages 1097–1105.

Z. Li and D. Hoiem. 2018. Learning without forgetting. *IEEE Transactions on Pattern Analysis and Machine Intelligence*, 40(12):2935–2947.

David Lopez-Paz et al. 2017. Gradient episodic memory for continual learning. In *Advances in Neural Information Processing Systems*, pages 6467–6476.

Arun Mallya and Svetlana Lazebnik. 2018. Packnet: Adding multiple tasks to a single network by iterative pruning. In *Proceedings of the IEEE Conference on Computer Vision and Pattern Recognition*, pages 7765–7773.

Brian W Matthews. 1975. Comparison of the predicted and observed secondary structure of t4 phage lysozyme. *Biochimica et Biophysica Acta (BBA)-Protein Structure*, 405(2):442–451.

Michael McCloskey and Neal J Cohen. 1989. Catastrophic interference in connectionist networks: The sequential learning problem. *Psychology of Learning and Motivation - Advances in Research and Theory*, 24(C):109–165.

Lili Mou, Zhao Meng, Rui Yan, Ge Li, Yan Xu, Lu Zhang, and Zhi Jin. 2016. How transferable are neural networks in nlp applications? In *Proceedings of the 2016 Conference on Empirical Methods in Natural Language Processing*, pages 479–489.

Cuong V. Nguyen, Alessandro Achille, Michael Lam, Tal Hassner, Vijay Mahadevan, and Stefano Soatto. 2019. Toward understanding catastrophic forgetting in continual learning. *CoRR*, abs/1908.01091.

Bo Pang and Lillian Lee. 2004. A sentimental education: Sentiment analysis using subjectivity summarization based on minimum cuts. In *Proceedings of the 42Nd Annual Meeting on Association for Computational Linguistics*, ACL '04, Stroudsburg, PA, USA. Association for Computational Linguistics.

Matthew E. Peters, Mark Neumann, Mohit Iyyer, Matt Gardner, Christopher Clark, Kenton Lee, and Luke Zettlemoyer. 2018a. Deep contextualized word representations. In *Proc. of NAACL*.

Matthew E. Peters, Mark Neumann, Mohit Iyyer, Matt Gardner, Christopher Clark, Kenton Lee, and Luke Zettlemoyer. 2018b. Deep contextualized word representations. In *Proceedings of the 2018 Conference of the North American Chapter of the Association for Computational Linguistics: Human Language Technologies, NAACL-HLT 2018, New Orleans, Louisiana, USA, June 1-6, 2018, Volume 1 (Long Papers)*, pages 2227–2237.

Matthew E. Peters, Sebastian Ruder, and Noah A. Smith. 2019. To tune or not to tune? adapting pretrained representations to diverse tasks. In

Proceedings of the 4th Workshop on Representation Learning for NLP, RepL4NLP@ACL 2019, Florence, Italy, August 2, 2019., pages 7–14.

Roger Ratcliff. 1990. Connectionist models of recognition memory: constraints imposed by learning and forgetting functions. *Psychological review*, 97(2):285.

Sylvestre-Alvise Rebuffi, Alexander Kolesnikov, Georg Sperl, and Christoph H Lampert. 2017. icarl: Incremental classifier and representation learning. In *Proceedings of the IEEE conference on Computer Vision and Pattern Recognition*, pages 2001–2010.

Joan Serra, Didac Suris, Marius Miron, and Alexandros Karatzoglou. 2018. Overcoming catastrophic forgetting with hard attention to the task. In *International Conference on Machine Learning*, pages 4555–4564.

Richard Socher, Alex Perelygin, Jean Wu, Jason Chuang, Christopher D Manning, Andrew Ng, and Christopher Potts. 2013. Recursive deep models for semantic compositionality over a sentiment treebank. In *Proceedings of the 2013 conference on empirical methods in natural language processing*, pages 1631–1642.

Rupesh K Srivastava, Jonathan Masci, Sohrob Kazerounian, Faustino Gomez, and Jürgen Schmidhuber. 2013. Compete to compute. In *Advances in neural information processing systems*, pages 2310–2318.

Ellen M Voorhees and Dawn M Tice. 1999. The trec-8 question answering track evaluation. In *TREC*, volume 1999, page 82. Citeseer.

Alex Warstadt, Amanpreet Singh, and Samuel R Bowman. 2018. Neural network acceptability judgments. *arXiv preprint arXiv:1805.12471*.

Dani Yogatama, Cyprien de Masson d'Autume, Jerome Connor, Tomás Kociský, Mike Chrzanowski, Lingpeng Kong, Angeliki Lazaridou, Wang Ling, Lei Yu, Chris Dyer, and Phil Blunsom. 2019. Learning and evaluating general linguistic intelligence. *CoRR*, abs/1901.11373.

Detecting Chemical Reactions in Patents

Hiyori Yoshikawa[1,3]**, Dat Quoc Nguyen**[1]**, Zenan Zhai**[1]**, Christian Druckenbrodt**[2]**,
Camilo Thorne**[2]**, Saber A. Akhondi**[2]**, Timothy Baldwin**[1]**, Karin Verspoor**[1]
[1]The University of Melbourne, Australia; [2]Elsevier; [3]Fujitsu Laboratories Ltd.
[1]{hiyori.yoshikawa,dqnguyen,zenan.zhai,tbaldwin,karin.verspoor}@unimelb.edu.au
[2]{c.druckenbrodt,c.thorne.1,s.akhondi}@elsevier.com

Abstract

Extracting chemical reactions from patents is a crucial task for chemists working on chemical exploration. In this paper we introduce the novel task of detecting the textual spans that describe or refer to chemical reactions within patents. We formulate this task as a paragraph-level sequence tagging problem, where the system is required to return a sequence of paragraphs that contain a description of a reaction. To address this new task, we construct an annotated dataset from an existing proprietary database of chemical reactions manually extracted from patents. We introduce several baseline methods for the task and evaluate them over our dataset. Through error analysis, we discuss what makes the task complex and challenging, and suggest possible directions for future research.

1 Introduction

Chemical patents are a crucial resource for chemical research and development activities. In fact, many compounds are reported first in patents and only a small fraction of them appears in the chemical literature after 1 to 3 years (Senger et al., 2015), meaning that chemists habitually search over both academic papers and patent databases. Moreover, as the number of chemical patents awarded each year is ever-increasing, there is an increasing urgency to perform patent searches to establish the novelty of chemical compounds (Akhondi et al., 2014). Text mining methods are a vital tool in this process, enabling a significant reduction in associated time and effort.

Most previous research in text mining of chemical information has focused on named entity recognition (NER) of chemical concepts, and several publicly-available NER corpora have been derived from both scientific literature (Kim et al., 2003; Corbett et al., 2007; Krallinger et al., 2015)

and chemical patents (Akhondi et al., 2014). Some studies have also addressed relation extraction between chemical entities and other concepts such as protein and diseases (Wei et al., 2015; Krallinger et al., 2017).

However, there has been limited work on automatically extracting chemical reactions from patents. A chemical patent usually contains a description of chemical reactions that are relevant to its claims. Figure 1 shows an example of a chemical reaction description. Generally speaking, a chemical reaction is a process where a set of chemical compounds is transformed into another set of chemical compounds. A reaction description may include the source chemical compounds, solvents and reagents involved in the reaction, reaction conditions, and materials obtained as a result of the reaction. Despite the fact that such information is crucial for a comprehensive understanding of chemical patents, there are — to the best of our knowledge — few methods or annotated resources that can be used for this purpose.

As a first step to extracting chemical reactions, a filtering step must take place to determine where reactions are described in a patent. In this paper, we introduce this new task of **chemical reaction detection**. The output of this task can be used as the input to (more complex) downstream tasks. For example, consider an event extraction system that extracts every step of a reaction as an individual event. Events in the first reaction of Figure 1 would be: (1) heating 2-pyridine-ethanol, triphenyl phosphine and carbon tetrachloride; (2) the addition of triphenyl phosphine; (3) heating them again; and so on. The application would also include estimating the relevance of chemical compounds to a given reaction, based on their role in the reaction (Akhondi et al., 2019). Such downstream tasks require as input a paragraph sequence corresponding to a reaction, in a repre-

P: *Example 1: Preparation of 2-(4-benzyloxybutyl)pyridine*
P: *2-(4-Benzyloxybutyl)pyridine is prepared in 5 steps according to the following reaction route.*

...

P: *(1) Preparation of 2-(2-chloroethyl)pyridine*
P: *2-Pyridine-ethanol (15.00 g, 122 mmol), triphenyl phosphine (38.40 g, 146 mmol) and carbon tetrachloride (100 mL) were put in a 500-mL flask, and heated under reflux. After 1.5 hours, triphenyl phosphine (9.60 g, 36.6 mmol) was added thereto and further heated for 30 minutes under reflux.*
P: *The reaction liquid was cooled down to room temperature, and then pentane (200 mL) was added thereto, and filtered using a Kiriyama funnel. The resultant filtrate was concentrated to give a crude product (17.07 g). This was distilled under reduced pressure to give 11.16 g (yield 65.8%, purity 97.1%) of 2-(2-chloroethyl)pyridine.* } reaction
P: *(2) Preparation of dimethyl 2-(2-pyridyl)ethylmalonate*
P: *2-(2-Chloroethyl)pyridine (10.35 g, 73.1 mmol), N,N-dimethylformamide (100 mL), dimethyl malonate (14.48 g, 110 mmol) and potassium carbonate (18.18 g, 132 mmol) were put in a 300-mL flask, and stirred. ...* } reaction

...

...

Figure 1: An example of chemical reaction description in a patent document (US20180072670A1). The symbol "P:" stands for the beginning of a paragraph.

sentation that preserves the order of the reaction substeps. Indeed, reactions are complex processes composed of sequentially ordered steps (much like recipes in cooking) and tend to be described sequentially. Thus, we formulate this task as a paragraph-level sequence tagging problem, where the output is a set of paragraphs containing the description of a reaction. Although the task formulation is simple, it is not straightforward to automate as it requires document-level understanding of the patent text, which tends to be highly ambiguous.

To measure the feasibility and identify the key challenges of this new task, we created an annotated dataset and established benchmark results over it, in the form of rule-based and machine learning methods.[1] The dataset is based on the chemical structure data from Reaxys®.[2] The database contains chemical reactions manually extracted from a very large number of patents. The reactions are associated with the patent from which they are extracted. As the primary purpose of the extraction is to populate a database of chemical reactions (some of which are extracted from non-textual sources) and not provide training data for NLP, it is not always possible to completely map back from the data to the source text. However, the large database enabled us to automatically create a potentially very large amount of training data that can be used to train state-of-the-art deep learning methods. For the experiments presented in this paper, we created an annotated corpus from a subset of Reaxys® reactions

---

[1]Contact the authors for data requests.

[2]Copyright ©2019 Elsevier Limited, except certain content provided by third parties. Reaxys is a trademark of Elsevier Limited.

and filtered out documents with low mapping coverage from the database to text, in an attempt to boost the fidelity of evaluation over that data. This culminated in training, development, and test sets consisting of 143 documents made up of >39,000 paragraphs in total.

2 Related Work

Patents are regarded as an important resource for chemical information, and a large volume of NLP research has focused on them (Fujii et al., 2007; Tseng et al., 2007; Gurulingappa et al., 2013; Southan, 2015; Rodriguez-Esteban and Bundschus, 2016; Akhondi et al., 2019). However, most previous work on chemical information extraction has focused on the NER task of extracting chemical names or chemistry-related concepts from literature (Kim et al., 2003; Corbett et al., 2007; Böhme et al., 2014; Akhondi et al., 2014; Krallinger et al., 2015). Some previous work has attempted to extract not only chemical names but also reaction procedures from the literature (Lawson et al., 2011; Wei et al., 2015; Mayfield et al., 2017; Krallinger et al., 2017). Among them, Lowe (2012) presents an integrated system that detects reaction text from chemical patents, and extracts chemicals and their roles in the corresponding reaction. The system is heavily rule-based and incorporates existing NLP libraries, and was reported to detect reactions with high accuracy. However, evaluation was limited to a small number of good-quality reaction texts, and the performance of the reaction detection sub-task was not evaluated in isolation.

Another line of work with an extensive literature is patent retrieval, where the task is to retrieve patent documents or passages given a query in the form of keywords, a sentence, or a document; Shalaby and Zadrozny (2019) survey this task extensively. A relevant shared task was organized as part of CLEF-IP 2012 (Piroi et al., 2012). In the sub-task titled "Passage Retrieval Starting From Claims", participants were required to extract passages from chemical patents that are relevant to a given claim. The difference between our task and theirs is that the output of our task is *all* chemical reactions mentioned in a given patent, independent of any claim. In addition, the CLEF-IP task does not require the identification of reaction spans. That is, they deal with each passage independently, ignoring ordering.

The proposed task can also be viewed as a text segmentation problem. Koshorek et al. (2018) formulated the text segmentation task on general domain corpora such as Wikipedia as a supervised learning problem, and proposed a two-level bidirectional LSTM model to learn to detect text spans. In particular, they used a softmax layer on top of a standard BiLTSM architecture for segmentation prediction. We experiment with a BiLTSM-CRF architecture as a document-level training method as described in Section 4, i.e. we use a CRF layer to obtain the document-level label sequence, instead of applying a softmax classifier on top of the BiLSTM.

3 Task and Dataset

3.1 Task Formulation

A patent document usually describes the reactions to produce the relevant compounds as part of its claims. As shown in Figure 1, a reaction may involve several steps to obtain the target compounds.[3] In our example, multiple contiguous paragraphs are used to describe a single reaction, and multiple reactions are necessary to obtain the final compounds.

As a reaction consists of a series of sub-steps executed over time, it is important to detect the beginning and the end of each reaction text accurately. Therefore, we define the task as a span detection problem rather than the simpler task of binary classification (i.e., classifying each paragraph as describing (part of) a reaction or not), which

---

[3]In this study we only focus on text data, although information of reactions can also be present in images and tables.

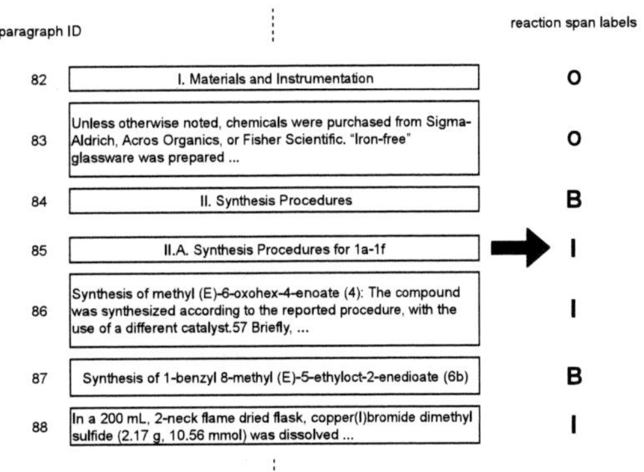

Figure 2: Illustration of our reaction span detection task.

would not be able to detect reactions as a whole or capture reaction substructure.

Figure 2 shows an example of an input and gold-standard output of the reaction span detection task. A patent document is given as a sequence of paragraphs. The task is to detect a span of contiguous paragraphs that describe a single chemical reaction. In our corpus, we provide paragraph-level label sequences over paragraphs in patent documents, following the IOB2 tagging scheme (Tjong et al., 1999).

The definition of "reaction spans" in our dataset follows the extraction rules of the original database. In principle, a reaction is extracted from a patent if the requisite information about the reaction (e.g., starting materials, reaction conditions and target compounds) is provided within the patent document and there is no obvious error or inconsistency in the description. Typically a reaction constitutes an example section or a subsection beginning with a title paragraph such as *Example 1*, *Step 1* and *Preparation of [product name]*, as shown in Figure 1. However, it is also commonly the case that an example section contains multiple reactions, in which case they have no title paragraph.

3.2 Data Preparation

Our corpus contains patents from the European Patent Office and the United States Patent and Trademark Office, all of which are written in English and freely available in a digital format. The corpus is based on the Reaxys® database, which contains reaction entries for each patent document manually created by experts in chemistry. A reaction entry has "locations" of the reaction in the corresponding patent document, mostly in terms

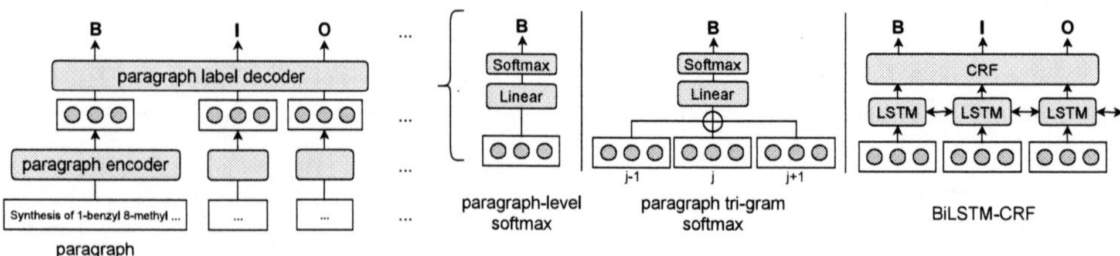

Figure 3: Our model architecture. The left figure illustrates the general architecture of the whole model, while the right figure details the decoder component.

of paragraph IDs (e.g., the reaction entry of *synthesis of methyl (E)-6-oxohex-4-enoate* in Figure 2 has a location property with value 84, 85, 86). We used this location information to automatically label the reaction text spans in the patent text. As the reaction data available in the database is extracted and curated from text, images, and tables based on specific guidelines and hence not directly aligned with NLP requirements, it is not always possible to completely map all the locations from Reaxys® database to text. First, the annotation was performed by a single expert worker for each patent document, without redundancy or explicit post-checking of the extraction. Second, some locations are missing in the original data. For example, as the manual extraction process is at the document level, a reaction is sometimes extracted only once regardless of how many times it is mentioned in the patent. As part of the mapping process, we filtered out potentially-incorrect paragraph spans using a set of rules. For instance, we discarded paragraph spans in which we could not find any of the chemical compounds or related information associated with the corresponding reaction in the database.

For evaluation, we applied the mapping process to a part of the database and selected patent documents with 100% mapping coverage (i.e. all reaction records in the database can be mapped to the text) and split them into training, development, and test partitions. As a result, we obtained training, development, and test sets consisting of 143 documents with >39,000 paragraphs in total. Although the test set is singly-annotated and no inter-annotator agreement is available, we manually checked a small subset to confirm that the annotation quality is sufficiently good to support high-fidelity evaluation. Table 1 presents a breakdown of the dataset.

A patent document consists of three main parts: title/abstract, claims, and description. We ex-

	Train	Dev	Test
# Documents	86	29	28
# Paragraphs	24,402	7,194	7,481
# Reaction spans	1,787	638	567
# Tokens / Paragraph	72.9	74.5	75.7

Table 1: Composition of the evaluation dataset. "# Tokens / Paragraph" stands for the average number of tokens in a paragraph based on OSCAR4 tokenization (Jessop et al., 2011).

tracted the text of the description part, where chemical reactions are described. For simplicity, we only use textual information, and ignore other types of data such as images describing chemical structures. Paragraphs that do not contain text (e.g., tables or references to images) are also discarded.

4 Our modeling approach

In this section, we describe our neural approach to reaction span detection. As illustrated in Figure 3, our general model architecture is composed of two main parts: a paragraph encoder and a paragraph label decoder. The encoder represents each paragraph as a vector that is then fed into the label decoder to determine the corresponding B/I/O label of the paragraph.

4.1 Paragraph encoder

We use a paragraph encoder to encode each paragraph p into vector v_p. Assume that the paragraph p consists of n tokens $w_1, w_2, \ldots, w_n$. We create a vector e_i to represent the ith word token w_i by concatenating its pre-trained word embedding $e_{w_i}^{\text{WE}}$, contextualized embedding $e_{w_i|p}^{\text{CW}}$, and an optional embedding $e_{f_i}^{\text{FT}}$ representing additional features f_i associated with w_i:

$$e_i = e_{w_i}^{\text{WE}} \oplus e_{w_i|p}^{\text{CW}} \oplus e_{f_i}^{\text{FT}} \quad (1)$$

We then use a BiLSTM paragraph encoder to

learn the paragraph vector v_p from a sequence $e_{1:n}$ of vectors $e_1, \ldots, e_n$. We compute the hidden states of the LSTMs corresponding to the ith token ($i \in \{1, \ldots, n\}$) as follows:

$$\overrightarrow{r_i} = \overrightarrow{\mathrm{LSTM}_e}(e_{1:i}) \qquad (2)$$

$$\overleftarrow{r_i} = \overleftarrow{\mathrm{LSTM}_e}(e_{i:n}) \qquad (3)$$

where $\overrightarrow{\mathrm{LSTM}_e}$ and $\overleftarrow{\mathrm{LSTM}_e}$ denote forward and backward LSTMs in the encoder, respectively. We then concatenate the final states of these two LSTMs to obtain the paragraph vector v_p:

$$v_p = \overrightarrow{r_n} \oplus \overleftarrow{r_1} \qquad (4)$$

4.2 Paragraph label decoder

Assume that we have an input document consisting of m paragraphs $p_{(1)}, p_{(2)}, ..., p_{(m)}$. The decoder will assign a B/I/O label to the jth paragraph $p_{(j)}$ based on the input paragraph vector representation(s) $v_{p_{(j)}}$ produced by the encoder as in Equation (4). We explore the following settings.

Paragraph-level softmax classifier: In this setting, we feed each vector $v_{p_{(j)}}$ into a softmax classifier for paragraph label prediction:

$$\mathbf{P}_{(j)} = \mathrm{Softmax}(\mathbf{W}^{\mathrm{PS}} v_{p_{(j)}} + b^{\mathrm{PS}}) \qquad (5)$$

where $\mathbf{P}_{(j)} \in \mathbb{R}^3$ is the final output of the network, and $\mathbf{W}^{\mathrm{PS}} \in \mathbb{R}^{3 \times 2k}$ and $b^{\mathrm{PS}} \in \mathbb{R}^3$ are a transformation weight matrix and a bias factor, respectively (here, k is the dimensionality of the $\overrightarrow{\mathrm{LSTM}_e}$ and $\overleftarrow{\mathrm{LSTM}_e}$ hidden states).

Paragraph-trigram softmax classifier: The paragraph-trigram softmax decoder extends the paragraph-level softmax decoder by taking the previous and next paragraphs of $p_{(j)}$ into account.[4] In particular, it is formalized as:

$$u_{p_{(j)}} = v_{p_{(j-1)}} \oplus v_{p_{(j)}} \oplus v_{p_{(j+1)}} \qquad (6)$$

$$\mathbf{P}_{(j)} = \mathrm{Softmax}(\mathbf{W}^{\mathrm{PT}} u_{p_{(j)}} + b^{\mathrm{PT}}) \qquad (7)$$

where $\mathbf{W}^{\mathrm{PT}} \in \mathbb{R}^{3 \times 6k}$ and $b^{\mathrm{PT}} \in \mathbb{R}^3$ are a transformation weight matrix and a bias factor, respectively.

We train each of the two softmax classifiers by minimizing the model negative log likelihood (i.e. cross-entropy loss). At inference time, we calculate the label probabilities for every paragraph us-

---

[4]When $j = 1$ and $j = m$ we use paragraphs $p_{(0)}$ and $p_{(m+1)}$, each of which consist of two special symbols $\langle \mathrm{S} \rangle$ and $\langle /\mathrm{S} \rangle$.

ing the learned classifier, and construct the label sequence with the highest joint probability score under the constraint of a valid IOB2 output (i.e. an I label must not come right after O).

BiLSTM-CRF classifier: In this setting, we use a BiLSTM-CRF architecture (Huang et al., 2015) to capture contextual information across paragraphs as well as label transitions. We first use another BiLSTM to learn latent feature vectors representing input paragraphs from a sequence $v_{p_{(1)}:p_{(m)}}$ of vectors $v_{p_{(1)}}, v_{p_{(2)}}, ..., v_{p_{(m)}}$, and then perform a linear transformation over each latent feature vector. Then output vector h_j for the jth paragraph ($j \in \{1, \ldots, m\}$) is computed as:

$$\overrightarrow{r_j} = \overrightarrow{\mathrm{LSTM}_d}(v_{p_{(1)}:p_{(j)}}) \qquad (8)$$

$$\overleftarrow{r_j} = \overleftarrow{\mathrm{LSTM}_d}(v_{p_{(j)}:p_{(m)}}) \qquad (9)$$

$$r_j = \overrightarrow{r_j} \oplus \overleftarrow{r_j} \qquad (10)$$

$$h_j = \mathbf{W}^{\mathrm{BC}} r_j + b^{\mathrm{BC}} \qquad (11)$$

where $\overrightarrow{\mathrm{LSTM}_d}$ and $\overleftarrow{\mathrm{LSTM}_d}$ denote forward and backward LSTMs in the decoder, respectively. $\mathbf{W}^{\mathrm{BC}} \in \mathbb{R}^{3 \times 2l}$ and $b^{\mathrm{BC}} \in \mathbb{R}^3$ are a transformation weight matrix and a bias factor, respectively (here, l is the dimensionality of the $\overrightarrow{\mathrm{LSTM}_d}$ and $\overleftarrow{\mathrm{LSTM}_d}$ hidden states).

Output vectors h_j are fed into a linear-chain CRF layer (Lafferty et al., 2001) for final B/I/O paragraph label prediction. A negative joint log likelihood loss is minimized when training, while the Viterbi algorithm is used for decoding.

5 Experimental Settings

5.1 Evaluation Metrics

We evaluate the model perfomance by using span-based metrics as described below.

We find that calculating micro-averaged scores over documents (i.e. the scores over the all spans in the datasets) leads to biased results. This is because the development and test sets consist of a small number of documents and style is consistent within a document, meaning that errors caused by the same writing style tend to accumulate and be overestimated. To mitigate this effect, we evaluate based on *document-level macro-averaged* recall, precision, and F-score, i.e. we compute the scores for each document, and use the average of document-level scores for model selection and final evaluation.

For model selection we use the span-based

scores based on a *strict match* strategy, where an output span is regarded as correct if the beginning and ending paragraphs strictly match those of the gold span. In some practical applications, it also makes sense to understand if the model can identify the *approximate* region where a reaction is described. Thus, for evaluation, we also compute the scores based on a *fuzzy match* strategy, where we calculate the number of matches by counting the number of gold spans that have at least one corresponding predicted output span whose beginning and ending paragraph indices are at most 1 paragraph away from the gold ones.

5.2 Implementation Details

5.2.1 Input Text

We use the text of each paragraph as input, with a maximum length of 128 tokens.[5] For tokenization, we used the OSCAR4 tokenizer (Jessop et al., 2011), as it is customized to chemical text mining.

Equation (1) formulates the input token-level representation for the BiLSTM paragraph encoder in the form of (context-insensitive) word embeddings, contextualized word embeddings, and feature embeddings. For the word embeddings $e_{w_i}^{\mathrm{WE}}$ and contextualized embeddings $e_{w_i|p}^{\mathrm{CW}}$, we employ Word2Vec (Mikolov et al., 2013) and ELMo (Peters et al., 2018), respectively, both pre-trained on chemical patent documents from Zhai et al. (2019). These embeddings are fixed during training. We denote our encoder employing only the pre-trained word and contextualized embeddings (i.e. $e_i = e_{w_i}^{\mathrm{WE}} \oplus e_{w_i|p}^{\mathrm{CW}}$) as **w2v +ELMo**.

We also explore additional learnable feature embeddings $e_{f_i}^{\mathrm{FT}}$ (in Equation 1) based on the output of a chemical named entity recognizer (Zhai et al., 2019). This named entity recognizer was trained on a patent corpus named Reaxys® Gold data (Akhondi et al., 2019). For self-containment purpose we show the entity label set of Reaxys® Gold data in Table 4 in the Appendix. As the label set has two levels of granularity, we use the output in two different ways: coarse-grained (left-hand side of the table) and fine-grained (right-hand side). We first obtain a token-level label sequence in the IOB2 format such as `[O, O, B-chemClass, I-chemClass, O]` for each paragraph and

then embed the labels into 5-dimensional vectors $e_{f_i}^{\mathrm{FT}}$. We refer to the paragraph encoder with additional input of coarse-grained NER labels as **w2v +ELMo +NER**$_{\text{COARSE}}$, and the one with the fine-grained labels as **w2v +ELMo +NER**$_{\text{FINE}}$.

5.2.2 Model Optimization

Our neural models are implemented using the AllenNLP framework (Gardner et al., 2018). With the paragraph-level and paragraph-trigram softmax classifiers, we train model parameters using the training set for 20 epochs and apply early stopping if no improvement in the loss over the development set is observed for 3 continuous epochs. With the BiLSTM-CRF classifier, we train model parameters for 30 epochs, and early stopping is applied after 10 epochs of no improvement. Experimental results with the decoder of paragraph-level softmax on the development set show the highest score when using **w2v +ELMo +NER**$_{\text{FINE}}$ input representation. Thus, for models with the paragraph-trigram softmax and BiLSTM-CRF decoders, we only explore the use of the **w2v +ELMo +NER**$_{\text{FINE}}$ input representation.

We use Adam (Kingma and Ba, 2015) as our optimizer for all experiments. We apply a grid search to select optimal hyper-parameters based on the document-level macro F-score over the development set. Table 5 in the Appendix shows the model hyper-parameters used for evaluation. For the model with the BiLSTM-CRF decoder, we initialize parameters of its paragraph encoder with those from the model trained with the paragraph-level softmax classifier, and fine-tune them together with the decoder parameters.

5.3 Baselines

5.3.1 Rule-based baseline

We additionally implement a rule-based baseline, based on common patterns in the first paragraphs of chemical reactions. For example, in the case where a chemical reaction description constitutes an Example part in a patent document, the first paragraph begins with phrases such as *Example 1*, *Step 1*, and *Preparation of [product name]*. We use a list of frequent patterns in the first paragraphs of chemical reaction descriptions to distinguish B paragraphs from I or O. Once a B paragraph is detected, we label succeeding paragraphs as I until a new B paragraph is detected.

---

[5]We also explored another option where we use only the first sentence of each paragraph. However, the experimental results show better performance when we use the entire paragraph in all cases.

Decoder	Input token representation	Strict match			Fuzzy match		
		$\mathcal{P}$	$\mathcal{R}$	$\mathcal{F}_1$	$\mathcal{P}$	$\mathcal{R}$	$\mathcal{F}_1$
Rule-based		.205	.381	.241	.278	.482	.319
Logistic		.421	.380	.376	.521	.462	.461
Paragraph-level softmax	W2V +ELMO	.352	.365	.336	.475	.457	.437
	W2V +ELMO +NER$_{\text{COARSE}}$	.340	.389	.337	.446	.468	.415
	W2V +ELMO +NER$_{\text{FINE}}$	.345	.383	.341	.479	.485	.447
Paragraph-trigram softmax	W2V +ELMO +NER$_{\text{FINE}}$	.513	.488	.482	.643	.573	.574
BiLSTM-CRF	W2V +ELMO +NER$_{\text{FINE}}$	**.658**	**.653**	**.640**	**.718**	**.708**	**.696**

Table 2: Performance of the baseline methods on reaction span detection, in terms of document-level macro-averaged precision ("$\mathcal{P}$"), recall ("$\mathcal{R}$"), and F-score ("$\mathcal{F}_1$"). "NER$_{\text{COARSE}}$" and "NER$_{\text{FINE}}$" indicate NER embeddings based on coarse- and fine-grained entity types, respectively.

5.3.2 Feature-based logistic regression

Another baseline we explore is the logistic regression classifier, where the output is calculated as:

$$\mathbf{P}_{(j)} = \text{Softmax}(\mathbf{W}^{\text{L}} \boldsymbol{\phi}_{p_{(j)}} + \boldsymbol{b}^{\text{L}}) \qquad (12)$$

where $\mathbf{P}_{(j)} \in \mathbb{R}^3$ is the final output of the network, $\mathbf{W}^{\text{L}} \in \mathbb{R}^{3 \times d}$ and $\boldsymbol{b}^{\text{L}} \in \mathbb{R}^3$ are a transformation weight matrix and a bias factor, and $\boldsymbol{\phi}_{p_{(j)}} \in \mathbb{R}^d$ is the concatenation of the following features:

- word count vectors of $p_{(j-1)}$, $p_{(j)}$ and $p_{(j+1)}$, where the ith entry of each vector is the number of times the ith token appears in the corresponding paragraph, and;

- 2-dimensional one-hot vectors for $p_{(j-1)}$, $p_{(j)}$ and $p_{(j+1)}$ indicating if the paragraph is a heading or a body paragraph.[6]

As preprocessing, we apply lowercasing and lemmatization using the NLTK WordNet Lemmatizer.[7] We also replace all numeric characters with a special character. We further apply the named entity recognizer presented in Section 5.2.1 with the fine-grained label set to replace all chemical names with special tokens corresponding to their entity types. The vocabulary consists of tokens that appear at least three times in the training set.

6 Results and Discussion

6.1 Overall Results

Table 2 shows the overall results on the test set. On the left-hand side of the table we show the re-

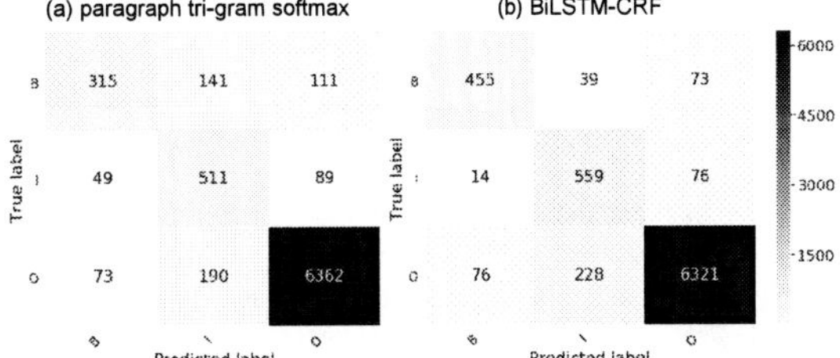

Figure 4: Confusion matrices of the paragraph-trigram softmax vs. BiLSTM-CRF model outputs, based on paragraph-level B/I/O labels.

sults in terms of strict match. The BiLSTM-CRF classifier achieves by far the best score in terms of both precision and recall, indicating that contextual information over paragraphs is key in this task. While the rule-based baseline achieves an exact-match recall of nearly 0.4, the precision is half this value, indicating a high number of false positives. Comparing the three different input features for paragraph-level softmax, we can see that the named entity features improve the recall very slightly, but overall have little impact on results.

The right-hand side of the table shows the results in terms of fuzzy match, where the BiLSTM-CRF model achieves an F-score around 70%.

6.2 Error Analysis

Figure 4 shows the confusion matrices of the model output based on the paragraph-level B/I/O labels. We compare the paragraph-trigram softmax and BiLSTM-CRF models, both with the W2V +ELMO +NER$_{\text{FINE}}$ input representation. We can observe that the BiLSTM-CRF output shows a large improvement in distinguishing be-

---

[6] The paragraph type information is also available in the original database.

[7] 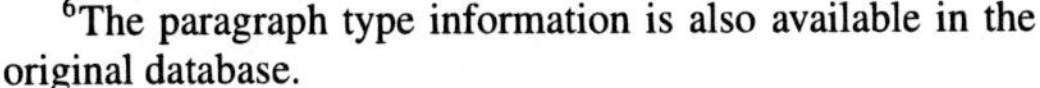https://www.nltk.org/

Ex.	Gold	ParSoftmax	Trigram	BiLSTM-CRF	Text
	B	B	B	B	*SYNTHETIC EXAMPLE 2*
	I	B	I	I	*Compound A2*
1	I	I	I	I	*1,4-dibromonaphthalene (7 g, 24.48 mmol) and 4-cyclohexyl-N-(4-isopropylphenyl)aniline ...*
	I	I	I	I	*1H NMR (400 MHz, CDCl3, δ):*
	I	I	I	I	*δ 8.04-7.985 (dd, 5H); 7.345-7.275 (m, 10H); 7.086-7.028 (m, 23H); 7.028-6.958 (m, 20H).*
	B	B	B	B	*Example 5. Preparation of SM-5: 2-Hydroxy-4'-trifluoromethylacetophenone*
2	I	I	I	I	*Step A. A 200 mL flask was charged with 4'-trifluoromethylacetophenone ...*
	B	I	I	B	*Step B. A 200 mL flask was charged with the crude of 2-Bromo-4'...*
	B	B	O	B	*Example 5*
	I	I	O	I	*The following Example illustrates a method for producing (R,Z)-dodec-5-ene-1,3-diol ...*
	I	I	O	I	*To a -78 C. solution of oct-1-yne (1.8 equiv.) in THF (0.5M) will be added ...*
3	B	I	B	B	*(R)-1-(benzyloxy)dodec-5-yn-3-ol will then taken up in hexane to generate ...*
	B	I	I	B	*(R,Z)-1-(benzyloxy)dodec-5-en-3-ol will be taken up in CH2Cl2 to generate ...*
	B	O	B	B	*Alternatively, the secondary alcohol of (R,Z)-1-(benzyloxy)dodec-5-en-3-ol may be ...*
	B	B	I	B	*(R,Z)-((1-(benzyloxy)dodec-5-en-3-yl)oxy)(tert-butyl)dimethylsilane will be taken up ...*
	B	I	I	B	*To a stirring 2.0M solution of (R,Z)-3-((tert-butyldimethylsilyl)oxy)dodec-5-en-1-ol ...*
	O	I	B	B	*7-(2-Methylphenylethyl)-Sancycline*
	O	I	I	I	*7-(2-Methylphenylethynyl)-sancycline (1 mmol) was taken in saturated ...*
4	B	I	B	B	*9-(4'-Acetyl phenyl) Minocycline*
	I	I	I	I	*In a clean, dry reaction vessel, was placed 9-iodominocycline (0.762 mmoles) ...*
	B	I	B	I	*7-(n-Propyl)-Sancycline*
	I	I	I	I	*7-propynyl sancycline was dissolved in a saturated methanol hydrochloric acid solvent. ...*
	B	B	B	B	*Example 25: Synthesis of Compound 15-Br-Boc*
5	I	I	I	I	*In a three-necked flask, compound 13-Br (3.4 g, 5.675 mmol), DMAP (0.139 g, ...*
	O	B	B	B	*Example 26: Synthesis of Compound 16-B-Boc*
	O	I	I	I	*In a three-necked flask, compound 14-B (2.726 g, 5.675 mmol), DMAP (0.139 g, ...*

Table 3: Output examples. Columns "ParSoftmax", "Trigram", and "BiLSTM-CRF" show the output of paragraph-level softmax, paragraph-trigram softmax and BiLSTM-CRF decoders, respectively, with the W2V +ELMO +NER$_{\text{FINE}}$ encoder.

tween B and I labels, indicating that long-term contextual information is crucial to correctly detecting the beginning of the reaction spans.

Table 3 shows system output examples from the test set. In Example 1, the first two paragraphs of the reaction span are its title and subtitle. The paragraph-level softmax model labels both the title and the subtitle as B, while the paragraph-trigram and BiLSTM-CRF model successfully classify the subtitle paragraph as I. In Example 2 and 3, there are multiple independent reactions in an Example part. In this case, the paragraph-level and paragraph-trigram classifiers often regard several reaction steps as one single reaction, while the BiLSTM-CRF model correctly separates out the individual reactions in both cases. Without context, it would be hard to distinguish the independent reactions from reaction steps inside a single reaction, as they have a common writing style (an example where a single reaction has several reaction steps can be found in Figure 1). As shown in Example 4, it is often the case that the title of a reaction span is the name of a chemical compound. All baseline classifiers often fail to detect such spans, even when chemical named entities are used as input features. Presumably, the

fact that the paragraph beginning with a compound name can occur at the beginning, within or outside a reaction span, makes it hard to leverage such patterns for span detection. In Example 5, the text span beginning with *Example 26* is written in exactly the same way as the previous *Example 25* except that *compound 14-B* is used instead of *compound 13-Br*. However, *Example 26* is not extracted as a reaction by the gold annotation while *Example 25* is extracted. This would be because the reaction was regarded as incorrect for technical reasons (e.g., the compound used in the paragraph is clearly incorrect), or was just discarded by the human expert because it is not an important reaction. Such cases are hard for the system to pick up on, as they require deep understanding of the context and background knowledge.

7 Conclusions

In this paper we introduced the chemical reaction detection task and formulated this task as a paragraph-level sequence tagging problem. We proposed heuristic and machine-learning based baseline methods to measure the feasibility of the task as well as to identify the key challenges. We also created an annotated dataset by mapping back reactions from the Reaxys® database to their source patents. We used this corpus to train and evaluate our baseline methods. The experimental results show that this task requires a deep understanding of patent document context, as well as chemical background knowledge. Indeed, the BiLSTM-CRF model trained at the document-level performed much better than the paragraph-level classification methods.

The performance of the baseline methods presented in this paper is still not satisfactory considering the complex downstream tasks such as event extraction. We believe that both the models and the corpus have potential to be improved. As future work, we plan to explore more efficient document-level training methods, and, in particular, methods that work well on noisy training sets. For instance, techniques successfully used for distant supervision (Mintz et al., 2009) may be effective. Furthermore, although we used only textual information, patent documents contain substantial visual information (e.g., images of compounds, or tables) that may be helpful to properly understand a reaction description. Longer term, we will also tackle finer-grained information extraction for chemical reactions utilizing the output of this task. This step involves extracting the details of the detected reactions, that is, inferring the underlying structure of the reactions themselves.

Acknowledgments

We would like to thank the anonymous reviewers for their valuable comments. This work was supported by an Australian Research Council Linkage Project grant (LP160101469). The computations in this paper were performed using the Spartan HPC-Cloud Hybrid (Lafayette et al., 2017) at the University of Melbourne.

References

Saber A. Akhondi, Alexander G. Klenner, Christian Tyrchan, Anil K. Manchala, Kiran Boppana, Daniel Lowe, Marc Zimmermann, Sarma A. R. P. Jagarlapudi, Roger Sayle, Jan A. Kors, and Sorel Muresan. 2014. Annotated Chemical Patent Corpus: A Gold Standard for Text Mining. *PLOS ONE*, 9(9):e107477.

Saber A. Akhondi, Hinnerk Rey, Markus Schwörer, Michael Maier, John Toomey, Heike Nau, Gabriele Ilchmann, Mark Sheehan, Matthias Irmer, Claudia Bobach, Marius Doornenbal, Michelle Gregory, and Jan A. Kors. 2019. Automatic identification of relevant chemical compounds from patents. *Database*, 2019.

Timo Böhme, Matthias Irmer, Anett Püschel, Claudia Bobach, Ulf Laube, and Lutz Weber. 2014. OCMiner: Text processing, annotation and relation extraction for the life sciences. In *SWAT4LS*.

Peter Corbett, Colin Batchelor, and Simone Teufel. 2007. Annotation of Chemical Named Entities. In *Proceedings of the Workshop on BioNLP 2007*, BioNLP '07, pages 57–64.

Atsushi Fujii, Makoto Iwayama, and Noriko Kando. 2007. Introduction to the special issue on patent processing. *Information Processing & Management*, 43(5):1149–1153.

Matt Gardner, Joel Grus, Mark Neumann, Oyvind Tafjord, Pradeep Dasigi, Nelson F Liu, Matthew Peters, Michael Schmitz, and Luke Zettlemoyer. 2018. AllenNLP: A deep semantic natural language processing platform. In *Proceedings of Workshop for NLP Open Source Software (NLP-OSS)*, pages 1–6.

Harsha Gurulingappa, Anirban Mudi, Luca Toldo, Martin Hofmann-Apitius, and Jignesh Bhate. 2013. Challenges in mining the literature for chemical information. *RSC Advances*, 3(37):16194–16211.

Zhiheng Huang, Wei Xu, and Kai Yu. 2015. Bidirectional LSTM-CRF Models for Sequence Tagging. *arXiv:1508.01991 [cs]*.

David M. Jessop, Sam E. Adams, Egon L. Willighagen, Lezan Hawizy, and Peter Murray-Rust. 2011. OSCAR4: A flexible architecture for chemical text-mining. *Journal of Cheminformatics*, 3(1):41.

J.-D. Kim, T. Ohta, Y. Tateisi, and J. Tsujii. 2003. GENIA corpus—a semantically annotated corpus for bio-textmining. *Bioinformatics*, 19(suppl_1):i180–i182.

Diederik P. Kingma and Jimmy Ba. 2015. Adam: A method for stochastic optimization. In *3rd International Conference on Learning Representations, ICLR 2015, San Diego, CA, USA, May 7-9, 2015, Conference Track Proceedings*.

Omri Koshorek, Adir Cohen, Noam Mor, Michael Rotman, and Jonathan Berant. 2018. Text Segmentation as a Supervised Learning Task. In *Proceedings of the 2018 Conference of the North American Chapter of the Association for Computational Linguistics: Human Language Technologies, Volume 2 (Short Papers)*, pages 469–473.

Martin Krallinger, Obdulia Rabal, Saber A Akhondi, et al. 2017. Overview of the BioCreative VI chemical-protein interaction Track. In *Proceedings of the Sixth BioCreative Challenge Evaluation Workshop*, volume 1, pages 141–146.

Martin Krallinger, Obdulia Rabal, Florian Leitner, Miguel Vazquez, David Salgado, Zhiyong Lu, Robert Leaman, Yanan Lu, Donghong Ji, Daniel M. Lowe, Roger A. Sayle, Riza Theresa Batista-Navarro, Rafal Rak, Torsten Huber, Tim Rocktäschel, Sérgio Matos, David Campos, Buzhou Tang, Hua Xu, Tsendsuren Munkhdalai, Keun Ho Ryu, SV Ramanan, Senthil Nathan, Slavko Žitnik, Marko Bajec, Lutz Weber, Matthias Irmer, Saber A. Akhondi, Jan A. Kors, Shuo Xu, Xin An, Utpal Kumar Sikdar, Asif Ekbal, Masaharu Yoshioka, Thaer M. Dieb, Miji Choi, Karin Verspoor, Madian Khabsa, C. Lee Giles, Hongfang Liu, Komandur Elayavilli Ravikumar, Andre Lamurias, Francisco M. Couto, Hong-Jie Dai, Richard Tzong-Han Tsai, Caglar Ata, Tolga Can, Anabel Usié, Rui Alves, Isabel Segura-Bedmar, Paloma Martínez, Julen Oyarzabal, and Alfonso Valencia. 2015. The CHEMDNER corpus of chemicals and drugs and its annotation principles. *Journal of Cheminformatics*, 7(1):S2.

Lev Lafayette, Greg Sauter, Linh Vu, and Bernard Meade. 2017. Spartan HPC-Cloud Hybrid: Delivering Performance and Flexibility.

John D Lafferty, Andrew McCallum, and Fernando CN Pereira. 2001. Conditional Random Fields: Probabilistic Models for Segmenting and Labeling Sequence Data. In *Proceedings of the Eighteenth International Conference on Machine Learning*, pages 282–289. Morgan Kaufmann Publishers Inc.

Alexander Johnston Lawson, Stefan Roller, Helmut Grotz, Janusz L. Wisniewski, and Libuse Goebels. 2011. Method and software for extracting chemical data.

Daniel M. Lowe. 2012. *Extraction of Chemical Structures and Reactions from the Literature*. Ph.D. thesis, University of Cambridge.

John Mayfield, Daniel Lowe, and Roger Sayle. 2017. CINF 13: Pistachio - Search and Faceting of Large Reaction Databases.

Tomas Mikolov, Ilya Sutskever, Kai Chen, Greg S Corrado, and Jeff Dean. 2013. Distributed Representations of Words and Phrases and their Compositionality. In *Advances in Neural Information Processing Systems 26*, pages 3111–3119.

Mike Mintz, Steven Bills, Rion Snow, and Dan Jurafsky. 2009. Distant supervision for relation extraction without labeled data. In *Proceedings of the Joint Conference of the 47th Annual Meeting of the ACL and the 4th International Joint Conference on Natural Language Processing of the AFNLP*, volume 2, pages 1003–1011.

Matthew Peters, Mark Neumann, Mohit Iyyer, Matt Gardner, Christopher Clark, Kenton Lee, and Luke Zettlemoyer. 2018. Deep Contextualized Word Representations. In *Proceedings of the 2018 Conference of the North American Chapter of the Association for Computational Linguistics: Human Language Technologies, Volume 1 (Long Papers)*, pages 2227–2237.

Florina Piroi, Mihai Lupu, Allan Hanbury, Alan P. Sexton, Friedemann Magdy, and Igor V. Filippov. 2012. CLEF-IP 2012: Retrieval Experiments in the Intellectual Property Domain. In *CLEF 2012 Evaluation Labs and Workshop, Online Working Notes*.

Raul Rodriguez-Esteban and Markus Bundschus. 2016. Text mining patents for biomedical knowledge. *Drug Discovery Today*, 21(6):997–1002.

Stefan Senger, Luca Bartek, George Papadatos, and Anna Gaulton. 2015. Managing expectations: Assessment of chemistry databases generated by automated extraction of chemical structures from patents. *Journal of Cheminformatics*, 7(1):49.

Walid Shalaby and Wlodek Zadrozny. 2019. Patent Retrieval: A Literature Review. *Knowledge and Information Systems*, 61(2):631–660.

Christopher Southan. 2015. Expanding opportunities for mining bioactive chemistry from patents. *Drug Discovery Today: Technologies*, 14:3–9.

Erik F. Tjong, Kim Sang, and Jorn Veenstra. 1999. Representing Text Chunks. In *Ninth Conference of the European Chapter of the Association for Computational Linguistics*.

Yuen-Hsien Tseng, Chi-Jen Lin, and Yu-I Lin. 2007. Text mining techniques for patent analysis. *Information Processing & Management*, 43(5):1216–1247.

Chih-Hsuan Wei, Yifan Peng, Robert Leaman, Allan Peter Davis, Carolyn J Mattingly, Jiao Li, Thomas C Wiegers, and Zhiyong Lu. 2015. Overview of the BioCreative V chemical disease relation (CDR) task. In *Proceedings of the Fifth BioCreative Challenge Evaluation Workshop*, volume 14.

Zenan Zhai, Dat Quoc Nguyen, Saber Akhondi, Camilo Thorne, Christian Druckenbrodt, Trevor Cohn, Michelle Gregory, and Karin Verspoor. 2019. Improving Chemical Named Entity Recognition in Patents with Contextualized Word Embeddings. In *Proceedings of the 18th BioNLP Workshop and Shared Task*, pages 328–338.

Decoder	Input token representation	Layers (enc)	Dim (enc)	LR
Paragraph-level softmax	w2v +ELMo	1	200	5×10^{-5}
	w2v +ELMo +NER$_{\text{COARSE}}$	2	200	5×10^{-5}
	w2v +ELMo +NER$_{\text{FINE}}$	2	100	5×10^{-5}

Decoder	Input token representation	Layers (dec)	Dim (dec)	LR
BiLSTM-CRF	w2v +ELMo +NER$_{\text{FINE}}$	2	100	1×10^{-3}

Table 5: The best hyperparameters on the development set. "LR" is the initial learning rate, "Layers (enc/dec)" is the number of LSTM layers; and "Dim (enc/dec)" is the dimensionality of the LSTM hidden states, where "enc/dec" indicate the LSTMs in the paragraph encoder and paragraph label decoder, respectively. "NER$_{\text{COARSE}}$" and "NER$_{\text{FINE}}$" mean NER tag embeddings based on coarse- and fine-grained entity types, respectively. The structure of the paragraph encoder used for the paragraph-trigram softmax and BiLSTM-CRF classifier is the same as the one for the paragraph-level softmax classifier, thus omitted from the table.

Coarse-grained	Fine-grained
chemClass	chemClass
	chemClass$_{\text{biomolecule}}$
	chemClass$_{\text{markush}}$
	chemClass$_{\text{mixture}}$
	chemClass$_{\text{mixture-part}}$
	chemClass$_{\text{polymer}}$
chemCompound	chemCompound
	chemCompound$_{\text{mixture-part}}$
	chemCompound$_{\text{prophetics}}$

Table 4: Entity types from Reaxys® gold-standard data.

Appendix

NER label sets

Table 4 shows the NER label sets that we used as additional features to include in the input representation as described in Section 5.2.1.

Hyper-parameters

Table 5 shows the optimal hyper-parameters we used for the final evaluation.

Identifying Patients with Pain in Emergency Departments using Conventional Machine Learning and Deep Learning

Thanh Vu[1]**, Anthony Nguyen**[1]**, Nathan J Brown**[2,3]**, James Hughes**[2,4]

[1] Australian e-Health Research Centre, CSIRO, Brisbane, Australia
[2] Emergency & Trauma Centre, Royal Brisbane & Women's Hospital, Brisbane, Australia
[3] Faculty of Medicine, University of Queensland, Brisbane, Australia
[4] School of Nursing, Queensland University of Technology, Brisbane, Australia
{thanh.vu, anthony.nguyen}@csiro.au
{nathan.brown3, james.hughes}@health.qld.gov.au

Abstract

Pain is the main symptom that patients present with to the emergency department (ED). Pain management, however, is often poorly done aspect of emergency care and patients with painful conditions can endure long waits before their pain is assessed or treated. To improve pain management quality, identifying whether or not an ED patient presents with pain is an important task and allows for further investigation of the quality of care provided. In this paper, machine learning was utilised to handle the task of automatically detecting patients who present at EDs with pain from retrospective data. Experimental results on a manually annotated dataset show that our proposed machine learning models achieve high performances, in which the highest accuracy and macro-averaged F_1 are 91.00% and 90.96%, respectively.

1 Introduction

There are over 8 million presentations to Australian public hospital emergency departments (EDs) each year (AIHW, 2018). Pain is the most common symptom for patients seeking care in EDs (Karwowski-Soulié et al., 2006; Hatherley et al., 2016; Todd, 2017; Varndell et al., 2018). In particular, a study of 726 presentations (Karwowski-Soulié et al., 2006) showed that 78% of patients presented to EDs with pain. Despite the large number of ED patients with pain, pain is often poorly assessed and treated within the ED (Hatherley et al., 2016; Varndell et al., 2018). This leads to increases in waiting times for patients until pain is assessed and pharmacological analgesia is offered (Hatherley et al., 2016; Varndell et al., 2018).

In this paper, we propose the task of identifying patients presenting to EDs with pain, with the view of improving care quality and the management of pain. In particular, the identification of patients presenting to EDs with pain allows for the scoping of groups who may be receiving poor pain care (Pletcher et al., 2008; Hwang et al., 2014; Todd, 2017). The ease of identification of patients with pain also allows for the evaluation of targeted interventions to improve care using large datasets.

However, manually handling the identification task at a large scale, such as tens, hundreds of thousands of ED patients is challenging as it requires expensive human effort to determine whether a patient presented to the ED with pain or not. To handle this problem, we propose to use machine learning including both conventional feature-based and deep learning models (Scholkopf and Smola, 2001; Liaw et al., 2002; Elman, 1990; LeCun et al., 1998; Chung et al., 2014) to automatically learn the hidden patterns to solve the task.

Machine learning research in healthcare has shown success in handling many other predictive tasks, such as cancer staging from pathology reports (McCowan et al., 2007), disease or diagnosis coding from health records (Koopman et al., 2015; Mullenbach et al., 2018), predicting in-hospital mortality, unplanned readmissions (Rajkomar et al., 2018), atrial fibrillation risk (Nguyen et al., 2019), and opioid overdose risk (Che et al., 2017; Lo-Ciganic et al., 2019). To this end, we construct a dataset of ED patients from an Australian hospital in order to evaluate our proposed machine learning models, in which each patient is assigned with either a "Pain" or "No-Pain" label if the patient is with or without the presence of pain, respectively. Our main contributions are as follows:

- We formally introduce the task of identifying whether or not a patient presented at an ED with pain.

- We propose conventional machine learning as well as deep learning models to handle the task.

- We perform extensive experiments on the task-specific annotated dataset to show the effectiveness of the models.

The remainder of the paper is structured as follows. In Section 2, we present related work on improving the pain management and care quality, as well as the application of machine learning in healthcare predictive tasks. Section 3 describes the pain identification task as well as how we constructed the annotated dataset. In Section 4, we first describe our machine learning models. We then report the experimental results of the models on the annotated dataset. Section 5 concludes the paper.

2 Related Work

An overview of research to help improve the pain management and care quality at emergency departments, as well as the application of machine learning in the healthcare domain, will be presented.

2.1 Pain-related Studies

Pain is the most common symptom of patients presenting at EDs (Cordell et al., 2002; Karwowski-Soulié et al., 2006). In particular, Cordell et al. (2002) and Karwowski-Soulié et al. (2006) revealed that pain accounts for up to 70% and 78% of ED visits, respectively. Much research attention has focused on the need for improving the pain management and care quality (Doherty et al., 2013; Georgiou et al., 2015; Hatherley et al., 2016; Todd, 2017; Varndell et al., 2018). Historically, the detection, assessment and management of pain are often neglected (Georgiou et al., 2015; Varndell et al., 2018). This results in patients being forced to wait extra time before getting assessed and/or treated (Doherty et al., 2013), which leads to negative outcomes for the patient and the healthcare system.

The use of opioids is a popular approach for pain treatment (Todd, 2017). However, recent studies of prescription opioid misuse and abuse revealed that in Australia, it has been increasing to levels of harm (Häuser et al., 2017). This leads to a more urgent need of improving the pain management and care quality in Australia, which motivates this study.

2.2 Machine Learning in Healthcare

With the availability of Electronic Medical Record (EMR) systems, electronic health records (EHRs) of patients, collected during the patient clinical encounters, have been increasingly available. This creates a great opportunity for using machine learning to improve care management and quality (McCowan et al., 2007; Koopman et al., 2015; Rajkomar et al., 2018; Mullenbach et al., 2018; Che et al., 2017). In particular, McCowan et al. (2007) utilised Support Vector Machine (SVM) (Scholkopf and Smola, 2001) to automatically infer and classify cancer stages from patient pathology reports. (Koopman et al., 2015) applied SVM to classify cancer-related International Classification of Diseases (ICD) codes from free-text death certificates.

Especially, with the huge amount of EHR data, deep learning has shown to obtain state-of-the-art (SOTA) results in many predictive tasks (Che et al., 2017; Rajkomar et al., 2018; Mullenbach et al., 2018). In particular, deep learning models based on recurrent neural network (RNN) (Elman, 1990) and convolutional neural network (CNN) (LeCun et al., 1998) have achieved SOTA performances in a number of tasks, such as large-scale ICD coding from hospital free-text discharge summaries (Mullenbach et al., 2018) and prediction of opioid overdose risk (Che et al., 2017). Che et al. (2017) presented an RNN-based model for classifying categories of opioid users and achieved robust results on a large-scale dataset of over a hundred thousand opioid users. Mullenbach et al. (2018) proposed a CNN-based model to tackle the ICD coding task and showed that the model yielded SOTA performances on the MIMIC III dataset (Johnson et al., 2016). Rajkomar et al. (2018) demonstrated that deep learning models achieved high accuracy for predictive tasks, such as in-hospital mortality, unplanned readmission and prolonged length of stay. In this study, we take the advantages of both conventional machine learning and deep learning models to handle a new task of pain-related identification which is described in Section 3.

3 Task Description and Dataset

In this section, the formulation of the task and the dataset used for the task evaluation is presented.

3.1 Task Description

Given a patient who presents at an ED, the aim is to identify whether or not that patient is with the presence of pain on admission. This task can be formulated as a two-class (binary) classification problem, in which the ED data of the patient was used to predict the pain class (i.e., either *"Pain"* to represent patients *with* pain or *"No-Pain"* to represent patients *without* pain).

Unstructured free-text ED data fields, namely "presenting problem" and "nurse assessment", were used for the classification task. These were the two free text fields that ED nurses fill out on a patient's arrival to the ED. Table 1 illustrates examples of patients with and without pain. Note that short-hand notations, abbreviations and typographical errors are common in the patient ED data, which presents additional challenges to the task.

Table 1: Examples of the ED data associated with patients with/without pain. The class of each patient was manually annotated.

Patient ED Data	Class
Presenting problem: 4/7 cough, tight chest , myalgia// recent dx t2dm; *Nurse assessment*: a=patent b= spontaneous, rr 19, reports it hurts to breath and having difficulty breathing c= strong reg radial pulse, tachycardic 120 very dry mucous membranes not maintaining oral intake d= gcs 15;	Pain
Presenting problem: mdma yesterday anxious insomnia subjective tongue swelling tachycardic; *Nurse assessment*: hr 120bpm dry tongue doe not appear swollen;	No-Pain

It is worth noting that the focus was on identifying patients with pain at admission. Other potentially useful ED information, such as ICD-10 diagnosis codes, would not be available until the patient is discharged.

3.2 Dataset

A dataset of patients presenting at EDs was constructed by randomly extracting 2,000 ED adult patients from an Australian hospital with the arrival date from August to October 2018[1]. The dataset was annotated by an experienced medical student under the supervision of a senior medical nurse, in which a patient was assigned a "Pain" label if the patient presented with pain,

---

Table 2: Basic dataset statistics

Dataset	#Patients	#Pain	#No-Pain
Training	1,200	574	626
Development	400	171	229
Test	400	193	207

and "No-Pain" otherwise. In particular, the annotator was provided with a list of pain related keywords (Hughes et al., 2019) to look for when reviewing the triage nursing assessment. In addition to these keywords, the annotator also reviewed the documentation for a pain score, such as "xx/10", "severe pain". When the annotator believed that the triage nursing assessment indicated pain but was outside of the definition, discussion was held between the student and the senior medical nurse about whether this indicated the patient arrived in pain. After annotating the data, the annotated dataset contained a total of 938 and 1,062 instances of "Pain" and "No-Pain" labels, respectively.

The annotated dataset was split into training, development and test sets containing 60%, 20%, 20% instances of the annotated dataset, respectively. Table 2 shows the dataset statistics.

4 Methods

This section details the machine learning models used for the pain classification task. Specifically, Support Vector Machine (SVM) and Random Forest (RF) were used as our conventional feature-based models, and Recurrent Neural Network (RNN) and Convolutional Neural Networks (CNN) were used as our deep learning models.

4.1 Conventional feature-based models

SVM (Scholkopf and Smola, 2001) and RF (Liaw et al., 2002) were used as our conventional feature-based models to handle the classification task. Figure 1 shows the general architecture of the conventional models. Here, both the models used the same set of lexical and semantic features according to (Yang et al., 2016; Vu et al., 2018) as follows:

Lexical features: Lexical features included n-grams at both word and character levels (i.e. sequences of n words or characters). n-grams at the character level were used to handle out-of-vocabulary (OOV) words. For each type of n-gram, only the top k most frequent n-grams from the training set were kept. The value of

---

[1]Research ethics was obtained from the Metro North Hospital and Health Service Human Research Ethics Committee.

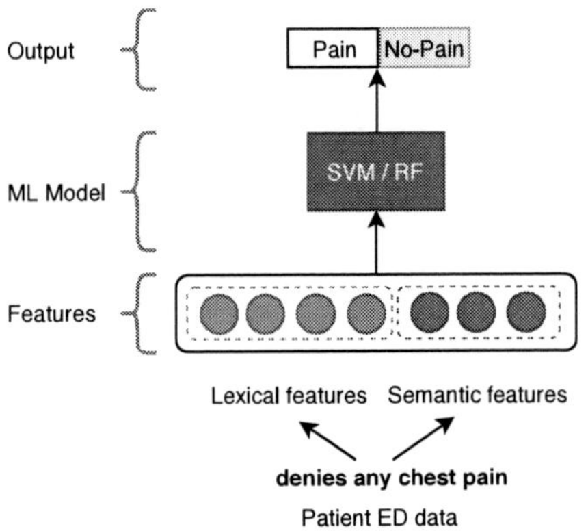

Figure 1: Conventional machine learning models. The model output is "No-Pain" for the input of "denies any chest pain".

each n-gram feature was calculated using the term frequency-inverse document frequency (tf-idf) weighting scheme.

Semantic features: Two approaches were applied to semantically represent the patient. Firstly, the average of pre-trained embeddings of words in the patient ED data was used as the representation of that patient. Secondly, latent semantic indexing (LSI) (Papadimitriou et al., 2000) was used to capture the underlying semantics of the dataset.

Implementation details: For the experimental dataset, tokens that contained no alphabetic or numeric characters were removed (for example, removing "//" but keeping "3/7"). All the remaining tokens were lowercased. The "presenting problem" and "nurse assessment" fields of a patient were concatenated to form the single text for the patient. Regarding lexical features, we set k, the top most frequent n-grams to 2,000 for both word and character levels. For the semantic features, fastText (Bojanowski et al., 2016) was applied to train a subword embedding model on a large-scale dataset of 8 million hospital clinical notes. We found that the best experimental results on the development set were achieved with the pre-trained embedding size of 200. Moreover, we set the LSI output size to 100.

The Scikit-learn implementations for both the SVM and RF models (Pedregosa et al., 2011) were used. For each model, a grid-search on hyper-parameters was performed to find the best performing model on the development set. Specifically, for each hyper-parameter setting, we trained the machine learning model using the training set

and then evaluate the trained model on the development set. The best-trained model was selected using the macro-averaged F_1 scores of "Pain" and "No-Pain" labels on the development set. After that, the best model was used for the evaluation on the test set.

For SVM, the "linear" kernel performed better than the "polynomial", "radial basis function (rbf)" and "sigmoid" kernels. The grid search was performed over *loss_function* $\in$ {"squared_hinge", "hinge"}; $C \in$ {0.1, 0.3, 0.5, 0.7, 0.9, 1.0, 3.0, 5.0}; *max_iteration* $\in$ {100, 200, 500, 1000, 2000}. We also set the *penalty_norm* parameter to l_2. The highest average-macro F_1 score was archived with *loss_function* = "hinge", $C = 0.3$, and *max_iteration* = 1000.

For RF, the grid search was performed over *max_depth* $\in [1-10]$ and *number_of_trees* $\in$ {10, 50, 100, 200, 300, 500, 1000}. A *max_depth* = 6 and *number_of_trees* = 500 produced the highest F_1 score on the development set.

4.2 Deep learning models

RNN (Elman, 1990) and CNN (LeCun et al., 1998) were used as deep learning models as they have proved to work well in the tasks of modelling sequence data (Mikolov et al., 2010) and text classification (Kim, 2014; Yang et al., 2016). Figure 2 shows the architecture of the deep learning models. For both models, the base/embedding layer was obtained by concatenating the pre-trained word embeddings (from a large-scale hospital clinical note dataset) with the character-level embeddings of that word (Kim et al., 2016). The pre-trained word embeddings were fixed, while character-level word embeddings were simultaneously trained with the other model parameters. The character-level word embeddings help handle the OOV words. The representations of words in the ED data of a patient were concatenated to form a sequence of word representation vectors.

RNN model: The sequence of word vectors were fed into an RNN encoder to learn the representation of the patient. As RNN has struggled with long-term dependencies, we applied a prominent variant of RNN, Gated recurrent unit (GRU) (Chung et al., 2014), which can handle the problem.[2] The hidden state vector of the last word in

---

[2]GRU performed better than long short-term memory (LSTM) (Hochreiter and Schmidhuber, 1997) as well as their bi-directional counterparts for this task in our experiments.

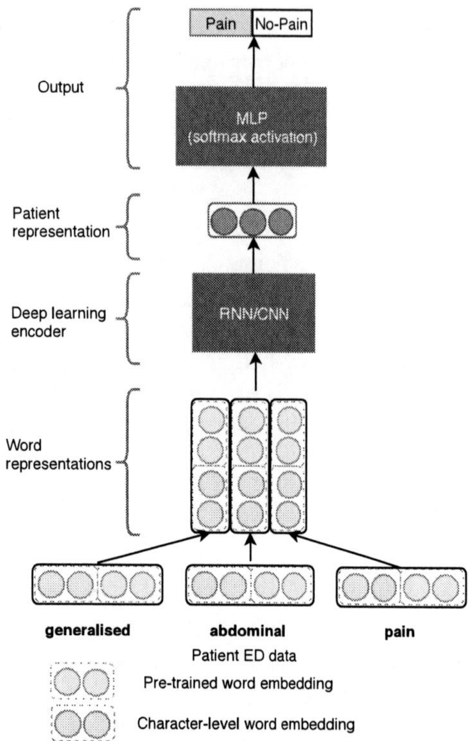

Figure 2: Deep learning models. The model output is "Pain" for the input of "generalised abdominal pain".

the patient data produced by GRU was used as the patient representation. Finally, the representation vector was fed into a one-hidden layer multilayer perceptron (MLP) with softmax output for classification which returns the class probabilities for the patient.

CNN model: The sequence of word vectors was fed into a CNN encoder which performed convolution operations and max-pooling to produce the representation vector of the patient. Similar to the RNN model, the representation vector was fed into a one-hidden layer MLP with softmax output to produce the class prediction.

Implementation details: The same pre-trained embeddings model and data preprocessing detailed in Section 4.1 was used. The deep learning models were implemented using Pytorch (Paszke et al., 2017). We trained each model using the Adam optimiser (Kingma and Ba, 2014) with the default learning rate of 0.001 and a fixed random seed. The batch size and the number of training epochs were respectively set to 32 and 50. The CNN-based model proposed by (Kim et al., 2016) was used to learn the character-level embeddings for each word, in which the window size and the num-

ber of filters were set to 2 and 50, respectively. For both models, we applied a dropout mechanism to both the word representations (before the encoder) and the patient representation (before MLP) with the probability of 0.5.

For RNN, a grid search was performed over $hidden\_size \in \{100, 200, 300, 400, 500\}$ and the number of layers, $n\_layers \in \{1, 2, 3, 4, 5\}$. The best performance was achieved with $hidden\_size = 400$ and $n\_layers = 5$. For CNN, we performed a grid search of the number of filters, $n\_filters \in \{100, 200, 300, 400, 500\}$ and the window sizes, $kernel\_sizes \in \{2, 3, 4, 5, (2, 3), (4, 5), (3, 4, 5)\}$. The setting of $n\_filters = 400$ and $kernel\_sizes = 3$ produced best performances.

4.3 Evaluation

Baseline: The proposed machine learning models were compared with a rule-based baseline, *RULE*. Specifically, the baseline used inclusion and exclusion criteria predefined by a senior ED nurse as detailed in a recent publication (Hughes et al., 2019), for example, terms containing "pain", "discomfort", "stab", "burn", "ache". In the baseline, Context/Negex (Chapman et al., 2011) was also used to handle negation in the patient ED data, for example, "denies neck pain".

Metrics: The metrics used to evaluate the models included *accuracy*, *precision*, *recall* and F_1 which are standard evaluation metrics for classification tasks. For all metrics, higher values represent better performances.

4.4 Results

Overall performance: Table 3 shows the main experimental results of the models on the test set. The rule-based model, RULE, achieves an accuracy of 84.75% indicating that the model performed well for this task. The drawback of this model is that it required expert knowledge for the construction of the inclusion and exclusion criteria. The results also show that all the proposed machine learning models achieved higher performances than RULE. Specifically, the machine learning models achieve absolute improvements of at least 3.3% over the RULE baseline with respect to the macro-averaged F_1 scores. This indicates that the proposed machine learning models can handle the task well even without expert knowledge.

Noteworthy, without feature engineering, the deep learning models (i.e., CNN and RNN) per-

Table 3: Experimental results (%) on the test set. $*$ indicates that the performance difference between the machine learning model and the RULE baseline is significant at the significance level α of 0.1 using the Approximate Randomisation test (Chinchor, 1992; Dror et al., 2018), with N= 5,000.

Model	Accuracy	Macro-averaged			Pain			No-Pain		
		Precision	Recall	F_1	Precision	Recall	F_1	Precision	Recall	F_1
RULE	84.75	84.87	84.63	84.69	86.26	81.35	83.73	83.49	87.92	85.65
SVM	88.00	88.13*	87.90*	87.96*	89.62	84.97	87.23*	86.64	90.82	88.68*
RF	88.00	88.31*	87.85*	87.93*	90.96*	83.42	87.03*	85.65	92.27*	88.84*
RNN	**91.00***	**91.21***	**90.88***	**90.96***	**93.37***	87.56*	**90.37***	89.04*	**94.20***	**91.55***
CNN	88.25	88.25*	88.30*	88.25*	86.50	**89.64***	88.04*	**90.00***	86.96	88.45

formed competitively or better than conventional models (i.e., SVM and RF). RNN produced the highest performance with an accuracy and macro-averaged F_1 score of 91.00% and 90.96%, which were 6.25% and 6.27% absolute higher than RULE, respectively. With regards to the "Pain" label, RNN achieved the highest precision of 93.37% and F_1 score of 90.37%. Meanwhile, CNN achieved the highest recall of 89.64%. In terms of the "No-Pain" label, CNN obtained the highest precision of 90.00%, while RNN achieved the highest recall of 94.20% and F_1 of 91.55%.

Table 3 also presents the statistical significance between the difference in performances between the machine learning models and the RULE baseline, using the Approximate Randomisation test (Chinchor, 1992; Dror et al., 2018), with N = 5,000 and the significance level α of 0.1. The Approximate Randomisation test is a popular non-parametric statistical significance test for NLP tasks (Chinchor, 1992; Dror et al., 2018). We found that the difference in performances between RNN and RULE were statistically significant across all classes as well as metrics. The deep learning models were also consistently better in terms of absolute values when compared to conventional models.

Ablation study: In the previous sections, deep learning models were shown to work better than conventional machine learning models. In this section, we evaluate the effectiveness of the pre-trained and character-level word embeddings on the performance of the deep learning models. Specifically, we perform an ablation study on the development set, in which we evaluate the best performing model, RNN, with different ablation settings as follows: w/o *char embeds*, w/o *word embeds* and w/o *both* denoting that the model was trained without character-level word embeddings, without pre-trained word embed-

dings[3] and neither the embeddings, respectively. We also presented the results of RNN when using only the "presenting problem", namely only *PP* and using only the nurse assessment, namely only *NA* ED data fields.[4]

As can be seen from Table 4, without character-level word embeddings slightly decreases the RNN performance. Without pre-trained word embedding significantly degrades the RNN performances by about 4%. The largest decline in the performance of about 4.8% was observed when both embedding types were not used. We further see that without using presenting problem data (i.e. "only NA") results in a significant decrease of more than 23% in the performance. This is perhaps caused by the fact that there were 276 out of 2,000 ($\sim$ 14%) patients who did not have any nursing assessment data. Another reason may be due to the presenting problem field being more informative in terms of containing more pain-related information than in the nurse assessment field. Further investigation revealed that 38% of the presenting problems in the development set contained pain-related keywords (detailed in the baseline, RULE) compared to 25.50% of the non-empty nurse assessment data. We also found that without using nurse assessment (i.e. "only PP") degrades the performance by about 3.8%. This indicates that the concatenation of the two free-text fields was important to the task.

4.5 Application

The immediate application of the research is to provide machine learning assistance to process and analyse very large datasets for the purposes of research or clinical audit. Apart from that, it can also be a potential real-time clinical application,

---

[3]In this case, the word embeddings were initialised randomly and then fine-tuned with the training of other model parameters.

[4]For the ED data field ablation study, we used the RNN with both pre-trained word and character-level embeddings.

Table 4: Ablation study performance (%) on the development set.

Model	Accuracy	F_1
RNN	90.00	89.80
w/o *char embeds*	$89.75_{-0.25}$	$89.61_{-0.19}$
w/o *word embeds*	$86.00_{-4.00}$	$85.50_{-4.30}$
w/o *both*	$85.25_{-4.75}$	$84.99_{-4.81}$
only *PP*	$86.25_{-3.75}$	$85.88_{-3.92}$
only *NA*	$67.42_{-22.58}$	$66.32_{-23.48}$

such as a smart support assistant to help improve the quality of triage related to presentations that involve or are likely to involve pain. Specifically, in the scenario of a patient who presents to triage, the triage nurse asks about the problem/symptoms and records in electronic notes. If pain or a condition likely to be associated with pain is recorded then the triage nurse should also ask the patient about the level of pain and record a pain score. The smart support assistant will monitor the electronic notes in real-time and if a pain score is not recorded in the notes when it should be, then it will provide a suggestion of adding the information to the triage nurse. Pain is a common symptom that the ED sees everyday but still does not do a good job at assessing. These applications are able to be expanded to different hospital departments and units, such as Intensive Care Units where assessing pain may also be challenging (Suominen et al., 2009).

4.6 Limitations and Future Work

As in the previous section, the best accuracy on the development set was 90%, achieved using RNN. This meant that there were 10% $\sim$ 40 instances, namely the "error" set, where RNN produced incorrect labels. The "error" set was reviewed by a senior ED nurse to determine the underlying reasons for the system discrepancies.

On review, we found cases where the ED nurse had difficultly in classifying pain. In these more difficult cases, half of the "error" cases could have been classified differently.[5] This shows that even with a medical background, there exist the more difficult cases where there may be uncertainty in the labels. In future, we plan to handle the uncertainty problem by involving multiple annotators and an adjudicator.

---

[5]This indicates that our proposed machine learning approaches could have achieved higher performances if the dataset labels relating to "error" cases were corrected.

Another limitation of the proposed deep learning model was that although it produced the highest performance, it was still difficult to understand and locate the evidence it used for prediction, which is an important aspect of text analytics in the healthcare domain. In future work, we aim to integrate neural attention mechanisms to our deep learning models to make it interpretable (Bahdanau et al., 2014; Luong et al., 2015; Vaswani et al., 2017).

5 Conclusions

In this paper, we presented the task of identifying patients who presented to EDs with pain. Both conventional feature-based machine learning and deep learning models were proposed to handle the task. Experimental results on a 2,000 ED patient annotated dataset showed that our machine learning models performed well on this task with the highest accuracy and macro-averaged F_1 score of 91.00% and 90.96%, respectively.

It was shown that the machine learning models achieved higher results than a rule-based baseline. Moreover, deep learning models performed competitively or better than conventional models. The ablation study indicated that pre-trained word embeddings and character-level word embeddings played an important role leading to the success of the deep learning models. These learnings are beneficial for similar research on other clinical tasks but also sets a solid foundation for further improving performances on the "pain" models as well as improve the clinical utility of the model through explainability, with the aim to scale the "pain" study to other hospitals and regions.

References

AIHW. 2018. Emergency department care 2017-2018: Australian hospital statistics. *Australian Institute of Health and Welfare*.

Dzmitry Bahdanau, Kyunghyun Cho, and Yoshua Bengio. 2014. Neural machine translation by jointly learning to align and translate. *arXiv preprint arXiv:1409.0473*.

Piotr Bojanowski, Edouard Grave, Armand Joulin, and Tomas Mikolov. 2016. Enriching word vectors with subword information. *arXiv preprint arXiv:1607.04606*.

Brian E Chapman, Sean Lee, Hyunseok Peter Kang, and Wendy W Chapman. 2011. Document-level classification of ct pulmonary angiography reports based on an extension of the context algorithm. *Journal of biomedical informatics*, 44(5):728–737.

Zhengping Che, Jennifer St Sauver, Hongfang Liu, and Yan Liu. 2017. Deep learning solutions for classifying patients on opioid use. In *AMIA Annual Symposium Proceedings*, volume 2017, page 525. American Medical Informatics Association.

Nancy Chinchor. 1992. The statistical significance of the muc-4 results. In *Proceedings of the 4th conference on Message understanding*, pages 30–50. Association for Computational Linguistics.

Junyoung Chung, Caglar Gulcehre, KyungHyun Cho, and Yoshua Bengio. 2014. Empirical evaluation of gated recurrent neural networks on sequence modeling. *arXiv preprint arXiv:1412.3555*.

William H Cordell, Kelly K Keene, Beverly K Giles, James B Jones, James H Jones, and Edward J Brizendine. 2002. The high prevalence of pain in emergency medical care. *The American journal of emergency medicine*, 20(3):165–169.

Steven Doherty, Jonathan Knott, Scott Bennetts, Mitra Jazayeri, and Sue Huckson. 2013. National project seeking to improve pain management in the emergency department setting: Findings from the nhmrcnics n ational p ain m anagement i nitiative. *Emergency Medicine Australasia*, 25(2):120–126.

Rotem Dror, Gili Baumer, Segev Shlomov, and Roi Reichart. 2018. The hitchhikers guide to testing statistical significance in natural language processing. In *Proceedings of the 56th Annual Meeting of the Association for Computational Linguistics (Volume 1: Long Papers)*, pages 1383–1392.

Jeffrey L Elman. 1990. Finding structure in time. *Cognitive science*, 14(2):179–211.

Evanthia Georgiou, Maria Hadjibalassi, Ekaterini Lambrinou, Panayiota Andreou, and Elizabeth DE Papathanassoglou. 2015. The impact of pain assessment on critically ill patients outcomes: a systematic review. *BioMed research international*, 2015.

Claire Hatherley, Natasha Jennings, and Rachel Cross. 2016. Time to analgesia and pain score documentation best practice standards for the emergency department–a literature review. *Australasian Emergency Nursing Journal*, 19(1):26–36.

Winfried Häuser, Stephan Schug, and Andrea D Furlan. 2017. The opioid epidemic and national guidelines for opioid therapy for chronic noncancer pain: a perspective from different continents. *Pain reports*, 2(3).

Sepp Hochreiter and Jürgen Schmidhuber. 1997. Long short-term memory. *Neural computation*, 9(8):1735–1780.

James A. Hughes, Nathan J. Brown, Jacqui Chiu, Brandon Allwood, and Kevin Chu. 2019. The relationship between time to analgesic administration and emergency department length of stay: A retrospective review. *Journal of Advanced Nursing*, 0(0):1–8.

Ula Hwang, Laura K Belland, Daniel A Handel, Kabir Yadav, Kennon Heard, Laura Rivera-Reyes, Amanda Eisenberg, Matthew J Noble, Sudha Mekala, Morgan Valley, et al. 2014. Is all pain is treated equally? a multicenter evaluation of acute pain care by age. *Pain®*, 155(12):2568–2574.

Alistair EW Johnson, Tom J Pollard, Lu Shen, H Lehman Li-wei, Mengling Feng, Mohammad Ghassemi, Benjamin Moody, Peter Szolovits, Leo Anthony Celi, and Roger G Mark. 2016. Mimic-iii, a freely accessible critical care database. *Scientific data*, 3:160035.

Fabienne Karwowski-Soulié, Stéphanie Lessenot-Tcherny, Agathe Lamarche-Vadel, Sébastien Bineau, Christine Ginsburg, Olivier Meyniard, Brigitte Mendoza, Pascale Fodella, Gwenaelle Vidal-Trecan, and Fabrice Brunet. 2006. Pain in an emergency department: an audit. *European Journal of Emergency Medicine*, 13(4):218–224.

Yoon Kim. 2014. Convolutional neural networks for sentence classification. *arXiv preprint arXiv:1408.5882*.

Yoon Kim, Yacine Jernite, David Sontag, and Alexander M Rush. 2016. Character-aware neural language models. In *Thirtieth AAAI Conference on Artificial Intelligence*.

Diederik P Kingma and Jimmy Ba. 2014. Adam: A method for stochastic optimization. *arXiv preprint arXiv:1412.6980*.

Bevan Koopman, Guido Zuccon, Anthony Nguyen, Anton Bergheim, and Narelle Grayson. 2015. Automatic icd-10 classification of cancers from free-text death certificates. *International journal of medical informatics*, 84(11):956–965.

Yann LeCun, Léon Bottou, Yoshua Bengio, Patrick Haffner, et al. 1998. Gradient-based learning applied to document recognition. *Proceedings of the IEEE*, 86(11):2278–2324.

Andy Liaw, Matthew Wiener, et al. 2002. Classification and regression by randomforest. *R news*, 2(3):18–22.

Wei-Hsuan Lo-Ciganic, James L Huang, Hao H Zhang, Jeremy C Weiss, Yonghui Wu, C Kent Kwoh, Julie M Donohue, Gerald Cochran, Adam J Gordon, Daniel C Malone, et al. 2019. Evaluation of machine-learning algorithms for predicting opioid overdose risk among medicare beneficiaries with opioid prescriptions. *JAMA network open*, 2(3):e190968–e190968.

Minh-Thang Luong, Hieu Pham, and Christopher D Manning. 2015. Effective approaches to attention-based neural machine translation. *arXiv preprint arXiv:1508.04025*.

Iain A McCowan, Darren C Moore, Anthony N Nguyen, Rayleen V Bowman, Belinda E Clarke, Edwina E Duhig, and Mary-Jane Fry. 2007. Collection of cancer stage data by classifying free-text medical reports. *Journal of the American Medical Informatics Association*, 14(6):736–745.

Tomáš Mikolov, Martin Karafiát, Lukáš Burget, Jan Černocký, and Sanjeev Khudanpur. 2010. Recurrent neural network based language model. In *Eleventh annual conference of the international speech communication association*.

James Mullenbach, Sarah Wiegreffe, Jon Duke, Jimeng Sun, and Jacob Eisenstein. 2018. Explainable prediction of medical codes from clinical text. *arXiv preprint arXiv:1802.05695*.

Dat Quoc Nguyen, Karin Verspoor, and Blanca Gallego Luxan. 2019. Risk prediction using electronic health records of patients with atrial fibrillation. In *Proceedings of the Advances in Data Science conference abstracts*.

Christos H Papadimitriou, Prabhakar Raghavan, Hisao Tamaki, and Santosh Vempala. 2000. Latent semantic indexing: A probabilistic analysis. *Journal of Computer and System Sciences*, 61(2):217–235.

Adam Paszke, Sam Gross, Soumith Chintala, Gregory Chanan, Edward Yang, Zachary DeVito, Zeming Lin, Alban Desmaison, Luca Antiga, and Adam Lerer. 2017. Automatic differentiation in PyTorch. In *NIPS Autodiff Workshop*.

F. Pedregosa, G. Varoquaux, A. Gramfort, V. Michel, B. Thirion, O. Grisel, M. Blondel, P. Prettenhofer, R. Weiss, V. Dubourg, J. Vanderplas, A. Passos, D. Cournapeau, M. Brucher, M. Perrot, and E. Duchesnay. 2011. Scikit-learn: Machine learning in Python. *Journal of Machine Learning Research*, 12:2825–2830.

Mark J Pletcher, Stefan G Kertesz, Michael A Kohn, and Ralph Gonzales. 2008. Trends in opioid prescribing by race/ethnicity for patients seeking care in us emergency departments. *Jama*, 299(1):70–78.

Alvin Rajkomar, Eyal Oren, Kai Chen, Andrew M Dai, Nissan Hajaj, Michaela Hardt, Peter J Liu, Xiaobing Liu, Jake Marcus, Mimi Sun, et al. 2018. Scalable and accurate deep learning with electronic health records. *NPJ Digital Medicine*, 1(1):18.

Bernhard Scholkopf and Alexander J Smola. 2001. *Learning with kernels: support vector machines, regularization, optimization, and beyond*. MIT press.

Hanna Suominen, Heljä Lundgrén-Laine, Sanna Salanterä, and Tapio Salakoski. 2009. Evaluating pain in intensive care. In *Nursing Informatics*, pages 192–196.

Knox H Todd. 2017. A review of current and emerging approaches to pain management in the emergency department. *Pain and therapy*, 6(2):193–202.

Wayne Varndell, Margaret Fry, and Doug Elliott. 2018. Quality and impact of nurse-initiated analgesia in the emergency department: A systematic review. *International emergency nursing*, 40:46–53.

Ashish Vaswani, Noam Shazeer, Niki Parmar, Jakob Uszkoreit, Llion Jones, Aidan N Gomez, Łukasz Kaiser, and Illia Polosukhin. 2017. Attention is all you need. In *Advances in neural information processing systems*, pages 5998–6008.

Thanh Vu, Dat Quoc Nguyen, Xuan-Son Vu, Dai Quoc Nguyen, Michael Catt, and Michael Trenell. 2018. Nihrio at semeval-2018 task 3: A simple and accurate neural network model for irony detection in twitter. *arXiv preprint arXiv:1804.00520*.

Zichao Yang, Diyi Yang, Chris Dyer, Xiaodong He, Alex Smola, and Eduard Hovy. 2016. Hierarchical attention networks for document classification. In *Proceedings of the 2016 conference of the North American chapter of the association for computational linguistics: human language technologies*, pages 1480–1489.

A neural joint model for Vietnamese word segmentation, POS tagging and dependency parsing

Dat Quoc Nguyen[1,2]
[1]The University of Melbourne, Australia
dqnguyen@unimelb.edu.au
[2]VinAI Research, Hanoi, Vietnam
v.datnq9@vinai.io

Abstract

We propose the first multi-task learning model for joint Vietnamese word segmentation, part-of-speech (POS) tagging and dependency parsing. In particular, our model extends the BIST graph-based dependency parser (Kiperwasser and Goldberg, 2016) with BiLSTM-CRF-based neural layers (Huang et al., 2015) for word segmentation and POS tagging. On Vietnamese benchmark datasets, experimental results show that our joint model obtains state-of-the-art or competitive performances.

1   Introduction

Dependency parsing (Kübler et al., 2009) is extremely useful in many downstream applications such as relation extraction (Bunescu and Mooney, 2005) and machine translation (Galley and Manning, 2009). POS tags are essential features used in dependency parsing. In real-world parsing, most parsers are used in a pipeline process with a precursor POS tagging model for producing predicted POS tags. In English where white space is a strong word boundary indicator, POS tagging is considered to be the first important step towards dependency parsing (Ballesteros et al., 2015).

Unlike English, for Vietnamese NLP, word segmentation is considered to be the key first step. This is because when written, white space is used in Vietnamese to separate syllables that constitute words, in addition to marking word boundaries (Nguyen et al., 2009). For example, a 4-syllable written text "Tôi là sinh viên" (I am student) forms 3 words "Tôi[I] là[am] sinh_viên[student]".[1] When parsing real-world Vietnamese text where gold word segmentation is not available, a pipeline process is defined that starts with a word segmenter to segment the text. The segmented text

---

[1]About 85% of Vietnamese word types are composed of at least two syllables and 80%+ of syllable types are words by themselves (Thang et al., 2008). For Vietnamese word segmentation, white space is only used to separate word tokens while underscore is used to separate syllables inside a word.

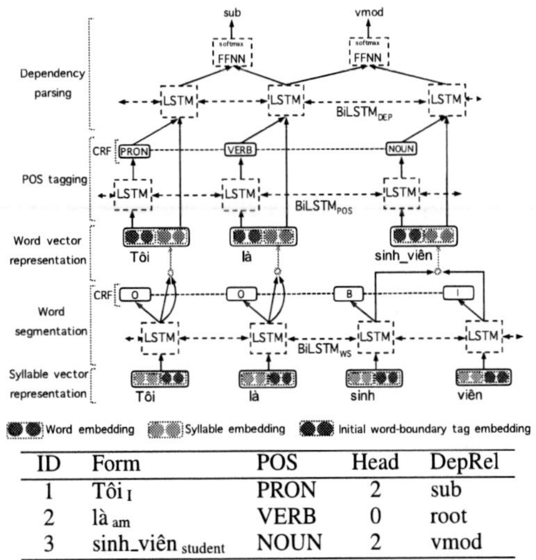

ID	Form	POS	Head	DepRel
1	Tôi[I]	PRON	2	sub
2	là[am]	VERB	0	root
3	sinh_viên[student]	NOUN	2	vmod

Figure 1: Illustration of our joint model. Linear transformations are not shown for simplification.

(e.g. "Tôi là sinh_viên") is provided as the input to the POS tagger, which automatically generates POS-annotated text (e.g. "Tôi/PRON là/VERB sinh_viên/NOUN") which is in turn fed to the parser. See Figure 1 for the final parsing output.

However, Vietnamese word segmenters and POS taggers have a non-trivial error rate, thus leading to error propagation. A solution to these problems is to develop models for jointly learning word segmentation, POS tagging and dependency parsing, such as those that have been actively explored for Chinese. These include traditional feature-based models (Hatori et al., 2012; Qian and Liu, 2012; Zhang et al., 2014, 2015) and neural models (Kurita et al., 2017; Li et al., 2018). These models construct *transition*-based frameworks at character level.

In this paper, we present a new multi-task learning model for joint word segmentation, POS tagging and dependency parsing. More specifically, our model can be viewed as an extension of the BIST *graph*-based dependency parser (Kiperwasser and Goldberg, 2016), that incorporates BiLSTM-CRF-based architectures (Huang et al., 2015) to predict the segmentation and POS tags. To the best of our knowledge, our model is the first one which is proposed to jointly learn these three tasks for Vietnamese. Experiments on Vietnamese benchmark datasets show that our model produces state-of-the-art or competitive results.

2 Our proposed model

As illustrated in Figure 1, our joint multi-task model can be viewed as a hierarchical mixture of three components: word segmentation, POS tagging and dependency parsing. In particular, our word segmentation component formalizes the Vietnamese word segmentation task as a sequence labeling problem, thus uses a BiLSTM-CRF architecture (Huang et al., 2015) to predict BIO word boundary tags from input syllables, resulting in a word-segmented sequence. As for word segmentation, our POS tagging component also uses a BiLSTM-CRF to predict POS tags from the sequence of segmented words. Based on the input segmented words and their predicted POS tags, our dependency parsing component uses a graph-based architecture similarly to the one from Kiperwasser and Goldberg (2016) to decode dependency arcs and labels.

Syllable vector representation: Given an input sentence $\mathcal{S}$ of m syllables s_1, s_2, ..., s_m, we apply an initial word segmenter to produce initial BIO word-boundary tags b_1, b_2, ..., b_m. Following the state-of-the-art Vietnamese word segmenter VnCoreNLP's RDRsegmenter (Nguyen et al., 2018b), our initial word segmenter is based on the lexicon-based longest matching strategy (Poowarawan, 1986). We create a vector $\mathbf{v}_i$ to represent each ith syllable in the input sentence $\mathcal{S}$ by concatenating its syllable embedding $\mathbf{e}_{s_i}^{(\text{s})}$ and its initial word-boundary tag embedding $\mathbf{e}_{b_i}^{(\text{B})}$:

$$\mathbf{v}_i = \mathbf{e}_{s_i}^{(\text{s})} \circ \mathbf{e}_{b_i}^{(\text{B})} \qquad (1)$$

Word segmentation (WSeg): The WSeg component uses a BiLSTM ($\text{BiLSTM}_{\text{WS}}$) to learn a latent feature vector representing the ith syllable from a sequence of vectors $\mathbf{v}_{1:m}$:

$$\mathbf{r}_i^{(\text{WS})} = \text{BiLSTM}_{\text{WS}}(\mathbf{v}_{1:m}, i) \qquad (2)$$

The WSeg component then uses a single-layer feed-forward network (FFNN_{WS}) to perform lin-

ear transformation over each latent feature vector:

$$\mathbf{h}_i^{(\text{WS})} = \text{FFNN}_{\text{WS}}(\mathbf{r}_i^{(\text{WS})}) \qquad (3)$$

Next, the WSeg component feeds output vectors $\mathbf{h}_i^{(\text{WS})}$ into a linear-chain CRF layer (Lafferty et al., 2001) for final BIO word-boundary tag prediction. A cross-entropy objective loss $\mathcal{L}_{\text{WS}}$ is computed during training, while the Viterbi algorithm is used for decoding.

Word vector representation: Assume that we form n words w_1, w_2, ..., w_n based on m syllables in the input sentence $\mathcal{S}$. Note that we use gold word segmentation when training, and use predicted segmentation produced by the WSeg component when decoding. We create a vector $\mathbf{x}_j$ to represent each jth word w_j by concatenating its word embedding $\mathbf{e}_{w_j}^{(\text{W})}$ and its syllable-level word embedding $\mathbf{e}_{w_j}^{(\text{SW})}$:

$$\mathbf{x}_j = \mathbf{e}_{w_j}^{(\text{W})} \circ \mathbf{e}_{w_j}^{(\text{SW})} \qquad (4)$$

Here, inspired by Bohnet et al. (2018), to obtain $\mathbf{e}_{w_j}^{(\text{SW})}$, we combine sentence-level context sensitive syllable encodings (from Equation 2) and feed it into a FFNN (FFNN_{SW}):

$$\mathbf{e}_{w_j}^{(\text{SW})} = \text{FFNN}_{\text{SW}}(\mathbf{r}_{f(w_j)}^{(\text{WS})} \circ \mathbf{r}_{l(w_j)}^{(\text{WS})}) \qquad (5)$$

where $f(w_j)$ and $l(w_j)$ denote indices of the first and last syllables of w_j in $\mathcal{S}$, respectively.

POS tagging: The POS tagging component first feeds a sequence of vectors $\mathbf{x}_{1:n}$ into a BiLSTM ($\text{BiLSTM}_{\text{POS}}$) to learn latent feature vectors representing input words, and passes each of these latent vectors as input to a FFNN (FFNN_{POS}):

$$\mathbf{r}_j^{(\text{POS})} = \text{BiLSTM}_{\text{POS}}(\mathbf{x}_{1:n}, j) \qquad (6)$$

$$\mathbf{h}_j^{(\text{POS})} = \text{FFNN}_{\text{POS}}(\mathbf{r}_j^{(\text{POS})}) \qquad (7)$$

Output vectors $\mathbf{h}_j^{(\text{POS})}$ are then fed into a CRF layer for POS tag prediction. A cross-entropy loss $\mathcal{L}_{\text{POS}}$ is computed for POS tagging when training.

Dependency parsing: Assume that the POS tagging component produces p_1, p_2, ..., p_n as predicted POS tags for the input words w_1, w_2, ..., w_n, respectively. Each jth predicted POS tag p_j is represented by an embedding $\mathbf{e}_{p_j}^{(\text{P})}$. We create a sequence of vectors $\mathbf{z}_{1:n}$ as input for the dependency parsing component, in which each $\mathbf{z}_j$ is resulted by concatenating the word vector representation $\mathbf{x}_j$ (from Equation 4) and the corresponding POS tag embedding $\mathbf{e}_{p_j}^{(\text{P})}$. The dependency parsing component uses a BiLSTM ($\text{BiLSTM}_{\text{DEP}}$) to learn latent feature representations from the input $\mathbf{z}_{1:n}$:

$$\mathbf{z}_j = \mathbf{x}_j \circ \mathbf{e}_{p_j}^{(\text{P})} \tag{8}$$

$$\mathbf{r}_j^{(\text{DEP})} = \text{BiLSTM}_{\text{DEP}}(\mathbf{z}_{1:n}, j) \tag{9}$$

Based on latent feature vectors $\mathbf{r}_j^{(\text{DEP})}$, either a transition-based or graph-based neural architecture can be applied for dependency parsing (Kiperwasser and Goldberg, 2016).

Nguyen et al. (2016) show that in both neural network-based and traditional feature-based categories, graph-based parsers perform better than transition-based parsers for Vietnamese. Thus, our parsing component is constructed similarly to the BIST graph-based dependency parser from Kiperwasser and Goldberg (2016). A difference is that we use FFNNs to split $\mathbf{r}_j^{(\text{DEP})}$ into *head* and *dependent* representations:

$$\mathbf{h}_j^{(\text{A-H})} = \text{FFNN}_{\text{Arc-Head}}\big(\mathbf{r}_j^{(\text{DEP})}\big) \tag{10}$$

$$\mathbf{h}_j^{(\text{A-D})} = \text{FFNN}_{\text{Arc-Dep}}\big(\mathbf{r}_j^{(\text{DEP})}\big) \tag{11}$$

$$\mathbf{h}_j^{(\text{L-H})} = \text{FFNN}_{\text{Label-Head}}\big(\mathbf{r}_j^{(\text{DEP})}\big) \tag{12}$$

$$\mathbf{h}_j^{(\text{L-D})} = \text{FFNN}_{\text{Label-Dep}}\big(\mathbf{r}_j^{(\text{DEP})}\big) \tag{13}$$

To score a potential dependency arc, we use a FFNN (FFNN_{ARC}) with a one-node output layer:

$$\text{score}(i, j) = \text{FFNN}_{\text{ARC}}\big(\mathbf{h}_i^{(\text{A-H})} \circ \mathbf{h}_j^{(\text{A-D})}\big) \tag{14}$$

Given scores of word pairs, we predict the highest scoring projective parse tree by using the Eisner (1996) decoding algorithm. This unlabeled parsing model is trained with a margin-based hinge loss $\mathcal{L}_{\text{ARC}}$ (Kiperwasser and Goldberg, 2016).

To label predicted arcs, we use another FFNN ($\text{FFNN}_{\text{LABEL}}$) with softmax output:

$$\boldsymbol{v}_{(i,j)} = \text{FFNN}_{\text{LABEL}}\big(\mathbf{h}_i^{(\text{L-H})} \circ \mathbf{h}_j^{(\text{L-D})}\big) \tag{15}$$

Based on vectors $\boldsymbol{v}_{(i,j)}$, a cross entropy loss $\mathcal{L}_{\text{LABEL}}$ for dependency label prediction is computed when training, using the gold labeled tree.

Joint multi-task learning: We train our model by summing $\mathcal{L}_{\text{WS}}$, $\mathcal{L}_{\text{POS}}$, $\mathcal{L}_{\text{ARC}}$ and $\mathcal{L}_{\text{LABEL}}$ losses prior to computing gradients. Model parameters are learned to minimize the sum of the losses.

Discussion: Our model is inspired by stack propagation based methods (Zhang and Weiss, 2016; Hashimoto et al., 2017) which are joint models for POS tagging and dependency parsing. For dependency parsing, the Stack-propagation model (Zhang and Weiss, 2016) uses a transition-based approach, and the joint multi-task model JMT (Hashimoto et al., 2017) uses a head selection based approach which produces a probability distribution over possible heads for each word (Zhang et al., 2017), while our model uses a graph-based approach.

Our model can be viewed as an extension of the joint POS tagging and dependency parsing model jPTDP-v2 (Nguyen and Verspoor, 2018),[2] where we incorporate a BiLSTM-CRF for word boundary prediction. Other improvements to jPTDP-v2 include: (i) instead of using 'local' single word-based character-level embeddings, we use 'global' sentence-level context for learning word embeddings (see equations 2 and 5), (ii) we use a CRF layer for POS tagging instead of a softmax layer, and (iii) following Dozat and Manning (2017), we employ *head* and *dependent* projection representations (in Equations 10–13) as feature vectors for dependency parsing rather than the top recurrent states (in Equation 9).

3 Experimental setup

Datasets: We follow the setup used in the Vietnamese NLP toolkit VnCoreNLP (Vu et al., 2018).

For word segmentation and POS tagging, we use standard datasets from the Vietnamese Language and Speech Processing (VLSP) 2013 shared tasks.[3] To train the word segmentation layer, we use 75K manually word-segmented sentences in which 70K sentences are used for training and 5K sentences are used for development. For POS tagging, we use 27,870 manually word-segmented and POS-annotated sentences in which 27K and 870 sentences are used for training and development, respectively. For both tasks, the test set consists of 2120 manually word-segmented and POS-annotated sentences.

To train the dependency parsing layer, we use the benchmark Vietnamese dependency treebank VnDT (v1.1) of 10,197 sentences (Nguyen et al., 2014), and follow a standard split to use 1,020 sentences for test, 200 sentences for development and the remaining 8,977 sentences for training.

Implementation: We implement our model (namely, **jointWPD**) using DyNet (Neubig et al.,

---

[2]On the benchmark English PTB-WSJ corpus, jPTDP-v2 does better than Stack-propagation, while obtaining similar performance to JMT.

[3]http://vlsp.org.vn/vlsp2013

	Model	WSeg	PTag	LAS	UAS
Unsegmented	Our jointWPD	97.81	94.05	71.50	77.23
	VnCoreNLP	97.90	94.06	68.84**	74.52**
	jPTDP-v2	97.90	93.82*	70.78**	76.80*
	Biaffine	97.90	94.06	72.59**	78.54**

Table 1: F_1 scores (in %) for word segmentation (WSeg), POS tagging (PTag) and dependency parsing (LAS and UAS) on *test* sets of unsegmented sentences. Scores are computed on all tokens (including punctuation), employing the CoNLL 2017 shared task evaluation script (Zeman et al., 2017). In all tables, $*$ and $**$ denote the statistically significant differences against jointWPD at p $\leq$ 0.05 and p $\leq$ 0.01, respectively. We compute sentence-level scores for each model and task, then use paired t-test to measure the significance level.

Model	WSeg	PTag	LAS	UAS
WS $\mapsto$ Pos $\mapsto$ Dep	98.48*	95.09*	70.68*	76.70*
Our jointWPD	98.66	95.35	71.13	77.01
(a) w/o Initial$_{\text{BIO}}$	98.25**	95.01*	70.34**	76.36**
(b) w/o CRF$_{\text{WSeg}}$	98.32**	95.06*	70.48**	76.47**
(c) w/o CRF$_{\text{PTag}}$	98.65	95.14*	71.00	76.94
(d) w/o PTag	98.63	95.10*	69.78**	76.03**

Table 2: F_1 scores on *development* sets of unsegmented sentences. (a): Without using initial word-boundary tag embedding, i.e., Equation 1 becomes $\mathbf{v}_i = \mathbf{e}_{s_i}^{(\mathrm{s})}$; (b): Using a softmax layer for word-boundary tag prediction instead of a CRF layer; (c): Using a softmax layer for POS tag prediction instead of a CRF layer; (d): Without using the POS tag embeddings for the parsing component, i.e. Equation 8 becomes $\mathbf{z}_j = \mathbf{x}_j$.

2017). We learn model parameters using Adam (Kingma and Ba, 2014), and run for 50 epochs. We compute the average of F_1 scores computed for word segmentation, POS tagging and (LAS) dependency parsing after each training epoch. We choose the model with the highest average score over the development sets to apply to the test sets. See Appendix for implementation details.

4 Main results

End-to-end results: Our scores on the test sets are presented in Table 1. We compare our scores with the VnCoreNLP toolkit (Vu et al., 2018) which produces the previous highest reported results on the same test sets for the three tasks. Note that published scores of VnCoreNLP for POS tagging and dependency parsing were reported using gold word segmentation, and its published scores for dependency parsing were reported using the previous VnDT v1.0. As the current released VnCoreNLP version is retrained using the VnDT v1.1 and we also use the same experimental setup, we thus rerun VnCoreNLP on the unsegmented test sentences and compute its scores.[4] Our jointWPD obtains a slightly lower word segmentation score and a similar POS tagging score against VnCoreNLP. However, jointWPD achieves 2.7% absolute higher LAS and UAS than VnCoreNLP.

We also show in Table 1 scores of the joint POS tagging and dependency parsing model jPTDP-v2 (Nguyen and Verspoor, 2018) and the state-of-the-art Biaffine dependency parser (Dozat and Manning, 2017). For Biaffine which requires automatically predicted POS tags, following Vu et al.

(2018), we produce the predicted POS tags on the whole VnDT treebank by using VnCoreNLP. We train both jPTDP-v2 and Biaffine with gold word segmentation.[5] For test, these models are fed with predicted word-segmented test sentences produced by VnCoreNLP. Our jointWPD performs significantly better than jPTDP-v2 on both POS tagging and dependency parsing tasks. However, jointWPD obtains 1.1+% lower LAS and UAS than Biaffine which uses a "*biaffine*" attention mechanism for predicting dependency arcs and labels. We will extend our parsing component with the biaffine attention mechanism to investigate the benefit for our joint model in future work.

Ablation analysis: Table 2 shows performance of a Pipeline strategy WS $\mapsto$ Pos $\mapsto$ Dep where we treat our word segmentation, POS tagging and dependency parsing components as independent networks, and train them separately. We find that jointWPD does significantly better than the Pipeline strategy on all three tasks.

Table 2 also presents ablation tests over 4 factors. When not using either initial word-boundary tag embeddings or the CRF layer for word-boundary tag prediction, all scores degrade by about 0.3+% absolutely. The 2 remaining factors, including (c) using a softmax classifier for

---

[4] See accuracy results w.r.t. the gold word segmentation in Table 3 in the Appendix.

[5] We reimplement jPTDP-v2 such that its POS tagging layer makes use of the VLSP 2013 POS tagging training set of 27K sentences, and then perform hyper-parameter tuning. The original jPTDP-v2 implementation only uses gold POS tags available in 8,977 training dependency trees, thus giving lower parsing performance than ours. For Biaffine, we use its updated version (Dozat et al., 2017) which won the CoNLL 2017 shared task on multilingual Universal Dependencies (UD) parsing from raw text (Zeman et al., 2017). Biaffine was also employed in all the top systems at the follow-up CoNLL 2018 shared task (Zeman et al., 2018).

POS tag prediction rather than a CRF layer and (d) removing POS tag embeddings, do not effect the word segmentation score. Both factors notably decrease the POS tagging score. Factor (c) slightly decreases LAS and UAS parsing scores. Factor (d) degrades the parsing scores by about 1.0+%, clearly showing the usefulness of POS tag information for the dependency parsing task.

5 Related work

Nguyen et al. (2018b) propose a transformation rule-based learning model RDRsegmenter for Vietnamese word segmentation, which obtains the highest performance to date. Nguyen et al. (2017) briefly review word segmentation and POS tagging approaches for Vietnamese. In addition, Nguyen et al. (2017) also present an empirical comparison between state-of-the-art feature- and neural network-based models for Vietnamese POS tagging, and show that a conventional feature-based model performs better than neural network-based models. In particular, on the VLSP 2013 POS tagging dataset, MarMoT (Mueller et al., 2013) obtains better accuracy than BiLSTM-CRF-based models with LSTM- and CNN-based character level word embeddings (Lample et al., 2016; Ma and Hovy, 2016). Vu et al. (2018) incorporate RDRsegmenter and MarMoT as the word segmentation and POS tagging components of Vn-CoreNLP, respectively.

Thi et al. (2013) propose a conversion method to automatically convert the manually built Vietnamese constituency treebank (Nguyen et al., 2009) into a dependency treebank. However, Thi et al. (2013) do not clarify how dependency labels are inferred; also, they ignore syntactic information encoded in grammatical function tags, and unable to deal with coordination and empty category cases.[6] Nguyen et al. (2014) later present a new conversion method to tackle all those issues, producing the high quality dependency treebank VnDT which is then widely used in Vietnamese dependency parsing research (Nguyen and Nguyen, 2015, 2016; Nguyen et al., 2016, 2018a; Vu et al., 2018). Recently, Nguyen (2018)

---

[6]Thi et al. (2013) reformed their dependency treebank with the UD annotation scheme to create a Vietnamese UD treebank in 2017. Note that the CoNLL 2017 & 2018 multilingual parsing shared tasks also provided F_1 scores for word segmentation, POS tagging and dependency parsing on this Vietnamese UD treebank. However, this UD treebank is small (containing about 1,400 training sentences), thus it might not be ideal to draw a reliable conclusion.

manually builds another Vietnamese dependency treebank—BKTreebank—consisting of about 7K sentences based on the Stanford Dependencies annotation scheme (Marneffe and Manning, 2008).

6 Conclusions and future work

In this paper, we have presented the first multi-task learning model for joint word segmentation, POS tagging and dependency parsing in Vietnamese. Experiments on Vietnamese benchmark datasets show that our joint multi-task model obtains results competitive with the state-of-the-art.

Che et al. (2018) show that deep contextualized word representations (Peters et al., 2018; Devlin et al., 2019) help improve the parsing performance. We will evaluate effects of the contextualized representations to our joint model. A Vietnamese syllable is analogous to a character in other languages such as Chinese and Japanese. Thus we will also evaluate the application of our model to those languages in future work.

Acknowledgments

I would like to thank Karin Verspoor and Vu Cong Duy Hoang as well as the anonymous reviewers for their feedback.

References

Miguel Ballesteros, Chris Dyer, and Noah A. Smith. 2015. Improved transition-based parsing by modeling characters instead of words with LSTMs. In *Proceedings of EMNLP*, pages 349–359.

Bernd Bohnet, Ryan McDonald, Gonçalo Simões, Daniel Andor, Emily Pitler, and Joshua Maynez. 2018. Morphosyntactic Tagging with a Meta-BiLSTM Model over Context Sensitive Token Encodings. In *Proceedings of ACL*, pages 2642–2652.

Razvan Bunescu and Raymond Mooney. 2005. A Shortest Path Dependency Kernel for Relation Extraction. In *Proceedings of HLT-EMNLP*, pages 724–731.

Wanxiang Che, Yijia Liu, Yuxuan Wang, Bo Zheng, and Ting Liu. 2018. Towards better UD parsing: Deep contextualized word embeddings, ensemble, and treebank concatenation. In *Proceedings of the CoNLL 2018 Shared Task*, pages 55–64.

Jacob Devlin, Ming-Wei Chang, Kenton Lee, and Kristina Toutanova. 2019. BERT: Pre-training of Deep Bidirectional Transformers for Language Understanding. In *Proceedings of NAACL-HLT*.

Timothy Dozat and Christopher D. Manning. 2017. Deep Biaffine Attention for Neural Dependency Parsing. In *Proceedings of ICLR*.

Timothy Dozat, Peng Qi, and Christopher D. Manning. 2017. Stanford's Graph-based Neural Dependency Parser at the CoNLL 2017 Shared Task. In *Proceedings of the CoNLL 2017 Shared Task*, pages 20–30.

Jason M. Eisner. 1996. Three New Probabilistic Models for Dependency Parsing: An Exploration. In *Proceedings of COLING*, pages 340–345.

Michel Galley and Christopher D. Manning. 2009. Quadratic-Time Dependency Parsing for Machine Translation. In *Proceedings of ACL-IJCNLP*, pages 773–781.

Kazuma Hashimoto, Caiming Xiong, Yoshimasa Tsuruoka, and Richard Socher. 2017. A joint many-task model: Growing a neural network for multiple NLP tasks. In *Proceedings of EMNLP*, pages 1923–1933.

Jun Hatori, Takuya Matsuzaki, Yusuke Miyao, and Jun'ichi Tsujii. 2012. Incremental Joint Approach to Word Segmentation, POS Tagging, and Dependency Parsing in Chinese. In *Proceedings of ACL*, pages 1045–1053.

Zhiheng Huang, Wei Xu, and Kai Yu. 2015. Bidirectional LSTM-CRF Models for Sequence Tagging. *arXiv preprint*, arXiv:1508.01991.

Diederik P. Kingma and Jimmy Ba. 2014. Adam: A Method for Stochastic Optimization. *arXiv preprint*, arXiv:1412.6980.

Eliyahu Kiperwasser and Yoav Goldberg. 2016. Simple and Accurate Dependency Parsing Using Bidirectional LSTM Feature Representations. *Transactions of ACL*, 4:313–327.

Sandra Kübler, Ryan McDonald, and Joakim Nivre. 2009. *Dependency Parsing*. Synthesis Lectures on Human Language Technologies, Morgan & cLaypool publishers.

Shuhei Kurita, Daisuke Kawahara, and Sadao Kurohashi. 2017. Neural Joint Model for Transition-based Chinese Syntactic Analysis. In *Proceedings of ACL*, pages 1204–1214.

John D. Lafferty, Andrew McCallum, and Fernando C. N. Pereira. 2001. Conditional Random Fields: Probabilistic Models for Segmenting and Labeling Sequence Data. In *Proceedings of ICML*, pages 282–289.

Guillaume Lample, Miguel Ballesteros, Sandeep Subramanian, Kazuya Kawakami, and Chris Dyer. 2016. Neural Architectures for Named Entity Recognition. In *Proceedings of NAACL-HLT*, pages 260–270.

Haonan Li, Zhisong Zhang, Yuqi Ju, and Hai Zhao. 2018. Neural Character-level Dependency Parsing for Chinese. In *Proceedings of AAAI*, pages 5205–5212.

Xuezhe Ma and Eduard Hovy. 2016. End-to-end Sequence Labeling via Bi-directional LSTM-CNNs-CRF. In *Proceedings of ACL*, pages 1064–1074.

Marie-catherine De Marneffe and Christopher D. Manning. 2008. The Stanford typed dependencies representation. In *Proceedings of the Coling 2008 workshop on Cross-Framework and Cross-Domain Parser Evaluation*, pages 1–8.

Thomas Mueller, Helmut Schmid, and Hinrich Schütze. 2013. Efficient higher-order CRFs for morphological tagging. In *Proceedings of EMNLP*, pages 322–332.

Graham Neubig, Chris Dyer, Yoav Goldberg, et al. 2017. DyNet: The Dynamic Neural Network Toolkit. *arXiv preprint*, arXiv:1701.03980.

Binh Duc Nguyen, Kiet Van Nguyen, and Ngan Luu-Thuy Nguyen. 2018a. LSTM Easy-first Dependency Parsing with Pre-trained Word Embeddings and Character-level Word Embeddings in Vietnamese. In *Proceedings of KSE*, pages 187–192.

Dat Quoc Nguyen, Mark Dras, and Mark Johnson. 2016. An empirical study for Vietnamese dependency parsing. In *Proceedings of ALTA*, pages 143–149.

Dat Quoc Nguyen, Dai Quoc Nguyen, Son Bao Pham, Phuong-Thai Nguyen, and Minh Le Nguyen. 2014. From Treebank Conversion to Automatic Dependency Parsing for Vietnamese. In *Proceedings of NLDB*, pages 196–207.

Dat Quoc Nguyen, Dai Quoc Nguyen, Thanh Vu, Mark Dras, and Mark Johnson. 2018b. A Fast and Accurate Vietnamese Word Segmenter. In *Proceedings of LREC*, pages 2582–2587.

Dat Quoc Nguyen and Karin Verspoor. 2018. An Improved Neural Network Model for Joint POS Tagging and Dependency Parsing. In *Proceedings of the CoNLL 2018 Shared Task*, pages 81–91.

Dat Quoc Nguyen, Thanh Vu, Dai Quoc Nguyen, Mark Dras, and Mark Johnson. 2017. From Word Segmentation to POS Tagging for Vietnamese. In *Proceedings of ALTA*, pages 108–113.

Kiem-Hieu Nguyen. 2018. BKTreebank: Building a Vietnamese Dependency Treebank. In *Proceedings LREC*, pages 2164–2168.

Kiet Van Nguyen and Ngan Luu-Thuy Nguyen. 2015. Error Analysis for Vietnamese Dependency Parsing. In *Proceedings of KSE*, pages 79–84.

Kiet Van Nguyen and Ngan Luu-Thuy Nguyen. 2016. Vietnamese transition-based dependency parsing with supertag features. In *Proceedings of KSE*, pages 175–180.

Phuong Thai Nguyen, Xuan Luong Vu, Thi Minh Huyen Nguyen, Van Hiep Nguyen, and Hong Phuong Le. 2009. Building a Large Syntactically-Annotated Corpus of Vietnamese. In *Proceedings of LAW*, pages 182–185.

Matthew Peters, Mark Neumann, Mohit Iyyer, Matt Gardner, Christopher Clark, Kenton Lee, and Luke Zettlemoyer. 2018. Deep contextualized word representations. In *Proceedings of NAACL-HLT*, pages 2227–2237.

Yuen Poowarawan. 1986. Dictionary-based Thai Syllable Separation. In *Proceedings of the Ninth Electronics Engineering Conference*, pages 409–418.

Xian Qian and Yang Liu. 2012. Joint Chinese Word Segmentation, POS Tagging and Parsing. In *Proceedings of EMNLP-CoNLL*, pages 501–511.

Nitish Srivastava, Geoffrey Hinton, Alex Krizhevsky, Ilya Sutskever, and Ruslan Salakhutdinov. 2014. Dropout: A Simple Way to Prevent Neural Networks from Overfitting. *Journal of Machine Learning Research*, 15:1929–1958.

Dinh Quang Thang, Le Hong Phuong, Nguyen Thi Minh Huyen, Nguyen Cam Tu, Mathias Rossignol, and Vu Xuan Luong. 2008. Word segmentation of Vietnamese texts: a comparison of approaches. In *Proceedings of LREC*, pages 1933–1936.

Luong Nguyen Thi, Linh Ha My, Hung Nguyen Viet, Huyen Nguyen Thi Minh, and Phuong Le Hong. 2013. Building a treebank for Vietnamese dependency parsing. In *Proceedings of RIVF*, pages 147–151.

Thanh Vu, Dat Quoc Nguyen, Dai Quoc Nguyen, Mark Dras, and Mark Johnson. 2018. VnCoreNLP: A Vietnamese Natural Language Processing Toolkit. In *Proceedings of NAACL: Demonstrations*, pages 56–60.

Daniel Zeman et al. 2017. CoNLL 2017 Shared Task: Multilingual Parsing from Raw Text to Universal Dependencies. In *Proceedings of the CoNLL 2017 Shared Task*, pages 1–19.

Daniel Zeman et al. 2018. CoNLL 2018 shared task: Multilingual parsing from raw text to universal dependencies. In *Proceedings of the CoNLL 2018 Shared Task*, pages 1–21.

Meishan Zhang, Yue Zhang, Wanxiang Che, and Ting Liu. 2014. Character-Level Chinese Dependency Parsing. In *Proceedings of ACL*, pages 1326–1336.

Xingxing Zhang, Jianpeng Cheng, and Mirella Lapata. 2017. Dependency Parsing as Head Selection. In *Proceedings of EACL*, pages 665–676.

Yuan Zhang, Chengtao Li, Regina Barzilay, and Kareem Darwish. 2015. Randomized Greedy Inference for Joint Segmentation, POS Tagging and Dependency Parsing. In *Proceedings of NAACL-HLT*, pages 42–52.

Yuan Zhang and David Weiss. 2016. Stack-propagation: Improved representation learning for syntax. In *Proceedings of ACL*, pages 1557–1566.

Appendix

Implementation details: When training, each task component is fed with the corresponding task-associated sentences. The dependency parsing training set is smallest in size (consisting of 8,977 sentences), thus for each training epoch, we sample the same number of sentences from the word segmentation and POS tagging training sets. We train our model with a fixed random seed and without mini-batches. Dropout (Srivastava et al., 2014) is applied with a 67% keep probability to the inputs of BiLSTMs and FFNNs. Following Kiperwasser and Goldberg (2016), we also use *word dropout* to learn embeddings for unknown syllables/words: we replace each syllable/word token s/w appearing $\#(s/w)$ times with a "unk" symbol with probability $\mathsf{p}_{unk}(s/w) = \frac{0.25}{0.25+\#(s/w)}$.

We initialize syllable and word embeddings with 100-dimensional pre-trained Word2Vec vectors as used in Nguyen et al. (2017), while the initial word-boundary and POS tag embeddings are randomly initialized. All these embeddings are then updated when training. The sizes of the output layers of FFNN_{WS}, FFNN_{POS} and $\text{FFNN}_{\text{LABEL}}$ are the number of BIO word-boundary tags (i.e. 3), the number of POS tags and the number of dependency relation types, respectively. We perform a minimal grid search of hyper-parameters, resulting in the size of the initial word-boundary tag embeddings at 25, the POS tag embedding size of 100, the size of the output layers of remaining FFNNs at 100, the number of BiLSTM layers at 2 and the size of LSTM hidden states in each layer at 128.

Additional results: Table 3 presents POS tagging and parsing accuracies w.r.t. gold word segmentation. In this case, for our jointWPD, we feed the POS tagging and parsing components with gold word-segmented sentences when decoding.

	Model	WSeg	PTag	LAS	UAS
Gold segment.	Our jointWPD	100.0	95.97	73.90	80.12
	VnCoreNLP	100.0	95.88	71.38**	77.35**
	jPTDP-v2	100.0	95.70*	73.12**	79.63*
	Biaffine	100.0	95.88	74.99**	81.19**

Table 3: POS tagging, LAS and UAS accuracy scores on the test sets w.r.t. gold word-segmented sentences. These scores are computed on all tokens (including punctuation). Recall that the LAS and UAS accuracies are computed on the VnDT v1.1 test set w.r.t. the automatically predicted POS tags.

Modelling Tibetan Verbal Morphology

Qianji Di   Ekaterina Vylomova   Timothy Baldwin

The University of Melbourne, Melbourne, Australia
Parkville, Victoria 3010, Australia
qdi@student.unimelb.edu.au {ekaterina.vylomova,tbaldwin}@unimelb.edu.au

Abstract

The Tibetan language, despite being spoken by 8 million people, is a low-resource language in NLP terms, and research to develop NLP tools and resources for the language has only just begun. In this paper, we focus on Tibetan verbal morphology — which is known to be quite irregular — and introduce a novel dataset for Tibetan verbal paradigms, comprising 1,433 lemmas with corresponding inflected forms. This enables the largest-scale NLP investigation to date on Tibetan morphological reinflection, wherein we compare the performance of several state-of-the-art models for morphological reinflection, and conduct an extensive error analysis. We show that 84% of errors are due to the irregularity of the Tibetan language.

1 Introduction

Tibetan is the language used by Tibetan people, in Tibetan areas in China — Tibet Autonomous Region, Qinghai Province, Sichuan Province, Gansu Province, and Yunnan Province — as well as parts of Nepal, Bhutan, India, and Pakistan. Among the languages of the Sino-Tibetan language family and Chinese national writing systems, the Tibetan language has one of the longest histories and most extensive bodies of literature. Although Tibetan is roughly divided into three dialects (Weizang, Khampa, and Amdo), the written language is uniform across all regions (Jitaiga, 2018).

The earliest work on Tibetan information processing began in the 1980s, focusing on fonts, character encoding support, and text input methods. This early work resulted in the ability to develop and share digital text resources in Tibetan, which benefited Tibetan scholars and the Tibetan diaspora (Zhijie, 2009). Tibetan information processing technology is rapidly developing, but some key problems remain, including the analysis of Tibetan verbs. Recent advances in Tibetan NLP have included the ability to automatically identify verbs, analyze the rules governing word form changing processes, and reveal various linguistic phenomena of Tibetan verbs (Zhijie and Rangzhuoma, 2010; Zhijie, 2005).

In this paper, we specifically focus on the Tibetan verbal inflection system, which is known for its irregularity (Suonanjiancuo, 2013). Specifically, we make use of the morphological reinflection task recently introduced under the umbrella of SIGMORPHON (Cotterell et al., 2018). We train several state-of-the-art machine learning models for reinflection and provide an extensive error analysis. We find that the original experimental data contained some errors, and the models do not cater to idiosyncrasies of the Tibetan language. After correcting errors in the data, experimental results improve. We also develop a new dataset for Tibetan verbs comprising 1,433 verbal lemmas with their present, past, future, and imperative forms.[1]

2 Tibetan Language

The Tibetan language belongs to the Tibetan branch of the Tibeto-Burman language group of the Sino-Tibetan language family. The Tibetan script is an abugida or alphasyllabary, whereby consonant–vowel sequences are written as a single unit. There are two schools of thought regarding the origin of Tibetan literature: some scholars be-

---

[1]The dataset is available at https://github.com/victoriadqj/Tibetan-Verb-Lexicon.

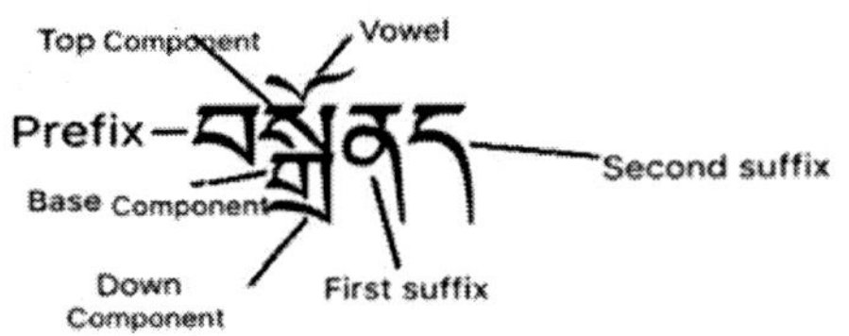

Figure 1: Lexicographic breakdown of a Tibetan word.

lieve that in the 7th century CE, the king Srongtsen Gampo in the Tubo era sent the Tibetan linguist Thombus Sangbu to North India to study Sanskrit, and that he created the Tibetan script based on Sanskrit (Wang, 1980). However, believers of the "Bon-ismo" religion hold that the Tibetan language evolved from Xiangxiong (Li et al., 2009).

Tibetan grammar is relatively rich, and verbs are inflected for tense and mood as fol-lows: present, past, future, and imperative. Taking གཅད *dep* "cut" as an example, the fu-ture form is གཅད *dep* "cut", past form is བཅད *dep* "cut", present form is གཅོད *di* "cut", and the imperative form is ཆོད *di* "cut"

In the Tibetan writing system, individual units (in the form of consonant–vowel se-quences) are often referred to as "compon-ents". One or more components constitute one "character", which is monosyllabic. One or more characters form a "word". Each syl-lable in Tibetan has a base component, which is a consonant and determines the base pro-nunciation of the syllable. Vowel symbols can be added above or below the base com-ponent to indicate different vowel sounds, in the form of top components above the base component, and one bottom component be-low it. Sometimes there is a prefix, indicating that the syllable is consonant-initial. There can also be one or two suffixes after the base component, indicating that the syllable has one or two consonants in addition to the base consonant. Figure 1 provides an example of the composition of a Tibetan word.

3   Related Work

Verbs are the core and fundamental ele-ments of Tibetan grammar.[2] In the "Tibetan Grammar Tutorial" (Jumian, 1982), the au-

thors elaborate on written verbs in Tibetan, and propose about 1,300 written syllables. Around 70% of verbs in their data undergo tense inflection, and the other 30% are in-variant under inflection; for only 20% of verbs is the imperative form different from the base lemma (Qu, 1985). Qu and Jing (2011) in "Sound Theory" defined categor-ies of Tibetan letters, and elaborated on the composition of Tibetan verbs, principles of transitiveness, as well as tenses. Later, Ji-taijia (2013) systematically studied functions of verbs in sentences and the relationship between verbs and other components in the sentence. Hill (2010) presented an overview of Tibetan verbal morphology. The author proposed to categorize Tibetan verbs into 11 paradigms, although there were still many ir-regular among frequently used ones. Still, scholars over the years have formed very different opinions on the morphosyntax of Tibetan.

Although we only consider Tibetan here, this work continues and further extends the work of Gorman et al. (2019). There, the authors conducted a detailed analysis of er-rors typically made by state-of-the-art mor-phological reinflection systems, in addition to introducing a novel error taxonomy that we utilize in this research.

4   Materials and Methods

4.1   The Task and Data

Following Gorman et al. (2019), we exper-iment with the morphological reinflection task (sub-task 1). The training data consists of triples of lemma, morphosyntactic fea-tures, and inflected form. In the test phase, the inflected form for an unseen lemma–morphological feature pair must be predicted.

We used the original datasets provided by Cotterell et al. (2018), which include two training sets for Tibetan, namely low-resource (100 samples) and medium-resource (158 samples).[3] Both test and development data comprise 50 samples. As part of this research, we develop a high-resource set of 1,433 instances.[4]

---

[2]This can be clearly concluded from the ancient Tibetan masterworks "Thirty Laud" and "Sound The-ory" (Qu and Jing, 2011)

[3]All encoded in UTF-8, based on the standard Tibetan Unicode mapping which was released in 1991.

[4]The format follows the UniMorph annotation scheme (Sylak-Glassman et al., 2015).

Model	Low	Med	High
Lemma Copy	0.44	0.44	0.44
SMP Baseline	**0.54**	0.48	**0.50**
A&G 2017	0.34	0.46	0.48
M&C 2018	0.42	**0.52**	0.46

Table 1: Results over the original datasets (best in bold).

Model	Nonce	Allomorphy
Lemma Copy	12	17
SMP Baseline	8	18
A&G 2017	10	16
M&C 2018	16	15

Table 2: Absolute number of errors on the test set made by each system trained in medium-resource setting.

4.2 Systems

For our experiments, we consider four models: (1) a naive baseline, whereby we simply return the lemma as the inflected form ("Lemma Copy"); (2) the baseline model used in SIGMORPHON 2017/2018 shared tasks (Cotterell et al. (2017, 2018): "SMP Baseline"); (3) Aharoni and Goldberg (2017)'s hard attention neural model ("A&G 2017"); and (4) Makarov and Clematide (2018)'s neural transduction models ("M&C 2018"). The latter two models achieved the highest scores in low- and medium-resource settings in the SIGMORPHON 2017/2018 shared tasks. Both are essentially neural seq-to-seq models (developed using Dynet framework (Neubig et al., 2017)) that rely on the assumption of nearly-monotonic alignment between a lemma and its inflected form, and learn a sequence of edit operations to perform string transduction.[5] The SMP Baseline model is non-neural, and first aligns strings using Levenshtein distance, and then extracts prefix- and suffix-based transformations.

5 Results

The results obtained by the four models are shown in Table 1. After manually reviewing errors across the four systems, we found not only system errors, but also errors in the data. In error analysis we employed the error taxonomy proposed by Gorman et al. (2019) and identified the following types: (1) target errors in the dataset; and (2) prediction errors. We further break down prediction errors into: (2.1) nonce-word errors (where a model generates a word which clearly violates lexicographic or morphophonetic constraints in the language); and (2.2) allomorphy errors

(where the wrong inflectional pattern is applied, i.e. a plausible inflection is generated, but it does not correspond to the indicated class).

5.1 Target Errors

Target errors are mainly due to errors in the Wiktionary source data[6] and incorrect extraction of paradigm tables, e.g. the lemma not existing in the lexicon, the inflected form not matching the indicated lemma, the positions of the inflected form and lemma being reversed, or even unrelated words appearing within a paradigm. Consider an example taken from the training data for the medium set. The lemma is ཞིག zhegh "arrange", the imperative form of which is said to be ཞིག zhegh "arrange". In practice, however, there's no such lemma or inflected form in Tibetan. It is most likely meant to be the lemma བཞིགས zhegh "arrange" and imperative form ཞིགས zhi "arrange". In this case, both the lemma and the inflected form are wrong. This type of error is quite common and amplifies the error rates.

5.2 Prediction errors

Table 2 presents the distribution of the number of prediction errors for each system trained in medium-resource setting. Below we present a more detailed analysis of each error category.

5.2.1 Nonce-word errors

This type of errors corresponds to illegal words, i.e. situations when the string generated by a system does not exist in Tibetan. We identify two sub-types of nonce-word errors in the Tibetan language.

The first one occurs because the Tibetan script is 2-dimensional (see Section 2),

---

[5]The hyperparameters are set to the values reported in the corresponding papers.

[6]Most language data in the UniMorph dataset was automatically extracted from Wiktionary.

whereby affixes may appear in a total of six positions relative to the base word. As can be seen in the following output:

(1) འཕོག *wugh* "cross water" + FUT → ཕོག (nonce-word)

The correct answer should be འཕོགས *wi* "will be crossing water", whereas the system predicted the suffix of the word but ignored the prefix and the second suffix. Since 2-dimensional scripts such as Tibetan are rare in the world's writing systems, researchers often do not consider this problem.

The second type relates to special cases in Tibetan. Some components are rarely used, and are unique variants of certain consonants as affixes. This often causes problems for learners of the Tibetan language. The following is an example of this case:

(2) དངས *ngi* "clear" + PRS → དྭངས *bi* (nonce-word)

Here, a special component representing the vowel ཱ *wha* should occur under the base component as an affix, meaning the correct answer is དྭངས *ngi* "clear".

5.2.2 Allomorphy errors

Allomorphy errors occur more often than nonce-word ones, and here we also classified them into two sub-types.

Firstly, the rules of Tibetan verb inflection are very complicated and irregular. For some of them, it is impossible for a system to learn the relevant rules through generalization over the training set. For instance, the present tense of the verb ཤི *hi* "die" is not predictable from its lemma འཆི *qie* "die". In this experiment, as can be seen in the example below, where the correct output should be ཟ *su* "eat", the system attempts to inflect based on rules that it has learned which are inappropriate for this word:

(3) བཟའ *sa* "eat" + PRS→ ཚོས *tsi* (nonce-word)

The second error type relates to vowels where the systems fail to predict the correct position of diacritics. Diacritics are vowels and can only be added above or below the base components, but systems fail to learn this constraint, and over-generate diacritic

Model	Low	Med	High
Lemma Copy	0.70	0.70	0.70
SMP Baseline	0.65	0.61	0.61
A&G 2017	0.19$^{.05}$	0.52$^{.03}$	**0.85**$^{.02}$
M&C 2018	**0.73**$^{.03}$	**0.72**$^{.02}$	0.76$^{.02}$

Table 3: Accuracy for the systems trained using the corrected dataset (best in bold).

positions. This kind of error also occurs when the models add an affix to the wrong position, or the order of affixes is incorrect, i.e. the models have predicted the components correctly but are unable to predict the correct order, as occurs in the following case (where the correct output is འདྲ *dep* "exhaust"):

(4) འདྲ *dep* "exhaust" + IMP →འདྲ *wegh* (nonce-word)

5.3 Results obtained on a new dataset

Since we found many target errors in the UniMorph data, we used the new verbal lexicon to improve the linguistic fidelity of the setup.

We manually counted 103 target errors out of 158 samples in the medium training set, which is 65% of the dataset. After correcting all the target errors in all sets according to the new lexicon, we reran our experiments.

Since both A&G 2017 and M&C 2018 use random parameter initialization, we ran the models with five different random seeds, and report their mean accuracy along with standard deviation. As Table 3 shows, in all three settings and across all three trained systems, the best accuracy increases substantially. Table 4 also provides the distribution of the number of prediction errors made on the corrected data. While there is clearly substantial room for improvement in the results, we believe these results to be much more reflective of the true ability of contemporary morphological reinflection systems to model Tibetan.

6 Conclusion

We focused on Tibetan verbal morphology in the context of sub-task-1 of the SIGMORPHON 2018 shared task. We considered a range of baselines and two state-of-the-art models trained in different data size

Model	Nonce	Allomorphy
Lemma Copy	0	15
SMP Baseline	5	16
A&G 2017	3	8
M&C 2018	8	14

Table 4: Absolute number of errors on the test set made by each system trained in high-resource setting (corrected data).

conditions. After conducting a detailed error analysis, we discovered that a significant percentage of errors relate to noise of the data and irregularity of Tibetan. We re-annotated the data and also developed a new Tibetan verbal lexicon comprising 1,433 lemmata with corresponding inflected forms. After re-running the model on the clean data, we observed a substantial improvement in terms of accuracy.

A possible research direction for future work would be to tailor the models to the idiosyncrasies of the Tibetan language.

References

Roee Aharoni and Yoav Goldberg. 2017. Morphological inflection generation with hard monotonic attention. In Proceedings of the 55th Annual Meeting of the Association for Computational Linguistics (Volume 1: Long Papers), pages 2004–2015, Vancouver, Canada.

Ryan Cotterell, Christo Kirov, John Sylak-Glassman, Géraldine Walther, Ekaterina Vylomova, Arya D. McCarthy, Katharina Kann, Sebastian Mielke, Garrett Nicolai, Miikka Silfverberg, David Yarowsky, Jason Eisner, and Mans Hulden. 2018. The CoNLL–SIGMORPHON 2018 shared task: Universal morphological reinflection. In Proceedings of the CoNLL–SIGMORPHON 2018 Shared Task: Universal Morphological Reinflection, pages 1–27, Brussels, Belgium.

Ryan Cotterell, Christo Kirov, John Sylak-Glassman, Géraldine Walther, Ekaterina Vylomova, Patrick Xia, Manaal Faruqui, Sandra Kübler, David Yarowsky, Jason Eisner, and Mans Hulden. 2017. CoNLL-SIGMORPHON 2017 shared task: Universal morphological reinflection in 52 languages. In Proceedings of the CoNLL SIGMORPHON 2017 Shared Task: Universal Morphological Reinflection, pages 1–30, Vancouver, Canada.

Kyle Gorman, Arya D. McCarthy, Ryan Cotterell, Ekaterina Vylomova, Miikka Silfverberg, and Magdalena Markowska. 2019. Weird inflects but OK: Making sense of morphological generation errors. In Proceedings of the 23rd Conference on Computational Natural Language Learning (CoNLL), pages 140–151, Hong Kong.

Nathan W Hill. 2010. A lexicon of Tibetan verb stems as reported by the grammatical tradition. Bayerische Akademie der Wissenschaften.

Jitaiga. 2018. The progress of Tibetan natural language processing. 34(1):1–11. Forum of Tibetan Development.

Jitaijia. 2013. Research on Tibetan Syntax.

Gesang Jumian. 1982. The category of Tibetan verbs. Minority Language of China, (5):27–39.

Yonghong Li, Yixin Zhou, Jing Shi, and Hongzhi Yu. 2009. On the origin of Tibetan language. Journal of Language and Literature Studies, (3):31–34.

Peter Makarov and Simon Clematide. 2018. Neural transition-based string transduction for limited-resource setting in morphology. In Proceedings of the 27th International Conference on Computational Linguistics, pages 83–93, Santa Fe, USA.

Graham Neubig, Chris Dyer, Yoav Goldberg, Austin Matthews, Waleed Ammar, Antonios Anastasopoulos, Miguel Ballesteros, David Chiang, Daniel Clothiaux, Trevor Cohn, Kevin Duh, Manaal Faruqui, Cynthia Gan, Dan Garrette, Yangfeng Ji, Lingpeng Kong, Adhiguna Kuncoro, Gaurav Kumar, Chaitanya Malaviya, Paul Michel, Yusuke Oda, Matthew Richardson, Naomi Saphra, Swabha Swayamdipta, and Pengcheng Yin. 2017. Dynet: The dynamic neural network toolkit. arXiv preprint arXiv:1701.03980.

Aitang Qu. 1985. The structure and evolution of the inflectional forms of Tibetan verbs. Minority Language of China, (1):1–15.

Aitang Qu and Song Jing. 2011. The 'theory of sound' and the principle of Tibetan creation. Minority Language of China, (5):15–25.

Suonanjiancuo. 2013. Study on the adhesion and inflection of Tibetan verbs. Journal of University of Tibet, (4):70–75.

John Sylak-Glassman, Christo Kirov, David Yarowsky, and Roger Que. 2015. A language-independent feature schema for inflectional morphology. In Proceedings of the 53rd Annual Meeting of the Association for Computational Linguistics and the 7th International

Joint Conference on Natural Language Processing (Volume 2: Short Papers), pages 674–680, Beijing, China.

Yao Wang. 1980. A brief account of Tibetan ancient historical documents. Journal of Xizang Minzu University, (2):11–37.

Cai Zhijie. 2005. Research on the development of Tibetan–Chinese–English electronic dictionary. Journal of Qinghai Norma University, (2):48–50.

Cai Zhijie. 2009. The design and realization of Tibetan spelling. Journal of Qinghai Normal University, (1):69–71.

Cai Zhijie and Cai Rangzhuoma. 2010. Design of BanZhiDa Tibetan lexicon. Journal of Chinese Information Processing, 24(5):46–50.

A multi-constraint structured hinge loss for named-entity recognition

Hanieh Poostchi
Nine Entertainment Co.
Willoughby NSW 2068, Australia
HPoostchi@nine.com.au

Massimo Piccardi
FEIT, University of Technology Sydney
Broadway NSW 2007, Australia
Massimo.Piccardi@uts.edu.au

Abstract

The negative log-likelihood or cross entropy is the usual training objective of NLP models owing to its versatility and empirical performance. However, training objectives which directly target the performance measure used to evaluate the task have the potential to lead to higher empirical accuracy. For this reason, in this short paper we propose using a multi-constraint structured hinge loss as the training objective of a contemporary named-entity recognition (NER) model. Experimental results over the challenging OntoNotes 5.0 dataset have shown that the proposed objective has been able to achieve an improvement of 0.62 CoNLL score points at a complete parity of testing set-up.

1 Introduction

All NLP models utilise a loss function as minimisation objective for model training. Choosing the most appropriate loss function for a particular task can play an important role in the performance of the trained models at test time and in-field. However, almost invariably the utilised loss function is the negative log-likelihood (NLL), also known as cross entropy. This is due to a number of attractive properties of the NLL such as its smoothness and differentiability in large regions of the parameter space. In addition, training with minimum NLL often leads to models of high empirical accuracy. However, this function is not exempt from shortcomings. To name two, 1) the NLL only rewards the probability of the ground-truth class and does not distinguish between the other classes, and 2) it does not impose explicit margins (or ratios) between the probability assigned to the ground-truth class and those assigned to the other classes. For this reason, other differentiable loss functions are regarded as appealing alternatives or complements to the NLL. Amongst them

are the hinge loss (Cortes and Vapnik, 1995) and the REINFORCE loss (Williams, 1992; Ranzato et al., 2016) which both attempt to directly optimise the performance measure used to evaluate the model's accuracy (e.g., the Hamming loss, the CoNLL score, the BLEU score etc). Both these losses can be used for the usual classification at token level or for the joint classification of all the tokens in a sentence (i.e., structured prediction) (Tsochantaridis et al., 2005). Given that targeting the evaluation loss during training may lead to improved performance at test time, in this short paper we explore the use of a structured hinge loss for named-entity recognition (NER). Our main contribution is the introduction of additional constraints between specific labelings aimed at increasing the accuracy of the learned model. Experimental results over a challenging NER dataset (OntoNotes 5.0, which is still far from accuracy saturation) show that the proposed approach has been able to achieve higher accuracy than both the NLL and a conventional structured hinge loss.

2 Related Work

In this section we briefly review the main literature on NER architectures and on structural loss functions. For a broader review of deep learning for NER, the reader can refer to (Li et al., 2018).

A current and well-known approach for NER combines a bidirectional LSTM with a CRF output layer to benefit from both their properties in sequential tagging (Huang et al., 2015). In this approach, the LSTM is used first to process each sentence token-by-token and produce an intermediate representation. Then, the CRF uses the intermediate representation as input to provide the joint prediction of all the labels. Lample et al. (2016) have extended this model with a second, auxiliary LSTM encoding each token character-by-character to also capture the regularities at character level. More recently, Peters et al. (2017; 2018) have proposed tagLM and ELMo to take advantage of the contextualised embeddings provided by pre-trained neural language models. Several other variants have been proposed since, including the Flair embedddings of Akbik et al. (2018) which currently hold the state-of-the-art accuracy over OntoNotes 5.0 (NB: besides a system hat uses gazetteers as extra resources to increase accuracy (Liu et al., 2019)). However, a bidirectional LSTM-CRF with ELMo embeddings can still be regarded as a very strong baseline for NER and, for this reason, it is used in the rest of this paper.

For what concerns alternative training objectives to the negative log-likelihood, Zhang at al. (2016) have proposed training an LSTM additioned with a linear output layer by using an SVM objective. In their model, the parameters of both the LSTM and the output layer have been learned jointly using a combination of sequence-level and frame-level regularised hinge losses. Similarly, Shi et al. (2016) have proposed adding a structural SVM output layer (Tsochantaridis et al., 2005) to an RNN to improve its discriminative capability. In 2012, Gimpel and Smith (2012) have proposed a structured ramp loss that leverages various styles of margins between predicted labelings. Recently, Edunov et al. (2018) have carried out an extensive review of structured loss functions, including hinge losses, cost-weighted likelihoods and reinforcement learning objectives. In a 2015 computer vision paper, Zhang and Piccardi (2015) have proposed adding extra constraints to a structured hinge loss to increase its accuracy in a task of activity segmentation in video. Inspired by that approach, in this paper we explore its application to NER, proposing three original combinations of dedicated constraints and margins.

3 Methodology

In this section, we first briefly review the structured hinge loss (3.1) and the utilised scoring function (3.2), and then introduce the proposed approach (3.3).

3.1 Structured hinge loss

Given a token sequence, $x = \{x_1 \dots x_t \dots x_T\}$, we note with $y = \{y_1 \dots y_t \dots y_T\}$ a labeling, i.e. a sequence of corresponding labels, one per token. We also assume to have a scoring function, $F(x, y; w)$ or $F(x, y)$ for brevity, which is able to assign a compatibility score to any such (x, y) pair. This function is completely defined by its set of parameters, w, and it is a structured predictor if the score of a labeling is computed jointly rather than independently for each label. Given these assumptions, the goal of a *structured hinge loss* is simply to ensure that the ground-truth labeling, y^g, for a given x is assigned a score larger than that of any other labeling, $y \neq y^g$, by a chosen margin, K:

$$F(x, y^g) - F(x, y) \geq K \quad \forall y \neq y^g \quad (1)$$

It is often useful to impose a margin that is the larger the more the labeling differs from the ground truth, and this can be achieved by setting the margin to be the evaluation loss ("margin rescaling" (Tsochantaridis et al., 2005)):

$$F(x, y^g) - F(x, y) \geq \Delta(y^g, y) \quad \forall y \neq y^g \quad (2)$$

However, the number of distinct labelings is exponential in the length of the sequence and it may not be possible to find a set of parameters which is able to satisfy all the constraints. In that case, the constraints are relaxed by introducing a non-negative term, $\xi \geq 0$, in Eq. 2 to minimally satisfy all the constraints:

$$F(x, y^g) - F(x, y) \geq \Delta(y^g, y) - \xi \quad \forall y \neq y^g$$

It is easy to see that the value of ξ is set by the most violated of the constraints, with y^* its corresponding labeling:

$$\xi = \max_y [-F(x, y^g) + F(x, y) + \Delta(y^g, y)] \quad (3)$$

$$y^* = \operatorname{argmax}_y [F(x, y) + \Delta(y^g, y)] \quad (4)$$

where we have omitted the first term in Eq. 4 since it does not depend on y. Note that since the search domain includes y^g, and $\Delta(y^g, y^g) = 0$, the above guarantees that $\xi \geq 0$. Eq. 3 is known as the *structured* hinge loss because of the interdependencies between the individual labels inside the scoring function and, possibly, the evaluation loss. In turn, the solution of Eq. 4 is known as the "loss-augmented" inference and is the crux of structured hinge loss minimisation. Given a training set, $\{x^i, y^i\}, i = 1 \dots N$, the training objective is therefore:

$$w^* = \operatorname{argmin}_w \sum_{i=1}^{N} \xi^i(w) \quad (5)$$

While the minimisation in Eq. 5 can be easily entertained by automated differentiation, the inference of the most-violating labelings must be performed externally with a dedicated algorithm.

3.2 Scoring function

The scoring function, $F(x, y; w)$, has been implemented as a BiLSTM-CRF (Lample et al., 2016), a popular NER model using a bidirectional LSTM as its feature layer and a CRF as its output layer. Its scoring function can be expressed as:

$$F(x, y; w) = \sum_{t=2}^{T} w_{y_{t-1}, y_t} + \sum_{t=1}^{T} f(y_t; w) \quad (6)$$

where $w_{i,j}$ are the transition weights for transitioning from label $y_{t-1} = i$ to label $y_t = j$, and $f(y_t; w)$ denotes the score assigned to label y_t by the BiLSTM layer. At its turn, the BiLSTM layer is organised as a bidirectional LSTM with trainable word and character embeddings as its inputs. At initialisation, the word embeddings can be assigned with either random or pre-trained values. At inference time, $\text{argmax}_y F(x, y; w)$ is provided by the Viterbi algorithm. For further details, please refer to (Lample et al., 2016).

3.3 The proposed multi-constraint structured hinge loss

Rather than constraining the optimisation problem with an exponential number of constraints, the structured hinge loss minimisation only considers the constraint setting the value of the loss:

$$\xi = [-F(x, y^g) + F(x, y^*) + \Delta(y^g, y^*)] \quad (7)$$

While such an approach makes the constrained minimisation feasible, we speculate that the addition of other constraints – either between the ground-truth labeling and other labelings, or between the other labelings themselves – may eventuate in a more performing model. To this aim, we have created a new set of labelings by arbitrarily introducing false positives in the ground-truth labelings of the training set. As false positives, we have decided to change the "Outside" label immediately preceding the first ground-truth entity of the training sentences into a "B-ORG" label. This is an altogether arbitrary change that creates mildly incorrect labelings: as such, we expect the scoring function to assign them scores lower than the corresponding ground truths, yet higher than more incorrect labelings. We note these new labelings as $u_i, i = 1 \ldots N$, reserving the subscript position for the sample index henceforth. Given these extra labelings, we propose three versions of a multi-constraint training loss:

- **Hinge-yu**: in this loss, we impose an extra constraint between the altered ground-truth labeling, u_i, and the remaining labelings. However, function $\Delta(u_i, y)$ cannot be used as margin since it expects to have a true labeling as its first argument. Therefore, following (Zhang and Piccardi, 2015) we set the margin to be $(\Delta(y_i, y) - \Delta(y_i, u_i))$. The labeling returned by the loss-augmented inference with this margin is the same as in the standard case (y_i^*) since the the second term in the margin $(\Delta(y_i, u_i))$ does not depend on y.

- **Double Hinge**: in this loss, we instead impose an extra constraint between the ground-truth labeling, y_i, and the altered ground truth, u_i. As margin, we can naturally use $\Delta(y_i, u_i)$.

- **Discounted Margin**: in this loss, we again impose an extra constraint between the altered ground-truth labeling, u_i, and the remaining labelings. As margin, we use the regular loss function, $\Delta(u_i, y)$, but "discounted" by a small discount factor since u_i is not an actual ground truth.

As evaluation loss for the margin, we have simply used the Hamming loss, since it naturally decomposes over the individual tokens of its arguments and it allows us to easily touch up the standard Viterbi algorithm to provide the required loss-augmented inference. Extending the loss-augmented inference to other, more specialised evaluation measures such as the CoNLL and MUC scores (Nadeau and Sekine, 2007) could be the scope of future work.

4 Experiments and results

4.1 Experimental set-up

We have carried out experiments over a challenging NER dataset, OntoNotes v5.0, which was first introduced in CoNLL 2012 as a shared task (Pradhan et al., 2012, 2013). This English dataset contains multi-token entities from 18 different categories, including amongst others, person, facility,

Table 1: The compared training objectives.

NLL	$l_{NLL} = -\sum_{i=1}^{N} \log p(y_i \mid x_i)$
Hinge Loss	$l_{Hinge} = \sum_{i=1}^{N} [-F(x_i, y_i) + F(x_i, y_i^*) + \Delta(y_i, y_i^*)]_+$ $y_i^* = \mathrm{argmax}_y\, F(x_i, y) + \Delta(y_i, y)$
Hinge-yu	$l_{Hinge-yu} = \sum_{i=1}^{N} [-F(x_i, y_i) + F(x_i, y_i^*) + \Delta(y_i, y_i^*)]_+$ $+ \sum_{i=1}^{N} [-F(x_i, u_i) + F(x_i, y_i^*) + \Delta(y_i, y_i^*) - \Delta(y_i, u_i)]_+$ $y_i^* = \mathrm{argmax}_y\, F(x_i, y) + \Delta(y_i, y)$
Double Hinge	$l_{DoubleHinge} = \sum_{i=1}^{N} [-F(x_i, y_i) + F(x_i, y_i^*) + \Delta(y_i, y_i^*)]_+$ $+ \sum_{i=1}^{N} [-F(x_i, y_i) + F(x_i, u_i) + \Delta(y_i, u_i)]_+$ $y_i^* = \mathrm{argmax}_y\, F(x_i, y) + \Delta(y_i, y)$
Discounted Margin	$l_{DiscountedMargin} = \sum_{i=1}^{N} [-F(x_i, y_i) + F(x_i, y_i^*) + \Delta(y_i, y_i^*)]_+$ $+ \sum_{i=1}^{N} [-F(x_i, u_i) + F(x_i, y_i^*) + df \times \Delta(u_i, y_i^*)]_+$ $y_i^* = \mathrm{argmax}_y\, F(x_i, y) + \Delta(y_i, y)$

Table 2: Comparison of the CoNLL scores for the OntoNotes 5.0 dataset with the different training objectives.

Training objective	CoNLL score
NLL	88.54 ± 0.13
Hinge Loss	88.81 ± 0.06
Hinge-yu	88.88 ± 0.10
Double Hinge	88.85 ± 0.13
Discounted Margin ($df = 0.925$)	$\mathbf{89.16 \pm 0.03}$

organisation, location, product, event, law, date and time, and is split over a training, validations and test sets. For the experiments, we have converted it to the IOB2 tagging scheme.

The experiments have been carried out using the DeLFT[1] implementation of the BiLSTM-CRF. In the experiments, the word embeddings have been initialised with a concatenation of fastText-300d[2] and ELMo-1024d[3] (DeLFT's default). All hyperparameters have also been left to their default values. Each training session has been run until convergence of the evaluation loss over the validation set or a maximum of 20 epochs. In the experiments, we have compared the following training objectives: 1) the NLL/cross entropy; 2) a standard structured hinge loss using the Hamming loss as margin ("Hinge Loss"), with no additional constraints; and 3-5) the three versions of the proposed multi-constraint structured hinge loss presented in Section 3.3. The discount factor, df, for

the Discounted Margin approach has been chosen in range $[0.85, 0.95]$ in 0.025 steps over the validation set. All the training objectives are displayed in Table 1.

For evaluation, we have used the CoNLL score, an entity-oriented variant of the F_1 score which is the standard evaluation measure for NER (Nadeau and Sekine, 2007). For every experiment, we have run three independent runs from different random seeds and reported their average score. In addition, for the most noteworthy pairwise comparisons, we have run one-tailed Welch's t-tests to test statistical significance (Hintze, 2019). As shown in (Colas et al., 2019), the Welch's t-test enjoys a good balance between Type I and Type II errors under a variety of assumptions for the underlying score distributions (beyond Gaussian), especially for small sample sizes.

4.2 Results and analysis

Table 2 shows the CoNLL scores achieved by the compared training objectives over the OntoNotes 5.0 test set as average of 3 independent runs. The table shows that even the standard structured hinge loss has achieved a higher score than the NLL ($+0.27$ percentage points). Even if the improvement is mild, the standard deviations over the

---

[1] https://github.com/kermitt2/delft

[2] https://dl.fbaipublicfiles.com/fasttext/vectors-english/crawl-300d-2M.vec.zip

[3] https://s3-us-west-2.amazonaws.com/allennlp/models/elmo/2x4096_512_2048cnn_2xhighway_5.5B/elmo_2x4096_512_2048cnn_2xhighway_5.5B_options.json

three runs are small and the p-value from a one-tailed Welch's t-test is < 0.05, showing that the improvement is statistically significant. In turn, all the versions of the proposed multi-constraint hinge loss have achieved higher scores than both the NLL and the standard structured hinge loss, with the Discounted Margin achieving the highest score. The improvement of the Discounted Margin over the NLL has been $+0.62$ percentage points, with a one-tailed Welch's t-test p-value < 0.01. While this improvement is still somehow limited, we wish to remark that it has leveraged only changes to the loss function in the code, and at a complete parity of model.

5 Conclusion

In this short paper, we have proposed a multi-constraint structured hinge loss to be used as training objective for a named-entity recognition model. The proposed loss enforces additional constraints with respect to the standard structured hinge loss with the aim of improving the test accuracy of the trained model. Experimental results over a challenging NER dataset (OntoNotes 5.0) have showed that the proposed loss has been able to achieve an improvement of 0.62 CoNLL score percentage points over the common negative log-likelihood. In the future, we aim to explore further combinations of constraints and margins, and possibly extend the proposed approach to other tasks.

References

Alan Akbik, Duncan Blythe, and Roland Vollgraf. 2018. Contextual string embeddings for sequence labeling. In *Proceedings of the 27th International Conference on Computational Linguistics*, pages 1638–1649.

Cédric Colas, Olivier Sigaud, and Pierre-Yves Oudeyer. 2019. A hitchhiker's guide to statistical comparisons of reinforcement learning algorithms. In *Reproducibility in Machine Learning, ICLR 2019 Workshop*, pages 1–23.

Corinna Cortes and Vladimir Vapnik. 1995. Support-vector networks. *Machine Learning*, 20(3):273–297.

Sergey Edunov, Myle Ott, Michael Auli, David Grangier, and Marc'Aurelio Ranzato. 2018. Classical structured prediction losses for sequence to sequence learning. In *Proceedings of the 2018 Conference of the North American Chapter of the Association for Computational Linguistics: Human Language Technologies*, pages 355–364.

Kevin Gimpel and Noah A. Smith. 2012. Structured ramp loss minimization for machine translation. In *Proceedings of the 2012 Annual Conference of the North American Chapter of the Association for Computational Linguistics: Human Language Technologies*, pages 221–231.

Jerry Hintze. 2019. T-test – two-sample. In *NCSS User's Guide II, Chapter 206*, pages 1–18.

Zhiheng Huang, Wei Xu, and Kai Yu. 2015. Bidirectional LSTM-CRF models for sequence tagging. *CoRR*, abs/1508.01991.

Guillaume Lample, Miguel Ballesteros, Sandeep Subramanian, Kazuya Kawakami, Chris DyerRemi Lebret, and Ronan Collobert. 2016. Neural architectures for named entity recognition. In *Proceedings of the 2016 Conference of the North American Chapter of the Association for Computational Linguistics: Human Language Technologies*, pages 260–270.

Jing Li, Aixin Sun, Jianglei Han, and Chenliang Li. 2018. A survey on deep learning for named entity recognition. *CoRR*, abs/1812.09449.

Tianyu Liu, Jin-Ge Yao, and Chin-Yew Lin. 2019. Towards improving neural named entity recognition with gazetteers. In *Proceedings of the 57th Conference of the Association for Computational Linguistics*, pages 5301–5307.

David Nadeau and Satoshi Sekine. 2007. A survey of named entity recognition and classification. *Linguisticae Investigationes*, 30(1):3–26.

Matthew Peters, Waleed Ammar, Chandra Bhagavatula, and Russell Power. 2017. Semi-supervised sequence tagging with bidirectional language models. In *Proceedings of the 55th Annual Meeting of the Association for Computational Linguistics*, pages 1756–1765.

Matthew Peters, Mark Neumann, Mohit Iyyer, Matt Gardner, Christopher Clark, Kenton Lee, and Luke Zettlemoyer. 2018. Deep contextualized word representations. In *Proceedings of the 2018 Conference of the North American Chapter of the Association for Computational Linguistics: Human Language Technologies*, pages 2227–2237.

Sameer Pradhan, Alessandro Moschitti, Nianwen Xue, Hwee Tou Ng, Anders Björkelund, Olga Uryupina, Yuchen Zhang, and Zhi Zhong. 2013. Towards robust linguistic analysis using OntoNotes. In *Proceedings of the Seventeenth Conference on Computational Natural Language Learning*, pages 143–152, Sofia, Bulgaria. Association for Computational Linguistics.

Sameer Pradhan, Alessandro Moschitti, Nianwen Xue, Olga Uryupina, and Yuchen Zhang. 2012. CoNLL-2012 shared task: Modeling multilingual unrestricted coreference in OntoNotes. In *Proceedings of the Sixteenth Conference on Computational Natural Language Learning*, Jeju, Korea.

Marc'Aurelio Ranzato, Sumit Chopra, Michael Auli, and Wojciech Zaremba. 2016. Sequence level training with recurrent neural networks. In *4th International Conference on Learning Representations*, pages 1–16.

Yangyang Shi, Kaisheng Yao, Hu Chen, Dong Yu, Yi-Cheng Pan, and Mei-Yuh Hwang. 2016. Recurrent support vector machines for slot tagging in spoken language understanding. In *Proceedings of the 2016 Conference of the North American Chapter of the Association for Computational Linguistics: Human Language Technologies*, pages 393–399.

Ioannis Tsochantaridis, Thorsten Joachims, Thomas Hofmann, and Yasemin Altun. 2005. Large margin methods for structured and interdependent output variables. *Journal of Machine Learning Research*, 6:1453–1484.

Ronald J. Williams. 1992. Simple statistical gradient-following algorithms for connectionist reinforcement learning. *Machine Learning*, 8:229–256.

Guopeng Zhang and Massimo Piccardi. 2015. Structural SVM with partial ranking for activity segmentation and classification. *IEEE Signal Process. Lett.*, 22(12):2344–2348.

Shi-Xiong Zhang, Rui Zhao, Chaojun Liu, Jinyu Li, and Yifan Gong. 2016. Recurrent support vector machines for speech recognition. In *Proceedings of the 2016 IEEE International Conference on Acoustics, Speech and Signal Processing*, pages 5885–5889.

Feature-guided Neural Model Training for Supervised Document Representation Learning

Aili Shen   Bahar Salehi   Jianzhong Qi   Timothy Baldwin
School of Computing and Information Systems
The University of Melbourne
Victoria, Australia
`ailis@student.unimelb.edu.au    baharsalehi@gmail.com`
`jianzhong.qi@unimelb.edu.au    tb@ldwin.net`

Abstract

With the advent of neural models, there has been a rapid move away from feature engineering, or at best, simplistically combining hand-crafted features with learned representations as side information. We propose a method that uses hand-crafted features to guide learning by explicitly attending to feature indicators when learning the relationship between the input and target variables. In experiments over two different tasks — quality assessment of Wikipedia articles and popularity prediction of online petitions— we demonstrate that the proposed method yields neural models that consistently outperform those that simply use hand-crafted features as side information.

1   Introduction and Background

Text classification/regression is a fundamental problem in natural language processing. Traditional methods make use of hand-crafted features, such as the length of a document, to represent a document. A classifier/regressor is built on top of such features to learn a model (Wang and Manning, 2012; Warncke-Wang et al., 2013, 2015; Dang and Ignat, 2016). Recently, neural models such as LSTMs (Hochreiter and Schmidhuber, 1997) and convolutional neural networks (CNNs: Kim (2014); Kalchbrenner et al. (2014)) have become the de facto for text classification/regression tasks, with one oft-cited advantage being that they are able to learn implicit features as part of the representation learning.

Studies employing neural models either eschew hand-crafted features or simplistically use hand-crafted features as side information. For example, Dang and Ignat (2017) propose to use a bidirectional LSTM ("bi-LSTM") to classify Wikipedia articles by their quality classes, and Shen et al. (2017) concatenate structural features (e.g., article length) and readability scores with bi-LSTM-

learned document representations for the same task. Subramanian et al. (2018) hand-engineer a set of features (e.g., the ratio of indefinite and definite articles), and concatenate them with CNN-learned document representations to predict the popularity of online petitions. Wu et al. (2018) explore the utility of hand-crafted features in NER by concatenating these features with character representations learned via an CNN and word embeddings. These representations are then fed into a bi-LSTM to identify named entities (with the help of a CRF) and re-construct the hand-crafted features in the output simultaneously, which is achieved by combining an auto-encoder loss with the NER loss.

The motivation underlying this work is that when hand-crafted features are represented by numerical vectors and concatenated with neural network representations, there is no information on what kind of feature each value represents. To make better use of hand-crafted features, we propose a feature-guided neural training method that guides the network to map feature indicators onto (explicit or implicit) features in the document. We evaluate the effectiveness of the proposed method over two datasets for two different tasks: (1) quality assessment of Wikipedia articles, and (2) popularity prediction of online petitions. Taking state-of-the-art approaches for the respective tasks, we achieve consistent improvements when using our model.

The closest work to our approach is the label-guided model training of Wang et al. (2018). They embed words and labels in the same embedding space, and compute a label-based attention score between a word and all possible labels, which is used to weight word embeddings in obtaining document representations. Our work differs in two aspects: (1) Wang et al. (2018) capture direct associations between labels and words, while we use the proxy of (potentially much higher-level) hand-crafted features to guide network learning; and (2) our method does not rely on the target variable being closely related to the semantics of a document, leading to better generalisability.

2 Methodology

Figure 1 is an illustration of our proposed approach, in the context of a stacked bi-LSTM, where two bi-LSTMs are applied to obtain the sentence and document level representations, respectively. Note that our method is not limited to LSTMs, as we show in Section 3.

A hand-crafted feature can consist of multiple feature indicators. For example, having *level 3+ headings* is one of the features in quality assessment of Wikipedia articles. This hand-crafted feature consists of two feature indicators (tokens) {"===", "===="}. We embed the document and feature indicators into a shared space. Then, as indicated in Figure 1, for each feature indicator, we compute cosine similarity between the feature indicator and word embeddings, followed by average-pooling to obtain a sentence score:

$$\text{score} = \frac{1}{N} \sum_{j=1}^{N} \frac{\mathbf{F}\mathbf{V}_j}{\|\mathbf{F}\|_2 \|\mathbf{V}_j\|_2}. \tag{1}$$

Here, $\mathbf{F}$ and $\mathbf{V}_j$ are embeddings of the feature indicator and the jth word in a sentence, respectively; $\|\mathbf{F}\|_2$ and $\|\mathbf{V}_j\|_2$ are the ℓ_2 norms of $\mathbf{F}$ and $\mathbf{V}_j$, respectively; and N is the number of words in a sentence. All scores based on the feature indicator are concatenated with sentence representations $\mathbf{Z}_1$, which are learned through a bi-LSTM layer (f_1). Then, another bi-LSTM layer (f_2) is applied to the concatenated sentence representations to obtain document representation $\mathbf{Z}_2$, which is followed by a dense layer (f_3) to compute $\mathbf{y}$.

The score computed in Equation 1 is for a single-token feature indicator. If a hand-crafted feature consists of multiple feature indicators (tokens, e.g., {"===", "===="}), the score becomes:

$$\text{score} = \frac{1}{M} \sum_{i=1}^{M} \frac{1}{N} \sum_{j=1}^{N} \frac{\mathbf{F}_i \mathbf{V}_j}{\|\mathbf{F}_i\|_2 \|\mathbf{V}_j\|_2}. \tag{2}$$

Here, M is the number of feature indicators in a hand-crafted feature, and $\mathbf{F}_i$ is the word embedding of the ith feature indicator in the feature.

For example, the feature *level 3+ headings* is one of structural features described in Shen et al.

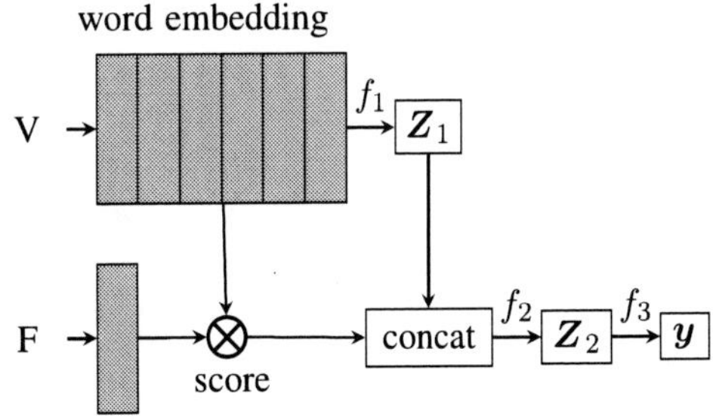

Figure 1: Illustration of our proposed method. Here, $\otimes$ denotes cosine similarity between the feature indicator and word embeddings; f_1 and f_2 denote bi-LSTM layers; f_3 denotes a dense layer; $\mathbf{Z}_1$ and $\mathbf{Z}_2$ denote sentence and document representations, respectively; $\mathbf{V}$ and $\mathbf{F}$ are the document input and feature indicators, respectively; and $\mathbf{y}$ is the target output.

(2017), which consists of two feature indicators {"===", "===="}. To obtain the similarity score for the feature *level 3+ headings*, we first compute the similarity score between each feature indicator "==="/"====" and word embeddings in the sentence, then apply average-pooling to obtain the similarity score for each feature indicator. We obtain the similarity score of *level 3+ headings* by averaging similarity scores among the feature indicators at the sentence level. Finally, the feature score is concatenated with the sentence representation, which is fed into a latter layer.

While we don't experiment with this in this paper, it is also possible to first average feature indicator embeddings and then compute the sentence score by Equation 1. This way, we can efficiently reduce the computation of similarity scores for hand-crafted features with a large number of feature indicators. In this paper, we use Equation 2, as the maximum number of feature indicators in a given hand-crated feature is less than $1,000$, and less than 10 in most cases.

3 Experiments

To test the effectiveness of our proposed method, we experiment with a Wikipedia document quality assessment task (Shen et al., 2019), and online petition signature prediction task (Subramanian et al., 2018), as detailed below. The reasons we chose these particular tasks are as follows. First, extensive domain-specific feature engineering had taken place in each case, that we could use as the basis of our feature indicators. Second, strong neural benchmarks have been established, based on extensive experimentation with both neural and non-neural models. Our experiments in this paper are based on the state-of-the-art.

We aim to explore the relative gains of our proposed method relative to the current state-of-the-art for the task, which in both cases is not based on contextualised embeddings. For BERT (Devlin et al., 2019) or other contextualised encoders, the same word in different contexts will end with different embeddings, leading to localized representations of feature indicators. As such, the proposed method is not directly applicable to models such as BERT, and novel research would be required to adapt the method to such models.

3.1 Wikipedia Document Quality Assessment

Dataset The Wikipedia dataset (Shen et al., 2019) consists of 29,794 English Wikipedia articles and their corresponding quality labels: Featured Article, Good Article, B-class Article, C-class Article, Start Article, and Stub Article, in descending order of document quality. The dataset is class-balanced and partitioned into training, development, and test splits (8:1:1). Documents are relatively long, and processed in a hierarchical manner, by constructing sentence representations, and composing these into a document representation.

Following Dang and Ignat (2017) and Shen et al. (2019), we formulate the quality assessment of Wikipedia articles as a multi-class classification problem, and all models are trained to minimise cross-entropy loss. We report average `accuracy` and standard deviation over 10 runs.

Hand-crafted features used to guide network learning here include: (1) references indicators; (2) links to other Wikipedia pages indicators; (3) citation templates indicators; (4) non-citation templates indicators; (5) categories linked in the article indicators; (6) image indicators; (7) infobox indicators; (8) level 2 headings indicators; and (9) level 3+ heading indicators. These features are from Dang and Ignat (2016) and Shen et al. (2017). Hand-crafted features in `Side-information` are based on counting the number of appearances of such feature indicators.

Model configuration We apply our proposed approach ("`Feature-guided`") over the four models detailed below. In each case, we contrast with two baselines: (1) `Vanilla`, makes no use of hand-crafted features; and (2) `Side-information` which uses the hand-crafted features as side information, by concatenating them with learned representations in the penultimate layer.

1. CNN_BiLSTM: apply convolution kernels with width 2, 3, and 4 (32 for each width size) to word embeddings within a sentence, and a tanh activation function to each; pass the output of the filters through a bi-LSTM.

2. AVERAGE_BiLSTM (Shen et al., 2017): average word embeddings to get the sentence representation, and run a bi-LSTM over the sequence of sentence representations.

3. STACKED_BiLSTM: feed the word embeddings in a sentence through a bi-LSTM, and the output through a max-pooling layer; finally, apply another bi-LSTM over the sentence representations.

4. STACKED_BiLSTM_ATT (Yang et al., 2016): use a hierarchical STACKED_BiLSTM, except that an attention mechanism with a context size of 100 is applied to the output of each bi-LSTM to weight words/sentences based on their importance in the sentence/document.

A max-pooling layer is applied to the output of the bi-LSTM at the sentence level for all models except STACKED_BiLSTM_ATT to get the document level representation, which is followed by two dense layers, one with a ReLU activation and one without any activation function. For all models, dropout layers are applied at both the sentence and document levels with a rate of 0.5 during training. For both CNN_BiLSTM and AVERAGE_BiLSTM, the bi-LSTM cell size is set to 256. For STACKED_BiLSTM and STACKED_BiLSTM_ATT, the cell size is set to 32 and 256 for the sentence and document level bi-LSTM, respectively.

We use 50-dimensional pre-trained word embeddings from GloVe (Pennington et al., 2014).[1] For OOV words, the word embeddings are randomly initialised based on sampling from a uniform distribution $U(-1, 1)$. All word embeddings

---

[1] We fine-tuned hyper-parameters over the development set for quality predictions of Wikipedia articles. 50-dimensional embeddings were chosen because `Vanilla` performs the best under this setting (meaning the baseline without features is as strong as possible).

Model	CNN_BiLSTM	Average_BiLSTM	Stacked_BiLSTM	Stacked_BiLSTM_ATT
Vanilla	57.12±0.58%	57.91±0.81%	57.60±0.65%	56.70±1.21%
Side-information	57.24±0.47%	59.04±0.33%	57.97±0.74%	57.44±0.62%
Feature-guided	**58.10±0.50%**[†]	**59.90±0.45%**[†]	**58.30±0.71%**	**58.30±0.65%**[†]

Table 1: accuracy over Wikipedia dataset. The best result is in **bold**, and marked with "†" if the improvement is statistically significant (based on a one-tailed Wilcoxon signed-rank test; $p < 0.05$).

are updated in the training process. We use a mini-batch size of 128 and a learning rate of 0.01. We train each model for 50 epochs. To prevent over-fitting, early stopping is adopted. All hyper-parameters are set empirically over the development data, and the models are optimised using Adam (Kingma and Ba, 2015).

Results The experimental results are presented in Table 1. We can see that our method outperforms both Vanilla and Side-information across all four network architectures, at a level of statistical significance for 3 out of the 4 models. It is worth noting that the performance of Stacked_BiLSTM_ATT is worse than that of Stacked_BiLSTM for both Vanilla and Side-information, due to attention in Stacked_BiLSTM_ATT not being as effective as max-pooling on this task. However, the performance of Stacked_BiLSTM_ATT is not worsened by incorporating the attention for our method, indicating that our feature-guided learning can guide the network to learn better.

3.2 Online Petition Signature Prediction

Dataset The online petitions dataset (Subramanian et al., 2018) consists of 10,950 UK petitions and their corresponding signature counts. Following Subramanian et al. (2018), we chronologically split the data into training, dev, and test (8:1:1).

We formulate signature count prediction as a regression problem, and all models are trained to minimise mean squared error. For evaluation, average mean absolute error ("MAE") and mean absolute percentage error ("MAPE") over 10 runs are reported. Here, MAPE is calculated as $\frac{100}{n} \sum_{1}^{n} \frac{|\hat{y}_i - y_i|}{y_i}$, where $\hat{y}_i$ and y_i are the predicted and ground-truth signature counts.

Hand-crafted features used to guide network learning here include: (1) indefinite vs. definite articles; (2) P1 singular and plural, P2, and P3 singular and plural pronouns; (3) subjective, positive, and negative words; and (4) biased words. These features are from Subramanian et al. (2018).

Model	MAE	MAPE
Vanilla	1.44	38.1
Side-information	1.45	39.0
Feature-guided	**1.42**[†]	**36.2**[†]

Table 2: Results over online petitions. The best result is indicated in **bold**, and marked with "†" if the improvement is statistically significant (based on a one-tailed Wilcoxon signed-rank test; $p < 0.05$).

Hand-crafted features in Side-information are based on counting the number of appearances of such feature words.

Model configuration We again compare our proposed Feature-guided approach with Side-information and Vanilla, in the form of a state-of-the-art CNN with convolution kernels of width 1, 2, and 3 (100 kernels for each width size) over word embeddings, with a ReLU applied to each. The outputs are passed through two dense layers, one with a tanh activation function and one with an ELU activation function, to obtain the final output.

A dropout layer is applied to the output of the convolution filters at a rate of 0.5 during training. We use a mini-batch size of 32, and a learning rate of $1e - 4$. All other hyper-parameters are the same as in the Wikipedia setting, except that the early stopping is based on MAE.

Results Table 2 summarises our results. We observe that our approach benefits Vanilla and Side-information once again, at a level of significance in terms of both MAE and MAPE. It is worth noting that Side-information performs worse than Vanilla, as it over-fits to features only present in the training data. In comparison, our method improves the model performance even in this case, as it identifies words semantically related to the feature indicators. For example, the word *increase*, not in the predefined list of positive words, has a high similarity score (> 0.8) with positive words *help*, *hope*, *give*, and *allow*.

4 Conclusion and Future Work

We proposed a method to guide network learning by attending to feature indicators associated with hand-crafted features. Experimental results over two tasks (quality assessment of Wikipedia articles, and popularity prediction of online petitions) show that our approach consistently outperforms two baselines, across a range of neural architectures. For future work, we are interested in exploring hand-crafted features from external sources, such as editor comments of a Wikipedia article.

References

Quang-Vinh Dang and Claudia-Lavinia Ignat. 2016. Measuring quality of collaboratively edited documents: the case of Wikipedia. In *Proceedings of the 2nd IEEE International Conference on Collaboration and Internet Computing*, pages 266–275.

Quang Vinh Dang and Claudia-Lavinia Ignat. 2017. An end-to-end learning solution for assessing the quality of Wikipedia articles. In *Proceedings of the 13th International Symposium on Open Collaboration*, pages 4:1–4:10.

Jacob Devlin, Ming-Wei Chang, Kenton Lee, and Kristina Toutanova. 2019. BERT: Pre-training of deep bidirectional transformers for language understanding. In *Proceedings of the 2019 Conference of the North American Chapter of the Association for Computational Linguistics: Human Language Technologies, (NAACL-HLT 2019)*, pages 4171–4186.

Sepp Hochreiter and Jürgen Schmidhuber. 1997. Long short-term memory. *Neural Computation*, 9(8):1735–1780.

Nal Kalchbrenner, Edward Grefenstette, and Phil Blunsom. 2014. A convolutional neural network for modelling sentences. In *Proceedings of the 52nd Annual Meeting of the Association for Computational Linguistics (ACL 2014)*, pages 655–665.

Yoon Kim. 2014. Convolutional neural networks for sentence classification. In *Proceedings of the 2014 Conference on Empirical Methods in Natural Language Processing (EMNLP 2014)*, pages 1746–1751.

Diederik P. Kingma and Jimmy Ba. 2015. Adam: A method for stochastic optimization. In *The 3rd International Conference on Learning Representations, (ICLR 2015)*.

Jeffrey Pennington, Richard Socher, and Christopher D. Manning. 2014. GloVe: Global vectors for word representation. In *Proceedings of the 2014 Conference on Empirical Methods in Natural Language Processing (EMNLP 2018)*, pages 1532–1543.

Aili Shen, Jianzhong Qi, and Timothy Baldwin. 2017. A hybrid model for quality assessment of Wikipedia articles. In *Proceedings of the Australasian Language Technology Association Workshop*, pages 43–52.

Aili Shen, Bahar Salehi, Timothy Baldwin, and Jianzhong Qi. 2019. A joint model for multimodal document quality assessment. In *Proceedings of the 19th ACM/IEEE-CS on Joint Conference on Digital Libraries (JCDL 2019)*, pages 107–110.

Shivashankar Subramanian, Timothy Baldwin, and Trevor Cohn. 2018. Content-based popularity prediction of online petitions using a deep regression model. In *Proceedings of the 56th Annual Meeting of the Association for Computational Linguistics, (ACL 2018)*, pages 182–188.

Guoyin Wang, Chunyuan Li, Wenlin Wang, Yizhe Zhang, Dinghan Shen, Xinyuan Zhang, Ricardo Henao, and Lawrence Carin. 2018. Joint embedding of words and labels for text classification. In *Proceedings of the 56th Annual Meeting of the Association for Computational Linguistics (ACL 2018)*, pages 2321–2331.

Sida I. Wang and Christopher D. Manning. 2012. Baselines and bigrams: Simple, good sentiment and topic classification. In *Proceedings of the 50th Annual Meeting of the Association for Computational Linguistics (ACL 2012)*, pages 90–94.

Morten Warncke-Wang, Vladislav R. Ayukaev, Brent Hecht, and Loren Terveen. 2015. The success and failure of quality improvement projects in peer production communities. In *Proceedings of the 18th ACM Conference on Computer-Supported Cooperative Work and Social Computing*, pages 743–756.

Morten Warncke-Wang, Dan Cosley, and John Riedl. 2013. Tell me more: An actionable quality model for Wikipedia. In *Proceedings of the 9th International Symposium on Open Collaboration*, pages 8:1–8:10.

Minghao Wu, Fei Liu, and Trevor Cohn. 2018. Evaluating the utility of hand-crafted features in sequence labelling. In *Proceedings of the 2014 Conference on Empirical Methods in Natural Language Processing (EMNLP 2018)*, page 28502856.

Zichao Yang, Diyi Yang, Chris Dyer, Xiaodong He, Alex Smola, and Eduard Hovy. 2016. Hierarchical attention networks for document classification. In *Proceedings of the 2016 Conference of the North American Chapter of the Association for Computational Linguistics: Human Language Technologies (NACCL-HLT 2016)*, pages 1480–1489.

Predicting Political Frames Across Policy Issues and Contexts

Shima Khanehzar   **Andrew Turpin**   **Gosia Mikolajczak**
School of Computing and Information Systems
The University of Melbourne
skhanehzar@student.unimelb.edu.au
{aturpin,malgorzata.mikolajczak}@unimelb.edu.au

Abstract

Politically-contested issues are often discussed with different emphases by different people. This emphasis is called a *frame*. In this paper, we examine the performance of classifiers trained using the media frames Corpus (MFC) (Card et al., 2015); a collection of US news labelled with fifteen different frame categories. Specifically, we compare pre-trained language models (XLNet, Bert, and Roberta), fine-tuned using MFC, against results from the literature and simpler models in their ability to predict frames from text. We also test these models on a new corpus that we have derived from Australian parliamentary speeches. Our experimental results first show that the fine-tuned models significantly outperform the current best methods on MFC. We also show that the model fine-tuned on US news articles can be convincingly applied to predict policy frames in Australian parliamentary speeches, though the accuracy is significantly reduced, suggesting potential discrepancy in framing strategies and/or text usage between US News and Australian Parliamentary Speeches.

1   Introduction

Politicians and the media often portray political issues in a subjective way in an attempt to shape public attitudes (Chong and Druckman, 2007). For example, a politician opposing the same-sex marriage (SSM) might frame the issue using the lens of tradition and religious beliefs, whereas a politician supporting SSM might frame a speech using fairness and equality as the base. Due to its complexity and linguistic subtleties, issue *framing* (Entman, 1993) remains challenging for automated text methods. To address these challenges, recent work by Boydstun et al. (2013) defines broad categories of common policy frames and annotates US News articles to build the media frames Corpus (MFC) (Card et al., 2015). Follow-up studies have used the MFC to investigate the accuracy of models that attempt to classify the dominant frames of US news articles. In this paper, we aim to extend this work and answer the following question: can recent pre-trained neural classifiers learn to predict dominant frames across issues and communication contexts? To answer this question, we provide the following contributions.

- We investigate the effectiveness of the pre-trained language models XLNet, Bert and Roberta in predicting dominant frames within each issue on the MFC.

- We investigate whether our models can learn to predict frame categories across issues. Our results show that we can apply trained models on a new issue without training data for that particular issue.

- We annotate a small subset of Australian parliamentary speeches on Same-Sex Marriage (SSM).

- We evaluate whether our models can learn to predict frames across communication contexts, applying the models fine-tuned on the MFC dataset on the Australian parliamentary speeches.

2   Background and Related Work

Natural Language Processing techniques have been applied to identify several aspects of the political discourse including ideology (Iyyer et al., 2014), sentiment (Godbole et al., 2007; Balahur et al., 2010), and stance (Mohammad et al., 2016).

Earlier studies focusing specifically on frame detection usually[1] employ topic modeling (Boydstun et al., 2013), (Nguyen, 2015), (Tsur et al.,

---

[1] for an exception, see Baumer et al. (2015) who use classifiers to identify the language of framing in the news

2015). This approach allows for automated detection of frames within specific corpora, but does not easily allow results and methods to be used across issues or contexts that are not part of the corpus on which the model is built. To address this shortcoming, Boydstun et al. (2013) proposed a list of 15 broad frames (e.g., Economic, Morality, or Legal; plus an "Other" category) commonly used when discussing different policy issues (such as abortion, immigration, foreign aid, etc.), and in different communication contexts (news stories, Twitter, party manifestos, legislative debates, etc.). The frames have been defined in the Policy Frame Codebook (PFC)

The **The Media Frames Corpus (MFC)** Card et al. (2015) includes news articles from 13 U.S. newspapers, covering five policy issues: *same-sex marriage, immigration, tobacco, gun control*, and the *death penalty*, published between 1980–2012. Approximately 12,000 articles have been annotated with the dominant frame from the list of categories proposed in PFC. The annotations also identify exact text spans associated with each of the 15 frames. Since the frame distribution is imbalanced and not reported in the original paper, here we show the the statistical distribution of the frameworks in table 1.

The MFC has been previously used for training and testing classification models. For example, Card et al. (2016) provide an unsupervised model that clusters articles with similar collections of "personas" (i.e., characterisations of entities) and demonstrate that these personas can help predict the coarse-grained framing annotations in the MFC.

The current best result for predicting the dominant frame of each article in the MFC comes from Ji and Smith (2017), who proposed a recursive neural discourse structure network with a new attention mechanism of the text for text categorization. They report the average accuracy across 10-fold cross-validation using the immigration issue which we report in Table 2 (column 4).

Field et al. (2018) used the MFC to investigate agenda-setting and framing in Russian News. They introduced embedding-based methods for projecting frames of one language into another (i.e., English to Russian). It is worth mentioning that their approach is applicable to languages suffering from lack of training data.

3   Method

In this paper, we explore three general approaches to classify text with the frames from the PFC. First, We create baseline models with Support Vector Machine (SVM) and Weighted Support Vector Machine (Weighted-SVM). SVMs are often used for text classification problems, as the algorithms perform classification by finding hyperplanes to differentiate the classes. Weighted-SVM is often used for dataset with skewed distribution to reduce bias, and it is more suitable for MFC, which has an imbalanced class distribution. We implement SVM and Weighted-SVM using the default parameters in the sklearn python library. Second, we use the MFC to form a lexicon (bag of words) for each frame and classify new texts using the Okapi text similarity metrics (Robertson and Zaragoza, 2009) from each lexicon. Last, we employ pre-trained language models, and fine-tune them with the MFC. Since our primary goal is to investigate if framing shares similar patterns across domains, we evaluate these models across issues and contexts. For across-issue evaluation, we fine-tune our models on four issues from the MFC (i.e., excluding immigration), and then evaluate them on the immigration subset. For across-context evaluation, we evaluate the models on a subset of the Australian Parliamentary Speeches (APS), which we describe in more detail below.

3.1   Framing Lexicons

Based on the approach by Field et al. (2018), a lexicon related to each frame f in the PFC is derived by taking the top 50 words with the highest pointwise mutual information $I(f, w) = \log p(w|f) - \log p(w)$, where w is a word. We compute $P(w|f)$ by taking the number of occurrences of w in all the text segments annotated with the secondary frame f in the MFC divided by the total number of words in those segments. Quantity $P(w)$ is computed similarly over the entire corpus. As in Field et al. (2018), we discard all words that occur in fewer than 0.5% of documents or in more than 98% of documents.

In order to classify a document into one of the 15 frames, we take the highest ranked lexicon using the document as a query against a collection of the 15 lexicons, measuring similarity using Okapi scoring (Robertson and Zaragoza, 2009). We use the default parameters in the Okapi formula as implemented in the Gensim Python Library.

Frame Category	MFC SSM	MFC no SSM	MFC IM	MFC no IM	APS
Economic	136	1400	414	1122	0
Capacity and Resources	4	245	210	39	0
Morality	405	406	76	735	6
Fairness and Equality	196	653	155	694	24
Legality Constitutionality Jurisdiction	1173	3747	957	3963	9
Policy Prescription and Evaluation	178	1938	473	1643	2
Crime and Punishment	20	2167	803	1384	0
Security and Defence	1	609	286	324	0
Health and Safety	50	1330	239	1141	0
Quality of Life	294	790	410	674	6
Cultural Identity	298	1335	556	1077	5
Public Sentiment	364	758	243	879	11
Political	1215	3547	969	3793	35
External Regulation and Reputation	22	290	132	180	2
Other	0	11	10	1	0
All	4356	19226	5933	17649	100

Table 1: Frame statistics in MFC and APS used in our experiments.

3.2 Neural models

Bert (Devlin et al., 2019) is a bi-directional language model based on now ubiquitous Transformers (Vaswani et al., 2017) with a Cloze Test objective, and trained on a large text corpus. The pre-trained Bert model can be fine-tuned with just one additional output layer to create state-of-the-art models for a wide range of tasks, such as question answering and language inference, without substantial task-specific architecture modifications. In this work, we add an extra task-specific neural layer followed by a non-linear layer and softmax for text classification on top of Bert. Then, the extra layers are jointly fine-tuned with the pre-trained Bert. A prominent limitation of Bert is that it takes at most 512 word tokens, which is often too small for document level tasks.

XLNet (Yang et al., 2019) is an unsupervised language representation learning method based on a novel generalized permutation language modeling objective. XLNet does not suffer from the pre-train-fine-tune discrepancy that Bert is subject to due to the Cloze Test objective during training. Additionally, XLNet employs Transformer-XL (Dai et al., 2019) as the backbone model, exhibiting excellent performance for language tasks involving long context. Overall, XLNet achieves high accuracy on various downstream language tasks including question answering, natural language inference, sentiment analysis, and document ranking.

Roberta (Liu et al., 2019) is an improved version of Bert trained on a larger dataset with longer sequences. It also modifies the original design of Bert by removing the next sentence prediction objective and dynamically changing the masking pattern during pre-training. The author of Roberta claims that Roberta is comparable with XLNet on all GLUE (Wang et al., 2019) tasks and SQUAD (Rajpurkar et al., 2016), and achieves the state-of-the-art performance on 4/9 of the GLUE tasks.

3.3 The APS Dataset

The Australian Parliamentary Speeches (APS) dataset includes transcripts of second reading speeches related to same-sex marriage (SSM) bills presented in the the House of Representatives of the Australian Parliament between 2004-2017. The data has been obtained from the Federal Parliament website. A random sample of 100 speeches was given to an honour student in political science, who was asked to identify 15 frame categories from the PFC, and to indicate the relevant passages representing each frame. The rater was also asked to indicate the dominant frame of each speech. We report the APS frame statistics in table 1.

| Training data | MFC SSM | MFC no SSM | MFC IM | MFC no IM |
| Testing data | MFC SSM | MFC SSM | MFC IM | MFC IM |
	(SISC)	(AISC)	(SISC)	(AISC)
Roberta-Base	**72.5**	**69.0**	**65.8**	**55.5**
Xlnet-Base-Case	72.1	67.9	64.1	54.7
Bert-Base-Case	70.6	67.2	62.5	53.4
SVM	64.5	60.59	57.2	47.24
Weighted-SVM	65.5	61.45	58.4	49.26
Framing Lexicons	66.2	62.34	58.3	49.44
Ji and Smith (2017)	–	–	**58.4**	–
Card et al. (2016)	–	–	56.8	–
Field et al. (2018)	–	–	57.3	–

Table 2: Mean accuracy of Same-Issue and Same-Context (SISC); Across-Issue and Same-Context (AISC) evaluated on both the Same-Sex Marriage (SSM) and Immigration (IM). The training and testing data are indicated in the heading of each column.

4 Experiments and Discussion

We divide our experiments into four parts: Same-Issue and Same-Context (SISC); Across-Issue and Same-Context (AISC); Same-Issue and Across-Context (SIAC); Across-Issue and Across-Context. We follow the same setup as in Card et al. (2016) and report average accuracy across 10-fold cross validation. We use the Bert-Base-Cased, Roberta-Base, Xlnet-Base-Cased models. We use the pre-trained model from Huggingface package. We set the maximum sequence length to 256 since the average number of tokens for SSM and IM are 253 and 254 respectively. For more details about the pre-trained models' parameters, we refer to the Huggingface package.

Same-Issue and Same-Context (SISC) We fine-tune and evaluate our models on the Same-Sex Marriage (SSM) and Immigration (IM) issues from the MFC dataset, and compare the results for IM with the previously proposed models, since to the best of our knowledge, IM is the only issue with results reported in previous work. Table 2 columns 2 and 4 show that the neural models outperform the basic classifier and lexicon-based methods. A paired t-test between Roberta-Base and Framing Lexicons method confirms the difference is statistically significant ($p < 0.001$). The difference between Roberta-Base and Xlnet-Base-Case is not statistically significant ($p = 0.061$), while the difference between Roberta-Base and Bert-Base-Case is ($p = 0.008$).

Across-Issue and Same-Context (AISC) To examine if our models can learn to predict frames across issues, we first exclude the SSM and IM data, respectively, from the MFC dataset and fine-tune our models on the data for the remaining issues. Then, we evaluate the models on the SSM and IM data and compare our results with the previously proposed models. Columns 3 and 5 of Table 2 show that there is a decrease from SISC in mean accuracy of about 4% for SSM, and 9% for IM. However, the classifiers are still well above chance, which is about 27.9% for SSM and 16.3% for IM if we default to the most common frame in the the respective issues.

Same-Issue and Across-Context (SIAC) To examine if our models can learn to predict frames across communication context, we fine-tune our models on the SSM data from the MFC, and then evaluate our models on the APS dataset. Table 3 (column 3) shows that there is a further drop in mean accuracy here for all models, but again still above chance, which is about 35.0% for APS if we default to the most common frame in the the respective issues.

Across-Issue and Across-Context (AIAC) To examine if our models can still learn to predict frames across both issue and communication context, we fine-tune our models on all other MFC data excluding SSM data, and then evaluate our models on APS dataset. Table 3 (column 2) shows that there is a further drop in mean accuracy here, about 9.3% on average for all models, compared to

SIAC, but again still above chance, which is about 35.0% for APS if we default to the most common frame in the the respective issues.

Training data	MFC no SSM	MFC SSM
Testing data	APS	APS
	(AIAC)	(SIAC)
Roberta-Base	41.0	43.0
Xlnet-Base-Case	**43.0**	46.0
Bert-Base-Case	40.0	**47.0**
SVM	32.0	35.0
Weighted-SVM	33.0	37.0
Framing Lexicons	34.0	38.0

Table 3: Mean accuracy of Same-Issue and Across-Context (SIAC); Across-Issue and Across-Context (AIAC) evaluated on both the APS dataset. The training and testing data are indicated in the heading of each column.

5 Discussion

The previous best mean accuracy for predicting the dominant frame on the Immigration subset of the MFC is 58.4%. Our best model (Roberta-Base) fine-tuned with data on the same issue improves the performance by 12.7%, and our best model (Roberta-large—not shown in Table **??**) fine-tuned on data not including the Immigration subset has 56.26% accuracy; still comparable performance against previous methods.

Our best model outperforms the previous best models on the MFC by a large margin. Notably, the performance of pre-trained language models is comparable to the previous best models, even with only fine-tuning on data not specific to the issue being classified, proving that pre-trained neural classifiers can learn to predict dominant frames across domains. However, fine-tuning on small amount of domain-specific data still outperforms the same models fine-tuned on out-of-domain datasets.

6 Conclusion

Using a pre-trained Roberta (Liu et al., 2019) model with added issue- and context-specific data to predict the dominant frame of a text improves upon the current state-of-the-art. Such a model that is trained on U.S. media articles can be convincingly applied to predict frames in Australian political speeches, though the accuracy is significantly reduced, suggesting potential discrepancy in framing strategy between US News and Australian Parliamentary Speeches, and/or different uses of language in the two contexts. Over the coming months, we will work on improving the size and quality of the APS data and examine ways to improve the prediction of dominant frames in Australian political text.

References

Alexandra Balahur, Ralf Steinberger, Mijail A. Kabadjov, Vanni Zavarella, Erik Van der Goot, Matina Halkia, Bruno Pouliquen, and Jenya Belyaeva. 2010. Sentiment analysis in the news. In *Proceedings of the International Conference on Language Resources and Evaluation, LREC 2010, 17-23 May 2010, Valletta, Malta*.

Eric Baumer, Elisha Elovic, Ying Qin, Francesca Polletta, and Geri Gay. 2015. Testing and comparing computational approaches for identifying the language of framing in political news. In *NAACL HLT 2015, The 2015 Conference of the North American Chapter of the Association for Computational Linguistics: Human Language Technologies, Denver, Colorado, USA, May 31 - June 5, 2015*, pages 1472–1482.

Amber E Boydstun, Justin H Gross, Philip Resnik, and Noah A Smith. 2013. Identifying media frames and frame dynamics within and across policy issues.

Dallas Card, Amber E Boydstun, Justin H Gross, Philip Resnik, and Noah A Smith. 2015. The media frames corpus: Annotations of frames across issues. In *Proceedings of the 53rd Annual Meeting of the Association for Computational Linguistics and the 7th International Joint Conference on Natural Language Processing (Volume 2: Short Papers)*, pages 438–444.

Dallas Card, Justin H. Gross, Amber E. Boydstun, and Noah A. Smith. 2016. Analyzing framing through the casts of characters in the news. In *Proceedings of the 2016 Conference on Empirical Methods in Natural Language Processing, EMNLP 2016, Austin, Texas, USA, November 1-4, 2016*, pages 1410–1420.

Dennis Chong and James N Druckman. 2007. Framing public opinion in competitive democracies. *American Political Science Review*, 101(4):637–655.

Zihang Dai, Zhilin Yang, Yiming Yang, Jaime G. Carbonell, Quoc Viet Le, and Ruslan Salakhutdinov. 2019. Transformer-xl: Attentive language models beyond a fixed-length context. In *Proceedings of the 57th Conference of the Association for Computational Linguistics, ACL 2019, Florence, Italy, July 28- August 2, 2019, Volume 1: Long Papers*, pages 2978–2988.

Jacob Devlin, Ming-Wei Chang, Kenton Lee, and Kristina Toutanova. 2019. BERT: Pre-training of deep bidirectional transformers for language understanding. In *Proceedings of the 2019 Conference of the North American Chapter of the Association for Computational Linguistics: Human Language Technologies, Volume 1 (Long and Short Papers)*, pages 4171–4186, Minneapolis, Minnesota. Association for Computational Linguistics.

Robert M Entman. 1993. Framing: Toward clarification of a fractured paradigm. *Journal of communication*, 43(4):51–58.

Anjalie Field, Doron Kliger, Shuly Wintner, Jennifer Pan, Dan Jurafsky, and Yulia Tsvetkov. 2018. Framing and agenda-setting in russian news: a computational analysis of intricate political strategies. In *Proceedings of the 2018 Conference on Empirical Methods in Natural Language Processing, Brussels, Belgium, October 31 - November 4, 2018*, pages 3570–3580.

Namrata Godbole, Manja Srinivasaiah, and Steven Skiena. 2007. Large-scale sentiment analysis for news and blogs. In *Proceedings of the First International Conference on Weblogs and Social Media, ICWSM 2007, Boulder, Colorado, USA, March 26-28, 2007*.

Mohit Iyyer, Peter Enns, Jordan Boyd-Graber, and Philip Resnik. 2014. Political ideology detection using recursive neural networks. In *Proceedings of the 52nd Annual Meeting of the Association for Computational Linguistics (Volume 1: Long Papers)*, pages 1113–1122, Baltimore, Maryland. Association for Computational Linguistics.

Yangfeng Ji and Noah A. Smith. 2017. Neural discourse structure for text categorization. In *Proceedings of the 55th Annual Meeting of the Association for Computational Linguistics, ACL 2017, Vancouver, Canada, July 30 - August 4, Volume 1: Long Papers*, pages 996–1005.

Yinhan Liu, Myle Ott, Naman Goyal, Jingfei Du, Mandar Joshi, Danqi Chen, Omer Levy, Mike Lewis, Luke Zettlemoyer, and Veselin Stoyanov. 2019. Roberta: A robustly optimized bert pretraining approach. *arXiv preprint arXiv:1907.11692*.

Saif Mohammad, Svetlana Kiritchenko, Parinaz Sobhani, Xiaodan Zhu, and Colin Cherry. 2016. SemEval-2016 task 6: Detecting stance in tweets. In *Proceedings of the 10th International Workshop on Semantic Evaluation (SemEval-2016)*, pages 31–41, San Diego, California. Association for Computational Linguistics.

Viet An Nguyen. 2015. *Guided Probabilistic Topic Models for Agenda-Setting and Framing*. Ph.D. thesis.

Pranav Rajpurkar, Jian Zhang, Konstantin Lopyrev, and Percy Liang. 2016. Squad: 100, 000+ questions for machine comprehension of text. In *Proceedings of the 2016 Conference on Empirical Methods in Natural Language Processing, EMNLP 2016, Austin, Texas, USA, November 1-4, 2016*, pages 2383–2392.

Stephen E. Robertson and Hugo Zaragoza. 2009. The probabilistic relevance framework: BM25 and beyond. *Foundations and Trends in Information Retrieval*, 3(4):333–389.

Oren Tsur, Dan Calacci, and David Lazer. 2015. A frame of mind: Using statistical models for detection of framing and agenda setting campaigns. In *Proceedings of the 53rd Annual Meeting of the Association for Computational Linguistics and the 7th International Joint Conference on Natural Language Processing of the Asian Federation of Natural Language Processing, ACL 2015, July 26-31, 2015, Beijing, China, Volume 1: Long Papers*, pages 1629–1638.

Ashish Vaswani, Noam Shazeer, Niki Parmar, Jakob Uszkoreit, Llion Jones, Aidan N. Gomez, Lukasz Kaiser, and Illia Polosukhin. 2017. Attention is all you need. In *Advances in Neural Information Processing Systems 30: Annual Conference on Neural Information Processing Systems 2017, 4-9 December 2017, Long Beach, CA, USA*, pages 5998–6008.

Alex Wang, Amanpreet Singh, Julian Michael, Felix Hill, Omer Levy, and Samuel R. Bowman. 2019. GLUE: A multi-task benchmark and analysis platform for natural language understanding. In *7th International Conference on Learning Representations, ICLR 2019, New Orleans, LA, USA, May 6-9, 2019*.

Zhilin Yang, Zihang Dai, Yiming Yang, Jaime G. Carbonell, Ruslan Salakhutdinov, and Quoc V. Le. 2019. Xlnet: Generalized autoregressive pretraining for language understanding. *CoRR*, abs/1906.08237.

Domain Adaptation for Low-Resource Neural Semantic Parsing

Alvin Kennardi[1], **Gabriela Ferraro**[1,2], and **Qing Wang**[1]

[1]Research School of Computer Science, Australian National University
[2]Data61, CSIRO
{alvin.kennardi, qing.wang}@anu.edu.au
gabriela.ferraro@data61.csiro.au

Abstract

One key challenge for building a semantic parser in new domains is the difficulty to annotate new datasets. In this paper, we propose a sequential transfer learning method as a domain adaptation method to tackle this issue. We show that we can obtain a model with better generalisation on a small dataset by transferring network parameters from a model trained with a bigger dataset with similar meaning representations. We evaluate our model with different datasets as well as versions of the datasets with different difficulty levels.

1 Introduction

Semantic parsing maps natural language sentences into meaning representations, for example, logical formulae, SQL queries, or executable codes. The successful implementation of the encoder-decoder architecture in the machine translation (Kalchbrenner and Blunsom, 2013; Sutskever et al., 2014) has driven researchers to apply this model into semantic parsing task (Dong and Lapata, 2016; Jia and Liang, 2016; Ling et al., 2016; Dong and Lapata, 2018). These neural semantic parsing models have achieved impressive results.

Semantic parsing datasets are usually domain and meaning representation dependent, thus making it difficult to re-use existing datasets for building general semantic parsers or semantic parsers in new domains. The process of annotating sentences with their meaning representations for modeling new domains or augmenting the existing datasets is expensive. Prior works proposed several strategies to tackle this issue, such as paraphrasing (Su and Yan, 2017), decoupling structure and lexicon (Herzig and Berant, 2018), and multi-task learning (Susanto and Lu, 2017; Herzig and Berant, 2017).

Our method aims to provide an alternative to the previous work. We perform transfer learning by training a model for one task using a dataset and fine-tuning the model using another related dataset. The idea of transfer learning is to utilize features, weights, or other knowledge acquired for one task to solve another related task. It has been extensively used for domain adaptation and building models to solve problems where only limited data is available (Pan and Yang, 2010). The fine-tuning transfer learning procedure has been successfully implemented in the encoder-decoder architecture for Neural Machine Translation Task (NMT) (Luong and Manning, 2015; Sennrich et al., 2016; Servan et al., 2016). In contrast with the multi-task learning, which jointly trains several tasks together, we perform transfer learning by training the first and second tasks in sequence.

Compared to models without transfer learning, our experiments shows that transfer learning gives a good prior for models trained with small datasets, hence improving model performance when only limited amounts of data are available.

Neural semantic parsing models are usually trained and tested using datasets in which variables are identified and anonymised before hand, thus considerably reducing the difficulty of the semantic parsing task (Finegan-Dollak et al., 2018). In this work, we use the un-anonymised versions of two semantic parsing datasets, as well as different data splits to provide extensive evaluation of our model.

To summarise, the contributions of this paper are as follows:

- Evaluation of transfer learning as domain adaptation for low-resource neural semantic parsing with different datasets and difficulty levels.

- Compilation and release of un-anonymised versions of ATIS and GeoQuery datasets for semantic parsing in lambda calculus formulae.[1]

2   Related Work

Encoder-decoder architectures based on neural networks have been successfully applied to semantic parsing (Dong and Lapata, 2016; Jia and Liang, 2016; Ling et al., 2016; Dong and Lapata, 2018). Since then, several ideas such as including attention mechanism (Dong and Lapata, 2016), multi-task learning (Susanto and Lu, 2017; Herzig and Berant, 2017; Fan et al., 2017), data augmentation (Jia and Liang, 2016; Kočiský et al., 2016) and two-steps (coarse-to-fine) decoder (Dong and Lapata, 2018) have been applied to semantic parsing models with the aim of boosting performance.

Similar to our work, others tried to overcome the lack of annotated data by leveraging existing datasets from related domains. Previous works from Herzig and Berant (2017) and Fan et al. (2017) used a multi-task framework to jointly learn the neural semantic parsing model and encourage parameter sharing between different datasets. The model proposed by Herzig and Berant (2017) used multiple knowledge bases in different domains to enhance the model performance. On the other hand, the work from Fan et al. (2017) leveraged access to a very large labeled dataset to help a small one. However, their models are trained using proprietary datasets, which are not publicly available, thus making model comparison unfeasible. The work proposed by Damonte et al. (2019) investigates the possibility of transfer learning to tackle the issue of lacking annotated data on neural semantic parsing. They used more complex model and data sets compared to our work.

Our work focuses on training a model using a larger dataset and fine-tune using another related low-resource dataset rather than multi-task learning. We also evaluate how additional training examples impact transfer learning models.

3   Methodology

3.1   Transfer Learning as Domain Adaptation

We adapt the formal definition of transfer learning from Pan and Yang (2010) to the neural semantic parsing problem involving a question q and a meaning representation f. A domain $\mathcal{D}$ consists

of input space $\mathcal{Q}$ and marginal probability $P(Q)$, where $Q = \{q_1, q_2, ..., q_n\} \subseteq \mathcal{Q}$. A domain can be denoted by $\mathcal{D} = \{\mathcal{Q}, P(Q)\}$. Given a domain $\mathcal{D} = \{\mathcal{Q}, P(Q)\}$, a task $\mathcal{T}$ consists of output space $\mathcal{F}$ and conditional probability $P(F|Q)$. A task can be denoted as $\mathcal{T} = \{\mathcal{F}, P(F|Q)\}$. In the semantic parsing problem, we want to learn conditional probability $P(F|Q)$ from the training set with training data (q_i, f_i), where $q_i \in \mathcal{Q}$ and $f_i \in \mathcal{F}$.

Suppose we have a *source domain* $\mathcal{D}_S$, with *source task* $\mathcal{T}_S$ and a *target domain* $\mathcal{D}_T$ with *target task* $\mathcal{T}_T$ where $0 < n_T << n_S$. Transfer learning uses the knowledge from D_S and T_S to improve the performance of T_T, where $D_S \neq D_T$, or $T_S \neq T_T$ (Pan and Yang, 2010).

Our transfer learning method starts by training a model in the *source domain* $\mathcal{D}_S$ to solve a *source task* T_S. Subsequently, we transfer the knowledge (i.e network parameters) to the model aimed to solve *target task* $\mathcal{T}_T$ and fine-tune the model using the *target domain* $\mathcal{D}_T$.

3.2   Model

In this work, we adopt the sequence-to-sequence with neural attention method from Dong and Lapata (2016). The model aims to map a question input $q = \langle x_1, x_2, ..., x_{|q|} \rangle$ to a meaning representation $f = \langle y_1, y_2, ..., y_{|f|} \rangle$. We want to compute the conditional probability of generating the meaning representation f given a question q as follows:

$$p(f|q) = \prod_{t=1}^{|f|} p(y_t|y_{<t}, q) \qquad (1)$$

The question input q is encoded using an encoder, and then a meaning representation f is generated using an attention decoder. The encoder hidden state $\mathbf{h}_t$ and cell state $\mathbf{c}_t$ at time step t can be computed as follows:

$$\mathbf{h}_t, \mathbf{c}_t = LSTM(\mathbf{h}_{t-1}, \mathbf{c}_{t-1}, \mathrm{E}(x_t)) \qquad (2)$$

where LSTM refers to a LSTM function described by Zaremba et al. (2014) and $E(.)$ is an embedding layer that returns a word vector representation of x_t. The hidden and cell state of the last encoder step are used to initialize the LSTM cell on the first decoder step, hence giving the context to the decoder. The LSTM encoder and decoder have different parameters.

The attention layers aim to include the encoder information to a meaning representation at each

---

[1]The code and datasets are available from `https://github.com/akennardi/Semantic-Parsing`

decoder step (Bahdanau et al., 2015; Luong et al., 2015). In an attention layer, we compute an attention score $s_{k,t}$ between the k-th encoder hidden state h_k and a decoder hidden state $\mathbf{h}_t$. The context vector c_t is a weighted sum of all encoder hidden vectors. We use the context vector $\mathbf{c}_t$ and the decoder hidden state $\mathbf{h}_t$, to obtain an attention hidden state vector $\mathbf{h}_t^{att}$ using equations as follows:

$$s_{k,t} = \frac{\exp\{\mathbf{h}_k \cdot \mathbf{h}_t\}}{\sum_{j=1}^{|q|} \exp\{\mathbf{h}_j \cdot \mathbf{h}_t\}}$$

$$\mathbf{c}_t = \sum_{k=1}^{|q|} s_{k,t}\mathbf{h}_k \qquad (3)$$

$$\mathbf{h}_t^{att} = \tanh(\mathbf{W}_1\mathbf{h}_t + \mathbf{W}_2\mathbf{c}_t)$$

The conditional probability of generating token y_t at time step t can be expressed as:

$$p(y_t|y_{<t}, q) = (softmax(\mathbf{W}_o\mathbf{h}_t^{att}))^T \mathbf{e}(y_t) \quad (4)$$

where $\mathbf{e}(y_t)$ is a one-hot vector with value 1 in the element of index y_t in the embedding layer and 0 otherwise.

We train our model to minimise the negative log-likelihood function over questions and formulae in the training set $\mathcal{T}$. The optimisation problem can be written as follows:

$$\text{minimise} \quad -\sum_{(q,f)\in\mathcal{T}} \log(p(f|q)) \qquad (5)$$

Given a question q, we used the model to generate the most probable sequence $\tilde{f}$ as follows:

$$\tilde{f} = arg\,max_{f'} p(f'|q) \qquad (6)$$

The model performs a greedy search to generate one token at a time to construct a sequence in lambda calculus.

4 Experiments

4.1 Datasets

For evaluation we used two semantic parsing datasets, namely ATIS and GeoQuery. The meaning representation of the datasets is lambda calculus. There are two types of dataset splits: question-split and query-split. In question-split, the training and test examples are divided based on the questions (Finegan-Dollak et al., 2018), thus based on the input sequence. Meanwhile, in query-split, the training and test examples are divided according to the similarity of their meaning representations

ATIS	
Question : cheapest fare from ci0 to ci1	
Formula : (min \$0 (exists \$1 (and (from \$1 ci0) (to \$1 ci1) (= (fare \$1) \$0))))	

ATIS Un-anonymised
Question : cheapest fare from Indianapolis to Seattle
Formula : (min \$0 (exists \$1 (and (from \$1 indianapolis) (to \$1 seattle) (= (fare \$1) \$0))))

GeoQuery
Question : what is the capital of s0
Formula : (capital:c s0)

GeoQuery Un-anonymised
Question : what is the capital of Georgia
Formula : (capital: georgia)

Table 1: Example of natural language questions and their meaning representation in lambda calculus.

Data Set	Train	Dev.	Test
ATIS	4,434	491	448
ATIS un-anonymised	4,029	504	504
GeoQuery	600	0	280
GeoQuery un-anonymised	583	15	279
GeoQuery un-anonymised + query-split	543	148	186

Table 2: Number of training (Train), development (Dev.), and testing (Test) instances for each dataset.

(Finegan-Dollak et al., 2018), thus based on the output sequences. Therefore, the query-split is more appropriate to evaluate the model's capability of composing output sequences, in this case, lambda calculus expressions.

The ATIS dataset (Price, 1990; Dahl et al., 1994; Zettlemoyer and Collins, 2007) consists of queries from a flight booking system. We obtained the un-anonymised version of ATIS by preprocessing the non-SQL ATIS dataset (Finegan-Dollak et al., 2018). Question variables in this dataset are not anonymised, but the formulae have variable identifiers. We removed the variable identifiers in logical formulae. The ATIS dataset split is question-split.

The GeoQuery dataset (Zelle and Mooney, 1996; Zettlemoyer and Collins, 2005) consists of queries about US geographical information. We annotated the un-anonymised version of GeoQuery based on non-SQL GeoQuery dataset (Finegan-Dollak et al., 2018), which has different meaning representations. We compared the question with the anonymised version and annotated lambda calculus formulae on the non-SQL GeoQuery dataset. We ran a script to put the variable back into the questions-formulae pairs, and split them into training, development and test sets based

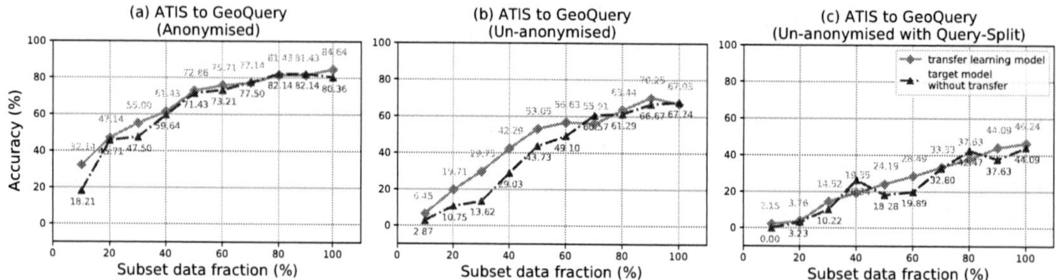

Figure 1: Learning curves from different transfer learning setups.

Source Domain	Target Domain
ATIS	GeoQuery
ATIS un-anonymised	GeoQuery un-anonymised
ATIS un-anonymised	GeoQuery un-anonymised with query-split

Table 3: Transfer learning experiments with ATIS and GeoQuery datasets.

on Finegan-Dollak et al. (2018). We also divided the GeoQuery un-anoymised dataset using query-split as proposed by Finegan-Dollak et al. (2018). Table 2 shows the details of each dataset.

4.2 Setup

We considered ATIS as a *Source Domain* dataset and GeoQuery as a *Target Domain* dataset. We believe that ATIS training samples are less similar, since it could only achieve a good model performance using more training samples. Thus it is more beneficial to use ATIS as *Source Domain*. We evenly divided the GeoQuery into 10 subsets of {10%, 20%,...,100%} fraction of the training set. With this setup, we simulate the situation where we have limited data in the target domain. This setup also allowed us to evaluate the effectiveness of transfer learning with sufficient training data. Details about the experiments setups are depicted in Table 3.

We set the model hyper-parameters following Dong and Lapata (2016) for GeoQuery. We optimised the objective function in Equation 5 using RMSProp algorithm (Tieleman and Hinton, 2012) with a decay rate of 0.95. The batch size was 20. We randomly initialised parameter from the uniform distribution $\mathcal{U}(-0.08, 008)$. The hidden unit size was 150, and the dropout rate was 0.5. We used 15 epoch to obtain a model from ATIS. We increased the number of epochs after transferring all network parameters to 150 and 180 for anonymised and un-anonymised GeoQuery, re-

spectively. Source and target models were trained with their own vocabularies to handle differences of vocabularies between two datasets. The evaluation metric was accuracy. We evaluated each model with inference described in Equation 6 on the full GeoQuery test set for every bucket. We reported exact match accuracy computed using equation as follows:

$$\text{Accuracy} = \frac{\text{\# of correct formulae}}{\text{\# test examples in the test set}} \quad (7)$$

4.3 Evaluation on Transfer Learning

We compared our transfer learning framework with the original target model (i.e. without transfer learning) in three different setups described in Section 4.2. Figure 1 shows the learning curves of those setups. The results from small GeoQuery subsets confirmed our hypothesis that the source model gives a stronger prior to the target model. The model obtained from transfer learning has 13.93%, 3.58%, and 2.15% accuracy improvement on the 10% fraction of GeoQuery, GeoQuery Un-anonymised, and GeoQuery Un-anonymised with Query-Split datasets respectively. Figure 1(a) and (b) clearly shows how the transfer learning improves the performance of the target models trained with small subsets. In Figure 1(c), the performance of the model with transfer learning are comparable to the original target model. However, the performance of original target model drops with additional training examples from 40% to 50% subset. On the other hand, the model with transfer learning does not have a sudden drop. A possible explanation to this result may be due to the difficulty of the original target model to learn from difficult training samples. The learning curves of the transfer learning models show smoother changes with additional training data as

No.	Question	Transfer Learning	Original Target Model
1	river in s0	(lambda $0 e (and (river:t $0) (loc:t $0 s0)))	(lambda $0 e (and (river:t $0) (loc:t $0 s0)) (size:i $0))
2	what is the capital of the smallest state	(capital:c (argmin $1 (state:t $1) (size:i $1)))	(capital:c (argmax $1 (state:t $1) (size:i $1)))
3	how many rivers does colorado have	(count $0 (and (river $0) (loc $0 colorado)))	(count $0 (and (state $0) (loc $0 usa)))
4	how large is texas	(size texas)	(argmax $0 (river $0) (density $0))
5	how many states does missouri border	(count $0 (and (state $0) (next_to $0 missouri)))	(count $0 (and (state $0) (next_to $0 delaware)))
6	how many states does the missouri river run through	(count $0 (and (state $0) (loc $0 missouri)))	(lambda $0 e (and (state $0) (loc $0 missouri)))

Table 4: Examples of Meaning Representations generated by the model trained with transfer learning and original target model using 10% fraction of various GeoQuery datasets.

compared to the original target model, indicating better model generalisation when the training data is small. With bigger subset (i.e 70% and more), the results from transfer learning models are comparable to the original models, indicating that the out-of-domain data does not impair the model performance. We show that our transfer learning method helps the target model to have a better performance when the training data is very small.

4.4 Error Analysis on Transfer Learning

We also looked into samples generated from the transfer learning models and original target models. Table 4 presents six samples from three different setups described in Table 3 with the target model trained with 10% subset of training examples. The first two samples are obtained from the models trained with GeoQuery. In the first example, the model trained with transfer learning can identify correct meaning representation, while the original target model generates wrong meaning representation due to the generation of extra tokens. The second example shows the model trained with transfer learning correctly identified the token "smallest" to generate "argmin" instead of "argmax".

The third and fourth samples show examples of meaning representations generated by the model trained with un-anonymised GeoQuery. In the third examples, the model with transfer learning correctly identified the entity "river". On the other hand, the model without transfer learning generates "state", which is more common in the training set. On the fourth example, the original target model generates an irrelevant meaning representation.

The last two samples are obtained from models trained with un-anonymised GeoQuery with query-split. The fifth example shows how the original target generates a wrong entity name "delaware" instead of "missouri". Similarly, the sixth example shows original target model produces a token "lambda" instead of "count". This error may be due to the fact that the original target model tends to generate the token they are familiar with in the training set. Examples described above shows how the model trained with transfer learning has a better ability to generate tokens that are different with training examples, thus improve the performance of the model.

5 Conclusion and Future Work

We proposed a transfer learning method by training a model using a larger dataset and fine-tuning with another related low-resource dataset. With this method, we can use a bigger dataset with a similar composition to improve the performance of a model trained with a smaller dataset.

For future work, it would be interesting to combine transfer learning and data selection methods so that the source model is trained only with the most similar instances in respect with the target domain. Another direction would be to explore transfer learning on a more complex model such as sequence-to-tree, which has a better performance than sequence-to-sequence models when trained with large datasets.

Acknowledgement

We would like to thank Xiang Li for his insight throughout the project. We would also like to thank the three anonymous reviewers for their valuable comments and insights. This work is a part of Individual Computing Project Course at the Australian National University taken by the first author with the same title.

References

Dzmitry Bahdanau, Kyunghyun Cho, and Yoshua Bengio. 2015. Neural machine translation by jointly learning to align and translate. In *3rd International Conference on Learning Representations, ICLR 2015, San Diego, CA, USA, May 7-9, 2015, Conference Track Proceedings*.

Deborah A. Dahl, Madeleine Bates, Michael Brown, William Fisher, Kate Hunicke-Smith, David Pallett, Christine Pao, Alexander Rudnicky, and Elizabeth Shriberg. 1994. Expanding the scope of the atis task: The atis-3 corpus. In *HUMAN LANGUAGE TECHNOLOGY: Proceedings of a Workshop held at Plainsboro, New Jersey, March 8-11, 1994*.

Marco Damonte, Rahul Goel, and Tagyoung Chung. 2019. Practical semantic parsing for spoken language understanding. *CoRR*, abs/1903.04521.

Li Dong and Mirella Lapata. 2016. Language to Logical Form with Neural Attention. In *Proceedings of the 54th Annual Meeting of the Association for Computational Linguistics (Volume 1: Long Papers)*, ACL 2016, pages 33–43, Berlin, Germany. Association for Computational Linguistics.

Li Dong and Mirella Lapata. 2018. Coarse-to-Fine Decoding for Neural Semantic Parsing. In *Proceedings of the 56th Annual Meeting of the Association for Computational Linguistics (Volume 1: Long Papers)*, ACL 2018, pages 731–742, Melbourne, Australia. Association for Computational Linguistics.

Xing Fan, Emilio Monti, Lambert Mathias, and Markus Dreyer. 2017. Transfer Learning for Neural Semantic Parsing. In *Proceedings of the 2nd Workshop on Representation Learning for NLP*, Rep4NLP 2017, pages 48–56, Vancouver, Canada. Association for Computational Linguistics.

Catherine Finegan-Dollak, Jonathan K. Kummerfeld, Li Zhang, Karthik Ramanathan, Sesh Sadasivam, Rui Zhang, and Dragomir Radev. 2018. Improving text-to-SQL evaluation methodology. In *Proceedings of the 56th Annual Meeting of the Association for Computational Linguistics (Volume 1: Long Papers)*, pages 351–360, Melbourne, Australia. Association for Computational Linguistics.

Jonathan Herzig and Jonathan Berant. 2017. Neural Semantic Parsing over Multiple Knowledge-bases. In *Proceedings of the 55th Annual Meeting of the Association for Computational Linguistics (Volume 2: Short Papers)*, ACL 2017, pages 623–628, Vancouver, Canada. Association for Computational Linguistics.

Jonathan Herzig and Jonathan Berant. 2018. Decoupling structure and lexicon for zero-shot semantic parsing. In *Proceedings of the 2018 Conference on Empirical Methods in Natural Language Processing*, pages 1619–1629, Brussels, Belgium. Association for Computational Linguistics.

Robin Jia and Percy Liang. 2016. Data Recombination for Neural Semantic Parsing. In *Proceedings of the 54th Annual Meeting of the Association for Computational Linguistics (Volume 1: Long Papers)*, ACL 2016, pages 12–22, Berlin, Germany. Association for Computational Linguistics.

Nal Kalchbrenner and Phil Blunsom. 2013. Recurrent Continuous Translation Models. In *Proceedings of the 2013 Conference on Empirical Methods in Natural Language Processing*, EMNLP 2013, pages 1700–1709, Seattle, Washington, USA. Association for Computational Linguistics.

Tomáš Kočiský, Gábor Melis, Edward Grefenstette, Chris Dyer, Wang Ling, Phil Blunsom, and Karl Moritz Hermann. 2016. Semantic Parsing with Semi-Supervised Sequential Autoencoders. In *Proceedings of the 2016 Conference on Empirical Methods in Natural Language Processing*, EMNLP 2016, pages 1078–1087, Austin, TX, USA. Association for Computational Linguistics.

Wang Ling, Phil Blunsom, Edward Grefenstette, Karl Moritz Hermann, Tomáš Kočiský, Fumin Wang, and Andrew Senior. 2016. Latent Predictor Networks for Code Generation. In *Proceedings of the 54th Annual Meeting of the Association for Computational Linguistics (Volume 1: Long Papers)*, ACL 2016, pages 599–609, Berlin, Germany. Association for Computational Linguistics.

Minh-Thang Luong and Christopher D. Manning. 2015. Stanford neural machine translation systems for spoken language domains. In *International Workshop on Spoken Language Translation*.

Thang Luong, Hieu Pham, and Christopher D. Manning. 2015. Effective approaches to attention-based neural machine translation. In *Proceedings of the 2015 Conference on Empirical Methods in Natural Language Processing*, pages 1412–1421, Lisbon, Portugal. Association for Computational Linguistics.

Sinno Jialin Pan and Qiang Yang. 2010. A survey on transfer learning. *Trans. on Knowledge and Data Eng.*, 22(10):1345–1359.

P. J. Price. 1990. Evaluation of spoken language systems: the ATIS domain. In *Speech and Natural Language: Proceedings of a Workshop Held at Hidden Valley, Pennsylvania, June 24-27,1990*.

Rico Sennrich, Barry Haddow, and Alexandra Birch. 2016. Improving neural machine translation models with monolingual data. In *Proceedings of the 54th Annual Meeting of the Association for Computational Linguistics (Volume 1: Long Papers)*, pages 86–96, Berlin, Germany. Association for Computational Linguistics.

Christophe Servan, Josep Maria Crego, and Jean Senellart. 2016. Domain specialization: a post-training domain adaptation for neural machine translation. *ArXiv*, abs/1612.06141.

Yu Su and Xifeng Yan. 2017. Cross-domain semantic parsing via paraphrasing. In *Proceedings of the 2017 Conference on Empirical Methods in Natural Language Processing*, pages 1235–1246, Copenhagen, Denmark. Association for Computational Linguistics.

Raymond Hendy Susanto and Wei Lu. 2017. Neural Architectures for Multilingual Semantic Parsing. In *Proceedings of the 55th Annual Meeting of the Association for Computational Linguistics (Volume 2: Short Papers)*, ACL 2017, pages 38–44, Vancouver, Canada. Association for Computational Linguistics.

Ilya Sutskever, Oriol Vinyals, and Quoc V. Le. 2014. Sequence to sequence learning with neural networks. *CoRR*, abs/1409.3215.

T. Tieleman and G. Hinton. 2012. Lecture 6.5— RmsProp: Divide the gradient by a running average of its recent magnitude. COURSERA: Neural Networks for Machine Learning.

Wojciech Zaremba, Ilya Sutskever, and Oriol Vinyals. 2014. Recurrent neural network regularization. *CoRR*, abs/1409.2329.

John M. Zelle and Raymond J. Mooney. 1996. Learning to Parse Database Queries Using Inductive Logic Programming. In *Proceedings of the 13th National Conference on Artificial Intelligence*, volume 2, pages 1050–1055, Portland, Oregon, USA. AAAI Press / The MIT Press.

Luke Zettlemoyer and Michael Collins. 2007. Online learning of relaxed CCG grammars for parsing to logical form. In *Proceedings of the 2007 Joint Conference on Empirical Methods in Natural Language Processing and Computational Natural Language Learning (EMNLP-CoNLL)*, pages 678–687, Prague, Czech Republic. Association for Computational Linguistics.

Luke S. Zettlemoyer and Michael Collins. 2005. Learning to map sentences to logical form: Structured classification with probabilistic categorial grammars. In *Proceedings of the Twenty-First Conference on Uncertainty in Artificial Intelligence*, UAI'05, pages 658–666, Arlington, Virginia, United States. AUAI Press.

A Pointer Network Architecture for Context-Dependent Semantic Parsing

Xuanli He♣   **Quan Hung Tran**♡   **Gholamreza Haffari**♣

♣Monash University, Australia
♡Adobe Research, San Jose, CA
{xuanli.he1, gholamreza.haffari}@monash.edu
qtran@adobe.com

Abstract

Semantic parsing targets at mapping human utterances into structured meaning representations, such as logical forms, programming snippets, SQL queries etc. In this work, we focus on logical form generation, which is extracted from an automated email assistant system. Since this task is dialogue-oriented, information across utterances must be well handled. Furthermore, certain inputs from users are used as arguments for the logical form, which requires a parser to distinguish the functional words and content words. Hence, an intelligent parser should be able to switch between generation mode and copy mode. In order to address the aforementioned issues, we equip the vanilla seq2seq model with a pointer network and a context-dependent architecture to generate more accurate logical forms. Our model achieves state-of-the-art performance on the email assistant task.

1   Introduction

Recently, due to the breakthrough of the deep learning, numerous and various tasks within the filed of natural language processing (NLP) have made impressive achievements (Vaswani et al., 2017; Devlin et al., 2018; Edunov et al., 2018). However, most these achievements are assessed by automatic metrics, which are relatively superficial and brittle, and can be easily tricked (Paulus et al., 2017; Jia and Liang, 2017; Läubli et al., 2018). Hence, understanding the underlying meaning of natural language sentences is crucial to NLP tasks.

As an appealing direction in natural language understanding, semantic parsing has been widely studied in the NLP community (Ling et al., 2016; Dong and Lapata, 2016; Jia and Liang, 2017). Semantic parsing aims at converting human utterances to machine executable representations. Most existing work focuses on parsing individual utterances independently, even they have an access to the contextual information. In spite of several pioneering efforts (Zettlemoyer and Collins, 2009; Srivastava et al., 2017), these pre-neural models suffer from complicated hand-crafted feature engineering, compared to their neural counterparts (Dong and Lapata, 2018; Rabinovich et al., 2017). One notable exception is the work of Suhr et al. (2018), who incorporate context into ATIS data with a neural approach.

In this work, we propose a neural semantic parser for email assistant task which incorporates the conversation context as well as a copy mechanism to fill-in the arguments of the logical forms from the input sentence. Our model achieves state-of-the-art (SOTA) performance. We further provide details analysis about where these improvements come from.

2   Models

To build our models, we follow a process of error-driven design. We first start with a simple seq2seq model, then we closely examine the errors, group them, and then propose a solution to each of these error groups. From our examination, we identify two main sources of errors of a seq2seq model: i) the overly strong influence of the language model component, and ii) the lack of contextual information. Thus we design our model to incorporate the *Pointer Mechanism* and *Context-dependent Mechanism* to solve these problems. From this point, we refer to the errors caused by the first source (language model) as *Copy-related errors*, and the ones caused by the second source (lack of context) as *Context-related errors*.

2.1   Word Copy using the Pointer Mechanism

With the basic seq2seq architecture, the model's generation is heavily influenced by the language

".

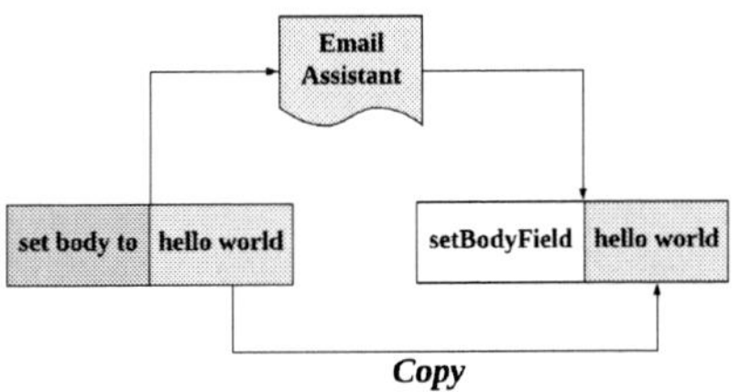

Figure 1: A example of semantic parsing on the email assistant system.

model aspect. Thus, it tends to use the strings it has seen in the training dataset (see Table 1).

current utterance:
set body to blue
logical form
reference: (setFieldFromString (getProbMutableField-ByFieldName body) (stringValue ” blue ”))
seq2seq: (setFieldFromString (getProbMutableFieldBy-FieldName body) (stringValue ” charlie is on his way ”))

Table 1: An error made by the base seq2seq model. Copy mechanism can fix it.

From this analysis, we realize that it would be crucial for the model to learn when to copy from the source sentence, and when to generate a new token. Thus, we incorporate the pointer mechanism into our base seq2seq approach.

As shown in Figure 1, for an email assistant system, users inputs are usually comprised of a functional part and a content part. A semantic parser should be able to distinguish and handle them in a different way. Specifically, the parser must generate a series of lambda-like functions for the functional part, while the content part should be copied to the argument slot.

Our pointer network is inspired by that of See et al. (2017) designed for the summarisation task. Given an utterance $\mathbf{x}$ and a logical form $\mathbf{y}$, at each time step t, we have a *soft* switch which determines the contributions of the token generator and the copier which uses a pointer over the words of the input utterance:

$$P(\mathbf{y}_t) = p_{gen}P_{vocab}(\mathbf{y}_t) + (1 - p_{gen}) \sum_{i:\mathbf{x}_i=\mathbf{y}_t} \alpha_i^t$$

where α_i^t is the attention score over the position i in the t-th generation step, and P_{vocab} is a probability distribution over the vocabulary. $p_{gen} \in [0, 1]$ is the *generation probability*, modelled as:

$$p_{gen} = \sigma(\mathbf{w}_c^T \mathbf{c}_t + \mathbf{w}_s^T \mathbf{s}_t + \mathbf{w}_x^T \mathbf{x}_t + b)$$

where $\mathbf{c}_t$ and $\mathbf{s}_t$ are the context vector and the decoder state respectively, while $\mathbf{w}_c^T$, $\mathbf{w}_s^T$, $\mathbf{w}_x^T$ and b are learnable parameters.

2.2 Conditioning on Conversation Context

Understanding conversations between a user and the system requires the comprehension of the flow of the discourse among sequence of utterances. Processing utterances independently within a conversation leads to misinterpreting users inputs, which will result in incorrect logical form generation (see Table 2). Therefore, we incorporate the context when processing the current utterance for a better generation.

dialog history
...
user: compose a new email. the recipient is mom. the subject is hello
user: cancel
...
current utterance:
cancel
logical form
reference: (undo)
seq2seq: (cancel)

Table 2: An error made by the base seq2seq model. It is clear that without the context information, the model cannot infer the correct logical form.

Basically, a conversation consists of a sequence of user utterances:$\{\mathbf{x}^1, ..., \mathbf{x}^T\}$ paired with a list of logical forms: $\{\mathbf{y}^1, ..., \mathbf{y}^T\}$. For a given utterance sequence $\mathbf{x}^i = \{\mathbf{x}_1^i, ..., \mathbf{x}_m^i\}$, a semantic parser should predict its associated logical form $\mathbf{y}^i = \{\mathbf{y}_1^i, ..., \mathbf{y}_n^i\}$. Inspired by Suhr et al. (2018), we introduce a hierarchical architecture to model both utterance-level and conversation-level information; see Figure 2. At the utterance level, we use an attentional seq2seq model to establish the mapping from an utterance $\mathbf{x}^i$ to its corresponding logical form $\mathbf{y}^i$:

$$\mathbf{h}_{1:m}^i = \text{Encoder}(\mathbf{x}_1^i, ..., \mathbf{x}_m^i), \quad (1)$$
$$\mathbf{c}_t^i = \text{Attention}(\mathbf{h}_{1:m}^i, \mathbf{s}_{t-1}^i), \quad (2)$$
$$\mathbf{y}_t^i, \mathbf{s}_t^i = \text{Decoder}(\mathbf{y}_{t-1}^i, \mathbf{s}_{t-1}^i, \mathbf{c}_t^i) \quad (3)$$

As the seq2seq model, we investigate the use of RNN-based and Transformer-based architectures. Furthermore, we make use of a conversation-level RNN to capture the wider conversational context:

$$\mathbf{g}_i = \text{RNN}(\mathbf{h}_m^i, \mathbf{g}_{i-1}) \quad (4)$$

where $\mathbf{h}_m^i$ is the last hidden state of the ith utterance, and $\mathbf{g}$ is the conversational hidden state.

In order to incorporate the conversational information into our model, we modify the Equ. 1 by injecting $\mathbf{g}_{i-1}$:

$$\mathbf{h}_{1:m}^{i} = \text{Encoder}([\mathbf{x}_1^i : \mathbf{g}_{i-1}], ..., [\mathbf{x}_m^i : \mathbf{g}_{i-1}])$$

where $[:]$ denotes a concatenation operation.

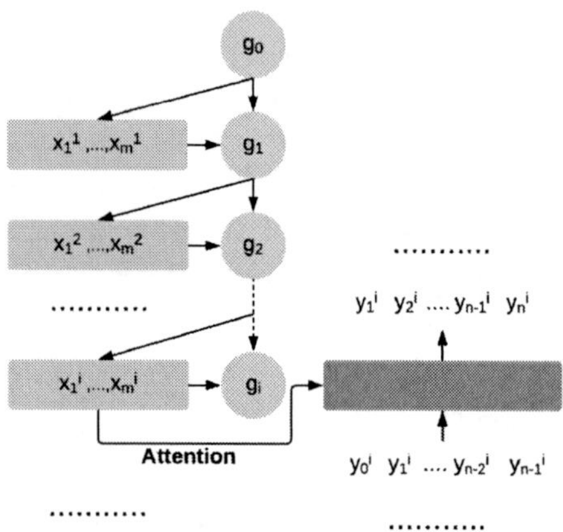

Figure 2: Overall architecture of our semantic parser. We omit the pointer network due to lack of space.

Similar to memory networks (Sukhbaatar et al., 2015), it is essential to give the decoder a direct access to the last k utterances, if we want to leverage the discourse information effectively. Hence, we concatenate the previous k utterance $\{\mathbf{x}_{i-k}, .., \mathbf{x}_{i-1}\}$ with the current utterance. Now Equ. 2 is rewritten as:

$$\mathbf{c}_t^i = \text{Attention}(\mathbf{h}_{1:m}^{i-k}, .., \mathbf{h}_{1:m}^{i-1}, \mathbf{h}_{1:m}^{i}, \mathbf{s}_{t-1}^i)$$

In addition, since the importance of the concatenated utterances is different, it is significant to differentiate these utterances to reduce confusion. Therefore, as suggested by Suhr et al. (2018), we add relative position embeddings $\mathrm{E}_{pos}[\cdot]$ to the utterances when we compute attention scores. Depending on their distances from the current utterance, we append $\mathrm{E}_{pos}[0], .., \mathrm{E}_{pos}[k]$ to the previous utterances respectively.

3 Experiments

Dataset Semantic paring is crucial to dialogue systems, especially for multi-turn conversations. Additionally, understanding users' intentions and extracting salient requirements play an important role in the dialogue-related semantic parsing. We use a dataset created by Srivastava et al. (2017) as a case study to explore the performance of semantic parsing in dialogue systems. This dataset is collected from an email assistant, which can help users to manage their emails. As shown in Table 3 Users can type some human sentences from the interface. Then the email assistant can automatically convert the natural sentences to the machine-understandable logical forms.

dialog history
... *user*: Define the concept " contact " *user*: add field " email " to concept " contact " *user*: create contact " Mom " ...
logical form
... (defineConcept (stringNoun " contact ")) (addFieldToConcept contact (stringNoun " email ")) (createInstanceByFullNames contact (stringNoun " mom ")) ...

Table 3: A partial conversation from the data

Following Srivastava et al. (2017), we partition the dataset into a training fold (93 conversations) and a test fold (20 conversations) as well. However, this partition might be different from Srivastava et al. (2017), as they only release the raw Email Assistant dataset. The total number of user utterances is 4759, the number of sessions is 113, and the mean/max of the number of utterances per interactive session is 42/273.

3.1 Main Results

Prior to this work, Srivastava et al. (2017) also incorporate the conversational context into a CCG parser (Zettlemoyer and Collins, 2007). CCG requires extensive hand-feature engineering to construct text-based features. However, neural semantic parsers have been demonstrating impressive improvement over various and numerous dataset (Suhr et al., 2018; Dong and Lapata, 2018). Hence, we explore both RNN-based (Bahdanau et al., 2014) and transformer-based (Vaswani et al., 2017) architectures for our attentional seq2seq model, denoted as *RNNS2S* and *Transformer* respectively. Hyperparameters, architecture details, and other experimental choices are detailed in the supplementary material. Unless otherwise mentioned, we use 3 previous utterances as the history. Since there is no validation set, we use 10-fold cross validation over the training set to find the best parameters.

Table 4 demonstrates the accuracy of different models. Our RNNS2S baseline already surpasses the previous SOTA result with a large margin. However, since we use our own partition, this comparison should not be as a reference. Both pointer network and conversational architecture dramatically advance the accuracy. Finally, our transformer model combining these two techniques obtains a new SOTA result.

	Accuracy
Previous methods	
Seq2seq (Srivastava et al., 2017)	52.3
SPCon (Srivastava et al., 2017)	62.3
Our models	
RNNS2S	68.0
RNNS2S + pointer	69.3
RNNS2S + context	69.8
RNNS2S + context + pointer	70.5
Transformer	69.3
Transformer + pointer	72.2
Transformer + context	71.0
Transformer + context + pointer	**73.4**

Table 4: Test accuracy on Email Assistant dataset. **Bold** indicates the best result. SPCon is the best CCG parser with contextual information in Srivastava et al. (2017)

3.2 Analysis

In this section we provide some deep analysis on our models. Since we see the same trend in both RNNS2S and Transformer, we only report the analysis of RNNS2S. The supplementary material reports the analysis of Transformer.

The effects of the copy mechanism We analyze the test data, and count the number of errors that can be rectified by introducing the pointer network for both vanilla and context-dependent seq2seq models. In the test set, we identify that a total of 37 errors made by the seq2seq model and 36 errors made by the seq2seq+context model can be rectified by the copy mechanism. According to Figure 3, our pointer network fixes at least half of the incorrect instances. Clearly, the pointer mechanism cannot solve all copy-related errors. After scrutinizing the system-generated results, we realize that the pointer network tends to retain the copy mode once it is triggered. This phenomenon is consistent with the observations by See et al. (2017). Consequently, the extra copies impinge on the accuracy of the system.

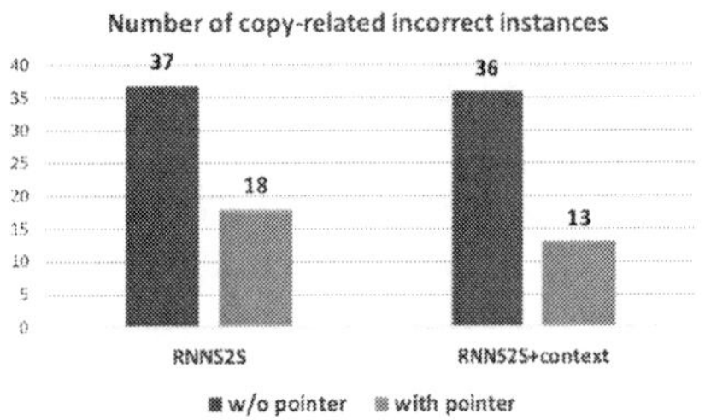

Figure 3: Number of copy-related incorrect instances that can be corrected by a pointer network.

The effects of the context-dependent mechanism. In the experiments, our context-dependent mechanism is shown to be able to address context-related errors, especially when user's input implies a complex and compositional command. These complex commands usually involve a series of complicated actions, as shown in Table 5. According to Table 6, our context-dependent model rectifies 27 out of 68 context-related errors.

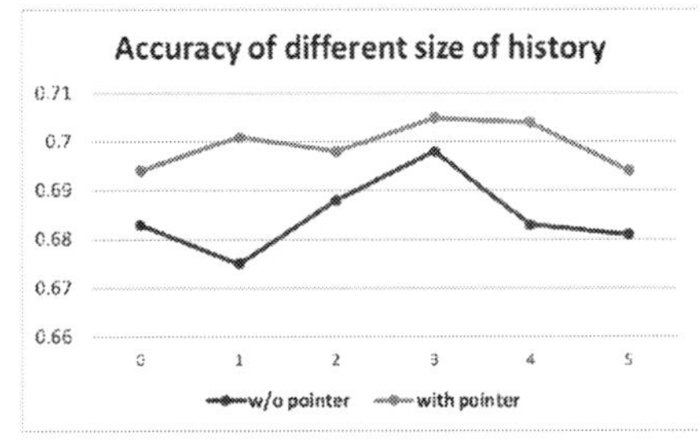

Figure 4: Accuracy of different size of history.

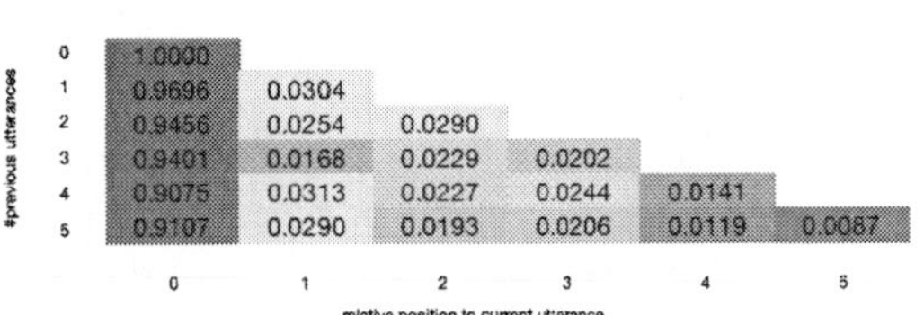

Figure 5: Heat map of different size of history.

Since we notice that previous utterances can also obfuscate the model, we conduct an ablation study over the size of history. As shown in Figure 4, incorporating 3 previous utterances reach the best performance. According to Figure 5, we believe that incorporating 3 previous utterances covers sufficient contextual information. Less than this number, the system cannot better utilize context, while the salient information is contaminated by the extra history. The same behavior is observed in Transformer model. We argue that the size of the effective history would be dependent

utterance:
Set recipient to Mom's email . Set subject to hello and send the email
logical form:
(doSeq (setFieldFromFieldVal (getProbMutableFieldByFieldName body) (evalField (getProbFieldByInstanceName-AndFieldName inbox body))) (doSeq (setFieldFromFieldVal (getProbMutableFieldByFieldName recipient_list) (eval-Field (getProbFieldByInstanceNameAndFieldName inbox sender))) (send email)))

Table 5: An example of complex and compositional commands.

	#incorrect
complex command	
RNNS2S	39
RNNS2S + context	20
context dependency	
RNNS2S	29
RNNS2S + context	21

Table 6: Incorrect instances of RNNS2S and context-dependent RNNS2S models in terms of complex commands and context dependency.

on different datasets, but they will demonstrate the same trend.

4 Conclusions

In this work, we explore a neural semantic parser architecture that incorporates conversational context and copy mechanism. These modelling improvements are solidly grounded by our analysis, and they significantly boost the performance of the base model. As a result, our best architecture establish a new state-of-the-art on the Email Assistant dataset. In the future, we would explore other architectural innovations for the system, for example, the neural denoising mechanisms.

5 Acknowledgement

We would like to thank three anonymous reviewers for their valuable comments and suggestions. This work was supported by the Multimodal Australian ScienceS Imaging and Visualisation Environment (MASSIVE).[1] This work is partly supported by the ARC Future Fellowship FT190100039 to G.H.

References

Dzmitry Bahdanau, Kyunghyun Cho, and Yoshua Bengio. 2014. Neural machine translation by jointly learning to align and translate. *arXiv preprint arXiv:1409.0473*.

Jacob Devlin, Ming-Wei Chang, Kenton Lee, and Kristina Toutanova. 2018. Bert: Pre-training of deep bidirectional transformers for language understanding.

Li Dong and Mirella Lapata. 2016. Language to logical form with neural attention. *arXiv preprint arXiv:1601.01280*.

Li Dong and Mirella Lapata. 2018. Coarse-to-fine decoding for neural semantic parsing. *arXiv preprint arXiv:1805.04793*.

Sergey Edunov, Myle Ott, Michael Auli, and David Grangier. 2018. Understanding back-translation at scale. *arXiv preprint arXiv:1808.09381*.

Robin Jia and Percy Liang. 2017. Adversarial examples for evaluating reading comprehension systems. *arXiv preprint arXiv:1707.07328*.

Diederik P Kingma and Jimmy Ba. 2014. Adam: A method for stochastic optimization. *arXiv preprint arXiv:1412.6980*.

Samuel Läubli, Rico Sennrich, and Martin Volk. 2018. Has machine translation achieved human parity? a case for document-level evaluation. *arXiv preprint arXiv:1808.07048*.

Wang Ling, Edward Grefenstette, Karl Moritz Hermann, Tomáš Kočiský, Andrew Senior, Fumin Wang, and Phil Blunsom. 2016. Latent predictor networks for code generation. *arXiv preprint arXiv:1603.06744*.

Romain Paulus, Caiming Xiong, and Richard Socher. 2017. A deep reinforced model for abstractive summarization. *arXiv preprint arXiv:1705.04304*.

Maxim Rabinovich, Mitchell Stern, and Dan Klein. 2017. Abstract syntax networks for code generation and semantic parsing. *arXiv preprint arXiv:1704.07535*.

Abigail See, Peter J Liu, and Christopher D Manning. 2017. Get to the point: Summarization with pointer-generator networks. *arXiv preprint arXiv:1704.04368*.

Shashank Srivastava, Amos Azaria, and Tom M Mitchell. 2017. Parsing natural language conversations using contextual cues. In *IJCAI*, pages 4089–4095.

Alane Suhr, Srinivasan Iyer, and Yoav Artzi. 2018. Learning to map context-dependent sentences to executable formal queries. *arXiv preprint arXiv:1804.06868*.

---

[1] https://www.massive.org.au/

Sainbayar Sukhbaatar, Jason Weston, Rob Fergus, et al. 2015. End-to-end memory networks. In *Advances in neural information processing systems*, pages 2440–2448.

Ashish Vaswani, Noam Shazeer, Niki Parmar, Jakob Uszkoreit, Llion Jones, Aidan N Gomez, Łukasz Kaiser, and Illia Polosukhin. 2017. Attention is all you need. In *Advances in Neural Information Processing Systems*, pages 5998–6008.

Luke Zettlemoyer and Michael Collins. 2007. Online learning of relaxed ccg grammars for parsing to logical form. In *Proceedings of the 2007 Joint Conference on Empirical Methods in Natural Language Processing and Computational Natural Language Learning (EMNLP-CoNLL)*, pages 678–687.

Luke S Zettlemoyer and Michael Collins. 2009. Learning context-dependent mappings from sentences to logical form. In *Proceedings of the Joint Conference of the 47th Annual Meeting of the ACL and the 4th International Joint Conference on Natural Language Processing of the AFNLP: Volume 2-Volume 2*, pages 976–984. Association for Computational Linguistics.

A   Implementation Details

In RNNS2S model, at the utterance level, a one-layer bidiretional RNNs for the encoder, while the decoder is a two-layer RNNs. We use a one-layer RNNs to represent the conversational information flow. All RNNs use LSTM cells, with a hidden size of 128. The sizes of word embeddings and position embeddings are 128 and 50 respectively. We train our models for 10 epochs by Adam optimizer (Kingma and Ba, 2014) with an initial learning rate of 0.001. The batch size of non-context training is 16, while the context variant is 1.

For Transformer model, we use 3 identical transformer blocks for both encoder and decoder. Within each block, the size of the embeddings is 256, while the feed forward network has 512 neurons. We set the size of heads to 4. The conversational encoder is a one-layer RNNs with the size of 256. The optimizer and training schedule is same as Vaswani et al. (2017), except $warmup\_steps = 500$. Due to the warmup steps, We train this model for 14 epochs. The batch size is same as that of RNNS2S.

B   Analysis of Transformer

The effects of the pointer mechanism According to Figure 6, half of the incorrect instances are fixed by the pointer mechanism.

	#incorrect
complex command	
Transformer	35
Transformer + context	24
context dependency	
Transformer	25
Transformer + context	16

Table 7:   Incorrect instances of Transformer and context-dependent Transformer models in terms of complex commands and context dependency.

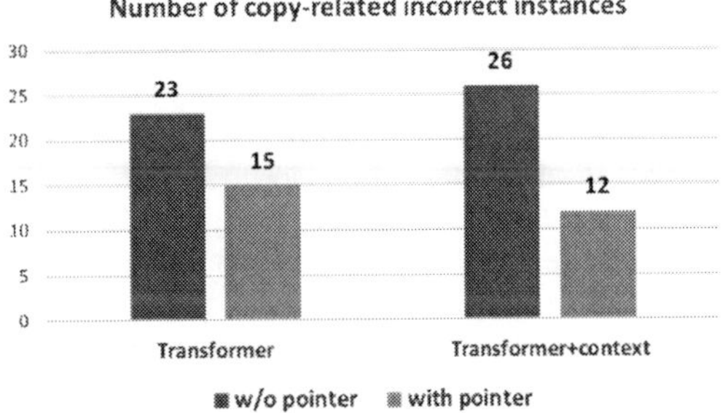

Figure 6: Number of copy-related incorrect instances that can be corrected by a pointer network.

The effects of the context-dependent mechanism. Similarly, incorporating the contextual information is able to address the context-oriented issues by a larger margin (see Table 7).

Finally, as observed in the main paper, having an access to the 3 previous utterances achieves the best performance.

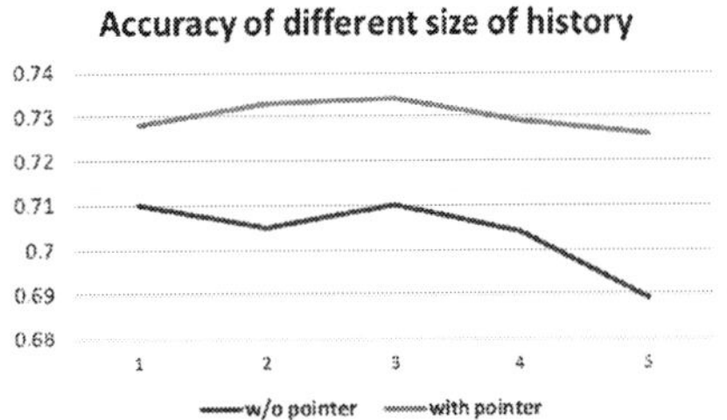

Figure 7: Accuracy of different size of history.

CNL^{ER}: A Controlled Natural Language for Specifying and Verbalising Entity Relationship Models

Bayzid Ashik Hossain, Gayathri Rajan and Rolf Schwitter
Department of Computing
Macquarie University, Sydney, Australia
{bayzid-ashik.hossain|rolf.schwitter}@mq.edu.au
gayathri.rajan@students.mq.edu.au

Abstract

The first step towards designing an information system is conceptual modelling where domain experts and knowledge engineers identify the necessary information together to build an information system. Entity relationship modelling is one of the most popular conceptual modelling techniques that represents an information system in terms of entities, attributes and relationships. Entity relationship models are constructed graphically but are often difficult to understand by domain experts. To overcome this problem, we suggest to verbalise these models in a controlled natural language. In this paper, we present CNL^{ER}, a controlled natural language for specifying and verbalising entity relationship (ER) models that not only solves the verbalisation problem for these models but also provides the benefits of automatic verification and validation, and semantic round-tripping which makes the communication process transparent between the domain experts and the knowledge engineers.

1 Introduction

An information system is a piece of software that has integrated components for organizing and analyzing data to aid decision making in an organization (Laudon and Laudon, 2015). One of the major roles of an information system is to accumulate data, turn it into information and later transform that information into organizational knowledge (Bourgeois, 2014). To be successful an information system always depends on a good design and conceptual modelling is the first step in the design process (Olivé, 2007). Information systems are best specified on the conceptual level using a language with names for individuals, concepts, and relations that occur in the application domain. Such a language is easy to understand by the domain experts and enhances correctness, compati-

bility, productivity and clarity in information system design (Halpin, 1998). Conceptual modelling involves different parties (e.g., domain experts and knowledge engineers) who brainstorm together to identify the necessary information for building the system (Hossain and Schwitter, 2018). After identifying the required information, knowledge engineers build a conceptual model of the information system by using conceptual modelling techniques such as entity relationship modelling (ERM) (Richard, 1990; Frantiska, 2018), object oriented modelling (UML) (O'Regan, 2017), or object role modelling (ORM) (Halpin, 2009).

One of the problems with these models is that they are constructed graphically and as a result they are often hard to understand for domain experts (Jarrar et al., 2006). Another problem with these conceptual modelling techniques is that they have no formal semantics; therefore, they are not machine comprehensible, do not support automatic verification and validation nor automatic reasoning (Calvanese, 2013).

To overcome these problems previous works used logic in parallel with traditional conceptual modelling techniques (Lutz, 2002; Berardi et al., 2005; Franconi et al., 2012). There are tools (Fillottrani et al., 2012; Lembo et al., 2016b,a) that allow knowledge engineers to draw the conceptual model and then translate the model constructs into a logical representation. This logical representation is then used to verify and validate the model. Using logic with traditional conceptual modelling techniques also introduces some problems like the difficulty to generate logical representations. Furthermore, it is not easy to understand these logical representations for domain experts since no well established methodology is available to make this process transparent (Calvanese, 2013).

Recent research on conceptual modelling showed that using a controlled natural language

"

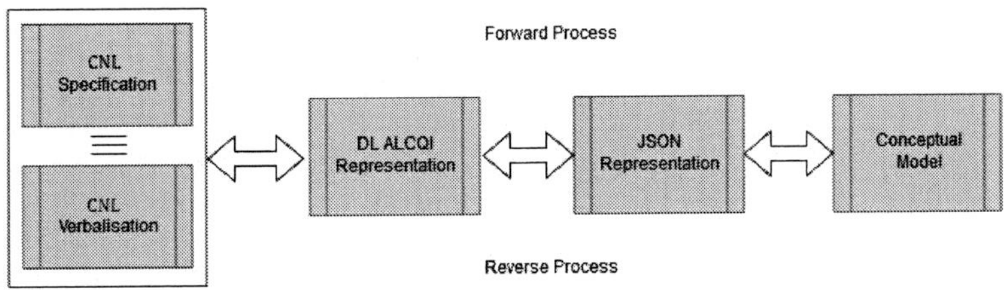

Figure 1: A CNL based conceptual modelling framework

(CNL) for specification and verbalisation can overcome the problems introduced by logic in the conceptual modelling process (Hossain and Schwitter, 2018). A CNL can be defined as a subset of natural language that is obtained by constraining the grammar and vocabulary in order to eliminate the ambiguity as well as the complexity of the language. A CNL can be designed in such a way that it has well defined computational properties and thus can be translated unambiguously into a formal representation (Schwitter, 2010). Using a CNL in conceptual modelling helps the domain experts to understand the conceptual models through specification and verbalisation, allows the machine to understand the models as the CNL can be translated into a formal representation, and therefore supports automated reasoning and question answering.

2 Motivation

The idea of using natural language for conceptual modelling is not new but previous approaches (Saeki et al., 1989; Mich, 1996; Harmain and Gaizauskas, 2003; Ambriola and Gervasi, 2006; Ibrahim and Ahmad, 2010) did not constrain the natural language enough and did not use logic to formally represent the conceptual models. Furthermore, the idea of semantic round-tripping from a specification to a conceptual model and from a conceptual model to a specification (verbalisation) is novel in this context. A recent survey (Störrle, 2017) on conceptual models showed that there are three modes of conceptual modelling: 1. informal modelling for cognition and communication; 2. semi-formal modelling for planning and documentation; and 3. formal modelling for generation and contracts. In the software industry 70-79% of the modelling is done informally (Störrle, 2017).

We want to use CNL in the conceptual modelling process to overcome the problems that occur in traditional conceptual modelling approaches. We want to bridge the gap between an informal and formal conceptual model. We also want to offer verbalisation for ERM. ERM is frequently used in the industry and has no verbalisation support. Existing tools that support creating ERM models do not provide the facility of writing specifications for conceptual models and therefore semantic round-tripping is not possible. We have developed a CNL-based conceptual modelling framework [Fig. 3] that supports the following points:

1. Writing textual specifications for the conceptual modelling process.

2. Description logic based common formal representation (DL $ALCQI$) for different conceptual models.

3. Generating a conceptual model from a written specification and the other way around.

4. Verification and validation of the written specification.

In this paper we present CNL^{ER}, a controlled natural language that is specially designed to specify and verbalize ERM constructs.

3 ERM Constructs

An ERM represents an information system in terms of entities, attributes and relationships (Song and Chen, 2009). ERM is mainly used to design relational databases and to do the planning and requirement analysis of an information system. The outcome of an ERM process is a graphical model often known as ER diagram (ERD). The basic components of an ERD are entities, attributes, and relationships [Fig. 2].

An *entity* is a real world object having independent existence (e.g., person, place, organisation) (Song and Chen, 2009). An entity is also known as a class or a concept. There are two types

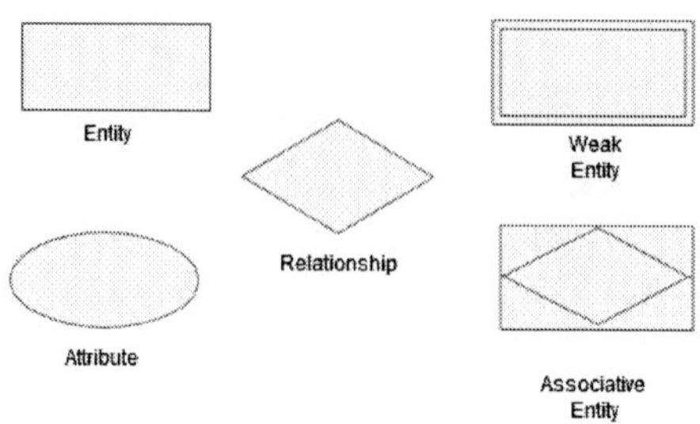

Figure 2: ERM constructs

of entities: (1) strong entities that have key attributes to uniquely identify each instance of an entity (e.g., student has student id as a key attribute); and (2) weak entities that do not have any key attributes and they depend on other strong entities to get identified (e.g., a room can not exist without a building, so "room" is a weak entity whereas "building" is a strong entity).

An *attribute* indicates a property or characteristic of an entity (Li and Chen, 2009). For example, if a student is an entity then "student name", "student id", and "phone number" would be the attributes for that student. Attributes help us to differentiate between entities. An attribute can be single valued (e.g., "student name") or multivalued (e.g., "skills"). A single valued attribute or a collection of single valued attributes that identify an instance of an entity uniquely is known as A key attribute or a primary key.

A *relationship* depicts the association between or among the entities. For example, if "student" and "program" are entities then in the fact "student is enrolled in program", the expression "is enrolled in" is the relationship between "student" and "program". Every relationship has a cardinality which defines the number of occurrences (minimum and maximum) of one entity that is related to a single occurrence of the other entity (Song and Chen, 2009). Based on the form of cardinality, we can divide a relationship in ERM into three types: one-to-one, one-to-many and many-to-many. Sometimes a many-to-many relationship acts as an entity itself which is known as an associative entity. An associative entity can have attributes that represent the properties of the corresponding relationship (Li and Chen, 2009). For example, if "student" and "course" are entities then the facts "every student studies 1 or more courses" and "every course is studied by 1 or more students" indicate that "student" and "course" have a many-

to-many relationship. So the relationship between these two entities can act as an associative entity. We can consider "study details" as an associative entity that can have "study start date" and "study end date" as attributes.

Entity Declaration

1. Student is an entity type.
2. Department is an entity type.
3. Course is an entity type.
4. Teacher is an entity type.
5. Enrolment is an entity type.
6. Section is an entity type.

Attribute Declaration

7. Student id is of integer data type.
8. Student name is of string data type.
9. Department number is of integer data type.
10. Department name is of string data type.
11. Teacher id is of integer data type.
12. Teacher name is of string data type.
13. Course id is of integer data type.
14. Course name is of string data type.
15. Enrolment semester is of integer data type.
16. Enrolment grade is of integer data type.
17. Section id is of integer data type.
18. Section name is of string data type.

Relationship Declaration

19. Student belongs to department.
20. Department contains student.
21. Teacher works in department.
22. Department employs teacher.
23. Course is offered by department.
24. Department offers course.
25. Course is offered in sections.
26. Teacher teaches students in course.
27. Enrolment associates
    "Teacher teaches students in course".

Constraint Declaration

28. Every student belongs to exactly 1 department.
29. Every department contains 1 or more students.
30. Every teacher works in exactly 1 department.
31. Every department employs 1 or more teachers.
32. Every course is offered by exactly 1 department.
33. Every department offers 1 or more courses.
34. Every enrolment includes exactly 1 teacher.
35. Every enrolment includes exactly 1 student.
36. Every enrolment includes exactly 1 course.
37. Every student owns exactly 1 student id and owns exactly 1 student name.
38. Every teacher owns exactly 1 teacher id and owns exactly 1 teacher name.
39. Every course owns exactly 1 course id and owns exactly 1 course name.
40. Every department owns exactly 1 department number and owns exactly 1 department name.
41. Every enrolment consists of exactly 1 enrolment semester and consists of exactly 1 enrolment grade.
42. Every section is dependent of exactly 1 course.

Table 1: Extended example scenario from the ER paper (Frantiska, 2018) expressed using CNL^{ER}

Listing 1: Grammar rules for entity declaration

```
% Input:  Student is an entity.
% Output: entity(A, student)

s([mode:M, type:entity, sem:L1-L2]) -->
  np([mode:M, num:sg, type:entity, pos:subj, sem:L1-L2]),
  [is, an, entity, type], ['.'].

np([mode:M, num:N, type:T, pos:P, sem:L1-L2]) -->
  noun([mode:M, num:N, type:T, pos:P, sem:L1-L2]).

noun([mode:proc, num:N, type:entity, pos:P, sem:[L1|L2]-[[L0|L1]|L2]]) -->
  lexical_rule([cat:noun, num:N, type:entity, pos:P, sem:L0]).

noun([mode:gen, num:N, type:entity, pos:P, sem:[[L0|L1]|L2]-[L1|L2]]) -->
  {lexicon([cat:noun, wform:WForm, num:N, type:entity, pos:P, arg:_X, sem:L0])},
  WForm.
```

4 CNL^{ER} for ERM Constructs

In this section we discuss how to express ERM constructs using CNL^{ER}. For this purpose, we have taken an example scenario from the paper (Frantiska, 2018) and extended it by adding a weak entity and modifying the associative entity. CNL^{ER} has a distinct sentence format to declare an entity in ERM. For example, to define the fact that a student is an entity, CNL^{ER} has the following sentence pattern with a noun (*student*) in subject position, followed by a copula (*is*) and the key phrase *an entity type* in object position (e.g., see sentences 1-6 in table [1]).

CNL^{ER} also has a particular sentence pattern to declare attributes in ERM. For example, to specify an attribute of type integer, CNL^{ER} uses a sentence that contains a previously declared entity name (e.g., *student*) followed by an attribute name (e.g., *id*); this forms a data property name (*student id*) which is followed by a copula (*is*), and the key phrase (e.g., *of integer data type*). For example, sentences 7-18 in Table [1] show the attribute declarations for the example scenario.

To declare a relationship, we use a declared entity type name (e.g., *student*) in subject position and a declared entity type name (e.g., *department*) in object position with a relationship name (e.g., *belongs to*) in between. (e.g., see sentences 19-27 in table [1] for relationship declarations).

To define cardinality constraints over the relationships, CNL^{ER} uses a quantifying expression followed by entities and attributes: a quantifier (*every*) in subject position and either a quantifier (*0 or more, 1 or more*) or a cardinality constraint

(*at least, at most, exactly*) in object position. For example, to define a one-to-one relationship cardinality between the entities "student" and "department", sentence (28) in table [1] is used, and to define a one-to-many relationship cardinality, sentence (29) in table [1] is used.

In order to define a many-to-many relationship in CNL^{ER}, we have to write two sentences that express the relationship between the entities in both direction. For example, to express a may-to-many relationship between "student" and "course", we have to write the following two sentences.

- *Every* student studies *1 or more* courses.

- *Every* course is studied by *1 or more* students.

To declare an associative entity in CNL^{ER} (e.g., "enrolment"), we have to declare the entity first. After that the entity needs to be linked with a many-to-many relationship using a predefined word "associates". The sentence 27 in table [1] declares an associative entity that links the ternary relationship among a teacher, a student and a unit. The relationship "includes" in the sentences 34, 35 and 36 of table [1] is predefined and can only be used together with an associative entity. An associative entity can have attributes like other entities. For example, sentence 41 in table [1] specifies attributes for the associative entity "enrolment".

To declare a weak entity in CNL^{ER}, we have to declare both strong and weak entities first as entities (e.g., "course" and "section" in table [1]). After that we need to specify that the weak entity is dependent of the strong entity. For example, to

123

declare that a section is a weak entity, sentence 42 specifies that "section" is a dependent of the "course" entity by using a predefined relationship "dependent of" in table [1].

5 Grammar

We use a definite clause grammar (DCG) (Pereira and Shieber, 2002) to process and translate a CNL^{ER} specification. The key advantage of using a DCG is that it implements a logic program that allows us to build a bi-directional grammar. The grammar translates the CNL^{ER} sentences into a corresponding internal description logic (DL) representation. This internal DL representation is further processed to generate an ERD.

A specification in CNL^{ER} consists of function words and content words. Function words (quantifiers, cardinality constraints and operators) describe the structure of the sentences and the number of these function words is fixed. In contrast, content words (nouns and verbs) are domain specific and are added to the lexicon during the writing process when they are declared. It is important to note that the bi-directional DCG contains grammar rules that translate every CNL^{ER} sentence into the internal DL representation and vice versa; this enable semantic round-tripping in our conceptual modelling framework. In this paper, we discuss the DCG rules that process some of the core ERM constructs. Below we discuss the grammar rules that process entity, attribute, relationship, constraint and associative entity declarations.

5.1 Entity Declaration

Listing [1] shows the grammar rules for an entity declaration. The first grammar rule states that a declarative sentence (s) consists of a noun phrase (np) and a key phrase ("*is an entity type*"), followed by a full stop (.). The grammar rule contains additional arguments that implement feature structures in the form of *attribute:value* pairs whereas the value can be a simple term or a complex term (for example in the form of a difference list: *[Head|Tail]-Tail*). The feature structure *mode:M* specifies whether the rule is used in the processing or generating mode and the feature structure *type:entity* specifies the type of the ERM construct. The feature structure *sem:L1-L2* is used to build up the semantic representation for an entity. The grammar rule for the noun phrase (np) con-

tains a feature structure (*num:N*) that deals with number agreement (singular or plural), a feature structure (*arg:X*) that defines the argument of an entity, and one (*pos:subj*) that specifies the position of the noun. Finally, the feature structure *cat:noun* specifies a noun and *wform:WForm* specifies a word form consisting of potentially multiple elements. To extract an entity from the input list, a lexical rule *lexical_rule/1* is used that generates lexical entries with their corresponding singular and plural forms (e.g., student and students) for that entity with the help of a morphological component.

5.2 Attribute Declaration

To process a sentence that is used to declare an attribute, we use similar grammar rules as shown in listing [1] but with a different key phrase (e.g., *of integer data type*). To process an attribute and its data type, a lexical rule is used that extracts the attribute from the input list by excluding the copula and the key phrase and by identifying the type (e.g., integer, string, date) from the key phrase. After that the lexical rule is used to insert the attribute and its type information into the lexicon.

5.3 Relationship Declaration

Listing [2] shows the grammar rules for a relationship declaration. The first grammar rule states again that a declarative sentence (s) consists of a noun phrase (np) and a verb phrase (vp), followed by a full stop (.). The feature structures for the mode declaration and the semantic representation are similar to the entity declaration whereas the feature structure *type:fact* specifies the ERM construct relationship.

The second grammar rule states that a verb phrase (vp) consists of a verb ($verb$) and a noun phrase (np). In the case of processing, the grammar rule for the verb consists of a lexical rule (*lexical_rule/1*) that extracts a relationship from the input list by identifying the noun phrases in the subject and object position. After that, the lexical rule adds the extracted relationship to the lexicon and adds the semantic representation (*L0*) for that relationship to the outgoing part (*[[L0|L1]|L2]*) of the difference list. In the case of generating, the grammar rule for a verb removes the semantic representation (*L0*) from the incoming part (*[[L0|L1]|L2]*) of the difference list and tries to find this representation in the lexicon in order to return the corresponding lexical entry.

Listing 2: Grammar rules for relationship declaration

```
% Input:  Student is enrolled in program.
% Output: [entity(A, student), relation(A, B, is_enrolled_in), entity(B, program)]

s([mode:M, type:fact, sem:L1-L3]) -->
  np([mode:M, num:N, type:fact, pos:subj, arg:X, sem:L1-L2]),
  vp([mode:M, num:N, type:fact, arg:X, sem:L2-L3]),
  ['.'].

vp([mode:M, num:N, type:fact, arg:X, sem:L1-L3])-->
  verb([mode:M, num:N, type:fact, arg:X, arg:Y, sem:L1-L2]),
  np([mode:M, num:_N, type:fact, pos:obj, arg:Y, sem:L2-L3]).

np([mode:M, num:N, type:T, pos:P, arg:X, sem:L1-L2) -->
  noun([mode:M, num:N, type:T, pos:P, arg:X, sem:L1-L2]).

noun([mode:proc, num:N, type:fact, pos:P, arg:X, sem:[L1|L2]-[[L0|L1]|L2]]) -->
  {lexicon([cat:noun, wform:WForm, num:N, type:entity, pos:P, arg:X, sem:L0])},
  WForm.

noun([mode:gen, num:N, type:fact, pos:P, arg:X, sem:[[L0|L1]|L2]-[L1|L2]]) -->
  {lexicon([cat:noun, wform:WForm, num:N, type:entity, pos:P, arg:X, sem:L0])},
  WForm.

verb([mode:proc, num:N, type:fact, arg:X, arg:Y, sem:[L1|L2]-[[L0|L1]|L2]]) -->
  lexical_rule([cat:verb, num:N, arg:X, arg:Y, sem:L0]).

verb([mode:gen, num:N, type:fact, arg:X, arg:Y, sem:[[L0|L1]|L2]-[L1|L2]])-->
  {lexicon([cat:verb, wform:WForm, num:N, type:brel, arg:X, arg:Y, sem:L0])},
  WForm.
```

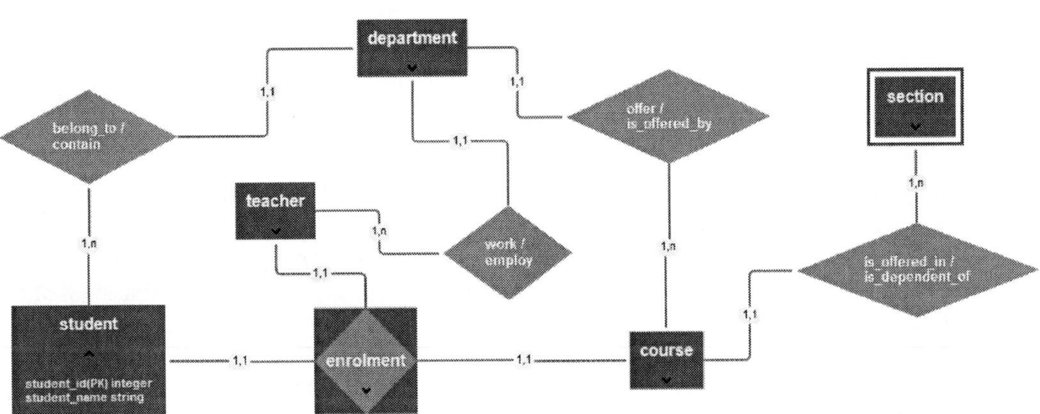

Figure 3: ERD of the example scenario (Frantiska, 2018) generated by the proposed CNL based conceptual modelling framework.

5.4 Constraint Declaration

To process a sentence that declares a cardinality constraint over a relationship, we use a grammar rule that is quite similar to the grammar rule in listing [2] with an additional quantifier (*qnt*) in subject position and a constraint (*cst*) in the object position. Note that the grammar rules for a quantifier and a cardinality constraint play an important role because they provide the relevant structure for the internal representation. For example, the grammar rule for the universal quantifier (*every*) results in a pattern of the form *sem:forall(X, Res ==> Sco)* that takes a restrictor (*Res*) that contains the information derived from the noun phrase in sub-

Listing 3: Grammar rules for associative entity declaration

```
% Fact Type "Association"
% Input:   Enrolment associates "student is enrolled in program".
% Output:  [entity(A, enrollment), associates(A, B), entity(C, student),
%           B#relation(C, D, is_enrolled_in), entity(D, program)]

s([mode:M, type:fact_ob, sem:L1-L4]) -->
  np([mode:M, num:N, type:fact, pos:subj, arg:X, sem:L1-L2]),
  verb([mode:M, wform:[associates], num:N, type:fact_ob, arg:X, arg:R, sem:L2-L3]),
  ['"'],
  s([mode:M, type:ob_fact, rel:R, sem:L3-L4]),
  ['"', '.'].

np([mode:M, num:N, type:T, pos:P, arg:X, sem:L1-L2) -->
  noun([mode:M, num:N, type:T, pos:P, arg:X, sem:L1-L2]).

noun([mode:proc, num:N, type:fact, pos:P, arg:X, sem:[L1|L2]-[[L0|L1]|L2]]) -->
  {lexicon([cat:noun, wform:WForm, num:N, type:entity, pos:P, arg:X, sem:L0])},
  WForm.

noun([mode:gen, num:N, type:fact, pos:P, arg:X, sem:[[L0|L1]|L2]-[L1|L2]]) -->
  {lexicon([cat:noun, wform:WForm, num:N, type:entity, pos:P, arg:X, sem:L0])},
  WForm.

verb([mode:proc, wform:WForm, num:N, type:fact_ob, arg:X, arg:Y,
      sem:[L1|L2]-[[L0|L1]|L2]]) -->
  {lexicon([cat:verb, wform:WForm, num:N, type:ob_rel, arg:X, arg:Y, sem:L0])},
  WForm.

verb([mode:gen, wform:WForm, num:N, type:fact_ob, arg:X, arg:Y,
      sem:[[L0|L1]|L2]-[L1|L2]]) -->
  {lexicon([cat:verb, wform:WForm, num:N, type:ob_rel, arg:X, arg:Y, sem:L0])},
  WForm.
```

ject position and the scope (*Sco*) that contains the information derived from the verb phrase and returns a pattern for an implication. In the case of a cardinality constraint that pattern might have the following form: *exists(X, Res & min(L) : Sco : max(U))*. Note also that the restrictor and scope are built up in these grammar rules with the help of specific feature structures.

5.5 Associative Entity Declaration

Listing [3] shows an excerpt of the grammar rules that are used to process and generate sentences for an associative entity. The first rule reuses the rule for a relationship and uses a key verb word (*associates*) to process an associative entity declaration. The first rule states that a sentence consists of a noun phrase (*np*) in subject position, a verb (*verb*) and a sentence in object position that refers to a particular relationship in the lexicon.

The grammar rule for *np* is the same as we used for the relationship declaration (see listing [2]) and for the ease of understanding we keep it in listing [3]. The feature structure *rel:R* in the sentence rule

in object position states that this is a "reified" relationship available in the lexicon and unlike the relationship rule stated in listing [2], it does not need to be processed by the lexical rule (*lexical_rule/1*).

This relationship could be a binary relationship or a ternary relationship. This grammar rule is used to link an entity to a relationship that makes the entity an associative entity.

6   Evaluation

We took an example scenario from the ER paper (Frantiska, 2018), extended the scenario and expressed the scenario in CNL^{ER} (see table [1]). After that we translated the CNL^{ER} specification into an internal DL representation and translated the resulting ERM constructs into a RuleML (Boley et al., 2010) JSON[1] representation (see figure 4). This JSON representation is used by our conceptual modelling tool for building an interactive diagram. The implementation of our conceptual modelling tool is based on the GoJS 2.0 frame-

---

[1]https://wiki.ruleml.org/index.php/RuleML_in_JSON

```
{"And":
    {"Atom":
        [{
              "Rel": "entity",
              "Ind": "department",
              "Var": "X"
         },
         {
              "Rel": "relation",
              "Ind": "employ",
              "Var": ["X","Y"]
         },
         {
              "Rel": "entity",
              "Ind": "teacher",
              "Var": "Y"
         }]
    }
}
```

Figure 4: RuleML JSON representation of the sentence (22) from table [1].

work[2].

The JSON representation is parsed to identify the entities, attributes and relationships for the resulting diagram. Unique entity names and relationship names are identified and added to a node array. Relationships are assessed individually to identify the links and added to a link array. These constructs are then translated into the internal GoJS representation that is used by the GoJS engine to render the diagram in a web browser (see figure 3). New entities, attributes and relationships can be added to a diagram and existing components can be modified or deleted by the user. Building a new diagram from scratch is also possible, since we designed the graphical editor for conceptual modelling as a standalone tool. When a diagram is saved, its internal GoJS representation is produced from which the internal JSON representation can be derived to generate the CNL^{ER} specification again.

To evaluate the controlled natural language CNL^{ER}, we then checked the expressiveness of the language in terms of ERM constructs. We compared the constructed diagram with the textual CNL^{ER} specification of the scenario and found that the diagram correctly represented all corresponding entities, attributes and relationships. Furthermore, it is possible to generate a semantically equivalent CNL^{ER} specification from the diagram in a round-tripping fashion.

---

[2] https://gojs.net/latest/index.html

7 Discussion

In this paper we presented CNL^{ER}, a controlled natural language that can be used to specify and verbalise ER models. Our main objective is to develop a controlled natural language based universal conceptual modelling framework where a domain expert can actively participate in the conceptual modelling process with a knowledge engineer. CNL^{ER} is a controlled natural language that can express ERM constructs in natural language and the language processor can translate it into a formal language (e.g., any serialization of DL *AL-CQI* (Lutz, 2002; Berardi et al., 2005; Franconi et al., 2012)). This formal representation can be further used for verification and validation. After that the formal representation can be processed to generate an ERD.

The goal of this work is to improve the current conceptual modelling process and enable domain domain experts to express their knowledge in a well defined subset of natural language that can be used as high-level interface language to construct conceptual models. Future work will investigate the scalability of CNL^{ER} by extending the coverage of the language so that also UML class diagrams (Calvanese, 2013) and ORM diagrams (Franconi et al., 2012) can be expressed in the same grammatical framework. These extensions involve parametrising and modularising the existing grammar to support additional modelling constructs.

8 Conclusion

CNL^{ER} is a high-level specification and verbalisation language for ER models that supports a controlled natural language based conceptual modelling approach. A textual specification of a conceptual model in CNL^{ER} can be translated via an internal representation into a JSON representation that is then used to generate an ER diagram. The translation works also in the other direction and supports the verbalisation of ER diagrams in CNL^{ER}. Because of these properties, CNL^{ER} has the potential to bridge the communication gap between a domain expert and a knowledge engineer in the domain of entity relationship modelling and makes the modelling process at the same time formal in a seemingly informal way.

References

Vincenzo Ambriola and Vincenzo Gervasi. 2006. On the systematic analysis of natural language requirements with circe. *Automated Software Engineering*, 13(1):107–167.

Daniela Berardi, Diego Calvanese, and Giuseppe De Giacomo. 2005. Reasoning on uml class diagrams. *Artificial Intelligence*, 168(1):70–118.

Harold Boley, Adrian Paschke, and Omair Shafiq. 2010. Ruleml 1.0: the overarching specification of web rules. In *International Workshop on Rules and Rule Markup Languages for the Semantic Web*, pages 162–178. Springer.

David Bourgeois. 2014. *Information systems for business and beyond*. The Saylor Foundation.

Diego Calvanese. 2013. *Description Logics for Conceptual Modeling Forms of reasoning on UML Class Diagrams*. EPCL Basic Training Camp.

Pablo R Fillottrani, Enrico Franconi, and Sergio Tessaris. 2012. The icom 3.0 intelligent conceptual modelling tool and methodology. *Semantic Web*, 3(3):293–306.

Enrico Franconi, Alessandro Mosca, and Dmitry Solomakhin. 2012. Orm2: formalisation and encoding in owl2. In *OTM Confederated International Conferences" On the Move to Meaningful Internet Systems"*, pages 368–378. Springer.

Joseph Frantiska. 2018. Entity-relationship diagrams. In *Visualization Tools for Learning Environment Development*, pages 21–30. Springer.

Terry Halpin. 1998. *ORM/NIAM Object-Role Modeling*. Springer Berlin Heidelberg, Berlin, Heidelberg.

Terry Halpin. 2009. Object-role modeling. In *Encyclopedia of Database Systems*, pages 1941–1946. Springer.

HM Harmain and Robert Gaizauskas. 2003. Cmbuilder: A natural language-based case tool for object-oriented analysis. *Automated Software Engineering*, 10(2):157–181.

Bayzid Ashik Hossain and Rolf Schwitter. 2018. Specifying conceptual models using restricted natural language. In *Proceedings of the Australasian Language Technology Association Workshop 2018*, pages 44–52, Dunedin, New Zealand.

Mohd Ibrahim and Rodina Ahmad. 2010. Class diagram extraction from textual requirements using natural language processing (nlp) techniques. In *2010 Second International Conference on Computer Research and Development*, pages 200–204. IEEE.

Mustafa Jarrar, C Maria, and Keet Paolo Dongilli. 2006. Multilingual verbalization of orm conceptual models and axiomatized ontologies.

Kenneth C. Laudon and Jane P. Laudon. 2015. *Management Information Systems: Managing the Digital Firm Plus MyMISLab with Pearson eText – Access Card Package*, 14th edition. Prentice Hall Press, Upper Saddle River, NJ, USA.

Domenico Lembo, Daniele Pantaleone, Valerio Santarelli, and Domenico Fabio Savo. 2016a. Easy owl drawing with the graphol visual ontology language. In *Fifteenth International Conference on the Principles of Knowledge Representation and Reasoning*.

Domenico Lembo, Daniele Pantaleone, Valerio Santarelli, and Domenico Fabio Savo. 2016b. Eddy: A graphical editor for owl 2 ontologies. In *IJCAI*, pages 4252–4253.

Qing Li and Yu-Liu Chen. 2009. *Entity-Relationship Diagram*, pages 125–139. Springer Berlin Heidelberg, Berlin, Heidelberg.

Carsten Lutz. 2002. Reasoning about entity relationship diagrams with complex attribute dependencies. In *Proceedings of the International Workshop in Description Logics 2002 (DL2002), number 53 in CEUR-WS (http://ceur-ws.org)*, pages 185–194.

Luisa Mich. 1996. Nl-oops: from natural language to object oriented requirements using the natural language processing system lolita. *Natural language engineering*, 2(2):161–187.

Antoni Olivé. 2007. *Conceptual Modeling of Information Systems*. Springer-Verlag, Berlin, Heidelberg.

Gerard O'Regan. 2017. Unified modelling language. In *Concise Guide to Software Engineering*, pages 225–238. Springer.

Fernando CN Pereira and Stuart M Shieber. 2002. *Prolog and natural-language analysis*. Microtome Publishing.

Barker Richard. 1990. *CASE Method: Entity Relationship Modelling*. Addition-Wesley Publishing Company, ORACLE Corporation UK Limited.

Motoshi Saeki, Hisayuki Horai, and Hajime Enomoto. 1989. Software development process from natural language specification. In *11th International Conference on Software Engineering*, pages 64–73. IEEE.

Rolf Schwitter. 2010. Controlled natural languages for knowledge representation. In *Proceedings of the 23rd International Conference on Computational Linguistics: Posters*, pages 1113–1121. Association for Computational Linguistics.

Il-Yeol Song and Peter P. Chen. 2009. *Entity Relationship Model*, pages 1003–1009. Springer US, Boston, MA.

Harald Störrle. 2017. How are conceptual models used in industrial software development?: A descriptive survey. In *Proceedings of the 21st International Conference on Evaluation and Assessment in Software Engineering*, pages 160–169. ACM.

Measuring English Readability for Vietnamese Speakers

Thuan Nguyen and Alexandra L. UITDENBOGERD
RMIT University - School of Science
124 La Trobe St
Melbourne VIC 3000
`john.nguyen09@outlook.com,sandra.uitdenbogerd@rmit.edu.au`

Abstract

Reading is important for language learners, but text difficulty needs to match a reader's skill level for efficient vocabulary acquisition. Traditional readability measures may not be effective for those who speak English as a second or additional language. This study examines English readability for Vietnamese native speakers (VL1). A collection of text difficulty judgements of nearly 100 English text passages was obtained from 12 VL1 participants, using a 5-point Likert scale. Using features from traditional readability measures, support vector machines and Dale-Chall features gave more accurate predictions than linear models using either Flesch or Dale-Chall features. VL1 participants' text judgements were strongly correlated with their past English test scores. This study introduces a first approximation to readability of English text for VL1, with suggestions for further improvements.

1 Introduction

Extensive reading, that is, reading a large amount of text at a comfortable level of difficulty, is an efficient way to improve language skills, as learners acquire vocabulary as they read, retain it for longer than if they use rote memorisation (Hermann, 2003), and greatly improve their receptive skills (Elley and Mangubhai, 1983). However, the level of difficulty of the text needs to match the learner, for example, to guess the meaning of new words, readers typically need to know at least 95% of the words (Laufer, 1989). Further, text needs to be well below the learner's frustration level (Klare, 1988). As most text written for native (L1) speakers is beyond the beginner and intermediate language learner, students need to start with simple or simplified text and work their way up to more advanced texts as they learn. Thus a method of

measuring the readability of text is crucial for language learners, and can be incorporated in to reading recommender systems.

There have been many proposed English text readability measurement techniques, most of which were modelled on native English-speaking (EL1) children, or texts written for them (for example (Flesch, 1948; Dale and Chall, 1948; Schwarm and Ostendorf, 2005)). English comprehension is different for people with different backgrounds and language skills, causing readability measurement techniques developed for EL1 to perform poorly for other L1-L2 combinations (Oller et al., 1972; Uitdenbogerd, 2005). The focus of this study was English readability for Vietnamese speakers (VL1). To our knowledge, no techniques have been built and tested specifically for this cohort.

While there is existing work on readability for non-native (L2) speakers, the majority is trained on data sets that assume texts written for different language levels match the comprehension experienced by L2 speakers. Examples include François and Miltsakaki (2012) for French L2 and Xia et al. (2016) for English. Xia et al. (2016) extended readability measurement techniques by adapting a model trained on texts for English L1 speakers using data from Cambridge English language tests at different Common European Framework of Reference for languages (CEFR) levels. While some studies use corpora that are fairly homogenous, it has been pointed out that other corpora reveal considerable inconsistency across text classes used as ground truth (François, 2014). Furthermore, there is evidence that expert or publisher-based ground truth is a poor surrogate for genuine language learner experience (Vajjala and Lucic, 2019).

This paper replicates two well-known readability measures, Flesch (1948) and Dale and Chall

(1948) by using their features and techniques, but building the model on new data collected from Vietnamese speakers. Prior research has shown that Machine Learning (ML) algorithms and Natural Language Processing (NLP) features provide better results than traditional formulae (François and Miltsakaki, 2012). Therefore, we also tested Support Vector Machines (SVMs) to produce the model for assessing English text readability as perceived by Vietnamese speakers.

Collecting appropriate ground truth was challenging, leading to a smallish data set with a skewed rating distribution. We report on the main techniques relevant to this project (Section 2), details about the ground truth data collection (Section 3), the results of applying linear models and SVMs, and further analysis and discussion of the data set and results.

2 Readability Measurement

Much research has demonstrated that extensive reading increases language acquisition (Hermann, 2003; Elley and Mangubhai, 1983; Laufer, 1989; Klare, 1988). Further research has tried to determine how to select appropriate reading material for learners through the development of readability measurement techniques, either simple metrics that can be applied manually to small samples, or more recently, complex predictive models using NLP features (for example François and Miltsakaki (2012)).

Readability for non-native speakers is likely to be affected by their knowledge of other languages. The principal way that this is experienced is through cognates (and loanwords), that is, words that are similar in appearance and meaning between a pair of languages. Their impact on readability of French for English speakers has been demonstrated (Uitdenbogerd, 2005).

Some studies measure readability (or complexity) of different units of language. While the majority of research estimates readability of whole documents, there is some work on readability of sentences (Pilán et al., 2014) as well as lexical complexity in isolation (Paetzold and Specia, 2016). In this work we look at text passages of 50-200 words in length, being short enough for participants to judge quickly, and long enough to provide context and features.

Flesch (1948) and Dale and Chall (1948) are two of the most popular readability measures for English, both of which extract two statistical features from text and calculate the difficulty level using a linear model. Both measures try to capture the syntactic complexity of a text using the average word count per sentence (WPS). Flesch (1948) captures vocabulary complexity via the average syllable count per word (SPW), whereas Dale and Chall (1948) use a predefined list of 3000 familiar words to calculate the percentage of difficult words (PDW).

The Flesch formula, shown below, produces a readability score that normally falls in the range 0–100 (theoretical maximum would be 121.22), with 0–30 being classed as very difficult, and 90–100 being very easy.

$$\text{RE} = 206.835 - 1.015(\frac{\text{\# wrds}}{\text{\# snts}}) - 84.6(\frac{\text{\# syll}}{\text{\# wrd}}) \quad (1)$$

Dale-Chall's formula calculates the grade-level of text.

$$\text{DC} = 0.0496(\frac{\text{\# words}}{\text{\# sents}}) + 0.1579(\frac{\text{\# hard words}}{\text{\# words}} * 100)$$
$$(2)$$

Schwarm and Ostendorf (2005) assessed text readability using SVMs and a combination of NLP features and statistical features. The present study also uses SVMs with statistical features from traditional models, but with ground truth data from Vietnamese speakers.

3 Vietnamese Ground truth data collection

Our aim was to collect a text corpus of a wide range of difficulty, and to collect human judgements of their perceived difficulty from VL1 speakers. The intention was to obtain multiple judgements per text to allow some analysis of how different individuals perceive the difficulty of the same text.

We selected a variety of texts to make up ten categories from four different sources: Oxford Bookworms graded readers for learners of English as a second language (EL2) consisting of five levels ranging from level 0 (Starter) to level 4, children's literature, young adult texts, and classic English literature. Oxford Bookworms texts were selected randomly from a digitised data-set. Three children's literature texts were arbitrarily selected from Project Gutenberg's Children's literature bookshelf. Four young adult texts were arbitrarily selected from a library's Young Adult section. The classical literature stories selected were the top three from a top ten list of classics found via a web search. Due to an oversight leading to original classic texts being used instead of the simplified version for Oxford Bookworms levels 5 and 6, there were three times as many texts from classical literature than other sources or levels. Despite the uneven representation of books, with *David Copperfield* and *The Woman in White* having ten samples each, versus only one to five samples for all others, each category was distinct, and had ten randomly selected extracts, allowing sufficient variety for testing readability, and providing a wide range of difficulty.

Extracting sentences from the books was via a script that randomly generated a starting sentence number, and the number of sentences to extract from that point. However, this process was not applied to young adult books since they were not electronically available, therefore a random number generator was used instead, to generate a page number, paragraph number and the number of sentences to extract. Ten texts from each level or source were randomly selected, each around 50-200 words in length, leading to a total of 100 texts. This text length and number of judgements was chosen to minimise the time commitment of volunteer participants and provide sufficient context to assess the readability of the text. It is a similar quantity to samples in previous studies (See for example, Björnsson (1968)). Text was presented to participants in a random order to eliminate ordering effects.

Participants were recruited via an invitation to complete an on-line survey posted in a large Facebook group for Vietnamese students in Australia. Twelve participants completed the entire questionnaire, resulting in 120 samples of data. One participant who did not complete all questions was excluded to avoid potential bias in the data-set toward specific participants' responses. The participants were Vietnamese students studying in Australia, the majority of whom had English IELTS levels 6 to 8, being equivalent to CEFR B2–C1/C2.

Participants were asked to read 10 texts with no time limit, each from a different reading level or source, and to choose an answer based on a 5-point Likert scale, with each point worded specifically for learners of English as a foreign language (Uitdenbogerd et al., 2017) as shown below.

1. The text was very easy. I knew every word.
2. The text was easy, but I did not understand some words.
3. The text was not easy, but I understood the story.
4. The text was difficult. I would need a dictionary.
5. The text was very difficult. A dictionary will not help me.

4 Linear models

Using the ground truth data-set obtained from Vietnamese speakers, we replicated methods used for traditional measures (Flesch, 1948; Dale and Chall, 1948). These new models were built using linear regression and statistical features of texts.

The Natural Language Toolkit (Loper and Bird, 2002) was used to extract the statistical features in the text, and scikit-learn (Pedregosa et al., 2011) was used for training and testing, as well as for calculating mean squared error (MSE). Syllable counts were based on those found in the Carnegie-Mellon Pronouncing Dictionary (cmudict). All words used in the study corpus were in cmudict.

These experiments replicate the techniques and features from Flesch and Dale-Chall, using the collected data-set to feed into the linear regression model. Bootstrapping was also attempted to compensate for the small data size and uneven distribution of responses.

The experiments were set up to train and test ten times on the collected data, the split ratio being 67% and 33% respectively, and each time splitting the data randomly. The aim was to build the model with the least mean squared error (MSE), which measures how well the linear model fits the data; and the least over-fitting amount, measured as the difference between the MSE of the training and test data sets. That is, a good model has a low MSE and a low measure of over-fitting. The coefficients of features of the best run become the recommended model for the given set of features.

When bootstrapping was applied, the data was sampled with replacement 100 times for each Likert scale point, from 1-3. No participants selected 5 (very difficult), and only one selected 4 (difficult), thus 4 was excluded.

4.1 Linear Model based on Flesch features

Table 1 shows the result of using WPS and SPW in the linear regression model based on VL1 judgements of English text difficulty.

The average train MSE and test MSE were 0.25 and 0.31 respectively. The best run produced an MSE of 0.23 for predicting unknown situations, having an over-fitting result of 0.05. The MSE was

Run no	Coeffs (WPS, SPW)	Train MSE	Test MSE	Over-fitting
1	0.005, 1.5	0.29	0.21	0.08
2	0.002, 1.4	0.28	0.23	0.05
3	-0.0004, 0.86	0.30	0.21	0.09
4	0.022, 0.59	0.15	0.51	0.36
5	0.016, 1.355	0.32	0.17	0.15
6	0.008, 1.367	0.30	0.19	0.11
7	0.003, 0.759	0.12	0.57	0.45
8	0.017, 0.459	0.18	0.46	0.28
9	0.013, 0.505	0.35	0.11	0.24
10	0.015, 0.647	0.19	0.41	0.22

Table 1: Results of replicating the Flesch formula

calculated using the following formula:

$$MSE = \frac{\sum_{i=1}^{n}(actual(i) - predicted(i))^2}{n}$$

where n is the number of test samples.

Therefore an average MSE of 0.31 in the test data suggests instability, since the distance between the data rating score and the predicted rating score is the middle of 2 rating levels.

The model can be represented as:

$$\text{VFlesch} = 0.002 * (\frac{\text{\# words}}{\text{\# sents}}) + 1.4 * (\frac{\text{\# sylls}}{\text{\# words}}) \quad (3)$$

This formula shows that the coefficient of SPW has more importance than WPS, at a vocabulary to grammar feature ratio of 700 (See Table 2). This suggests that the original Flesch model, which has a feature ratio of 83.4, has less emphasis on vocabulary, and would therefore be less effective for Vietnamese speakers. On looking at the second and third best runs based on over-fitting score, it can be seen that WPS is consistently small, and in one case is negative, indicating that sentence length can virtually be ignored to get a good estimate of readability for this cohort of speakers. The run with a coefficient ratio most similar to the original Flesch score is Run 5, which has a vocabulary to grammar coefficient ratio of 84.7 and is in the middle of the runs when compared by over-fitting amount, indicating that the new coefficients would be more stable.

Applying bootstrapping increased the error significantly with average MSE of 0.54 and resulted in an unpredictable model, so was not helpful in this case.

4.2 Linear Model based on Dale-Chall Features

In Table 3 we report on the model based on WPS and PDW, which are taken from the Dale-Chall formula.

The MSE in predicting training data and test data respectively are 0.28 and 0.24 for the best model, and its coefficients for percentage of difficult words and average word count per sentence are 0.015 and 0.020 respectively. The average MSE across 10 runs are 0.31 and 0.20. This model has less error than the Flesch-based model. The coefficients produced by the runs are also more stable than the Flesch ones, suggesting that the Dale-Chall vocabulary feature is superior. None of the runs produced coefficients with a similar ratio of PDW to WPS as the original Dale-Chall formula (approximately 3.18).

The resulting formula for this model is as follows:

$$\text{VDC} = 0.020(\frac{\text{\# words}}{\text{\# sents}}) + 0.015(\frac{\text{\# hard words}}{\text{\# words}} * 100) \quad (4)$$

In this model, the coefficients of the two features are quite similar to each other. That is, unlike for Flesch, in the Dale-Chall formula WPS is relatively more important for VL1 than vocabulary, since the PDW was weighted 3.18 times more than WPS in the original Dale-Chall formula, but in this model is only 0.75 times (shown in Table 2).

In the previous model, applying bootstrapping increased the error significantly. We also applied bootstrapping in this model to confirm if features are the factor that causes the significant increase in error. Indeed, using bootstrapped data produced a very high level of error (> 0.60 MSE). Therefore, it is safe to conclude that bootstrapping does not work very well with linear models of this data-set.

Additionally, we tested a modified version of the Dale-Chall word list that was potentially more suitable for VL1. The Vietnamese first author of the present study — who found many of the words on the original list unfamiliar and therefore difficult — modified the list by removing any words that seemed difficult. We acknowledge that this is not a robust approach, however it was a good first approximation, and a more representative list for VL1 may be future work. The results of the modified word list were very similar to the original results. Further analysis showed that 26 of the 100 texts contained a slightly higher number of difficult words when using the modified list, 2 texts with 3, 4 with 2 and 20 with 1 respectively, being less than 3% change in a PDW score. Mean (0.35), standard deviation (0.07) and maximum (0.6) PDW remained about the same for both

	Coefficients			Vocab/Grammar Ratios		VL1 Ratio/Orig. Ratio
Coeff. Type	WPS Grammar	SPW Vocab	PDW Vocab	SPW/WPS	PDW/WPS	
Original Flesch	1.015	84.6		83.4		
Best VFlesch	0.002	1.4		700		8.4
Original Dale-Chall	0.0496		0.158		3.18	
Best VDC	0.02		0.015		0.75	0.24

Table 2: Vocabulary to grammar coefficient ratios for Flesch, Dale-Chall, and the best linear model runs with VL1 data.

Run no	Coeffs (PDW, WPS)	Train MSE	Test MSE	Over-fitting
1	0.013, 0.014	0.32	0.16	0.16
2	0.010, 0.011	0.34	0.12	0.22
3	0.014, 0.006	0.33	0.16	0.17
4	0.012, 0.020	0.32	0.17	0.15
5	0.014, 0.015	0.25	0.31	0.06
6	0.003, 0.020	0.20	0.40	0.20
7	0.015, 0.020	0.28	0.24	0.04
8	0.009, 0.010	0.35	0.11	0.24
9	0.014, 0.014	0.34	0.13	0.11
10	0.014, 0.013	0.32	0.16	0.16

Table 3: Results of replicating the Dale-Chall formula

versions and the minimum increased from 0.18 to 0.19.

To summarise, the model produced by using features from Dale-Chall gave a lower error rate than the model using Flesch features, and the features appeared to be more stable.

4.3 Combined features from Flesch and Dale-Chall formulas

The features used in this experiment are taken from Flesch and Dale-Chall formulas, which are: WPS, SPW and PDW. Our hypothesis is that this will not affect the model's performance because the Flesch and Dale-Chall formulae try to represent the vocabulary complexity by SPW or PDW respectively, and there may not be much gain by combining the two features. The result confirmed this by producing an MSE of 0.27, which does not provide any improvement on previous models. The two vocabulary features have a correlation of 0.53 for our data-set.

4.4 Using Dale-Chall and Flesch score as a feature

The results of the original Dale-Chall formula and our linear model are in different formats, that is the Dale-Chall score is a grade level ranging from 0-10+ and our model is a difficulty level ranging from 1-5. Therefore, it is not straightforward to

scale the result from our model to Dale-Chall and vice versa. Therefore to compare our model with the original Dale-Chall formula we calculated the Dale-Chall score for the text using the original weights and then used it as a feature (Table 4) to calculate the error rate as for previous experiments.

Run no	Coeffs (Dale-Chall)	Train MSE	Test MSE	Over-fitting
1	0.078	0.31	0.19	0.12
2	0.119	0.27	0.26	0.01
3	0.097	0.34	0.13	0.21
4	0.017	0.19	0.44	0.15
5	0.080	0.16	0.49	0.27

Table 4: Results of using Dale-Chall as a feature

The errors of the model fluctuated and produced different results for each random train and test data split resulting high average prediction error across multiple runs. This indicates in some cases the result from Dale-Chall formula does not resemble participant ratings, for example some cases produce a test error of almost 0.50 (run 4 and 5), meaning the model is not learning anything. We conclude that while the *features* in Dale-Chall formula worked best for VL1, the original Dale-Chall formula is less effective for Vietnamese speakers.

When running the same validation against the original Flesch reading ease score, even though the MSE were lower than using original DC as a feature, the same error fluctuation pattern occurs (See Table 5). This suggests that the original Flesch gives a better result than the original DC for VL1, but is still less effective for Vietnamese speakers than than the model trained on DC features with VL1 data.

5 Using SVMs on statistical features

ML is known to be effective in text classification, and has also been applied to text readability (Schwarm and Ostendorf, 2005). Here we ap-

Run no	Coeffs (Flesch)	Train MSE	Test MSE	Over-fitting
1	-0.013	0.31	0.15	0.24
2	-0.008	0.15	0.49	0.34
3	-0.011	0.30	0.19	0.11
4	-0.012	0.29	0.20	0.04
5	-0.009	0.23	0.31	0.14

Table 5: Results of using Flesch as a feature

ply SVMs with a radial basis kernel function to determine whether they will improve readability assessment of English for VL1.

We tested three feature sets: Flesch only, Dale-Chall only, and the combined features of both. The split ratio was different for this experiment, being 70% training data and 30% test data due to the small data-set. As the data-set was quite small for SVMs to be effective we also used bootstrapping to re-sample the data-set from 120 samples to 300 samples, despite the method increasing the error rate in the previous experiments.

We used cross-validation, with the training and test data split randomly for each cross-validation. The experiment was to start with 5 runs and increased to 10 runs for each data-set. The aim of this was to observe the MSE and the variance to see if more cross-validation increases variance, which might indicate an unreliable model. The reason 5-10 runs were chosen is that for each run we generated a random cross-validation to train and test, and since the data is small, after 10 runs it is possible that the model will be over-trained and produce an unreliable prediction model.

The results of using raw data are shown in Table 6 and Table 7.

Feature set	MSE (+/- var.)
Flesch Features	0.14 (+/- 0.08)
Dale-Chall Features	0.15 (+/- 0.09)
Combined features	0.15 (+/- 0.09)

Table 6: 5 runs of SVMs on raw data

Feature set	MSE (+/- var.)
Flesch Features	0.19 (+/- 0.13)
Dale-Chall Features	0.19 (+/- 0.13)
Combined features	0.19 (+/- 0.13)

Table 7: 10 runs of SVMs on raw data

Observing the results, there are two things to notice. Firstly, the MSE increases significantly and the variance also increases, which indicates

that the model becomes over-fitted to the data and increased validation increases the error. This can be caused by the small data-set since ML requires large data-sets to be effective.

The data was then re-sampled using the bootstrap method to increase to 300 samples, even though 300 is not a large number for ML (previous ML experiments all have roughly more than 1000 data-points (François and Miltsakaki, 2012; Schwarm and Ostendorf, 2005)), but since it is re-sampled from 120 data-points, then 300 is a reasonable number. The results are shown in Table 8 and Table 9.

Feature set	MSE (+/- var.)
Flesch Features	0.39 (+/- 0.07)
Dale-Chall Features	0.21 (+/- 0.05)
Combined features	0.28 (+/- 0.03)

Table 8: Five runs of SVMs on bootstrapped data

Feature set	MSE (+/- var.)
Flesch Features	0.38 (+/- 0.07)
Dale-Chall Features	0.21 (+/- 0.06)
Combined features	0.27 (+/- 0.07)

Table 9: Ten runs of SVMs on bootstrapped data

In this experiment with the bootstrap method, the results stay almost consistent, even with more cross-validation. This model is confirmed to be more effective, since ML requires a large data-set. The model also gives a better performance than the linear models because it isn't prone to over-fitting, even though the bootstrap method increases MSE.

Additionally, features from the Dale-Chall formula have the best performance across the three feature sets tested. Features from Flesch produced the worst performance, being even worse than linear models, while combined features were not far behind and were comparable to results of linear models.

6 Analysis

In this section we examine some properties of the judgements that were collected, including English skill level of participants, and how that related to their text ratings. We also examine general properties of the texts in each category in the hope of shedding some light on the slightly contradictory results occurring in the readability models.

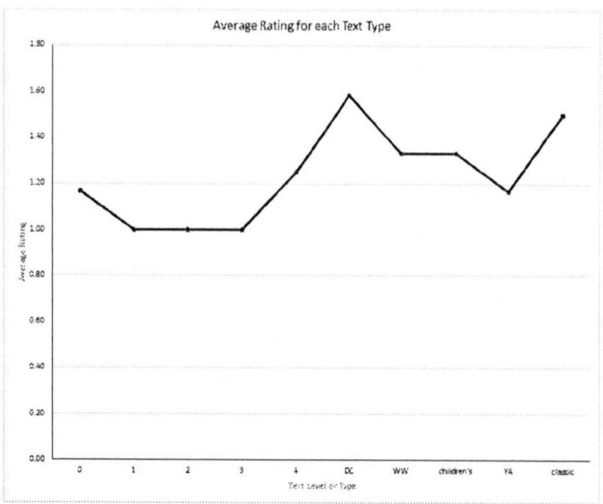

Figure 1: Average rating over twelve human judgements for each type of text.

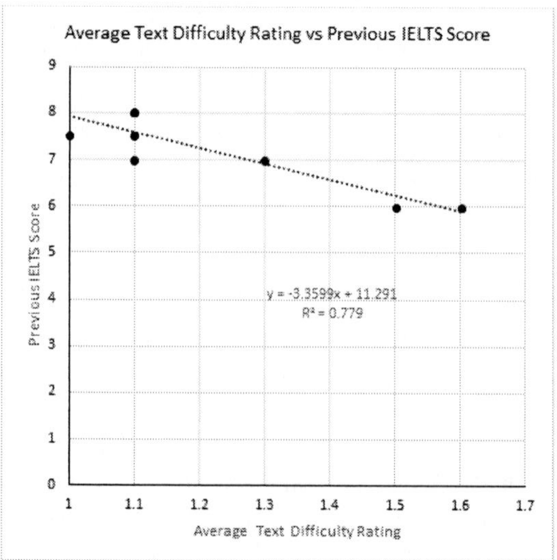

Figure 2: Average rating given by each participant versus their most recent IELTS score.

6.1 Judgements

We collected 10 judgements for each category of text, each from a different participant. Due to the method of random allocation of texts to participants, not all texts in the collection received judgements and some texts received up to four judgements. There were 6–8 text samples judged from each category. Figure 1 shows the average judgements for each text category. When a regression line is fit between the five Oxford Bookworms levels and their averages, the resulting equation had a slope of 0.017 and an R^2 of 0.05, suggesting a very poor fit. This is likely because all the Bookworms texts were too easy for the pool of participants, leading to insufficient difference in ratings across the levels. It can be observed that levels 1-3 all had the same average rating of 1. That is, every participant rated all texts of those levels as being very easy. For level 0, one participant gave a rating of 3 to a text (10). The same participant was the only one to rate any text with a 4 (difficult), and had the highest average ratings of difficulty. Two participants rated all texts as very easy, and therefore provided no information to the models of readability.

Nine of the twelve participants had provided their past IELTS test score. We compared their average ratings and their past IELTS test score (See Figure 2). The R^2 was 0.779, thus a high correlation (0.88). The rating distribution, however, was exponential, with 99, 19, 3, 1 and 0 ratings respectively from very easy to very difficult (fitting a line to the log of the non-zero rating counts has an R^2 of 0.99).

The only text to be given a rating above 3 by any participant was an extract from David Copperfield, which was presented as below.

> Mr. Micawber was extremely glad to see me, but a little confused too. He would have conducted me immediately into the presence of Uriah, but I declined.
>
> 'I know the house of old, you recollect,' said I, 'and will find my way upstairs. How do you like the law, Mr. Micawber?'
>
> 'My dear Copperfield,' he replied. 'To a man possessed of the higher imaginative powers, the objection to legal studies is the amount of detail which they involve. Even in our professional correspondence,' said Mr. Micawber, glancing at some letters he was writing, 'the mind is not at liberty to soar to any exalted form of expression. Still, it is a great pursuit. A great pursuit!'

Of the public domain texts, The Woman in White (WW in Figure 1) was generally considered easier than the pool of classic literature by participants. Bookworms texts were generally considered easy, and David Copperfield was the most difficult.

6.2 Analysis of Text Features

On examining the relationship between the extracted features and the texts in each category (See Table 10), it was clear that the Bookworms text extracts had an almost monotonically increasing average sentence length from Level 0 (6.1) to 4 (13.95). All other texts had a higher average sentence length (15.6–22.5) except the YA text category (13.2).

Text Category	SPW	PDW	WPS
Children's lit.	1.26	17.7%	17.21
Level 0	1.19	21.9%	6.10
Level 1	1.19	22.8%	7.94
Level 2	1.20	16.2%	12.07
Level 3	1.23	15.5%	10.32
Level 4	1.31	24.9%	13.95
David Copperfield	1.32	22.5%	22.54
The Woman in White	1.29	18.4%	15.56
Top 3 classics	1.35	22.1%	20.33
Young Adult	1.29	24.7%	13.22

Table 10: Features averaged across each text category

While the average SPW increased monotonically for the Bookworm text levels, with all but Level 4 having a lower average SPW than other text categories, the PDW average varied considerably, with Level 4 having the highest average PDW across all categories of text. Clearly, the Dale-Chall word list is not a factor in setting the levels of Oxford Bookworm texts. Interestingly, the easiest non-Bookworm category based on average judgements (YA), had the second highest average PDW. A correlation across texts between SPW and WPS of 0.33 is probably due to the constraints placed on Oxford Bookworm text. While there was a fairly high correlation between SPW and PDW (0.53), clearly there were systematic differences.

7 Discussion of Results and Limitations

The models applied to the data did not display huge differences in effectiveness, but the Dale-Chall features generally outperformed the Flesch ones, in both the regression and SVM-based models. In the Flesch case, vocabulary became much more important as a feature relative to sentence length, compared to the original Flesch formula, whereas for Dale-Chall vocabulary was slightly less important than in the original formula.

Despite inconsistency in the relative importance of vocabulary to sentence length for Vietnamese speakers between feature sets, the collected text ratings showed a strong relationship with the level of English language skill of the participants, as measured by IELTS tests. On average across participants, text ratings appeared to follow logical trends, with Bookworm texts being easy, and classical literature being more challenging.

There were several limitations to our preliminary study, some of which can be addressed in future analysis, but most would require a new experiment with a greater number of participants. As with most empirical research, the more data available, the more robust the results. For any techniques that involve machine learning and many features, large sets of data are required. From a statistical perspective, having only about 100 data points only allows one to build good models involving multiple predictors if the effect size is expected to be large. We did, however, have a reasonable fit for both linear models on two features.

One of the difficulties was a mismatch between the participants and the experimental apparatus. Because of their relatively high level English background, being in the range IELTS 6–8 (for those who completed an IELTS test), the majority of the texts were too easy. This didn't provide enough discrimination between texts in the lower levels of difficulty. Based on an examination of the relationship between ratings and IELTS background, the current apparatus would require participants who have a much lower IELTS level.

There may have been a better model produced if the Likert scale was more fine-grained, to allow a greater spread of rating scores. For example, the research that developed the Lix readability model used a nine-point scale (Björnsson, 1968). However, one advantage of the Likert scale used here is that it should create more consistent ratings across participants, due to the precise wording for each point on the scale. Despite this, there is a drawback, in that the wording emphasises lexical difficulty. For a future study the wording should remove that emphasis to reduce potential bias toward vocabulary.

To make the test less onerous for lower level participants the wording would need to be further changed. Asking beginners to *read* a difficult text would result in them spending considerable time trying to decipher it, whereas what is required is a quick judgement as to its difficulty. So future questionnaires should ask participants to *look at* the text instead.

The most difficult text, as judged by Vietnamese participants, had long sentences and fairly long words, and a moderate percentage of difficult words, based on the Dale-Chall list. The texts judged the easiest had shorter sentences and words, and somewhat fewer difficult words. However, there was not a direct linear relationship between published simplified texts and human judgements. Perhaps there would be a linear relationship if the experiment had a different combination of participants and rating scale, but the current experiment does not provide evidence that the use of published scales as ground truth for human perception of reading difficulty is any more than a convenient substitute.

7.1 Future Work

We have been considering how to obtain a larger set of judgements from participants with lower levels of English comprehension, to provide a better spread of readability ratings. Using existing crowd-sourcing platforms is not really an option, since those who use them would already need a functional level of English to navigate the platforms. To our knowledge there is no equivalent platform available in Vietnamese.

We contemplated using students studying English in Vietnam, but this was unlikely to result in many participants due to the constraints on recruitment. An alternative may be using social media sites that are popular in Vietnam to advertise to participants, or providing a free Massive Open On-line Course (MOOC) for the collection of data from students. Evidence from this study and elsewhere (Jacob and Uitdenbogerd, 2019) suggests that to obtain enough participants with beginner or intermediate L2 skills, it is essential to recruit and present the study in their L1, or ratings will be exponential in distribution.

This initial study was limited to three traditional readability features. Further work would involve a wider range of features, with particular focus on those that are related to the human experience of reading (Crossley et al., 2008). However, a larger set of human judgements is needed before meaningful experimentation with ML techniques can be contemplated.

It may be useful to create a validated equivalent to the Dale-Chall list for Vietnamese speakers beyond our initial attempt at modifying the list with the input from a single Vietnamese participant. Due to the French colonial background of Vietnam there are also French-Vietnamese cognates (for example, ga tô for gateau) which may impact readability by being more memorable (Beinborn et al., 2014). However, the impact is likely to be much less than for more related language pairs such as Spanish-Italian, or French-English.

In this work we focused on the readability of passages of English text for speakers with Vietnamese L1. We are currently also working with other language backgrounds. Difficulty varies greatly across text, which with traditional formulae was managed by taking multiple samples. Flesch (1948) recommended 25-30 samples for measuring a book's readability, if the whole book is not being analysed, and Björnsson (1968) used 20 100-word samples for lexical complexity and 20 ten-sentence samples for grammatical complexity. We may explore sentence-level readability in future (Pilán et al., 2014).

8 Conclusion

This study is the first to attempt to measure English readability for Vietnamese speakers. Our contribution consists of a small data-set of human judgements of English text by Vietnamese volunteers, and the application of linear regression and SVM models to predict readability, using traditional readability features.

SVMs produced a model with the best performance in terms of MSE. Bootstrapping increased the MSE in linear models, but helped significantly in building an effective SVM model.

The features from Dale-Chall performed consistently well across all models (linear regression and SVMs). The small data-set prevented the rigorous use of a large feature set, despite a combination of statistical features and NLP features being likely to produce a better model (François and Miltsakaki, 2012). Thus future work includes applying more features to a larger data-set, preferably with a better match between text samples and participants, and using the Vietnamese data-set to tune a model produced from a larger data-set (Xia et al., 2016).

Acknowledgments

We thank Mr Patrick Jacob for suggesting different methodologies in the experiment.

References

Lisa Beinborn, Torsten Zesch, and Iryna Gurevych. 2014. Readability for foreign language learning: The importance of cognates. *ITL-International Journal of Applied Linguistics*, 165(2):136–162.

Carl-Hugo Björnsson. 1968. *Läsbarhet: hur skall man som författare nå fram till läsarna?* Bokförlaget Liber.

Scott A Crossley, Jerry Greenfield, and Danielle S McNamara. 2008. Assessing text readability using cognitively based indices. *Tesol Quarterly*, 42(3):475–493.

Edgar Dale and Jeanne S. Chall. 1948. A formula for predicting readability: Instructions. *Educational Research Bulletin*, 27(2):37–54.

Warwick B Elley and Francis Mangubhai. 1983. The impact of reading on second language learning. *Reading research quarterly*, pages 53–67.

R Flesch. 1948. A new readability yardstick. *Journal of Applied Psychology*, 32(3):221–233.

Thomas François and Eleni Miltsakaki. 2012. Do NLP and machine learning improve traditional readability formulas? In *Proceedings of the First Workshop on Predicting and Improving Text Readability for Target Reader Populations*, PITR '12, pages 49–57, Stroudsburg, PA, USA. Association for Computational Linguistics.

Thomas François. 2014. An analysis of a French as a foreign language corpus for readability assessment. In *Proceedings of the third workshop on NLP for computer-assisted language learning*, pages 13–32.

Frank Hermann. 2003. Differential effects of reading and memorization of paired associates on vocabulary acquisition in adult learners of english as a second language. *TESL-EJ*, 7(1):1–16.

Patrick Jacob and Alexandra L. Uitdenbogerd. 2019. In *Australasian Language Technology Workshop ALTW 2019*.

George R Klare. 1988. The formative years. In Beverly L. Zakaluk and S. Jay Samuels, editors, *Readability: Its past, present, and future*, pages 14–34. ERIC.

Batia Laufer. 1989. What percentage of text-lexis is essential for comprehension? In Christer Laurén and Marianne Nordman, editors, *Special language: From humans thinking to thinking machines*, pages 316–323.

Edward Loper and Steven Bird. 2002. NLTK: The natural language toolkit. In *Proceedings of the ACL-02 Workshop on Effective Tools and Methodologies for Teaching Natural Language Processing and Computational Linguistics - Volume 1*, ETMTNLP '02, pages 63–70, Stroudsburg, PA, USA. Association for Computational Linguistics.

John W Oller, J Donald Bowen, Ton That Dien, and Victor W Mason. 1972. Cloze tests in English, Thai, and Vietnamese: Native and non-native performance. *Language Learning*, 22(1):1–15.

Gustavo Paetzold and Lucia Specia. 2016. Semeval 2016 task 11: Complex word identification. In *Proceedings of the 10th International Workshop on Semantic Evaluation (SemEval-2016)*, pages 560–569.

F. Pedregosa, G. Varoquaux, A. Gramfort, V. Michel, B. Thirion, O. Grisel, M. Blondel, P. Prettenhofer, R. Weiss, V. Dubourg, J. Vanderplas, A. Passos, D. Cournapeau, M. Brucher, M. Perrot, and E. Duchesnay. 2011. Scikit-learn: Machine learning in Python. *Journal of Machine Learning Research*, 12:2825–2830.

Ildikó Pilán, Elena Volodina, and Richard Johansson. 2014. Rule-based and machine learning approaches for second language sentence-level readability. In *Proceedings of the ninth workshop on innovative use of NLP for building educational applications*, pages 174–184.

Sarah E. Schwarm and Mari Ostendorf. 2005. Reading level assessment using support vector machines and statistical language models. In *Proceedings of the 43rd Annual Meeting on Association for Computational Linguistics*, ACL '05, pages 523–530, Stroudsburg, PA, USA. Association for Computational Linguistics.

A. L. Uitdenbogerd, S. Kablaoui, and A. Martin. 2017. Defining a unified model of vocabulary acquisition via extensive reading : Final report. Grant Report for the Office for Learning and Teaching.

A.L. Uitdenbogerd. 2005. Readability of French as a foreign language and its uses. *J. Kay, A. Turpin and R. Wilkinson (ed.) ADCS 2005: Proceedings of the Tenth Australasian Document Computing Symposium*, pages 19–25.

Sowmya Vajjala and Ivana Lucic. 2019. On understanding the relation between expert annotations of text readability and target reader comprehension. In *Proceedings of the Fourteenth Workshop on Innovative Use of NLP for Building Educational Applications*, pages 349–359, Florence, Italy. Association for Computational Linguistics.

Menglin Xia, Ekaterina Kochmar, and Ted Briscoe. 2016. Text readability assessment for second language learners. In *Proceedings of the 11th Workshop on Innovative Use of NLP for Building Educational Applications*, pages 12–22.

Does Multi-Task Learning Always Help?
An Evaluation on Health Informatics Tasks

Aditya Joshi, Sarvnaz Karimi, Ross Sparks, Cécile Paris, C Raina MacIntyre
CSIRO Data61, Sydney, Australia
Kirby Institute, University of New South Wales, Sydney, Australia
{firstname.lastname}@csiro.au , r.macintyre@unsw.edu.au

Abstract

Multi-Task Learning (MTL) has been an attractive approach to deal with limited labeled datasets or leverage related tasks, for a variety of NLP problems. We examine the benefit of MTL for three specific pairs of health informatics tasks that deal with: (a) overlapping symptoms for the same classification problem (personal health mention classification for influenza and for a set of symptoms); (b) overlapping medical concepts for related classification problems (vaccine usage and drug usage detection); and, (c) related classification problems (vaccination intent and vaccination relevance detection). We experiment with a simple neural architecture: a shared layer followed by task-specific dense layers. The novelty of this work is that it compares alternatives for shared layers for these pairs of tasks. While our observations agree with the promise of MTL as compared to single-task learning, for health informatics, we show that the benefit also comes with caveats in terms of the choice of shared layers and the relatedness between the participating tasks.

1   Introduction

Health informatics is the discipline concerned with the systematic processing of data, information and knowledge in medicine and healthcare (Hasman, 1998). Health informatics tasks tend to be specific in terms of parameters such as symptoms, regions of interest or the phenomenon to be detected. As a result, datasets for different health informatics tasks have been reported. However, it remains to be seen if these datasets or classification tasks help each other in terms of how similar the participating datasets or tasks are. In this paper, we examine the utility of Multi-Task Learning (MTL) for several pairs of health informatics tasks that are related in different ways.

MTL pertains to the class of learning algorithms that jointly train predictors for more than one task. In Natural Language Processing (NLP) research, MTL using deep learning has been used either to learn shared representations for related tasks, or to deal with limited labeled datasets (Xue et al., 2007; Zhang and Yeung, 2012; Søgaard and Goldberg, 2016; Ruder, 2017; Liu et al., 2017) for a variety of NLP problems such as sentiment analysis (Huang et al., 2013; Mishra et al., 2017). Most of this work that uses MTL presents architectures utilising multiple shared and task-specific layers. In contrast, we wish to see if the benefit comes from the simplistic notion of 'learning these classifiers together'. Therefore, we use a basic architecture for our MTL experiments consisting of a single shared layer and single task-specific layers, and experiment with different alternatives for the shared layer. This simplicity allows us to understand the benefit of MTL in comparison with Single-Task Learning (STL) for different configurations of shared layers, for task pairs that are related in different ways.

We experiment with datasets of English tweets for three pairs of boolean classification problems. The first pair deals with two datasets which were annotated for the same classification problem but differed in their scope in terms of illnesses that they cover. The second pair deals with different classification problems with some overlap in terms of the scope of medical concepts taken into account. The third pair deals with related classification problems: one problem influences the probability of output of the other.

Through our experiments with simple architectures for popular tasks in health informatics, we examine the question:
'Does multi-task learning always help?'

2   Related Work

MTL has been applied to a variety of text classification tasks (Søgaard and Goldberg, 2016; Xue et al., 2007; Ruder, 2017; Zhang and Yeung, 2012; Liu et al., 2017). The impact of task relatedness on MTL has been explored in case of statistical prediction models (Zhang and Yeung, 2012; Ben-David and Schuller, 2003). In the case of deep learning-based models, Bingel and Søgaard (2017) show how fundamental NLP tasks (such as MWE detection, POS tagging and so on) of different complexities perform when paired. (Mishra et al., 2017) use MTL for two related tasks in opinion mining: sentiment classificaton and sarcasm classification. (Wu and Huang, 2016) use MTL for personalisation of sentiment classification where global and local classifiers are jointly learned. A survey of MTL approaches using deep learning is by (Ruder, 2017).

In the context of health informatics, MTL has been applied in different kinds of tasks. Zou et al. (2018) predict influenza counts based on search counts for different geographical regions - however, they do not use a neural architecture. The task in itself is similar to Pair 1 in our experiments. Chowdhury et al. (2018) use MTL for pharmacovigilance, where each tweet is labeled with adverse drug reaction and indication labels. This is similar to the drug usage detection task in our experiments. For this, they use bi-directional LSTM as the shared layer, in addition to other task-specific layers before and after the shared layer. Benton et al. (2017) use MTL for prediction of mental health signals. Their architecture uses multi-layer perceptrons as shared layers. Bingel and Søgaard (2017) use bi-directional LSTM as the shared layer and compares different pairs of NLP tasks. In contrast, we experiment with three alternatives of shared sentence representations. The above are classification formulations for health informatics. MTL has also been used for other tasks such as biomedical entity extraction (Crichton et al., 2017), non-textual data based on medical tests to predict disease progression (Zhou et al., 2011) and so on.

We use datasets introduced in past work for our experiments. The sources of these datasets are described in the appropriate sections. In addition to the differences with past work as described above, to the best of our knowledge, the results of a MTL model have not been reported for the tasks and the task pairs that we consider. Our systematic analysis in terms of parameters of tasks and our experimentation with different shared layers sets us apart from past work.

3   Task Pairs Under Consideration

We consider three task pairs for our experimentation. These task pairs are related in different ways allowing an investigation into understanding configurations in terms of task relatedness in which MTL may be useful. The three configurations can be described as follows:

1. **Overlapping symptoms for the same classification problem**: The first pair corresponds to the same classification problem: personal health mention detection, *i.e.*, to predict if a given tweet reports an incidence of an illness, for overlapping concepts. For example, '*I have been sneezing since morning*' is a true instance, while '*Strong perfumes may cause sneezing*' is a false instance. Although the definition of the classification tasks is the same, we consider a pair of datasets that cover overlapping symptoms. The first dataset is labeled for personal health mentions of **influenza**, while the second dataset is labeled for personal health mentions of **multiple symptoms**, namely, cough, cold, fever and diarrhoea. Thus, this pair represents a configuration where the overarching classification task is the same but the set of multiple symptoms overlaps with the symptoms of influenza[1]. We refer to this as *Pair 1*.

2. **Overlapping medical concepts for different classification problems**: As *Pair 2*, we consider a pair of classification problems involving overlapping medical concepts. The tasks are: (1) **Vaccination behaviour detection**: To classify whether or not a person has received or intends to receive a vaccine; and, (2) **Drug usage detection**: To classify whether or not a person has received or intends to receive a medicinal drug. The relationship between these tasks arises because of the relationship between the medical concepts. For example, '*I got a flu shot yesterday*' is an instance of vaccine usage while '*I*

<hr>

[1] https://www.cdc.gov/flu/consumer/symptoms.htm; Last accessed on 3rd September, 2019.

took a pain-killer yesterday' is an instance of drug usage. Since a 'vaccine' is a specific type of a general medical entity 'drug'[2], we expect that the classification tasks may be semantically different but deal with overlapping medical concepts.

3. **Related classification problems**: Finally, *Pair 3* corresponds to the configuration of related classification problems. The two classification problems that we consider are: (1) **Vaccine relevance detection**: To classify whether or not a tweet is relevant to vaccination; and, (2) **Vaccine intent detection**: To classify whether or not a tweet expresses intent to receive a vaccine. The classification tasks in pair 3 bear a notion of implication between them, because a tweet relevant to vaccines can alone express intent to receive a vaccine. For example, *'I don't think I will get a flu shot this year'* is relevant to vaccines but does not express vaccine intent.

For tasks in Pairs 1 and 2, we use datasets which contain labels for either of the tasks. Since the tasks in Pair 3 are related classification problems, each instance contains labels for both the tasks. The datasets were provided by three separate papers and may not contain purposeful overlaps.

4   MTL Architecture

We experiment with basic MTL architectures so as to understand the contribution of MTL to a fundamental architecture. The basic outline of our MTL architecture is shown in Figure 1. The input text is converted to a vector of embeddings using an embedding layer. This then goes to the shared sentence representation (hereafter referred to as the 'shared layer' for the sake of brevity), followed by the dropout layer. The dropout layer serves as an input to two dense layers, one for each classification task. The dotted rectangle in the architecture represents the shared layer. This layer is expected to capture the shared representation across the different classification tasks. In order to compare the role of different shared layers, we experiment with three configurations of neural layers as alternatives for the shared layer: BiLSTM, Convolutional, and BiLSTM followed by Convolutional. These are

represented as B, C and $B + C$ in the rest of the paper.

In the case of Pairs 1 & 2, each instance carries values for exactly one of the two tasks because they were derived from two sources. Therefore, we consider it to be a case of missing labels. For each instance, we add a mask value of minus one (-1) for the label which is not present. We use a customised loss function which skips instances that bear the mask value. This means that instances that do not carry a label for a classification task are not incorporated when calculating the loss. For Pair 3, both labels are available for each instance. In this case, both labels are incorporated in computing the training loss.

5   Experimental Setup

All our tasks involve boolean text classification. We refer to the labels as 'true' and 'false' in the rest of the paper, although the semantics of these labels depend on the classification problem. We use the following datasets for our experiments:

- **Pair 1**:
    - As the *'influenza'* dataset, We use the dataset by Lamb et al. (2013) for influenza. The dataset contains 2,661 tweets (of which 1,304 are labeled as true). The original paper reports an n-gram baseline of 67%.
    - As the *'multiple symptoms'* dataset, we use a dataset of 9,006 tweets (of which 2,306 are labeled as true) by (Robinson et al., 2015). The tweets consist of illnesses, such as cough, cold, fever, and diarrhoea. No cross-validation results on this dataset have been reported in the original paper.

- **Pair 2**:
    - For vaccination usage detection, we use the dataset provided as a shared task as reported in Weissenbacher et al. (2018). The dataset consists of 5,751 tweets (of which 1,692 are true). The winning team by Joshi et al. (2018) reported a F-score of 80.87% for 10-fold cross-validation.
    - For drug usage detection, we use 13,409 tweets (of which 3,167 are true) provided by Jiang et al. (2016). No cross-

---

[2] https://www.cdc.gov/vaccines/vac-gen/ imz-basics.htm; Last accessed on 3rd September, 2019.

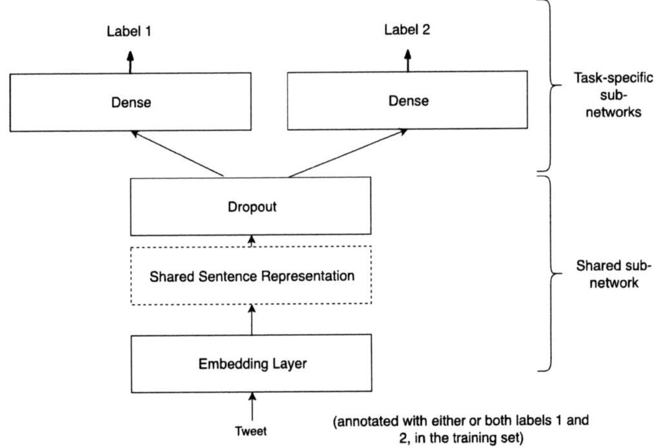

Figure 1: Our MTL architecture.

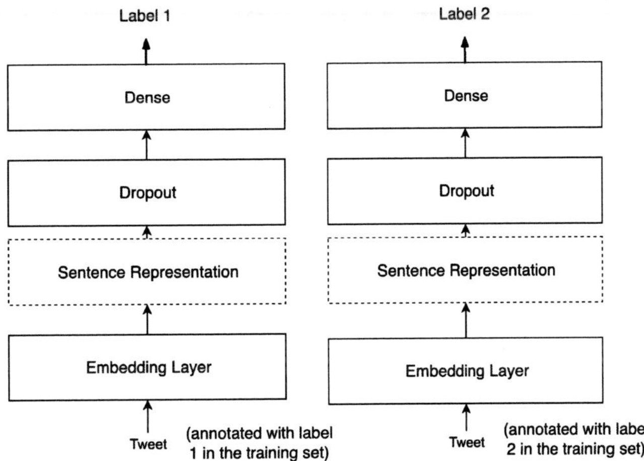

Figure 2: STL architecture corresponding to our MTL architecture.

validation results on this dataset have been reported in the original paper.

- **Pair 3**: We use a dataset of 10,688 tweets by Dredze et al. (2016). Out of these, 9,517 are labeled true for vaccine relevance while 3,097 are labeled true for vaccine intent. No experimental evaluation for these tasks has been reported in the paper or its derivative papers, to the best of our knowledge.

Since these datasets have been reported in past papers, we use Tweepy[3] to download the datasets of tweets using their identifiers. To implement the deep learning models, we use Keras (Chollet, 2015), with the Adam optimiser and binary cross-entropy as the loss function during training, with

___

[3]http://www.tweepy.org/; Last accessed on 3rd September, 2019.

a dropout of 0.25 and number of units for intermediate layers as 25. We use word embeddings with 200 dimensions, pre-trained on a Twitter corpus using GLoVe (Pennington et al., 2014). These embeddings have been trained on 2 billion tweets with 27 billion tokens.

The general outline of our experimentation is a comparison of MTL with the equivalent single-task learning (STL) version. The corresponding STL architecture is shown in Figure 2. This architecture is identical to MTL, except that it separately learns the classifiers for the two tasks. The STL version uses one dense layer to obtain the classification output after the embedding layer and a layer to capture the semantic representation (the equivalent of the shared layer in MTL). For all our experiments, we report average accuracy and F-score values on ten-fold cross-validation.

	STL		MTL	
Shared Layer	Acc.	F-score	Acc.	F-score
Influenza				
B	76.52	75.90	77.85	**76.41**
C	76.74	**76.75**	73.46	66.79
B+C	75.84	74.41	77.89	**76.86**
Multiple symptoms				
B	78.49	48.48	75.34	**56.50**
C	74.91	**54.43**	79.58	44.29
B+C	78.39	45.34	79.28	**51.31**

Table 1: Accuracy and F-score (%) for Pair 1: Personal health mention detection for influenza and personal health mention detection for multiple symptoms.

	STL		MTL	
Shared Layer	Acc.	F-score	Acc.	F-score
Vaccine Usage Detection				
B	85.46	74.85	85.90	**76.82**
C	85.53	**75.50**	85.59	75.47
B+C	84.28	73.49	85.62	**75.59**
Drug Usage Detection				
B	78.78	53.74	79.27	**56.47**
C	77.20	**55.59**	80.74	54.59
B+C	78.09	52.79	80.71	**56.83**

Table 2: Accuracy and F-score (%) for Pair 2: Vaccination usage detection and drug usage detection.

	STL		MTL	
Shared Layer	Acc.	F-score	Acc.	F-score
Vaccine Relevance Detection				
B	97.71	**98.80**	97.40	98.64
C	97.60	**98.75**	97.27	98.58
B+C	97.56	98.73	97.86	**98.88**
Vaccine Intent Detection				
B	75.72	75.29	86.55	**78.93**
C	86.03	**76.93**	83.88	75.00
B+C	85.62	75.59	85.82	**77.15**

Table 3: Accuracy and F-score (%) for Pair 3: Vaccine relevance detection and vaccine intent detection.

6 Results

The effectiveness of Pair 1 for the three shared layers BiLSTM (B), Convolutional (C), and BiLSTM plus Convolutional (B+C) is shown in Table 1. These values are higher than the reported baseline for the influenza detection task. For both tasks, B and B+C result in an improvement when MTL is used. The highest improvement is 6% in case of influenza for B+C. However, there is a degradation when the shared layer is C. The improvement in case of B and B+C for 'Multiple symptoms' is statistically significant ($p < 0.05$, paired t-test). The improvement in the case of influenza, however, is not statistically significant.

The corresponding effectiveness of Pair 2 is shown in Table 2 for the pair: vaccine usage detection and drug usage detection. The best F-score for vaccine usage detection is 76.82%, when a BiLSTM layer is used as a shared representation in the MTL architecture. The best F-score for drug usage detection is 56.83%, when a combination of BiLSTM and convolutional layers is used in a corresponding setting. We observe that, for vaccine usage detection, there is an improvement of 2-3% in case of either B or B+C. The improvement is not statistically significant. Similar trends are observed for Pair 3, as shown in Table 3. We observe that the F-scores are also high (around 97-98%) for vaccine relevance detection, purely due to the skew in the dataset. However, we observe that, in this case, the improvement in F-score when MTL is used is observed only in the case of B+C. Since vaccine intent *implies* vaccine relevance, our results show that MTL may not be beneficial for re-lated classification tasks where one task implies another.

It is possible that the benefit of MTL depends on the size of the training set from the conjugate task (*i.e.*, tweets labeled for drug usage detection in order to improve the effectiveness of vaccine usage detection). Therefore, the impact of the size of training dataset on accuracy of four tasks of pairs 1 and 2, for the best performing architecture is shown in Figure 3. In general, the performance improves with an increase in training set size. The improvement is higher for Pair 2 than Pair 1. The datasets in Pair 2 were created using separate sets of keywords (drug names versus vaccine names, in specific), while the ones in Pair 1 were created using overlapping sets of keywords. Thus, the extent of relatedness or similarity governs the performance gain due to MTL. It may be noted that this comparison is not relevant for Pair 3 since every

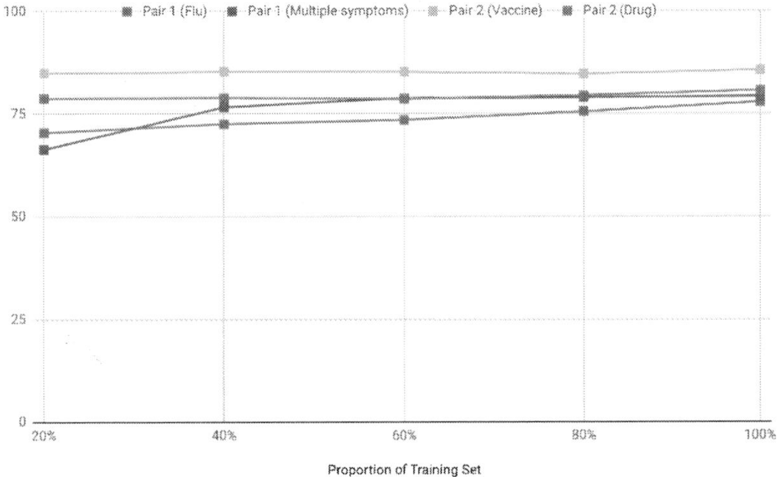

Figure 3: Change in accuracy values with an increase in the proportion of training set from the additional task in the pair for pairs 1 and 2.

instance in the dataset contains both the labels.

7 Error Analysis

We analyse the errors in two parts. In the first part, we compare errors made by the architectures that use STL and MTL. This helps to understand situations in which MTL does better than STL. In the second part, we evaluate errors made by MTL. These can serve as pointers for future work.

We manually analyse 50 randomly selected erroneous instances each from STL and MTL for all pairs of tasks. The benefit of MTL over STL was observed in the following cases for Pairs 1 and 2:

- **Pair 1**: For personal health mention detection, false positives were observed in the form of tweets that express the fear of flu (for example, the tweet '*i feel like im getting sick!=[UGH piggy flu stay away!*' was misclassified) in the case of STL but not in MTL. Errors due to figurative language (for example, '*because theres times when i want to just check my facebook feed and not feel sick to my stomach*') occurred with STL (6 out of 50) more often than with MTL (2 out of 50).

- **Pair 2**: Errors in tweets where the speaker was reluctant to take a drug (for example, the tweet '*do i take my migraine medicine and pray for no interactions or do i take a muscle relaxant or tramadol and hope for the best*' was mis-classified) were reduced when MTL

(1 out of 50) was used instead of STL (8 out of 50).

We observe no specific patterns of errors for Pair 3 when we compare the mis-classified instances for STL and MTL.

In contrast, an analysis of errors obtained from MTL showed the following patterns:

- Errors in **Pair 1** include long tweets which contain a rant along with a personal health mention (11 out of 50). For example, '*8 hrs sleep still feel like shit laying in pitch black listening to my belly make some weird arsed noises think im gunna hurl again*'.

- Errors in **Pair 2** include (a) Apprehensions/fears expressed before a flu shot/Intent to receive a flu shot (16 out of 50, in case of vaccination usage detection); (b) Mentions of a drug for dramatic effect (14 out of 50, in case of drug usage detection). For example, '*i dont usually remember drunk dreams. unless combined w melatonin*'.

These show that MTL may be unable to guard against topic drifts observed due to rants, apprehensions or dramatisation.

8 Conclusions & Future Work

We evaluate multi-task learning (MTL) for three pairs of similar health informatics tasks dealing with: (1) Overlapping symptoms (detection of influenza and multiple symptoms); (2) General/specific medical concepts (detection of the usage of drugs and vaccines); and, (3) Related classification problems (vaccine relevance detection and vaccine intent detection). We compare STL with MTL where the pair of tasks are jointly learned for three kinds of shared sentence representations. In general, for shared layers based on BiLSTM and BiLSTM + Convolutional, MTL helps the three pairs. However, this improvement is not observed when the Convolutional layer is used as a shared representation. The improvement, wherever applicable, is around 2-4% for all the pairs. While MTL has been considered almost a 'silver bullet' in situations where related classification problems or datasets are available, our results highlight the caveats therein. We observe that the benefit of MTL depends on the type of shared layer and the relationship between the tasks under consideration.

Our results show that MTL can help to leverage different datasets annotated for related health informatics tasks. This is potentially useful since specialised tasks are common in health informatics and large datasets may or may not be available. It remains to be verified if the benefit can be generalised for other tasks. Similarly, while we present the relatedness between the participating tasks in a qualitative manner, their similarity could be empirically determined as a future work. A correlation between the similarity of classification tasks and the expected benefit of MTL is a possible future work.

References

Shai Ben-David and Reba Schuller. 2003. Exploiting task relatedness for multiple task learning. In *Learning Theory and Kernel Machines*, pages 567–580. Springer.

Adrian Benton, Margaret Mitchell, and Dirk Hovy. 2017. Multitask learning for mental health conditions with limited social media data. In *Proceedings of the Conference of the European Chapter of the Association for Computational Linguistics*, pages 152–162, Valencia, Spain.

Joachim Bingel and Anders Søgaard. 2017. Identifying beneficial task relations for multi-task learning in deep neural networks. In *Proceedings of the Conference of the European Chapter of the Association for Computational Linguistics*, pages 164–169, Valencia, Spain.

Franois Chollet. 2015. Keras. `https://github.com/fchollet/keras`.

Shaika Chowdhury, Chenwei Zhang, and Philip S Yu. 2018. Multi-task pharmacovigilance mining from social media posts. In *Proceedings of the World Wide Web Conference*, pages 117–126, Lyon, France. International World Wide Web Conferences Steering Committee.

Gamal Crichton, Sampo Pyysalo, Billy Chiu, and Anna Korhonen. 2017. A neural network multi-task learning approach to biomedical named entity recognition. *BMC bioinformatics*, 18(1):368.

Mark Dredze, David Broniatowski, Michael Smith, and Karen M Hilyard. 2016. Understanding vaccine refusal: why we need social media now. *American journal of preventive medicine*, 50(4):550–552.

Arie Hasman. 1998. Education and health informatics. *International journal of medical informatics*, 52(1-3):209–216.

Shu Huang, Wei Peng, Jingxuan Li, and Dongwon Lee. 2013. Sentiment and topic analysis on social media: A multi-task multi-label classification approach. In *Proceedings of the Annual ACM web science conference*, pages 172–181, Paris, France.

Keyuan Jiang, Ricardo Calix, and Matrika Gupta. 2016. Construction of a personal experience tweet corpus for health surveillance. In *Proceedings of the ACL Workshop on biomedical natural language processing*, pages 128–135, Berlin, Germany.

Aditya Joshi, Xiang Dai, Sarvnaz Karimi, Ross Sparks, Cecile Paris, and C Raina MacIntyre. 2018. Shot or not: Comparison of nlp approaches for vaccination behaviour detection. In *Proceedings of the EMNLP Workshop SMM4H: The 3rd Social Media Mining for Health Applications Workshop & Shared Task*, pages 43–47.

Alex Lamb, Michael Paul, and Mark Dredze. 2013. Separating fact from fear: Tracking flu infections on Twitter. In *Proceedings of the Conference of the North American Chapter of the Association for Computational Linguistics: Human Language Technologies*, pages 789–795, Atlanta, Georgia.

Pengfei Liu, Xipeng Qiu, and Xuanjing Huang. 2017. Adversarial multi-task learning for text classification. In *Proceedings of the Annual Meeting of the Association for Computational Linguistics*, pages 1–10, Vancouver, Canada.

Abhijit Mishra, Kuntal Dey, and Pushpak Bhattacharyya. 2017. Learning cognitive features from gaze data for sentiment and sarcasm classification using convolutional neural network. In *Proceedings of the Annual Meeting of the Association for Computational Linguistics*, pages 377–387, Vancouver, Canada.

Jeffrey Pennington, Richard Socher, and Christopher Manning. 2014. Glove: Global vectors for word representation. In *Proceedings of the conference on empirical methods in natural language processing*, pages 1532–1543, Doha, Qatar.

Bella Robinson, Ross Sparks, Robert Power, and Mark Cameron. 2015. Social media monitoring for health indicators. In *International Congress on Modelling and Simulation*, Gold Coast, Australia.

Sebastian Ruder. 2017. An overview of multi-task learning in deep neural networks. *arXiv preprint arXiv:1706.05098*.

Anders Søgaard and Yoav Goldberg. 2016. Deep multi-task learning with low level tasks supervised at lower layers. In *Proceedings of the Annual Meeting of the Association for Computational Linguistics*, volume 2, pages 231–235, Berlin, Germany.

Davy Weissenbacher, Abeed Sarker, Michael Paul, and Graciela Gonzalez-Hernandez. 2018. Overview of the third social media mining for health (SMM4H) shared tasks at EMNLP 2018. In *Proceedings of the EMNLP Workshop on The Social Media Mining for Health Applications Workshop and Shared Task*, pages 13–16, Brussels, Belgium.

Fangzhao Wu and Yongfeng Huang. 2016. Personalized microblog sentiment classification via multi-task learning. In *Proceedings of the 13th AAAI Conference on Artificial Intelligence*.

Ya Xue, Xuejun Liao, Lawrence Carin, and Balaji Krishnapuram. 2007. Multi-task learning for classification with dirichlet process priors. *Journal of Machine Learning Research*, 8(Jan):35–63.

Yu Zhang and Dit-Yan Yeung. 2012. A convex formulation for learning task relationships in multi-task learning. *arXiv preprint arXiv:1203.3536*.

Jiayu Zhou, Lei Yuan, Jun Liu, and Jieping Ye. 2011. A multi-task learning formulation for predicting disease progression. In *Proceedings of the 17th ACM SIGKDD international conference on Knowledge discovery and data mining*, pages 814–822. ACM.

Bin Zou, Vasileios Lampos, and Ingemar Cox. 2018. Multi-task learning improves disease models from web search. In *Proceedings of the World Wide Web Conference*, pages 87–96, Lyon, France. International World Wide Web Conferences Steering Committee.

An Improved Coarse-to-Fine Method for Solving Generation Tasks

Wenyu Guan[1,2], Qianying Liu[3], Guangzhi Han[2], Bin Wang[4] and Sujian Li[1]
[1] Key Laboratory of Computational Linguistics, MOE, Peking University
[2] School of Software and Microelectronics, Peking University
[3] Graduate School of Informatics, Kyoto University
[4] Xiaomi AI Lab, Xiaomi Inc.
{guanwy, hanguangzhi10, lisujian}@pku.edu.cn
ying@nlp.ist.i.kyoto-u.ac.jp, wangbin11@xiaomi.com

Abstract

The coarse-to-fine (coarse2fine) methods have recently been widely used in the generation tasks. The methods first generate a rough sketch in the coarse stage and then use the sketch to get the final result in the fine stage. However, they usually lack the correction ability when getting a wrong sketch. To solve this problem, in this paper, we propose an improved coarse2fine model with a control mechanism, with which our method can control the influence of the sketch on the final results in the fine stage. Even if the sketch is wrong, our model still has the opportunity to get a correct result. We have experimented our model on the tasks of semantic parsing and math word problem solving. The results have shown the effectiveness of our proposed model.

1 Introduction

The coarse-to-fine (coarse2fine) methods have been applied in many generation tasks such as machine translation (Xia et al., 2017) , abstract writing (Wang et al., 2018b) and semantic parsing (Dong and Lapata, 2018). They have shown excellent performances but still have many disadvantages. Traditional coarse2fine models usually tackle one task in two stages. In the first stage (coarse stage), a low-level seq2seq model is used to generate a rough sketch, which makes the data more compact and alleviates the problem of data sparsity. Some examples of sketches are shown in Table 1. Besides, Sketches in this stage are also easier to generate. Then, in the fine stage, both text and previous sketches will be input to another high-level seq2seq model to predict the final result so that the high-level model can produce a precise output.

In the coarse2fine models, the concept of template sketch provides a new view of compiling a rough template, but how to guarantee its quality is still a problem. Meanwhile, details from the fine stage will be filled into sketches to produce the final result, so the quality of sketches serves an essential influence on the result. If the generated sketches are in high quality, the coarse2fine model performs well. Otherwise, we fail to get an excellent output. The main reason is that the sketch is misleading and has no possibility to be corrected once it is wrong.

In this paper, we propose an improved coarse2fine model to solve this problem. It has a similar framework which consists of two levels of seq2seq models. First, the model predicts a rough sketch in the coarse stage. In the fine stage, compared with traditional coarse2fine model, we use the generated sketches in the coarse stage as assistant information to help the decoder. Besides, We set a weight to control the degree of how the sketch affects the fine stage. Higher weight means that the fine stage is strictly guided by the sketch. Lower weight will decrease the impact of the sketch on the final output and give the model more flexibility to generate the result which does not rely on the sketch. For different tasks, we will tune the weights by experience and make a balance between the sketch guidance and the model's correction ability.

Our model is a universal framework which can apply on many generation tasks. In this work, we apply it on two semantic parsing tasks (text2logic and text2code) and math word problem (MWP) solving task. Experimental results show that our model achieves a better performance than some baseline models in these tasks.

2 Related Work

In this section, we briefly introduce the tasks where we experimented our model and also the

Tasks	Type	Example
	logic	(argmin $0 (and (place:t $0) (loc:t $0 s0)) (elevation:i $0))
Text2logic	sketch	(argmin #1 (and place:t @1 loc:t @2) elevation:i @1)
	text	what is the lowest point in s0 ?
	code	decode = curry(_proxy_method, method=bytes.decode)
Text2code	sketch	NAME = NAME(NAME, NAME=NAME.NAME)
	text	call the function curry with 2 arguments: _proxy_method and method set to bytes.decode[bytes.decode], substitute the result for decode.
	equation	$x = 150 + 2 - 50$
MWP	sketch	$x = \langle num \rangle + \langle num \rangle - \langle num \rangle$
	text	There are 150 science books, and the storybooks are 50 books less than the science books. How many books are there in the storybooks?

Table 1: Examples of text, sketches and generating goals in different datasets.

method we applied.

2.1 Semantic Parsing

Semantic parsing is a task of translating natural language into computer executable language such as logic form, code in computer language and SQL query. Traditional semantic parsing usually adopts rule based method Tang and Mooney (2000); Wong and Mooney (2007); Andreas et al. (2013). Recently, with the development of neural network techniques, there are many new semantic parsing models with neural methods. Of them, Seq2seq models have been widely applied in semantic parsing tasks. The encoder encodes the text and the decoder predicts the logic symbols (Dong and Lapata, 2016). The seq2tree model encodes inputs by LSTM and generates the logic form by conditioning the output sequences or trees on the encoding vectors.(Dong and Lapata, 2016). Abstract syntax networks (ASN) represent the output as the abstract syntax trees (ASTs) (Rabinovich et al., 2017). Its decoder uses a dynamically-determined modular structure paralleling the structure of the output tree.

2.2 Math Word Problem

Math word problem (MWP) aims to teach computers to read the questions in natural language and generate the corresponding math equations. The methods of solving math word problems can be mainly classified into two categories. The first category is the template-based models which summarize some templates through locating similar questions from a given dataset and then fill the concrete numbers into the templates to solve problems (Huang et al., 2017; Wang et al., 2017).

Some cases of math word problems, math equations, templates and sketches are shown in Table 2 These methods are intuitive, but it is difficult to obtain high-quality templates due to data sparsity and transfer them to other datasets. The second category of methods mainly exploits the seq2seq framework to generate the solution equations (Wang et al., 2018a). Recently this kind of methods have shown outstanding performance without manual feature engineering, but they are prone to generate wrong numbers due to its generation flexibility. Some researches have applied reinforcement learning (Huang et al., 2018) or a stack (Chiang and Chen, 2018) to improve the decoding process.

2.3 Coarse-to-fine method

Generalized coarse-to-fine method divides problems into different stages and solves them from coarse to fine. This method is widely applied in computer vision (Gangaputra and Geman, 2006; Pedersoli et al., 2011; Wen et al., 2019) and natural language process (Mei et al., 2016; Choi et al., 2017). The special coarse-to-fine method in this paper is based on end-to-end framework. It has two seq2seq models, generating target data from a coarse stage to a fine stage. Xia et al. (2017) proposed *polish mechanism* with two levels of decoders. The first decoder generates a raw sequence and the second decoder polishes and refines the raw sentence with deliberation. Their model performs excellently on machine translation and text summarization, which is also the first time to use this kind of coarse-to-fine model. Wang et al. (2018b) used a similar framework to write paper abstracts. In the fields of semantic pars-

Question	Woodpeckers can eat 645 pests per day, and frogs can eat 608 pests in 8 days. How many insects do woodpeckers eat more than frogs every day?
Equation	$x = 645 - 608/8$
Template	$x = \langle num1 \rangle - \langle num2 \rangle / \langle num3 \rangle$
Numbers	$\{\langle num1 \rangle : 645, \langle num2 \rangle : 608, \langle num3 \rangle : 8\}$
Question	The garment factory originally planned to make 1080 sets of suits, which would be completed in 20 days. Actually they finished 72 sets per day, How many sets they produced everyday more than the original plan?
Equation	$x = 72 - 1080/20$
Template	$x = \langle num3 \rangle - \langle num1 \rangle / \langle num2 \rangle$
Numbers	$\{\langle num1 \rangle : 1080, \langle num2 \rangle : 20, \langle num3 \rangle : 72\}$
Question	The shirt factory produced 640 shirts in the past 4 days, but now it produces 350 shirts per day. How many shirts it produces each day more than it used to ?
Equation	$x = 350 - 640/4$
Template	$x = \langle num3 \rangle - \langle num1 \rangle / \langle num2 \rangle$
Numbers	$\{\langle num1 \rangle : 640, \langle num2 \rangle : 4, \langle num3 \rangle : 350\}$
Sketch	$x = \langle num \rangle - \langle num \rangle / \langle num \rangle$

Table 2: Examples of math word problems with different equations but same sketches.

ing, Dong and Lapata (2018) applied a two-level coarse-to-fine model in text2logic, text2python and text2SQL. This framework also shows significant improvement in these parsing tasks.

3 Problem Formulation

In this work, we aim at generating structured languages. Each instance contains a piece of text in natural language with m words $\{w_i\}_1^m$, generating the target output $\{e_i\}_1^{|e|}$. We learn sketches $\{s_i\}_1^{|s|}$ from $\{w_i\}_1^m$. We decompose the probability distribution $p(e|w)$ into a combination of sketch's conditional probability:

$$p(e|w) = p(e|s, w)p(s|w) \quad (1)$$

In this paper, we compute $p(e|s, w)$ and $p(s|w)$ step by step:

$$p(s|w) = \prod_{t=1}^{|s|} p(s_t|s_{1,\dots,t-1}, w) \quad (2)$$

$$p(e|s, w) = \prod_{t=1}^{|e|} p(e_t|e_{1,\dots,t-1}, s, w) \quad (3)$$

3.1 Framework

The coarse2fine model consists of four main components: text encoder, sketch decoder, sketch encoder, and final decoder.

During the coarse stage, the text encoder and sketch decoder predicate sketch by computing $p(s|w)$ step by step. Then, in fine stage, the sketch encoder will encode the sketch and the decoder takes the text encoder's output and sketch to compute the probability distribution. The framework is shown in Figure 1.

3.2 Coarse Stage

In the coarse stage, a basic seq2seq architecture is used to generate sketches. Firstly, question text is split into tokens and sent into an embedding layer. Then, a two-layer bidirectional LSTM (Hochreiter and Schmidhuber, 1997) will read the embedded word one-by-one and produce a sequence of hidden states $\{q_i\}_1^m$:

$$q_i^f = LSTM(emb(w_i), q_{i-1}^f) \quad (4)$$

$$q_i^b = LSTM(emb(w_i), q_{i+1}^b) \quad (5)$$

$$q_i = [q_i^f, q_i^b] \quad (6)$$

Each decoding step, the embedding vector of previously symbol and previous hidden state are sent to LSTM. Then, we calculate the probability distribution of the sketch through attention mech-

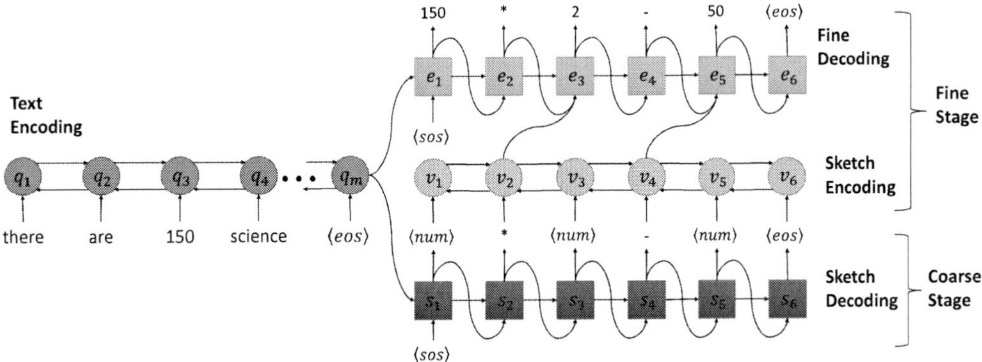

Figure 1: Improved Coarse-to-Fine Model framework.

anism:

$$h_j = LSTM(emb(s_{j-1}), h_{j-1}) \tag{7}$$

$$a_{ji} = softmax(q_i h_j) \tag{8}$$

$$c_j = \sum_{i=0}^{m} a_{ji} h_j \tag{9}$$

$$p(s_j | s_{1,...,j-1}, w) = softmax(U[tanh(W[c_j; h_j] + b_{attn})] + b) \tag{10}$$

h_j is the decoder hidden state in j step, a_{ji} is the attention score, c_j is the context vector. Beyond that, U, W, b_{attn} and b are model's parameters.

3.3 Fine Stage

In this stage, the fine decoder uses the sketch as assistant information to predict the final result. At the beginning of the fine stage, a bidirectional LSTM is used as sketch encoder to encode the sketch. After taking the encoded sketch as a part of the input, the fine decoder has perceptions of the whole sketch in low-level meaning. The process of sketch encoding is similar to question encoding, while the difference is that the input of (4) and (5) are changed to sketch symbols $\{s_i\}_1^{|s|}$.

Then, the fine decoder will use the encoded sketch to help its decoding process. As shown in Figure 1, fine decoder shares the same common text encoder with sketch decoder. The decoding process of fine stage is also similar to sketch decoding (7)-(10), but the input of LSTM is designed

as follows:

$$i_t = \begin{cases} \lambda \cdot v_{t-1} + (1 - \lambda) emb(e_{t-1}), \\ \qquad\qquad e_{t-1}\text{is determined by} s_{t-1} \\ emb(e_{t-1}), \quad \text{otherwise} \end{cases} \tag{11}$$

$$h_t = LSTM(i_t, h_{t-1}) \tag{12}$$

If e_{t-1} is determined by s_{t-1}, the input is the combination of the embedding of e_{t-1} and the sketch encoder's output v_{t-1}. Otherwise, it is set as the embedding of e_{t-1}. We assume the number of sketch decoding outputs is the same shape as the ones from fine decoding. So the e_t and the s_t are aligned one by one. λ is a hyper parameter that controls the combination of v_{t-1} and $emb(e_{t-1})$, ranging from 0 to 1. It indicates how much the fine decoder is guided by sketches. If λ is 1, the process of fine decode will be strictly guided by the sketch. Once the sketch is wrong, the fine decoder has little possibilities to generate a correct result. On the contrary, if λ is 0, the coarse stage will become useless and our model will degrade into one stage model. Like equations (7)-(10), we compute the final probability distribution according to w and s step by step. And $p(e_t|e_{1,...,t-1}, s, w)$ is calculated analogously equation (10).

3.4 Model Training

As shown in equation (1), our goal is to maximize the likelihood of sketches and optimize the final results. It can be trained in a supervised way with gold sketches and results. The objective function aims to maximize L:

$$L = L_{ske} + L_{res} \tag{13}$$

$$L_{ske} = \sum_{(s,w)} \log p(s|w) \tag{14}$$

$$L_{res} = \sum_{(s,w,e)} \log p(e|s,w) \tag{15}$$

(s, w, e) belongs to training pairs. When the model is in testing mode, the final result is computed according $\hat{s} = \arg\max_{s'} p(s'|w)$ and $\hat{e} = \arg\max_{e'} p(e'|w, s)$. s' and e' are sketch candidates and result candidates.

4 Experiments

4.1 Dataset

Text-to-Logic In this task, we conduct our model on GEO dataset, which contains 880 sentences and their corresponding logical queries. Following Dong and Lapata(2018)'s work, we extract the sketches from λ-calculus-based meaning representations. These sketches ignore the arguments and variables and concentrate on operators and logic structures. "\$" means an ignored argument and "#" represents an omitted token.

Text-to-Code We chose the Django dataset which has 18805 pairs of natural language expression texts and python codes. We get the sketches by replacing the objects, numbers, functions, and variables with their type names. The symbols of the basic framework are reversed, such as keyword and operators.

MWP Math23k is one of the most popular math word problem datasets which has 23,162 Chinese algebra problems. Each item contains a question in Chinese, a math equation and a answer to the question. To get sketches, we use a placeholder $\langle num \rangle$ to replace the detail numbers in math equations, so sketches only include operators ("+-*/") and $\langle num \rangle$. Another large-scale MWP dataset is Dolphin23K, but its authors just release a construction tool, so we can't get the standard data. All the experiments on it are finished by the dataset's author and they never release the code. Because we can't evaluate the result fairly, we give up conducting our experiment on Dolphin23K. Examples of original data and sketches of these three datasets are shown in Table 1.

Dataset	Train	Dev	Test
GEO	600	100	180
Django	16000	1000	1805
Math23k	21162	1000	1000

Table 3: Statics of datasets

Task	Emb	Hidden	Epoch	LR
Text2logic	150	250	50	0.005
Text2code	200	300	150	0.005
MWP	128	512	150	0.01

Table 4: Model parameters and training settings

4.2 Preprocess

To compare the result equally, we made our preprocessing in accord with Dong and Lapata (2018)'s experiment as much as possible. For GEO, we followed Dong and Lapata's work, transforming all words into lower type and replacing the entity mentions with a sign and a counting number. And for Django, we chosed to use the processed data given by Yin and Neubig (2017). They tokenized and POS tagged sentences using NLTK. In MWP, we followed Wang et al.'s work. To reduce the influence of OOV, we normalized numbers as the order of their appearance. Examples of some processed cases of Math23k are shown in Table 2, who have same sketches.

4.3 Results

We has compared our improved coarse2fine model with different published models. The optimizer is Adam and many details of training and testing are shown in Table 3 and Table 4. To compare the result equally, we chose the same model parameters as Dong and Lapata (2018) in semantic parsing tasks. Accuracy in this paper (except the MWP) is calculated by comparing the generated result to the gold result(sketches, logic expressions and Python codes), while, in MWP, the accuracy means that whether the math formula predicated by our model it is equal to the given answer.

The results of text2logic are presented in Table 5. Dong and Lapata has experimented the seq2seq and seq2tree method in this task. Seq2tree is a novel framework that has the ability to generate a sequence in hierarchical tree structure. It has an excellent performance in semantic parsing tasks. And Rabinovich et al. has used an abstract syntax tree to generate logic expressions. In our ex-

Model	Acc
Seq2seq (Dong and Lapata, 2016)	84.6%
Seq2tree (Dong and Lapata, 2016)	87.1%
Asn (Rabinovich et al., 2017)	85.7%
Asn+supatt (Rabinovich et al., 2017)	87.1%
One stage	85.0%
Coarse2fine (Dong and Lapata, 2018)	88.2%
Improved coarse2fine	**88.6%**

Table 5: Results of text2logic on GEO

Model	Acc
Seq2seq+unk replacement	45.1%
Seq2tree+unk replacement	39.4%
Lpn+copy (Ling et al.)	62.3%
Snm+copy (Yin and Neubig, 2017)	71.6%
One stage	69.5%
Coarse2fine (Dong and Lapata, 2018)	74.1%
Improved coarse2fine	**76.1%**

Table 6: Results of text2code on Django

Model	Acc
Self-Attention (Robaidek et al., 2018)	56.8%
Bi-LSTM (Robaidek et al., 2018)	57.9%
Seq2seq+stack (Chiang and Chen, 2018)	65.8%
T-RNN (Wang et al., 2019)	66.9%
Coarse2fine	66.7%
Improved coarse2fine	**67.9%**

Table 7: Result of MWP on Math 23K.

periment, the sketch decoder can get 89.3% accuracy and the highest accuracy of logic expression is 88.6% when λ is 0.9. Compared to Dong and Lapata's model, our accuracy rise by 0.4%.

Table 6 reports the results of text2code task. The accuracy of sketches in this task is 77.4%. First two lines are Dong and Lapata's experiments with seq2seq model and seq2tree model. In addition, Ling et al. has designed Latent-Predictor-Network with copy mechanism. And a syntactic neural model also shows good performance in code generation (Yin and Neubig, 2017). As we can see, our model has an outstanding performance in Django dataset. We achieve 76.1% accuracy when λ is 0.6.

The results of MWP are shown in Table 7. As mentioned in Section 2.2, models can be classified into various categories according to the way they get the equation. Classification models get templates through classifier based on Bi-LSTM or Self-Attention (Robaidek et al., 2018). Generation models get equations based on seq2seq models. They are improved with many assistant components. Chiang and Chen (2018) has used a stack, so they could build a tree structure math formula by pushing and popping generated items. Wang et al. (2019) has designed a template-based model which could predict the tree structure formula from bottom to up. In our experiment, sketches have 68.3% accuracy, whereas the accuracy of our

model reaches 67.9% when λ is 0.3.

4.4 Further Test and Analysis

We present the performance with different hyper parameter λ in Table 8. For semantic parsing tasks, our model has a more obvious improvement in text2code. When λ is 1, the model is equal to Dong and Lapata's model and it has 74.9% accuracy. With the decrease of λ, the influence of sketch declines. In the range of (1, 0.6), the lower λ gives the fine decoder more chances to generate a correct result. When λ is lower than 0.6, correct sketches' help will be decreased, which leads to a poor result . The model should keep λ in a appropriate value, so it can take coarse2fine model's advantage and have chances to predict a correct result even the sketch is wrong.

We are the first one to apply coarse2fine method in MWP task. To check whether using sketches makes a good contribution to this task, we suspend the coarse stage and give gold sketches to sketch encoder[1]. The hyper parameter λ is set to 1 so the equation generation will be strictly guided by the sketch. We compared it with one stage model (Wang et al., 2018a). As shown in Figure 2, our model can improve its accuracy highly and shows faster convergence speed after applying gold sketches. Also, its accuracy hits 77.0% under such circumstances.

5 Conclusions

We propose an improved coarse-to-fine generating model in this paper, which takes the advantages of using sketches to help the generating process. When the sketches have mistakes, our model still has a chance to generate a correct result, which will be conducive to the final accuracy. Besides, it is a general framework for many tasks and easy

---

[1]Giving gold sketches to the sketch encoder in the former two tasks has been accomplished by Dong and Lapata. The accuracies are 93.9% and 83.0%

Task	λ 1	0.8	0.6	0.4	0.2
Text2logic	88.2%	88.5%	87.8%	86.5%	85.2%
Text2django	74.9%	76.0%	76.1%	75.2%	74.9%
MWP	66.7%	66.9%	67.4%	67.8%	67.8%

Table 8: Accuracy of three tasks with different hyper parameters.

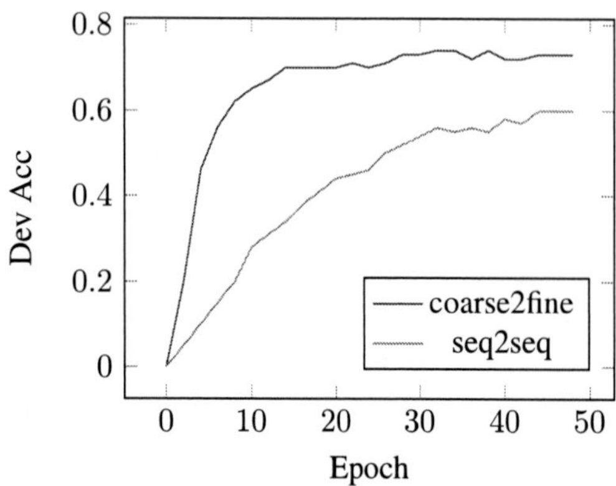

Figure 2: Training record of coarse2fine model and seq2seq model.

to follow. We have conducted our model in many generation tasks (text2logic, text2code, MWP). As a result, compared with the basic model, our accuracy has increased by 0.4%, 2.0%, 1.2% respectively in these three tasks.

Acknowledgments

We thank the anonymous reviewers for their helpful comments on this paper. This work was partially supported by National Natural Science Foundation of China (61572049 and 61876009). The corresponding author is Sujian Li.

References

Jacob Andreas, Andreas Vlachos, and Stephen Clark. 2013. Semantic parsing as machine translation. In *Proceedings of the 51st Annual Meeting of the Association for Computational Linguistics (Volume 2: Short Papers)*, pages 47–52.

Ting-Rui Chiang and Yun-Nung Chen. 2018. Semantically-aligned equation generation for solving and reasoning math word problems. *arXiv preprint arXiv:1811.00720*.

Eunsol Choi, Daniel Hewlett, Jakob Uszkoreit, Illia Polosukhin, Alexandre Lacoste, and Jonathan Berant. 2017. Coarse-to-fine question answering for long documents. In *Proceedings of the 55th Annual Meeting of the Association for Computational Linguistics (Volume 1: Long Papers)*, pages 209–220.

Li Dong and Mirella Lapata. 2016. Language to logical form with neural attention. In *Proceedings of the 54th Annual Meeting of the Association for Computational Linguistics (Volume 1: Long Papers)*, volume 1, pages 33–43.

Li Dong and Mirella Lapata. 2018. Coarse-to-fine decoding for neural semantic parsing. In *Proceedings of the 56th Annual Meeting of the Association for Computational Linguistics (Volume 1: Long Papers)*, pages 731–742.

Sachin Gangaputra and Donald Geman. 2006. A design principle for coarse-to-fine classification. In *Proceedings of the 2006 IEEE Computer Society Conference on Computer Vision and Pattern Recognition-Volume 2*, pages 1877–1884. IEEE Computer Society.

Sepp Hochreiter and Jürgen Schmidhuber. 1997. Long short-term memory. *Neural computation*, 9(8):1735–1780.

Danqing Huang, Jing Liu, Chin-Yew Lin, and Jian Yin. 2018. Neural math word problem solver with reinforcement learning. In *Proceedings of the 27th International Conference on Computational Linguistics*, pages 213–223.

Danqing Huang, Shuming Shi, Chin-Yew Lin, and Jian Yin. 2017. Learning fine-grained expressions to solve math word problems. In *Proceedings of the 2017 Conference on Empirical Methods in Natural Language Processing*, pages 805–814.

Wang Ling, Edward Grefenstette, Karl Moritz Hermann, Tomáš Kociský, Andrew Senior, Fumin Wang, and Phil Blunsom. Latent predictor networks for code generation.

Hongyuan Mei, TTI UChicago, Mohit Bansal, and Matthew R Walter. 2016. What to talk about and how? selective generation using lstms with coarse-to-fine alignment. In *Proceedings of NAACL-HLT*, pages 720–730.

Marco Pedersoli, Andrea Vedaldi, and Jordi Gonzàlez. 2011. A coarse-to-fine approach for fast deformable object detection. In *CVPR 2011*, pages 1353–1360. IEEE.

Maxim Rabinovich, Mitchell Stern, and Dan Klein. 2017. Abstract syntax networks for code generation and semantic parsing. In *Proceedings of the 55th Annual Meeting of the Association for Computational Linguistics (Volume 1: Long Papers)*, pages 1139–1149.

Benjamin Robaidek, Rik Koncel-Kedziorski, and Hannaneh Hajishirzi. 2018. Data-driven methods for solving algebra word problems. *arXiv preprint arXiv:1804.10718*.

Lappoon R Tang and Raymond J Mooney. 2000. Automated construction of database interfaces: Integrating statistical and relational learning for semantic parsing. In *Proceedings of the 2000 Joint SIGDAT conference on Empirical methods in natural language processing and very large corpora: held in conjunction with the 38th Annual Meeting of the Association for Computational Linguistics-Volume 13*, pages 133–141. Association for Computational Linguistics.

Lei Wang, Yan Wang, Deng Cai, Dongxiang Zhang, and Xiaojiang Liu. 2018a. Translating a math word problem to a expression tree. In *Proceedings of the 2018 Conference on Empirical Methods in Natural Language Processing*, pages 1064–1069.

Lei Wang, Dongxiang Zhang, Jipeng Zhang, Xing Xu, Lianli Gao, Bingtian Dai, and Heng Tao Shen. 2019. Template-based math word problem solvers with recursive neural networks.

Qingyun Wang, Zhihao Zhou, Lifu Huang, Spencer Whitehead, Boliang Zhang, Heng Ji, and Kevin Knight. 2018b. Paper abstract writing through editing mechanism. In *Proceedings of the 56th Annual Meeting of the Association for Computational Linguistics (Volume 2: Short Papers)*, pages 260–265.

Yan Wang, Xiaojiang Liu, and Shuming Shi. 2017. Deep neural solver for math word problems. In *Proceedings of the 2017 Conference on Empirical Methods in Natural Language Processing*, pages 845–854.

Yang Wen, Bin Sheng, Ping Li, Weiyao Lin, and David Dagan Feng. 2019. Deep color guided coarse-to-fine convolutional network cascade for depth image super-resolution. *IEEE Transactions on Image Processing*, 28(2):994–1006.

Yuk Wah Wong and Raymond Mooney. 2007. Learning synchronous grammars for semantic parsing with lambda calculus. In *Proceedings of the 45th Annual Meeting of the Association of Computational Linguistics*, pages 960–967.

Yingce Xia, Fei Tian, Lijun Wu, Jianxin Lin, Tao Qin, Nenghai Yu, and Tie-Yan Liu. 2017. Deliberation networks: Sequence generation beyond one-pass decoding. In *Advances in Neural Information Processing Systems*, pages 1784–1794.

Pengcheng Yin and Graham Neubig. 2017. A syntactic neural model for general-purpose code generation. In *Proceedings of the 55th Annual Meeting of the Association for Computational Linguistics (Volume 1: Long Papers)*, pages 440–450.

Emerald 110k:
A Multidisciplinary Dataset for Abstract Sentence Classification

Connor Stead [1]   Stephen Smith [1]   Peter Busch [1]   Savanid Vatanasakdakul [2]

[1] Department of Computing, Macquarie University, Australia
[2] Carnegie Mellon University, Qatar

connor.stead@hdr.mq.edu.au stephen.smith@mq.edu.au
peter.busch@mq.edu.au savanid@cmu.edu

Abstract

Background: Datasets available for abstract sentence classification modelling are predominately comprised of abstracts sourced from biomedical research.
Aims: To contribute a large non-biomedical multidisciplinary dataset for abstract sentence classification model research.
Method: Bulk extract and transformation of Emerald Group Publishing structured abstracts indexed on Scopus.
Results: We present the largest multidisciplinary dataset for abstract sentence classification modelling, consisting of 1,050,397 sentences from 103,457 abstracts.

1   Introduction

Abstracts enable researchers to efficiently determine the relevance of literature to their research (Rowley, 1982, Collision, 1971, Cleveland and Cleveland, 2013). The desire to optimise this efficiency has resulted in the adoption of structured abstracts, which feature explicit headings reflecting key characteristics of a study. Examples of these headings include: aim, method, results and contributions. The alternative to structured abstracts are those where sentences addressing such characteristics are not specified.

Compared to unstructured alternatives, structured abstracts are perceived to offer greater value for researchers (Sharma and Harrison, 2006, Taddio et al., 1994 and Guimarães, 2006); permit advanced access to research findings (Mosteller et al., 2004), contain more relevant information (Budgen et al., 2008) and are easier to read (Kitchenham et al., 2008 and Budgen et al., 2008). Structured abstracts also increase the likelihood that relevant research is discovered (Eldredge, 2006, Mulrow, 1987, Haynes et al., 1990, Hartley,

1997, Bayley et al., 2002 and Bayley and Eldredge, 2003).

Natural language processing (NLP) has been used to automate the structuring of unstructured abstracts (Gonçalves et al., 2018; Jin and Szolovits, 2018, Dernoncourt et al., 2016); which is achieved through the development of Abstract Sentence Classification Models (ASCM), capable of classifying sentences sourced from unstructured abstracts into structured abstract headings.

This paper presents a novel dataset to advance ASCM research. The dataset introduced is unlike those already leveraged in ASCM development, primarily as it is comprised of abstracts originating from disciplines not yet explored in current research. The adoption of our dataset in future model development will enable the benchmarking of ASCM capability in new disciplines.

2   Related Work

There are numerous datasets available to researchers seeking to develop ASCM. These are outlined in table 1, an extension of the table presented by Dernoncourt and Lee (2017, p. 3). We extend their table by identifying the abstract's disciplinary domain. The size represents the number of abstracts reflected in the dataset. The 'manual' flag identifies if sentences were manually classified into structured abstract headings by the authors (Y) or were pre-structured in the original abstract (N).

The number of datasets available for ASCM does not directly correspond to the number of ASCM studies, as researchers re-use datasets to benchmark performance and to test novel algorithms. Further, studies may develop a dataset for model development without contributing the dataset as an artefact. Dernoncourt and Lee (2017) also presented a dataset in a standalone paper, much like this body of work. Table 2 provides a summary of ASCM development efforts, along with the dataset used in model development.

Dataset	Size	Manual	Domain
Hara et al. (2007)	200	Y	BM (RCT)
Hirohata et al. (2008)	104k	N	BM
Chung (2009)	327	Y	BM (RCT)
Boudin et al. (2010)	29k	N	BM
Kim et al. (2011)	1k	Y	BM
Huang et al. (2011)	23k	N	BM
Robinson (2012)	1k	N	BM (RCT)
Zhao et al. (2012)	20k	Y	BM
Davis and Mollá (2012)	194	N	BM (RCT)
Huang et al. (2013)	20k	N	BM (RCT)
Dernoncourt and Lee (2017)	196k	N	BM (RCT)

Table 1: Existing ASCM datasets, BM = Biomedicine
RCT = Randomised Controlled Trials.

It is evident the dataset contributed by Kim et al. (2011) and Dernoncourt and Lee (2017) enjoys significant adoption in ASCM development. This dataset represents in practice the concern that the almost exclusive benefactor of advancements in ASCM studies are researchers in the biomedical discipline, and that the abstracts of non-biomedical disciplines have predominately not been included in model development.

There are a few studies representing exceptions to the biomedical exclusive trend. These are identified in table 2 with an asterisk (*). The first example is Teufel and Moens (1998), who developed a Naive Bayes classifier using sentences retrieved from 201 computational linguistics and cognitive science abstracts, achieving 68.6% precision (p. 24). Further non-biomedical examples include Wu et al. (2006) who used the computer and information science academic index Citeseer as an abstract source and Liu et al. (2013) who used ScienceDirect, a primarily scientific and health science academic literature index. These datasets are not available for researcher utilisation.

In response to the lack of disciplinary diversity, we are exploring greater non-biomedical grounded ASCM development. We desire to increase the likelihood that ASCM capability can become a viable inter-disciplinary mechanism to increase research discovery and accessibility. As part of our research, we have created a novel multi-disciplinary abstract sentence dataset for future ASCM development. The dataset development process is outlined in the following section.

Study	Dataset
Teufel and Moens (1998) *	Study developed (Computation and language archive)
McKnight and Srinivasan (2003)	Study developed (Medline)
Shimbo et al. (2003)	Study developed (Medline)
Ito et al. (2004)	Study developed (Medline)
Yamamoto and Takagi (2005)	Study developed (Medline)
Wu et al. (2006) *	Study developed (Citeseer)
Lin et al. (2006)	Study developed
Xu et al. (2006)	Study developed (RCT – source unknown)
Ruch et al. (2007)	Study developed (Medline)
Hirohata et al. (2008)	Study developed (Medline)
Chung (2009)	Study developed (Medline)
Kim et al. (2011)	Study developed (Medline)
Lui (2012)	Kim et al., 2011
Verbeke et al. (2012)	Kim et al., 2011
Liu et al. (2013) *	Study developed (Science Direct)
Hassanzadeh et al. (2014)	Kim et al., 2011
Dernoncourt et al. (2016)	Kim et al., 2011 Dernoncourt et al., 2016
Nam et al. (2016)	Study developed (PubMed)
Jin and Szolovits (2018)	Kim et al., 2011 Dernoncourt and Lee, 2017
Gonçalves et al. (2018)	Dernoncourt and Lee, 2017

Table 2: Existing ASCM studies.

3 Dataset Development

We present a novel abstract sentence dataset for ASCM research. The dataset contains sentences retrieved from multi-disciplinary non-biomedical journal abstracts. Each sentence is classified as belonging to one of the following heading classes:

- Purpose
- Design/methodology/approach
- Findings
- Originality/value
- Social implications
- Practical implications
- Research limitations/implications

3.1 Abstract Identification

As of 2019, Emerald Group Publishing (henceforth: Emerald) publishes over 300 double-blind peer reviewed journals (Emerald Group Publishing, 2019). Emerald journals publish research from management, information science and engineering disciplines. This includes fields such as aerospace technology, management information systems, corporate governance, marketing, computing, accounting, public health, supply chain management and tourism (Emerald Group Publishing, 2019).

In 2005 Emerald began mandating the use of structured abstracts in their journal publications (Emerald Group Publishing Limited, 2005). The multidisciplinary nature of Emerald's journal portfolio combined with their mandated structured abstract adoption policy has resulted in a unique opportunity for ASCM development. However, existing ASCM research has failed to leverage Emerald journal abstracts for model development.

3.2 Abstract Extract

The Scopus academic literature index was utilised to obtain Emerald journal abstracts. This was due to the availability of an API to access Scopus content, as well as the reach and scope of the index. An initial examination of Scopus identified 336 Emerald journals available where research was published between 2005 and 2019. This count indicated that the Emerald portfolio was widely available through Scopus.

After determining the availability of Emerald journals on Scopus, we developed a Python program capable of autonomously querying Scopus for Emerald journal records, downloading results and storing them on a local machine. This was made possible by Elsevier's Scopus API (https://dev.elsevier.com/) and the Python package Pybliometrics (https://github.com/pybliometrics-dev/pybliometrics).

The program processed a CSV file containing a list of Emerald journal ISSN codes. The program iterated over each observation in the CSV, querying Scopus for all publications from the journal between 2004 and 2019. The year 2004 was chosen as it was possible that some journals adopted structured abstracts prior to 2005, the time in which Emerald mandated the use of structured abstracts across their publications (Emerald Group Publishing Limited, 2005). The downloaded observations did not include the full text of the article, only metadata such as: DOI, article title, authors, publication date and the abstract.

There were 138,613 journal article metadata observations retrieved from the Scopus queries. These were exported into a Microsoft Excel workbook for manual unstructured/structured abstract classification. An abstract was deemed to be structured if it featured the Emerald structured abstract headings and these headings were used to separate components of what would otherwise have been free text abstracts. As a result, 109,608 abstracts were classified as structured, with the remaining abstracts discarded.

3.3 Abstract Sentence Transformation

Existing datasets utilised in ASCM research are presented as sentence level observations, featuring a sentence string with its corresponding structured abstract class. To ensure easy adoption in model development, it was necessary to deconstruct the abstracts into sentences, whilst maintaining the structured abstract class they reflected.

A program was developed which processed each abstract, identifying the locations of the structured headings and treating them as delimiters. This segmented the base abstract string into heading level substrings. We then used a tokenizer to split these into sentence strings, which were reviewed to identify data quality issues such as: sentences incorrectly split from the tokenizer (for example, seeing i.e. as an end of sentence condition), presence of a copyright indicator as the last sentence observation and invalid heading classes.

Any data quality issues identified were managed either through sentence modification or removal of the base abstract; which ensured the dataset contained all sentences from base abstracts.

3.4 Resulting Dataset

Post sentence transformation, we formed a dataset consisting of 1,050,397 sentences originating from 103,457 abstracts. A heading level summary of the sentence abstract count is provided in table 3. Sentence per abstract and token per sentence frequency as well as descriptive statistics are provided in figures 1 and 2. We note the low frequency for the 'Social implications' class. Table 4 identifies the sentence and abstract counts for the top 15 (of 406) journals featuring abstracts. This demonstrates its multidisciplinary nature.

We named our dataset Emerald 110k, following the ASCM dataset naming convention set by

Dernoncourt and Lee (2017) with their biomedical dataset PubMed 200k. The 110k reflects the 103,457 Emerald abstracts from which sentences originate. Our dataset is available via GitHub (https://github.com/connorstead/emerald_ascm) in .CSV, .SAS7BDAT and Python .PKL to enable cross platform utilisation.

Heading	Sentences	Abstracts
Purpose	198,277	103,394
Design/methodology/approach	223,312	101,328
Findings	269,321	103,268
Originality/value	187,986	102,559
Social implications	26	15
Practical implications	92,243	48,689
Research limitations /implications	79,232	40,544

Table 3: Heading level summary of resulting dataset

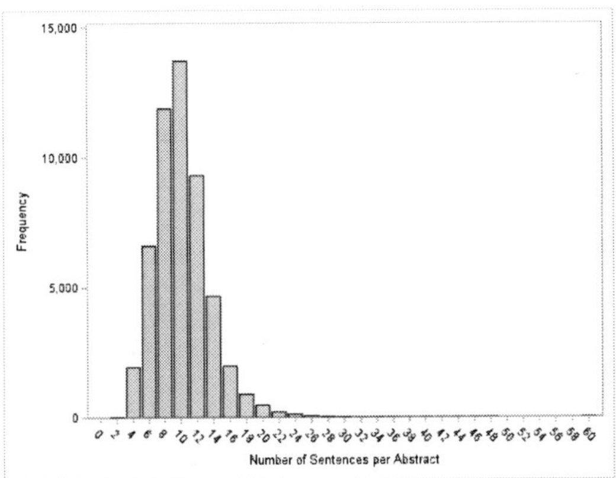

Figure 1: Sentence per Abstract Frequency. Minimum: 1 Maximum: 60 Mean: 10.1530 Standard Deviation: 3.4253 Skewness: 1.2720 Kurtosis: 5.2848

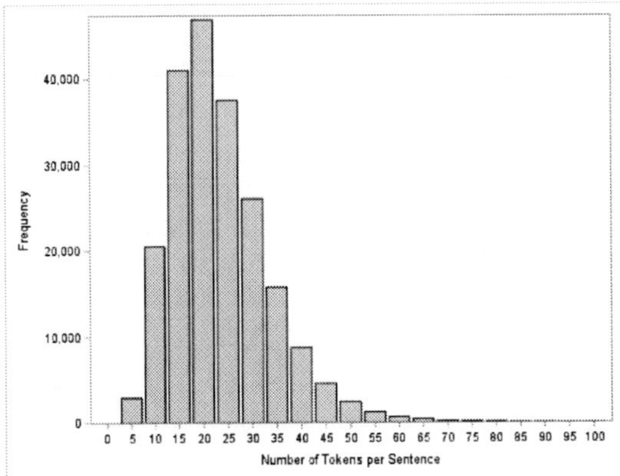

Figure 2: Tokens per Sentence Frequency. Minimum: 1 Maximum: 309 Mean: 23.34 Standard Deviation: 10.4790 Skewness: 1.3217 Kurtosis: 5.5276

Journal (ISSN)	Sentences	Abstracts
International Journal for Computation and Mathematics in Electrical and Electronic Engineering (03321649)	16,659	1,627
British Food Journal (0007070X)	15,821	1,477
Kybernetes (0368492X)	14,676	1,513
Management Decision (00251747)	14,518	1,455
International Journal of Numerical Methods for Heat and Fluid Flow (09615539)	12,365	1,217
European Journal of Marketing (03090566)	12,283	1,136
Industrial Management and Data Systems (02635577)	10,728	978
International Journal of Contemporary Hospitality Management (09596119)	10,629	1,046
Engineering Computations (02644401)	10,471	1,026
International Journal of Social Economics (03068293)	9,730	970
Industrial Lubrication and Tribology (00368792)	9,611	941
Rapid Prototyping Journal (13552546)	9,593	863
Strategic Direction (02580543)	9,355	1,267
Benchmarking (14635771)	9,343	815
Journal of Knowledge Management (13673270)	9,017	859

Table 4: Sentence and abstract frequency for the top 15 journals in the dataset (ordered by sentence count)

4 Conclusion and Ongoing Research

This paper explored the development of a novel dataset for ASCM research. The novelty of this dataset is primarily due to its composition of abstract sentences from a range of non-biomedical disciplinary literature. Our dataset is also the second largest dataset available. It offers a unique opportunity for ASCM researchers to explore the performance of their models outside of biomedical abstract datasets.

Our future research is concerned with expanding ASCM outside of biomedicine and providing associated advancements to new disciplines. Accordingly, we are utilizing this dataset in our own exploration of state of the art ASCM development. We also intend to update this dataset as additional Emerald structured abstracts are published each year, whilst seeking to identify new sources of structured abstracts for ASCM research.

5 Acknowledgements

The authors wish to acknowledge the Australian Government Research Training Program Scholarship which enabled this research to take place.

6 References

Bayley, L., & Eldredge, J. (2003). The structured abstract: an essential tool for researchers. Hypothesis, 17(1), 11-13.

Bayley, L., Wallace, A., & Brice, A. (2002). Evidence based librarianship implementation committee. research results, dissemination task force recommendations. Hypothesis, 16(1), 6-8.

Boudin, F., Nie, J.-Y., Bartlett, J. C., Grad, R., Pluye, P., & Dawes, M. (2010). Combining classifiers for robust PICO element detection. BMC Medical Informatics Decision Making, 10(1), 29.

Budgen, D., Kitchenham, B. A., Charters, S. M., Turner, M., Brereton, P., & Linkman, S. G. (2008). Presenting software engineering results using structured abstracts: a randomised experiment. Empirical Software Engineering, 13(4), 435-468.

Chung, G. Y. (2009). Sentence retrieval for abstracts of randomized controlled trials. BMC Medical Informatics Decision Making, 9(1), 10.

Cleveland, A. D., & Cleveland, D. B. (2013). Introduction to indexing and abstracting. Santa Barbara, California: ABC-CLIO.

Collison, R. L. (1971). Abstracts and abstracting services. Santa Barbara, California: ABC-CLIO.

Davis-Desmond, P., & Mollá, D. (2012). Detection of evidence in clinical research papers. Paper presented at the Proceedings of the Fifth Australasian Workshop on Health Informatics and Knowledge Management-Volume 129.

Dernoncourt, F., & Lee, J. Y. (2017). Pubmed 200k rct: a dataset for sequential sentence classification in medical abstracts. arXiv preprint arXiv:.06071.

Dernoncourt, F., Lee, J. Y., & Szolovits, P. (2016). Neural networks for joint sentence classification in medical paper abstracts. arXiv preprint arXiv:.05251.

Eldredge, J. (2006). Evidence-based librarianship: the EBL process. Library hi tech, 24(3), 341-354.

Emerald Group Publishing Limited. (2005). Emerald structured abstracts have arrived! Journal of Managerial Psychology, 20(1).

Emerald Group Publishing Limited. (2019). Emerald | Product Information | Journals. Retrieved from https://www.emeraldgrouppublishing.com/products/journals/index.htm

Gonçalves, S., Cortez, P., & Moro, S. (2018). A Deep Learning Approach for Sentence Classification of Scientific Abstracts. Paper presented at the International Conference on Artificial Neural Networks.

Guimarães, C. A. (2006). Structured abstracts: narrative review. Acta cirurgica brasileira, 21(4), 263-268.

Hara, K., & Matsumoto, Y. (2007). Extracting clinical trial design information from MEDLINE abstracts. New Generation Computing, 25(3), 263-275.

Hartley, J. (1997). Is it appropriate to use structured abstracts in social science journals? Learned Publishing, 10(4), 313-317.

Hassanzadeh, H., Groza, T., & Hunter, J. (2014). Identifying scientific artefacts in biomedical literature: The Evidence Based Medicine use case. Journal of Biomedical Informatics, 49, 159-170.

Haynes, R. B., Mulrow, C. D., Huth, E. J., Altman, D. G., & Gardner, M. J. (1990). More informative abstracts revisited. Annals of internal medicine, 113(1), 69-76.

Hirohata, K., Okazaki, N., Ananiadou, S., & Ishizuka, M. (2008). Identifying sections in scientific abstracts using conditional random fields. Paper presented at the Proceedings of the Third International Joint Conference on Natural Language Processing: Volume-I.

Huang, K.-C., Chiang, I.-J., Xiao, F., Liao, C.-C., Liu, C. C.-H., & Wong, J.-M. (2013). PICO element detection in medical text without metadata: Are first sentences enough? Journal of Biomedical Informatics, 46(5), 940-946.

Huang, K.-C., Liu, C. C.-H., Yang, S.-S., Xiao, F., Wong, J.-M., Liao, C.-C., & Chiang, I.-J. (2011). Classification of PICO elements by text features systematically extracted from PubMed abstracts. Paper presented at the 2011 IEEE International Conference on Granular Computing.

Ito, T., Shimbo, M., Yamasaki, T., & Matsumoto, Y. (2004). Semi-supervised sentence classification for medline documents. Methods, 138, 141-146.

Jin, D., & Szolovits, P. (2018). Hierarchical Neural Networks for Sequential Sentence Classification in Medical Scientific Abstracts. arXiv preprint arXiv:.06161.

Kim, S. N., Martinez, D., Cavedon, L., & Yencken, L. (2011). Automatic classification of sentences to support evidence based medicine. Paper presented at the BMC bioinformatics.

Kitchenham, B. A., Brereton, O. P., Owen, S., Butcher, J., & Jefferies, C. (2008). Length and readability of structured software engineering abstracts. IET software, 2(1), 37-45.

Lin, J., Karakos, D., Demner-Fushman, D., & Khudanpur, S. (2006). Generative content models for structural analysis of medical abstracts. Paper presented at the Proceedings of the hlt-naacl bionlp workshop on linking natural language and biology.

Liu, Y., Wu, F., Liu, M., & Liu, B. (2013). Abstract sentence classification for scientific papers based on transductive SVM. Computer Information Science, 6(4), 125.

Lui, M. (2012). Feature stacking for sentence classification in evidence-based medicine. Paper presented at the Proceedings of the Australasian Language Technology Association Workshop 2012.

McKnight, L., & Srinivasan, P. (2003). Categorization of sentence types in medical abstracts. Paper presented at the AMIA Annual Symposium Proceedings.

Mosteller, F., Nave, B., & Miech, E. J. (2004). Why we need a structured abstract in education research. Educational Researcher, 33(1), 29-34.

Mulrow, C. D. (1987). The medical review article: state of the science. Annals of internal medicine, 106(3), 485-488.

Nam, S., Kim, S.-K., Kim, H.-G., Ngo, V., & Zong, N. (2016). Structuralizing biomedical abstracts with discriminative linguistic features. Computers in Biology Medicine, 79, 276-285.

Robinson, K. A., Saldanha, I. J., & Mckoy, N. A. (2011). Development of a framework to identify research gaps from systematic reviews. Journal of Clinical Epidemiology, 64(12), 1325-1330.

Rowley, J. E. (1982). Abstracting and indexing. London: Clive Bingley.

Ruch, P., Boyer, C., Chichester, C., Tbahriti, I., Geissbühler, A., Fabry, P., . . . Lovis, C. (2007). Using argumentation to extract key sentences from biomedical abstracts. International Journal of Medical Informatics, 76(2-3), 195-200.

Sharma, S., & Harrison, J. E. (2006). Structured abstracts: do they improve the quality of information in abstracts? American journal of orthodontics dentofacial orthopedics, 130(4), 523-530.

Shimbo, M., Yamasaki, T., & Matsumoto, Y. (2003). Using sectioning information for text retrieval: a case study with the medline abstracts. Paper presented at the Proceedings of Second International Workshop on Active Mining (AM'03).

Taddio, A., Pain, T., Fassos, F. F., Boon, H., Ilersich, A. L., & Einarson, T. R. (1994). Quality of nonstructured and structured abstracts of original research articles in the British Medical Journal, the Canadian Medical Association Journal and the Journal of the American Medical Association. CMAJ: Canadian Medical Association Journal, 150(10), 1611.

Teufel, S., & Moens, M. (1998). Sentence extraction and rhetorical classification for flexible abstracts. Paper presented at the AAAI Spring Symposium on Intelligent Text summarization.

Verbeke, M., Van Asch, V., Morante, R., Frasconi, P., Daelemans, W., & De Raedt, L. (2012). A statistical relational learning approach to identifying evidence based medicine categories. Paper presented at the Proceedings of the 2012 Joint Conference on Empirical Methods in Natural Language Processing and Computational Natural Language Learning.

Wu, J.-C., Chang, Y.-C., Liou, H.-C., & Chang, J. S. (2006). Computational analysis of move structures in academic abstracts. Paper presented at the Proceedings of the COLING/ACL on Interactive presentation sessions.

Xu, R., Supekar, K., Huang, Y., Das, A., & Garber, A. (2006). Combining text classification and hidden markov modeling techniques for structuring randomized clinical trial abstracts. Paper presented at the AMIA Annual Symposium Proceedings.

Yamamoto, Y., & Takagi, T. (2005). A sentence classification system for multi biomedical literature summarization. Paper presented at the 21st International Conference on Data Engineering Workshops (ICDEW'05).

Zhao, J., Bysani, P., & Kan, M.-Y. (2012). Exploiting classification correlations for the extraction of evidence-based practice information. Paper presented at the AMIA Annual Symposium Proceedings.

FindHer: a Filter to Find Women Experts

Gabriela Ferraro
CSIRO Data61, Canberra, Australia
Australian National University, Australia
gabriela.ferraro@data61.csiro.au

Zoe Piper
CSIRO, Canberra, Australia
zoe.piper@csiro.au

Rebecca Hinton
CSIRO, Canberra, Australia
rebecca.hinton@csiro.au

Abstract

Women are underrepresented in many spheres of our societies, including research. A common excuse for exclusively male line-ups is that suitable women could not be found. One way of promoting visibility of women in industry and academia is to explicitly provide solutions to find them. Expert Connect is a publicly searchable database of Australia's researchers that now includes FindHer, a filter to find women experts in any field of research. In this industry paper, we evaluate Natural Language Processing and Computer Vision technologies for gender determination within the aim of automating gender profile tagging for FindHer. We found current off-the-shelf tools are highly effective in detecting gender from names and photos. Nevertheless, a human-in-the-loop approach should be preferred to a fully automatic one, since ethical concerns might arise.

1 Introduction

Women representation remains critically low in a range of fields, including the research sector (Larivire et al., 2013; West et al., 2013; Mihaljevic-Brandt et al., 2016; Bonham and Stefan, 2017). A common excuse for exclusively male line-ups is that suitable women could not be found. This has led to a proliferation of initiatives encouraging women to list their details in various skills and expertise related directories. These directories are then promoted to conference organisers, company boards, investor groups, the media and beyond.

These directories do promote women and improve their chance of discovery; they also put the onus on women to create and update their profiles across multiple platforms. This can be time-consuming and repetitive. What is more, it may or may not result in extra opportunities since often the only people looking at these directories are people who already know they want to engage a woman. We can be smarter about how we manage the public data that already exists. We want to meet the challenge of someone saying that "a suitable woman could not be found". In short, we need to put gender-based information in places where people are already looking.

Expert Connect[1] is a publicly searchable database of Australian research expertise designed to boost industry-researcher collaboration. Since International Women's Day in 2019, Expert Connect can now be filtered to find women experts in any field of research using FindHer.[2] Currently, only 15 percent of the Expert Connect data is included in the filter (with over 4,500 women profiled). It's not a perfect process, but we are continually working on improvements with the number of women profiled continuing to grow.

Work like this raises ethical considerations. In Section 3.1, we discuss some of the issues we considered in the process of submitting our ethics approval for this work. We present experiments on automatic gender determination using off-the-shelf Natural Language Processing (NLP) and Computer Vision (CV) technologies. Our aim is to assess the feasibility of off-the-shelf technologies to support the classification of expert profiles according to gender. Our study shows that current technologies achieved high precision in gender classification using peoples names and profile's photos. However, automatically assigning the correct gender to people's profiles is far from perfect.

The rest of the paper is organised as follows: Section 2 includes a description of the methods we evaluate for gender determination. Section 3 is about the experiments carried-out and the results

---

[1] https://expertconnect.global/
[2] https://expertfindher.global/

found. In Section 4 we conclude this paper and present some ideas for future work.

2   Gender Determination Methods

2.1   Title lookup

Title lookup is a simple and effective deterministic method. Titles are usually one or more words prefixing peoples names such as Miss, Dr., President, among many others. Titles might signify gender, an official position, or a professional or academic qualification. It is not uncommon that people use titles in their public profiles, for example, in the Expert Connect platform. This is the most reliable source of gender since people assign themselves titles to with which they identified. The women titles we use are the following: *Mrs.*, *Ms.*, *Miss*, and *Sister*.

Note that other titles commonly found in expert profiles such as Dr., Professor President, are gender neutral and not useful for gender determination. This method works as follows: given a user profile, if the profile contained a title, then the gender associated with that title is assigned as the user's gender.

2.2   Name lookup

Name lookup is a widely used deterministic method that relies on directories or databases of female and male names. In our experiments, we use two lists of Australian scientist female names: *500 women scientists* and *Women in science Australia*, which contained 150 female names. Since Australia is a multicultural society the lists include diverse names, for example, **Shaghik**, **Jessica**, and **Samia**, just to mention a few. This method works as follows: given a user profile, the user name string is looked up in the names list, and if found, the gender associated with the name is assigned as the user's gender.

2.3   Genderize

Genderize is an existing third-party webservice for infering the gender of a first name. The service can be accessed through a free API and has a limit of 1000 queries per day. Genderize utilised big datasets of information from user profiles across major social networks across 79 countries and 89 languages. The response includes a confidence value and a count, which represents the number of data entries used to calculate the response. This method works as follows: given a user profile, the user name string (not including the surname) is sent to the API[3], and returns the probability estimate of its gender. The API also accept two optional parameters, *location-id* and *language-id*, which not used in our experiments.

2.4   Chicksexer

Chicksexer is a Python package designed to perform gender classification. It is based on a machine learning classifier that uses a character level multilayer LSTM network (Hochreiter and Schmidhuber, 1997). The model is trained using names with gender annotation from Dbpedia Person Data,[4] Popular baby names in the US,[5] and names datasets curated by Milos Bejda.[6] The output prediction includes the probability assigned to each gender class. This method works as follows: given a user profile, the user name string (not including the surname) is sent to the predict-gender function, which returns a probability estimate of its gender.

2.5   Facifier

Facifier is an emotion and gender detector developed in Python and OpenCV,[7] It is a machine learning based classifier that uses HaarCascade (Viola and Jones, 2001) to detect human faces in photos and a gender classifier. The gender classifier is trained with the KDEF[8] dataset consisting of 4900 images, and 2000 images from the IMDB dataset.[9]

2.6   CNN-Gender

CNN-Gender (Levi and Hassner, 2015) uses Convolutional Neuronal Networks for gender determination using images. We used a TensorFlow reimplementation.[10] The model is trained with the Adience dataset,[11] which contains 26,580 images.

	Female	Males
Names	568	263
Images	3934	3147

Table 1: Evaluation data for names and images

	Title lookup	%
Ms.	1	0.03
Mrs.	8	0.25
Miss	0	0
Sister	0	0
Total females	9	0.28
Mr.	19	0.60
Dr.	322	10
Prof.	66	2
	Name lookup	%
Females	64	11

Table 2: Title and Name lookup and experiment results. Title percentage is calculated over the total number of users in Expert Connect: 3157. Name percentage is calculated over the total number of females in the Names dataset: 568.

3 Experiments and Results

We use two datasets to evaluate the methods described in Section 2, Names and Images, respectively. Details about the datasets are shown in Table 1. The Names dataset was compiled by querying the Expert Connect database. Duplicate names and second names were removed, thus the dataset consists of single-term names. The Images dataset was compiled by querying the Expert Connect database and manually classifying user profile photos as female or male. Note that the datasets were only used for testing and never for training the methods.

Results for lookup methods are shown in Table 2. As expected, lookup methods have a poor coverage. Only 0.28 percent of the users indicate

[3] https://pypi.org/project/Genderize/
[4] https://wiki.dbpedia.org/downloads-2016-10
[5] https://www.ssa.gov/oact/babynames/
[6] https://mbejda.github.io/
[7] https://opencv.org/
[8] http://kdef.se/
[9] https://data.vision.ee.ethz.ch/cvl/rrothe/imdb-wiki/
[10] https://github.com/dpressel/rude-carnie
[11] http://www.openu.ac.il/home/hassner/Adience/data.html

	Precision	Recall	F1
Chicksexer	0.982	0.876	0.925
Genderize	0.925	0.901	0.912
Facifier	0.421	0.738	0.534
CNN gender	0.933	0.861	0.895

Table 3: Off-the-shelve methods for gender determination experiment results

their gender using female titles. This is not surprising since female titles like Miss, Mrs. and Ms. indicate marital status and might be considered obsolete in modern societies.

For anecdotal purposes we also investigated the use of other titles. We found that only 0.6 percent of the users chose to set their title as Mr. (male title). Academic titles such as Dr. and Prof. seem to be preferred when choosing a title for professional profiles, showing that 10 percent of the users are identified as Drs. Nevertheless, only a small percentage of the profiles in Expert Connect include a title.

The Names lookup approach covers 11 percent of the total number of females in the Names dataset, demonstrating that catalogues are usually incomplete, and therefore, an unreliable source for finding female researchers.

Results for off-the-shelf methods are presented in Table 3. Both named-based methods achieved high precision and recall. Chicksexer performs slightly better than Genderize. Another advantage of Chicksexer is that is it trainable, and its source code is available under an open source license. To understand why named-based methods can make incorrect predictions, we investigated some false negative instances given by Chicksexer. We randomly chose 25 names, and found half of them are non-western, e.g., Vikneswary, Fincina Anumitra, Ya-juan, among others. Some names are unisex, e.g., Sasha, Ali; and some users used short versions of their names, which made them gender neutral or unisex, e.g., Cat, Steph, Nicky, Charlie, and Billie. Some false negatives are likely to be reduced by including culturally diverse examples for training. However, predictions for gender neutral names are likely to remain confused when using only names for gender determination, either for humans or machines.

The image-based methods show a considerable difference in performance between them. Facifier achieved modest results when applied to the images from the Expert Connect database, with 0.421 Precision, 0.738 Recall, and an F1-score of 0.534. An error analysis on its output indicate that Facifier sometimes struggles to capture the face in images, and therefore is not able to predict the gender class. Note also that the datasets used to train Facifier are considerably smaller than the ones used in CNN-gender, hence a fair comparison between Facifier and CNN-gender is not possible. CNN-gender achieved high Precision: 0.933, high Recall: 0.861, and an F1-score of 0.895.

To better understand CNN-gender errors, we examined some false positive and false negative instances. We randomly select 25 false positive instances, and could not find a clear pattern among them. In 4 images males have long hair, in 4 images they are using glasses, and in 3 images the person appears small at a corner of the image. Similarly, we randomly select 25 false negative instances. This time we found clear patterns between them. In 20 images females are using glasses. In in all of them females have short hair or a pony tail, which make them look as if they have short hair. Although these traits are not strictly male ones, the datasets are probably biased, as there are many training instances of females with long hair, and males with short hair. For human judges it was very easy to determine the gender of the false positive and false negative instances, however the automatic classifier struggled to correctly predict them.

3.1 Ethical Concerns and Limitations

The study presented in this paper and the FindHer filter has ethical approval. The ExpertConnect Platform clearly let people know that they have a profile irrespective to gender. To ensure transparency, how the FindHer filter works is available to the public.

The authors are aware that names and images cannot be used to unambiguously determine the gender of a user, and that a user might not identify with the prototypical gender they look like, nor with their given name. All the methods studied in this paper see gender in a binary way: a name or an image can be either female or male. This poses a clear limitation since in modern societies gender is seen as a spectrum, rather than in a binary way.

As shown in this study, automatic gender binary determination methods are far from perfect and it is still in beta. Ethical considerations might arise if the wrong gender is assigned to a user. Therefore, the FindHer team use automatic methods for classifying profiles according to their gender and confidence scores, which are later manually assessed before updating the gender of users' profiles.

4 Conclusion and Future Work

Gender inequality persist around the world. Considerable effort and resources are currently invested to mitigate this issue and to promote gender equality. FindHer is an example of such efforts, as it allows anyone to explicitly find woman experts in Australia via a Web platform. In order to automate gender determination of expert profiles, we have studied the performance of off-the-shelf language and computer vision technologies, which use given names and profile photos, respectively. Our experiments show the assessed methods are successful, and performance is likely to be higher if name-based and image-based methods are combined. There are many other sources of names such as name repositories, administration records and country specific birth list. Performance can also be improved by re-training name-based methods using culturally diverse sets of names, so that the tools will reflect the cultural diversity of Australian society.

5 Acknowledgements

The authors would like to thank the ALTW reviewers for their thoughtful feedback. Special thanks to Stephen Wan for providing helpful feedback and for proofreading this paper; and to Trevor Fairhurst for his valuable contributions at the early stages of this project.

References

Kevin Bonham and Melanie I. Stefan. 2017. Women are underrepresented in computational biology: An analysis of the scholarly literature in biology, computer science and computational biology. *PLOS Computational Biology*, 13:e1005134.

Sepp Hochreiter and Jürgen Schmidhuber. 1997. Long short-term memory. *Neural Comput.*, 9(8):1735–1780.

Vincent Larivire, Chaoqun Ni, Yves Gingras, Blaise Cronin, and Cassidy Sugimoto. 2013. Bibliometrics: Global gender disparities in science. *Nature*, 504:211–3.

Gil Levi and Tal Hassner. 2015. Age and gender classification using convolutional neural networks. *2015*

IEEE Conference on Computer Vision and Pattern Recognition Workshops (CVPRW), pages 34–42.

Helena Mihaljevic-Brandt, Lucia Santamaria, and Marco Tullney. 2016. The effect of gender in the publication patterns in mathematics. *PLOS ONE*, 11:e0165367.

Paul Viola and Michael Jones. 2001. Rapid object detection using a boosted cascade of simple features. volume 1, pages I–511.

Jevin West, Jennifer Jacquet, Molly King, Shelley Correll, and Carl Bergstrom. 2013. The role of gender in scholarly authorship. *PloS one*, 8:e66212.

Difficulty-aware Distractor Generation for Gap-Fill Items

Chak Yan Yeung, John Lee, Benjamin Tsou
Department of Linguistics and Translation
City University of Hong Kong
cyyeung91@gmail.com, {jsylee, rlbtsou}@cityu.edu.hk

Abstract

Many computer-assisted language learning (CALL) systems offer gap-fill items, often with multiple choices in order to facilitate immediate feedback. Automatic distractor generation can therefore be helpful in providing the multiple choices. While existing algorithms focus on proposing the most plausible distractors, many realistic scenarios make use of distractors at a variety of difficulty levels. This paper evaluates the use of a neural language model to rank distractors in terms of difficulty. Experiments show that BERT outperforms semantic similarity measures, in terms of both correlation to human judgment and classification accuracy of distractor plausibility.

1 Introduction

Many computer-assisted language learning (CALL) systems offer gap-fill items, also known as cloze or fill-in-the-blank items. A gap-fill item consists of a carrier sentence in which one word — called the key, or *target word* — is blanked out. Table 1 shows an example carrier sentence whose target word is 'served'.

To enable automatic feedback, multiple choices are sometimes provided for filling the gap. As shown in Table 1, these choices include the target word itself and several distractors. Judicious selection of distractors is important for generating effective items. A distractor should produce a sentence that seems plausible, yet unacceptable. Language pedagogy literature generally recommends that the target word and distractors belong to the same word class (Heaton, 1989), and be semantically related, ideally "false synonyms" (Goodrich, 1977). An empirical study confirmed that distractors indeed tend to be syntactically and semantically homogenous (Pho et al., 2014).

To reduce the manual effort and time needed for selecting distractors, there has been much interest

He ____ as class representative for two years.
(a) served   [target word]   (b) acted   [distractor]   (c) brought [distractor]

Table 1: A multiple-choice gap-fill item consists of a carrier sentence with a blank, and choices for filling the blank. In this example, the choices include two distractors and the target word (correct answer).

in developing algorithms for automatic distractor generation. Existing algorithms typically take a two-step approach (Jiang and Lee, 2017; Susanti et al., 2018). The first step generates distractor candidates, typically in a list ranked according to measures of semantic similarity and collocation strength. The second step removes candidates that are acceptable answers, using n-gram and collocation frequency or other criteria.

Evaluations on distractor generation tend to be limited to the highest-ranked distractors, for example the top-ranked or top three candidates only (Jiang and Lee, 2017; Susanti et al., 2018). Many practical scenarios, however, require not only the most challenging distractors, but distractors across the spectrum of plausibility. When authoring test items, for example, it can be useful to generate items at various difficulty levels for comprehensive assessment. In a CALL system, it can be effective to personalize distractor difficulty according to the user's language proficiency.

It is informative, then, to evaluate distractor algorithms on their ability to generate distractors at different levels of plausibility. We therefore propose to investigate the correlation between the estimated ranking of distractors and human judgment on plausibility. This research direction has indeed been taken up in item generation in the natural sciences (Liang et al., 2018; Gao et al., 2019). However, to the best of our knowledge, it has not yet been attempted for gap-fill items for language learning.

Language models provide a natural framework for this task by predicting how likely a word appears in a gap within the sentence. This paper is the first attempt to apply BERT (Devlin et al., 2019), a state-of-the-art model trained on the masked language modeling objective, on the task of distractor ranking. Experimental results show that BERT outperforms semantic similarity measures, in terms of both correlation to human judgment and classification accuracy of distractor plausibility.

The rest of the paper is organized as follows. In Section 2, we review related research areas. In Section 3, we outline our approach for distractor generation. In Section 4, we report experimental results on ranking distractors for gap-fill items for learning Chinese as a foreign language. Finally, we conclude in Section 5.

2   Previous work

For the target word in a carrier sentence, a distractor generation algorithm aims to optimize two objectives: the distractor should look plausible for filling in the gap; but it should also *not* produce an acceptable sentence. Reflecting the twin goals, most existing algorithms perform two tasks (Jiang and Lee, 2017; Susanti et al., 2018). The first, Candidate Generation, identifies all possible distractor candidates. The second, Candidate Filtering, seeks to remove those candidates that are also acceptable answers, leaving only the distractors that are "reliable", i.e., those that yield an incorrect sentence.

Section 2.1 reviews existing approaches for the Candidate Generation task, which is the research focus of this paper. Section 2.2 then surveys related tasks in computer-assisted learning that have adopted evaluation on candidate ranking.

2.1   Candidate Generation

In most approaches, a distractor needs to have the same part-of-speech (POS) as the target word (Coniam, 1997). In addition, a number of features have been explored for ranking the candidates:

Word co-occurrence. Since a distractor should collocate strongly with a word in the carrier sentence (Hoshino, 2013), candidates are evaluated according to their co-occurrence frequencies with other words in the sentence. Various definitions of co-occurrence have been used, including bigram counts (Susanti et al., 2018) and, more generally, n-grams in a context window centered on the distractor (Liu et al., 2005); dependency relations (Sakaguchi et al., 2013); grammatical relations in a Word Sketch (Smith et al., 2010); as well as pointwise mutual information (PMI) (Jiang and Lee, 2017).

Learner error. Typical or frequent learner mistakes can be effective as distractors. When generating gap-fill items for prepositions, distractors based on learner errors were indeed found to be more challenging than those selected according to word co-occurrence (Lee et al., 2016). Distractor candidates have been mined from learner corpora and further selected with a discriminative model (Sakaguchi et al., 2013).

Semantic similarity. The distractor should be semantically close to the target word. Similarity can be quantified by semantic distance in Word-Net (Pino et al., 2008; Chen et al., 2015), thesauri (Sumita et al., 2005; Smith et al., 2010), ontologies (Karamanis et al., 2006), hand-crafted rules (Chen et al., 2006), and word embeddings (Jiang and Lee, 2017; Susanti et al., 2018). Other approaches have also explored synonym of synonyms (Knoop and Wilske, 2013); and words that are semantically similar to the target word in some sense, but not in the particular sense in the carrier sentence (Zesch and Melamud, 2014).

A study on gap-fill items for learning Chinese as a foreign language compared the quality of distractors generated by a number of criteria, including spelling, word co-occurrence and semantic similarity (Jiang and Lee, 2017). Experimental results show that a semantic similarity measure, based on the `word2vec` model (Mikolov et al., 2013), yields distractors that are significantly more plausible than those generated by spelling similarity, and by word co-occurrence strength as estimated by PMI.

2.2   Evaluation on candidate ranking

Although the output of most distractor generation algorithms is a ranked list, most previous studies on distractor quality in gap-fill items have limited their attention to the top-ranked distractors. To the best of our knowledge, quantitative evaluations on *ranking* quality have been reported for item generation in the natural sciences, but not yet for language learning; furthermore, the focus has been on question-answering items, rather than gap-fill items.

Given a dataset of distractors and non-distractors, Liang et al. (2018) trained ranking models to rank the distractors higher. Experimental results suggested that random forest and Lambda MART performed best. However, the evaluation was restricted to pairwise prediction of distractor difficulty.

Gao et al. (2019) addressed the task of generating questions from a paragraph. Using bidirectional LSTMs, their system classified questions as either "easy" or "difficult". While their evaluation methodology was similar to the one advocated by this paper, it is applied to question generation rather than distractor generation.

3 Approach

Following most previous approaches, we adopt a two-step process for distractor generation: the first step generates distractor candidates, and the second step filters out candidates that constitute acceptable answers. Our research focus is on the first step, to which we introduce a re-ranking process with a neural language model.

3.1 Baseline

Our baseline uses semantic similarity measures, which have been reported in previous research to yield the best performance in identifying plausible distractor candidates (Section 2.1).

Word embeddings have been shown to be effective in measuring word similarity and relatedness in a large range of NLP tasks, including distractor generation (Jiang and Lee, 2017). We used word embeddings trained by Skipgram with negative sampling on Baidu Encyclopedia (Li et al., 2018). Specifically, we calculated cosine similarity between the word embeddings of the distractor candidate and the target word, and obtained candidates with the highest scores.

3.2 Re-ranking

The appropriateness of a distractor may depend not only on the target word but also on the context of the carrier sentence. Consider the word *served* as the target word. In the context of food being served at a restaurant, the word *brought* may be a plausible distractor since it is semantically close to the target word. However, in the context of serving in a position, the word *acted* would be a more plausible distractor, for example for the carrier sentences in Table 1. Hence, we propose to re-rank the distractors in the baseline list (Section 3.1) with a language model.

BERT (Devlin et al., 2019) is a state-of-the-art neural language model based on the Transformer architecture (Vaswani et al., 2017). The model is bi-directional, i.e., trained to predict the identity of a masked word based on both the words that precede and follow it. It has been shown to be effective in a variety of natural language processing tasks. This paper is the first to apply it to distractor generation.

Using its PyTorch implementation[1], we masked the target word in each carrier sentence and harvested the words most highly ranked by BERT for the masked position. We then re-ranked the candidates in the baseline list according to their relative ranking in BERT.

An alternative to re-ranking would be to directly use the ranked list from BERT. We did not adopt this approach because the list can include distractor candidates that are not semantically similar to the target word.

4 Experiments

We first present our dataset (Section 4.1), and then analyze experimental results (Section 4.2).

4.1 Data

We derived our evaluation data from the dataset compiled by Jiang and Lee (2017), which consists of 37 carrier sentences taken from a number of textbooks for Chinese as a foreign language. The target words include 37 distinct nouns and verbs.

To construct a pool of distractor candidates for the target word in each sentence, we intersected these two sets: the 20 words that are most similar to the target word according to the baseline algorithm (Section 3.1); and the 50 most likely words for the masked position according to BERT (Section 3.2).

Out of this pool, we randomly selected a total of 172 distractor candidates for human annotation. Five human raters, all native speakers of Chinese, independently annotated each candidate according to the scheme used in Jiang and Lee (2017).

___
[1]https://pypi.org/project/pytorch-pretrained-bert/

Method	Correlation		Classification
	Pearson's r	**Spearman's rho**	**accuracy**
Baseline	-0.233	-0.263	42.52%
Re-ranking	**-0.455**	**-0.487**	**60.63%**

Table 2: Evaluation of the baseline (Section 3.1) and re-ranking (Section 3.2) methods on correlation to human judgment on plausibility (left); and on classification of distractor plausibility (right).

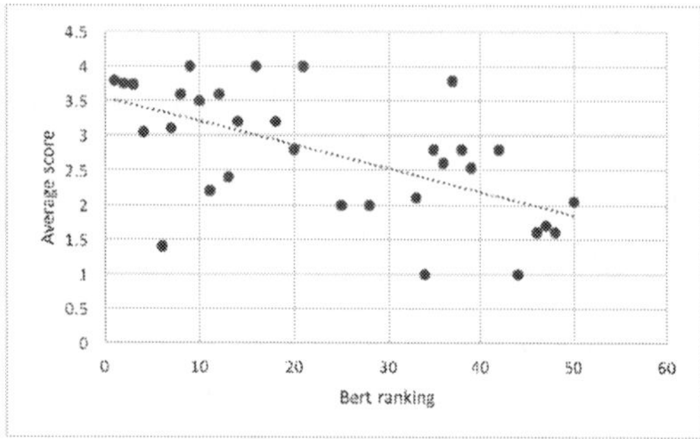

Figure 1: Correlation between human scores on the plausibility of the distractor candidates, and their ranking in BERT (Section 3.2).

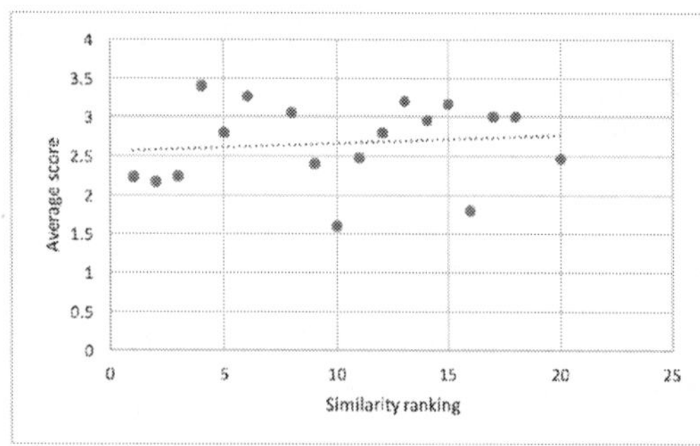

Figure 2: Correlation between human scores on the plausibility of the distractor candidates, and their semantic similarity ranking (Section 3.1).

Each distractor candidate can be rated as "Obviously wrong", "Somewhat plausible", "Plausible", or "Correct" (and hence unacceptable as a distractor). The pairwise Kappa for the five human raters was 0.420, which is considered a "Moderate" level of agreement (Landis and Koch, 1977).

4.2 Results

Correlation with human judgment. Table 2 shows the level of correlation between the automatically produced distractor ranking and the average human rating.[2] A larger negative coefficient indicates a higher degree of correlation, since distractors with higher plausibility scores should have a smaller rank number. BERT achieved a Pearson correlation coefficient of -0.455; visualized in Figure 1, the correlation is statistically significant ($p = 0.002$). In contrast, the coefficient for the semantic similarity baseline was only -0.233; visualized in Figure 2, the correlation is not statistically significant ($p = 0.123$). The trend was similar with Spearman's rho, for which BERT achieved a coefficient of -0.487, which is statistically significant ($p = 0.0007$). The baseline obtained a coefficient of -0.263, which is not statistically significant ($p = 0.081$).

Generation accuracy. We generated distractors by setting thresholds in the re-ranked list for different plausibility levels. We tuned the thresholds by leave-one-out cross-validation to optimize accuracy in classifying a candidate as "Correct", "Plausible"[3], or "Less Plausible". The gold label is the majority label out of the five raters. As shown in Table 2, BERT achieved 60.63% classification accuracy, outperforming the similarity baseline, which achieved 42.52% by always predicting the majority label "Less plausible". For our dataset, the optimized thresholds for BERT were to classify candidates ranked 1 to 10 as "Correct"; those ranked 11 to 39 as "Plausible"; and the rest as "Less Plausible".

5 Conclusions

To support automatic generation of gap-fill items with distractors at a variety of plausibility levels, we have introduced distractor ranking as a new evaluation framework for distractor generation. This study is the first to apply BERT to the task of distractor ranking. Experimental results show that it outperforms semantic similarity measures in terms of both correlation to human judgment on distractor plausibility, and classification accuracy of distractor plausibility.

---

[2]We assigned score 1 to the "Obviously wrong" candidates, score 2 to "Somewhat plausible", score 3 to "Plausible" and score 4 to "Correct" distractors.

[3]The "Plausible" and "Somewhat Plausible" labels in the human annotation were collapsed into the "Plausible" label.

Acknowledgment

This work was supported by the Innovation and Technology Fund (Ref: ITS/389/17) of the Innovation and Technology Commission, the Government of the Hong Kong Special Administrative Region. We thank Ka Po Chow for his assistance. The first author completed this research at City University of Hong Kong and now works at Google.

References

Chia-Yin Chen, Hsien-Chin Liou, and Jason S. Chang. 2006. FAST: An Automatic Generation System for Grammar Tests. In *Proc. COLING/ACL Interactive Presentation Sessions*.

Tao Chen, Naijia Zheng, Yue Zhao, Muthu Kumar Chandrasekaran, and Min-Yen Kan. 2015. Interactive Second Language Learning from News Websites. In *Proc. 2nd Workshop on Natural Language Processing Techniques for Educational Applications*.

David Coniam. 1997. A Preliminary Inquiry into Using Corpus Word Frequency Data in the Automatic Generation of English Language Cloze Tests. *CALICO Journal*, 14(2-4):15–33.

Jacob Devlin, Ming-Wei Chang, Kenton Lee, and Kristina Toutanova. 2019. BERT: Pretraining of Deep Bidirectional Transformers for Language Understanding. In *Proc. NAACL-HLT*.

Yifan Gao, Lidong Bing, Wang Chen, Michael R. Lyu, and Irwin King. 2019. Difficulty Controllable Generation of Reading Comprehension Questions. In *Proc. 28th International Joint Conference on Artificial Intelligence (IJCAI)*.

Hubbard C. Goodrich. 1977. Distractor Efficiency in Foreign Language Testing. *TESOL Quarterly*, 11(1):69–78.

J. B. Heaton. 1989. *Writing English Language Tests*. Longman.

Yuko Hoshino. 2013. Relationship between Types of Distractor and Difficulty of Multiple-Choice Vocabulary Tests in Sentential Context. *Language Testing in Asia*, 3(16).

Shu Jiang and John Lee. 2017. Distractor Generation for Chinese Fill-in-the-blank Items. In *Proc. 12th Workshop on Innovative Use of NLP for Building Educational Applications*, page 143–148.

Nikiforos Karamanis, Le An Ha, and Ruslan Mitkov. 2006. Generating Multiple-Choice Test Items from Medical Text: A Pilot Study. In *Proc. 4th International Natural Language Generation Conference*.

Susanne Knoop and Sabrina Wilske. 2013. WordGap: Automatic Generation of Gap-Filling Vocabulary Exercises for Mobile Learning. In *Proc. Second Workshop on NLP for Computer-assisted Language Learning, NODALIDA*.

J. Richard Landis and Gary G. Koch. 1977. The Measurement of Observer Agreement for Categorical Data. *Biometrics*, 33:159–174.

John Lee, Donald Sturgeon, and Mengqi Luo. 2016. A CALL System for Learning Preposition Usage. In *Proc. ACL*.

Shen Li, Zhe Zhao, Renfen Hu, Wensi Li, Tao Liu, and Xiaoyang Du. 2018. Analogical Reasoning on Chinese Morphological and Semantic Relations. *arXiv preprint arXiv:1805.06504*.

Chen Liang, Xiao Yang, Neisarg Dave, Drew Wham, Bart Pursel, and C. Lee Giles. 2018. Distractor Generation for Multiple Choice Questions using Learning to Rank. In *Proc. 13th Workshop on Innovative Use of NLP for Building Educational Applications*, pages 284–290.

Chao-Lin Liu, Chun-Hung Wang, Zhao-Ming Gao, and Shang-Ming Huang. 2005. Applications of Lexical Information for Algorithmically Composing Multiple-Choice Cloze Items. In *Proc. 2nd Workshop on Building Educational Applications Using NLP*, pages 1–8.

Tomas Mikolov, Kai Chen, Greg Corrado, and Jeffrey Dean. 2013. Efficient Estimation of Word Representations in Vector Space. In *Proc. International Conference on Learning Representations (ICLR)*.

Van-Minh Pho, Thibault André, Anne-Laure Ligozat, B. Grau, G. Illouz, and Thomas François. 2014. Multiple Choice Question Corpus Analysis for Distractor Characterization. In *Proc. LREC*.

Juan Pino, M. Heilman, and Maxine Eskenazi. 2008. A Selection Strategy to Improve Cloze Question Quality. In *Proc. Workshop on Intelligent Tutoring Systems for Ill-Defined Domains, 9th International Conference on Intelligent Tutoring Systems*.

Keisuke Sakaguchi, Yuki Arase, and Mamoru Komachi. 2013. Discriminative Approach to Fill-in-the-Blank Quiz Generation for Language Learners. In *Proc. ACL*.

Simon Smith, P. V. S. Avinesh, and Adam Kilgarriff. 2010. Gap-fill Tests for Language Learners: Corpus-Driven Item Generation. In *Proc. 8th International Conference on Natural Language Processing (ICON)*.

Eiichiro Sumita, Fumiaki Sugaya, and Seiichi Yamamoto. 2005. Measuring Non-native Speakers' Proficiency of English by Using a Test with Automatically-Generated Fill-in-the-Blank Questions. In *Proc. 2nd Workshop on Building Educational Applications using NLP*.

Yuni Susanti, Takenobu Tokunaga, Hitoshi Nishikawa, and Hiroyuki Obari. 2018. Automatic Distractor Generation for Multiple-choice English Vocabulary Questions. *Research and Practice in Technology Enhanced Learning*, 13(15).

Ashish Vaswani, Noam Shazeer, Niki Parmar, Jakob Uszkoreit, Llion Jones, Aidan N. Gomez, Lukasz Kaiser, and Illia Polosukhin. 2017. Attention is All You Need. *Advances in Neural Information Processing Systems*, pages 6000–6010.

Torsten Zesch and Oren Melamud. 2014. Automatic Generation of Challenging Distractors Using Context-Sensitive Inference Rules. In *Proc. Workshop on Innovative Use of NLP for Building Educational Applications (BEA)*.

Investigating the Effect of Lexical Segmentation in Transformer-based Models on Medical Datasets

Vincent Nguyen
Australian National University
CSIRO Data61
vincent.nguyen@anu.edu.au

Sarvnaz Karimi
CSIRO Data61
Sydney, Australia
sarvnaz.karimi@csiro.au

Zhenchang Xing
Australian National University
Canberra, Australia
zhenchang.xing@anu.edu.au

Abstract

Transformer-based models have been popular recently and have improved performance for many Natural Language Processing (NLP) Tasks, including those in the biomedical field. Previous research suggests that, when using these models, an in-domain vocabulary is more suitable than using an open-domain vocabulary. We investigate the effects of a specialised in-domain vocabulary trained from scratch on a biomedical corpus. Our research suggests that, although the in-domain vocabulary is useful, it is usually constrained by the corpora size because these models needs to be trained from scratch. Instead, it is more useful to have more data, perform additional pretraining steps with a corpus-specific vocabulary.[1]

1 Introduction

In the natural language processing domain, there is a requirement for a fixed-sized vocabulary during training which could lead to *Out-Of-Vocabulary (OOV)* problem (Luong et al., 2015). This problem is when the fixed vocabulary model encounters an unseen word during inference, and the model is unable to handle it appropriately. Word-Piece tokenisation, initially used in machine translation systems (Wu et al., 2016), has been widely successful in addressing the OOV problem by segmenting unseen words into *word pieces* as a representation for the unknown word. Previous research has either replaced unseen words with a special token (Luong et al., 2015), used character word embeddings (Labeau and Allauzen, 2017) as a fall-back, or ignored these words completely. These techniques have shortcomings as they do not attempt to represent the unseen word or require additional processing and memory as with character embeddings. WordPiece tokenisation is

---

[1] Our code is publicly available at Lexical-Segmentation-Transformer.

WordPiece: *arthralgias → art-hra-al-gia-s*
Ideal: *arthralgias → arthr-algias*
arthr- means joints, -algias means pain

Figure 1: Word segmentation in WordPiece and the ideal segmentation using medical morphemes.

a trade-off, where there is no need for special handling of out-of-vocabulary, as unseen words are segmented into sub-word units. It allows a limited vocabulary to represent an infinitely sized vocabulary space.

Models that successfully use WordPiece tokenisation include the transformer-based architectures: BERT (Devlin et al., 2019), RoBERTa (Liu et al., 2019), and XLNet (Yang et al., 2019). BERT uses WordPieces as morphemes to aid the contextual representation of words. BERT performs at a state-of-the-art level on the GLUE tasks (Wang et al., 2019) due to its ability to fine-tune specifically to each task. Given this success, the model has also been applied to the biomedical domain through models such as BioBERT (Lee et al., 2019), which applies additional pretraining on the MEDLINE and PubMed corpora for biomedical text representation. However, these BioBERT models sometimes do not perform well on biomedical tasks, and in some instances are even worse than vanilla BERT (Zhu et al., 2019; Peng et al., 2019; Nguyen et al., 2019).

We hypothesise that a reason for this failure could be due to the vocabulary limitation of BioBERT, where the authors keep the open-domain vocabulary of BERT. This is problematic because the original BERT vocabulary is not suited for the biomedical domain due to the lack of medical suffixes and prefixes in its vocabulary leading to incorrect segmentation of the words (see the example in Figure 1). This is important because the suffixes and prefixes (the morphemes) in medical terminology carry distinct meanings, and almost the entire medical vocabulary can be constructed from prefix and suffix combinations (Stanfield et al., 2008). Thus, we aim to validate the importance of having the additional biomedical vocabulary for downstream tasks.

2 Background

Most of biomedical natural language processing is adapted from open-domain state-of-the-art techniques, from word embeddings (Chiu et al., 2016), to BiLSTM-CRF (Kalyan and Sangeetha, 2019). BERT is a deeply bidirectional encoder that is based on the transformer architecture. It uses self-attention as a mechanism of encoding input contextually by attending to different aspects of the sentence using multi-headed self-attention head, passed through layer normalisation and a Multi-Layer Perceptrons (MLP). The BERT model has been successful in the open-domain as it scored State-of-the-Art (SOTA) performance on the SQUAD (Rajpurkar et al., 2016) and GLUE datasets because it addresses the polysemy problem (Molla and Gonzlez, 2007), through contextual clues, for richer representations.

However, it was realised that directly applying the model to a closed domain can be problematic due to two factors: (1) The BERT model is trained on Wikipedia and BookCorpus meaning that the internal representations for specialised words may not be properly learned for a specialised domain; and, (2) The internal vocabulary that BERT has learned is suitable for tasks in the open-domain and a separate or additional vocabulary is needed (Beltagy et al., 2019).

To address the first problem, BioBERT takes the original BERT model and performs additional pretraining steps on academic biomedical literature, PubMed and MEDLINE, to improve downstream medical tasks. However, BioBERT does not change the open-domain vocabulary to a medically-focused one. Furthermore, the language in academic corpora is different to clinical text and patient language. These issues resulted in lower than expected performance on biomedical datasets, such the MEDIQA (Ben Abacha et al., 2019; Nguyen et al., 2019) and in some cases worse than the original BERT models (Zhu et al., 2019) from which they were trained from.

Alleviating the dataset problem, Clinical BERT (Alsentzer et al., 2019), performs further pretraining steps for the BioBERT and BERT models on domain-specific corpora showing marked improvements on downstream clinical tasks. However, they did not change the internal vocabulary of the models as this would require training the models from scratch which may limit performance.

Addressing both the vocabulary and the dataset problem, SciBERT was trained from scratch on the Semantic Scholar corpus and a specialised SentencePiece vocabulary trained on the corpus.

Our paper is a first look empirical study into the effect of vocabulary and dataset in applying BERT-based models to downstream tasks. Although our study is limited in scope, it still explores an important problem and our research suggests that some of previous studies may have drawn incorrect conclusions.

2.1 Sub-word Models

The original WordPiece algorithm addresses the OOV problem and handles arbitrary sequences of characters found on the web. This algorithm greedily maximises the likelihood of the vocabulary over the training data. The algorithm is similar to the byte-pair encoding algorithm, which uses frequency rather than likelihood to train the model. By using word pieces, the tokenisation procedure can break down OOV words into their word subunits. For instance, jumped can be broken down into `jump ##ed`.

The SentencePiece algorithm (Kudo and Richardson, 2018) is similar to WordPiece except that it performs direct training from raw sentences with language independence. It treats all sentences as a sequence of Unicode characters without a special reliance on spaces, allowing for reliable multi-lingual de-tokenisation.

3 Methods

We propose vocabulary adaption to investigate the segmentation problems for medical text in BERT models and their variants. We propose two different methods to achieve this: (1) Adding additional vocabulary from a common medical vocabulary of suffixes and prefixes[2] to the existing BERT vocabulary and perform additional pretraining steps; and, (2) Training a separate SentencePiece tokeniser and pretraining a BERT model from scratch on the medical corpus. We compare

---

[2]GlobalRPh Common Medical Suffixes and Prefixes (Accessed Nov 2019)

Model	NLI		RQE		QA	
	Dev Acc.	Test Acc.	Dev Acc.	Test Acc.	Dev Acc.	Test Acc.
Medical vocab 10k steps	0.781	0.743	0.778	0.487	0.739	0.655
Medical Vocab (intermediate)	0.795	0.721	0.762	**0.500**	0.718	0.657
Medical Vocab (final)	0.791	0.751	0.748	**0.500**	0.731	0.634
Medical Vocab (final) - Medical Vocab	0.741	**0.798**	0.768	0.478	0.731	0.640
SentencePiece Vocab (intermediate)	0.769	0.684	0.745	0.491	**0.782**	0.665
SentencePiece Vocab (final)	0.666	0.684	0.431	**0.500**	0.641	0.513
BioBERT v1.0 PMC	0.809	0.768	0.775	0.487	0.778	**0.721**
BioBERT v1.0 PubMed+PMC	0.828	0.778	0.775	0.474	0.765	0.708
BioBERT v1.0 PubMed	0.815	0.775	0.791	0.465	0.744	0.704
BioBERT v1.1 PubMed	**0.833**	0.790	**0.808**	0.487	0.778	0.677
SciBERT + BaseVocab	0.799	0.773	0.745	0.487	0.735	0.697
SciBERT + SciVocab	0.817	0.783	0.785	0.483	0.761	0.713
BERT base	0.786	0.736	0.742	0.483	0.709	0.655

Table 1: Comparing accuracy of all models in three tasks using the MEDIQA datasets.

these methods against BERT, BioBERT and SciB-ERT models on downstream medical tasks.

3.1 Datasets

We use PubMed Central (PMC)[3] corpus for pre-training our BERT Model. It consists of two million articles, 300 million sentences and one billion tokens at the time of writing. Note that we use the full text of the articles, not just the abstracts, as this was shown to be effective in SciBERT (Belt-agy et al., 2019).

For fine-tuning, we select the MEDIQA datasets (Ben Abacha et al., 2019) which contains three tasks: MEDical Natural Language Inference (MEDNLI) (Johnson et al., 2016), Recognising Question Entailment (RQE) (Abacha and Demner-Fushman, 2016), and Question Answering (QA).

3.2 Preprocessing

In order to comply with BERT's formatting for pretraining, for tokenisation and sentence segmentation, we use ScispaCy (Neumann et al., 2019), with a biomedical model (en_core_sci_sm) for its speed and ability to parse biomedical data. We then train a SentencePiece model with a fixed vocabulary size of 32,000 on a subset of 20 million PubMed text articles to extract a vocabulary that maximises likelihood over the dataset. We then adapt the SentencePiece vocabulary to be compatible with BERT by pruning '_' characters, replacing them with '##' and removing start and end of sequence tokens.

3.3 Pretraining

Due to the large size of PMC and time and computing resources limitation, we randomly select a subset of 60 million sentences for pretraining. We use the default settings for pretraining the BERT model as described in the original paper. We also use the same pretraining schedule as the original BERT implementation where the model is first trained on a sequence length of 128, which we call the *intermediate model*, until convergence before being trained on a sequence length of 512, the *final model*. We set the learning rate of 1e-4 for the SentencePiece model as this is being trained from scratch and 2e-5 for the Medical Vocabulary model.

3.4 Fine-tuning

After pretraining, we fine-tune our model to each task in the dataset. We use a learning rate of 5e-5 for five epochs. We also use a fixed seed of 42 for all libraries. We train our model on the official training data and report our results on the development and test sets of each task.

We fine-tune 12 models to three separate tasks and evaluate on both the development and the test sets due to distribution mismatch (the test sets were made much later than the original training/development sets). We fine-tuned the BERT base model plus medical vocabulary with the models pretrained for 10k, 90k (intermediate), 100k (final) steps and a final model without the medical vocabulary. Similarly, we pretrain the BERT model with a PubMed SentencePiece vocabulary on models for 90k (intermediate) and 100k steps (final). We fine-tune all the BioBERT models,

---

[3]PubMed Central Dump

where all v1.0 models are trained on abstracts of a specific corpus (e.g., Pubmed or PMC), and the v1.1 model is trained on the full-text corpus. We also fine-tune the SciBERT models with BERT base vocabulary (BaseVocab) and Semantic Scholar SentencePiece vocabulary (SciVocab). Finally, we fine-tune our baseline (BERT base). We report our results in Table 1.

4 Results and Discussions

Overall, we found that fine-tuned models , with the exception of our SentencePiece model and Medical Vocab model for QA, outperformed the *BERT base* baseline.

For the NLI task, the SentencePiece models and the Medical Vocab (final) model performed worse on the development set, however the Medical Vocab (final) - Medical Vocab model performed best on the test set. All other models performed scored higher than the BERT base model. The BioBERT models, on average, performed best here as the task involved inference from a medical sentence (a clinical note) to a normalised sentence (summary).

On the RQE dataset, all models performed reasonably on the development set, with the PubMED models scoring the best, with the exception of the final SentencePiece model as the task required interpretation of patient language in addition to academic. However, all models performed poorly on the test set, with no model scoring higher than random guess due to a marginal distribution mismatch between the training, development sets against the test set.

On the QA dataset, the task involved interpreting a patient's naturally formed question to a medical answer from medical articles. Here, BioBERT performed the best on the test set.

In summary, all models performed similarly with only mild discrepancies which we discuss in the following section.

4.1 SciVocab versus BaseVocab

We find that the SciVocab model performed better than the BaseVocab model (see Table 1, rows 11-12). BaseVocab is trained similarly to our medical vocab model where BERT base was fine-tuned with additional data before further tuned to a downstream task. The reason the SciVocab model performed better is that it had learned better representations during the training phase while the BaseVocab model learned noisier representations due

to a vocabulary mismatch between the Semantic Scholar dataset and the BERT vocabulary. However, the SciVocab may not be as beneficial due to the academic nature of the vocabulary as the MEDIQA contains a mix of both academic medical terminology and natural patient questions.

4.2 BioBERT versus SciBERT SciVocab

The BioBERT and SciBERT models are both pre-trained/tuned on academic biomedical literature. However, there are two keys differences to note, SciBERT is trained from scratch as it is not possible to completely alter the BERT vocabulary while maintaining the original weights. We found that, contrary to previous research (Zhu et al., 2019), citing a development accuracy of 43% (RQE) and 68% (NLI), the BioBERT models performed better on the development and test sets of the MEDIQA datasets. We attribute BioBERT's strength to the fact that it was fine-tuned rather than trained from scratch, and thus incorporates both open-domain and biomedical-domain knowledge. Further evaluation with a purely biomedical reasoning task such as clinical term extraction (Si et al., 2019) may be suitable for further comparison.

We found that the BioBERT models performed better than previously reported and that the size of corpus matters in the performance of the model as the full-text corpus model is generally better.

4.3 Medical versus SentencePiece Vocab

We found that, on two of the tasks, the medical vocab model performed better due to the nature of the task. The SentencePiece vocab is adapted only for the PMC corpus, which is academically written without misspellings or colloquialism, in contrast with the datasets. That is, having a corpus specific vocabulary might not be sufficient even within the same domain due to the different nature of writing styles; academic and general audience. Furthermore, we found that the SentencePiece vocab do not contain all the punctuation tokens, which further hurts performance when it comes to understanding questions as '?' is replaced with 'unk'.

Consistent with SciBERT and BaseVocab vocabulary overlap, there was a 40% overlap in vocabulary between BERT base vocabulary and the PMC SentencePiece vocabulary, highlighting the vocabulary mismatch between two corpora. Also, there is a 4% overlap in the added medical suffix/prefix vocabulary and the SentencePiece vocabulary suggesting that the PMC corpus was likely not training the representations of the added prefix and suffix tokens correctly because they do not appear frequently enough. Finally, due to the relatively smaller size of pretraining dataset compared with all the other models, the SentencePiece model most likely overfit as the performance across all datasets worsened with more training steps (see Table 1, rows 6-7).

However, the training with the PMC corpus allowed for better adaption to the downstream tasks. Our models did not perform as well as BioBERT as they are trained on a smaller subset than the original models. We also find that the intermediate SentencePiece model performs better than the final model, and this is because the downstream task had only short sequences, introducing noise and overfitting. The medical vocab model, rather than the SentencePiece model, is more robust against this noise as it is not trained from scratch.

4.4 BioBERT versus Medical Vocab

Although trained similarly, all the BioBERT models outperformed our pretrained models across all datasets. For a direct comparison, we compare *BioBERT v1.1 PubMED* as this shares the same dataset and pretraining procedures. The only notable differences between the BioBERT model and ours is that: 1) 3% of the Medical vocab model is augmented with medical suffix/prefix and 2) We trained only a subset of PubMED on the Medical vocab model. We do a preliminary test by removing additional vocabulary (Table 1, row 4) in our model for a comparison against dataset size. We saw that the performance of the model increased slightly on average, leading to the conclusion that the extra vocabulary was hurting performance as they were not well trained. Overall, we also find that the accuracy is still lower than the BioBERT model, suggesting that additional dataset size is crucial to achieving a better performance.

4.5 Effect of Corpus and Vocabulary

In all the models, although vocabulary helps (e.g., SciVocab vs. BaseVocab), this effect is limited to the pretraining phase when learning representations, but when applying to a downstream task, it is more important to have additional corpus data that is suited to the downstream task. This effect is shown where SciBERT basevocab (fine-tuned from the BERT base model) performed better than the BERT base model. The additional corpus data is useful in the case of BioBERT vs. SciVocab as BioBERT is fine-tuned with additional data on top of the BookCorpus and Wikipedia datasets of the BERT model.

We hypothesise that the best way to maximise all these effects is instead of fine-tuning from one corpus to the other, to combine both the open-domain and target domain corpora and pretrained the model from scratch with a well-tuned vocabulary. We leave this to future work.

5 Limitations and Future Work

There are several limitations to our study which we leave as directions for future work: (1) we only trained on a subset of the PMC dataset for pretraining the Medical Vocab and SentencePiece models as it was computationally intensive to use the full set; (2) we only trained and evaluated on BERT base models. For a complete comparison we need to pretrain all the BioBERT models, SciBERT models, our models and also, for completeness, clinical BERT using the BERT large model, and then 3) we would need to train on datasets of varying sizes to see the effect of the corpus. Furthermore, investigation of character embeddings as a segmentation strategy over the use of wordpieces, avoiding the need for a vocabulary could be useful. However, this would require factorisation of the embedding space to reduce the computational cost of increased sequence length (Lan et al., 2019).

Furthermore, empirically, we did not conduct a significance test due to the use of a fixed seed for all randomisation to emphasise reproducibility, however, in future, re-running each experiment without a fixed seed multiple times to produce reliable statistics is desirable in future work.

6 Conclusions

Previous research suggests that using open-domain vocabulary in BERT-based models affects downstream tasks compatibility and leads to a loss in effectiveness. However, our research suggests that this is not the case. An open-domain vocabulary is more useful than an in-domain vocabulary trained on less data, if it is additionally trained on an in-domain corpus.

Acknowledgements

This research is supported by the Australian Research Training Program and the CSIRO Research Office Postgraduate Scholarship.

References

Ben Abacha and Demner-Fushman. 2016. Recognizing Question Entailment for Medical Question Answering. *American Medical Informatics Association Annual Symposium Proceedings*, 2016:310–318.

Emily Alsentzer, John Murphy, William Boag, Wei-Hung Weng, Di Jindi, Tristan Naumann, and Matthew McDermott. 2019. Publicly available clinical BERT embeddings. In *Proceedings of the 2nd Clinical Natural Language Processing Workshop*, pages 72–78, Minneapolis, Minnesota, USA. Association for Computational Linguistics.

Iz Beltagy, Kyle Lo, and Arman Cohan. 2019. SciBERT: A pretrained language model for scientific text. In *Proceedings of the 2019 Conference on Empirical Methods in Natural Language Processing and the 9th International Joint Conference on Natural Language Processing (EMNLP-IJCNLP)*, pages 3606–3611, Hong Kong, China. Association for Computational Linguistics.

Asma Ben Abacha, Chaitanya Shivade, and Dina Demner-Fushman. 2019. Overview of the MEDIQA 2019 shared task on textual inference, question entailment and question answering. In *Proceedings of the 18th BioNLP Workshop and Shared Task*, pages 370–379, Florence, Italy.

Billy Chiu, Gamal Crichton, Anna Korhonen, and Sampo Pyysalo. 2016. How to train good word embeddings for biomedical NLP. In *Proceedings of the 15th Workshop on Biomedical Natural Language Processing*, pages 166–174, Berlin, Germany.

Jacob Devlin, Ming-Wei Chang, Kenton Lee, and Kristina Toutanova. 2019. BERT: Pre-training of deep bidirectional transformers for language understanding. In *Proceedings of the 2019 Conference of the North American Chapter of the Association for Computational Linguistics: Human Language Technologies, Volume 1 (Long and Short Papers)*, pages 4171–4186, Minneapolis, Minnesota. Association for Computational Linguistics.

Alistair Johnson, Tom Pollard, Lu Shen, Li-wei Lehman, Mengling Feng, Mohammad Ghassemi, Benjamin Moody, Peter Szolovits, Anthony Celi, and Roger Mark. 2016. MIMIC-III, a freely accessible critical care database. *Scientific Data*, 3:160035.

K.S Kalyan and S. Sangeetha. 2019. SECNLP: A survey of embeddings in clinical natural language processing. *Computing Research Repository*, abs/1903.01039.

Taku Kudo and John Richardson. 2018. SentencePiece: A simple and language independent subword tokenizer and detokenizer for neural text processing. In *Proceedings of the 2018 Conference on Empirical Methods in Natural Language Processing: System Demonstrations*, pages 66–71, Brussels, Belgium. Association for Computational Linguistics.

Matthieu Labeau and Alexandre Allauzen. 2017. Character and subword-based word representation for neural language modeling prediction. In *Proceedings of the First Workshop on Subword and Character Level Models in NLP*, pages 1–13, Copenhagen, Denmark. Association for Computational Linguistics.

Zhenzhong Lan, Mingda Chen, Sebastian Goodman, Kevin Gimpel, Piyush Sharma, and Radu Soricut. 2019. ALBERT: A Lite BERT for Self-supervised Learning of Language Representations. *Computing Research Repository*, arXiv:1909.11942.

Jinhyuk Lee, Wonjin Yoon, Sungdong Kim, Donghyeon Kim, Sunkyu Kim, Chan Ho So, and Jaewoo Kang. 2019. BioBERT: a pre-trained biomedical language representation model for biomedical text mining. *Bioinformatics*.

Yinhan Liu, Myle Ott, Naman Goyal, Jingfei Du, Mandar Joshi, Danqi Chen, Omer Levy, Mike Lewis, Luke Zettlemoyer, and Veselin Stoyanov. 2019. RoBERTa: A robustly optimized BERT pretraining approach. *Computing Research Repository*, abs/1907.11692.

Thang Luong, Ilya Sutskever, Quoc Le, Oriol Vinyals, and Wojciech Zaremba. 2015. Addressing the rare word problem in neural machine translation. In *Proceedings of the 53rd Annual Meeting of the Association for Computational Linguistics and the 7th International Joint Conference on Natural Language Processing (Volume 1: Long Papers)*, pages 11–19, Beijing, China. Association for Computational Linguistics.

Diego Molla and Jos Gonzlez. 2007. Question answering in restricted domains: An overview. *Computational Linguistics*, 33:41–61.

Mark Neumann, Daniel King, Iz Beltagy, and Waleed Ammar. 2019. ScispaCy: Fast and robust models for biomedical natural language processing. In *Proceedings of the 18th BioNLP Workshop and Shared Task*, pages 319–327, Florence, Italy.

Vincent Nguyen, Sarvnaz Karimi, and Zhenchang Xing. 2019. ANU-CSIRO at MEDIQA 2019: Question answering using deep contextual knowledge. In *Proceedings of the 18th BioNLP Workshop and Shared Task*, pages 478–487, Florence, Italy.

Yifan Peng, Shankai Yan, and Zhiyong Lu. 2019. Transfer learning in biomedical natural language processing: An evaluation of BERT and ELMo on ten benchmarking datasets. In *Proceedings of the Workshop on Biomedical Natural Language Processing*, pages 58–65, Florence, Italy.

Pranav Rajpurkar, Jian Zhang, Konstantin Lopyrev, and Percy Liang. 2016. Squad: 100, 000+ questions for machine comprehension of text. *Computing Research Repository*, abs/1606.05250.

Yuqi Si, Jingqi Wang, Hua Xu, and Kirk Roberts. 2019. Enhancing clinical concept extraction with contextual embedding. *Computing Research Repository*, abs/1902.08691.

P. Stanfield, Y.H. Hui, and N. Cross. 2008. *Essential Medical Terminology*. Jones and Bartlett. Chapter 2.

Alex Wang, Amanpreet Singh, Julian Michael, Felix Hill, Omer Levy, and Samuel R. Bowman. 2019. GLUE: A multi-task benchmark and analysis platform for natural language understanding. In *In the Proceedings of International Conference on Learning Representations*, pages 353–355, Brussels, Belgium.

Yonghui Wu, Mike Schuster, Zhifeng Chen, Quoc V. Le, Mohammad Norouzi, Wolfgang Macherey, Maxim Krikun, Yuan Cao, Qin Gao, Klaus Macherey, Jeff Klingner, Apurva Shah, Melvin Johnson, Xiaobing Liu, Łukasz Kaiser, Stephan Gouws, Yoshikiyo Kato, Taku Kudo, Hideto Kazawa, Keith Stevens, George Kurian, Nishant Patil, Wei Wang, Cliff Young, Jason Smith, Jason Riesa, Alex Rudnick, Oriol Vinyals, Greg Corrado, Macduff Hughes, and Jeffrey Dean. 2016. Google's Neural Machine Translation System: Bridging the Gap between Human and Machine Translation. *Computing Research Repository*, page arXiv:1609.08144.

Zhilin Yang, Zihang Dai, Yiming Yang, Jaime Carbonell, Ruslan Salakhutdinov, and Quoc V. Le. 2019. XLNet: Generalized Autoregressive Pretraining for Language Understanding. *Computing Research Repository*, page arXiv:1906.08237.

Wei Zhu, Xiaofeng Zhou, Keqiang Wang, Xun Luo, Xiepeng Li, Yuan Ni, and Guotong Xie. 2019. PANLP at MEDIQA 2019: Pre-trained language models, transfer learning and knowledge distillation. In *Proceedings of the 18th BioNLP Workshop and Shared Task*, pages 380–388, Florence, Italy.

Neural Versus Non-Neural Text Simplification: A Case Study

Islam Nassar[†*]   **Michelle Ananda-Rajah**[†‡*]   **Gholamreza Haffari**[†*]

†Faculty of Information Technology, Monash University, VIC, Australia.
‡ Department of Infectious Diseases, The Alfred Hospital and Central Clinical School.
*{firstname.lastname}@monash.edu

Abstract

We propose a modular rule-based system for Text Simplification and show that it outperforms the state-of-the-art neural-based simplification system in terms of simplicity. We compare the output of both systems to highlight the differences between the two approaches. Further, we present an adaptation of our system to handle domain-specific tasks, where we employ a hybrid approach of our rule-based system and phrase-based machine translation to simplify medical discharge summaries in a low-resource situation. We compile a small medical simplification dataset to evaluate our proposed solution.

1   Introduction

Text Simplification is loosely defined as reducing the linguistic complexity of text, without changing its meaning, to suit a wider range of audience such as: non-native speakers, children, or people with language impairments. It is usually achieved by applying rewrite rules to perform two types of operations: (1) lexical simplification, where difficult words are substituted with more common alternatives; and (2) syntactic simplification, where complex sentence structures are split, reordered, or deleted to produce simpler more readable structure. To implement those rewrite rules, researchers employ various methods broadly categorized into two categories: rule-based methods and data-driven methods (Siddharthan, 2014).

In rule-based methods, the rules are hand-crafted a priori then applied to new text at simplification time. Examples of such rules include dictionary-based lookups for lexical simplification (Kurohashi & Sakai, 1999) or rules aiming at sentence restructuring into more readable formats. (A. Siddharthan, 2002; Vickrey & Koller, 2008). In contrast, data-driven methods frame the simplification process as a monolingual Machine Translation problem where the rewrite rules are learned from a parallel corpus of complex-simple sentences. This enables researchers to leverage the advances in Machine Translation to address the simplification task.

Considering the breakthrough achieved by Neural Machine Translation, we ask the questions: Could similar success be achieved in Text Simplification by employing neural architectures? Would rule-based methods be more effective since simplification is a fundamentally different task than translation?

To answer these questions, first, we propose a non-neural general-purpose rule-based simplification system. We, then, show how it can be adapted to address domain-specific simplification tasks by leveraging a small parallel dataset from the target domain. Subsequently, we compare the output of our system with that of a recently proposed neural-based simplification system (Zhang & Lapata, 2017). In our study, we focus on two simplification domains: (1) general-purpose English, for which we run our tests using Wikipedia-based datasets; and (2) medical English, for which we compile a small medical parallel corpus of complex-simple pairs and use it to test our systems. We show that our rule-based system outperforms the neural system, in terms of simplicity, both qualitatively and quantitatively. Finally, we reflect on the output of both systems to pinpoint the shortcomings of each approach and encourage researchers to address them in future research.

2   Rule-Based Simplification System

In this section, we describe our proposed rule-based simplification system. It comprises two modules corresponding to the two major operations of text simplification: lexical and syntactic simplification.

2.1 Lexical Simplification

The lexical module operates in two phases: simpler synonyms extraction, and lexical substitution. In the first phase, the system builds a synonyms dictionary for all the words appearing in the input text and apply a simplicity criterion to only keep synonyms which are simpler than the original words. In the second phase, the system decides which words should be substituted with which synonyms based on the context of the original words in their sentences.

Simpler Synonyms Extraction   Given an input sentence, this phase starts with tokenization and part-of-speech (PoS) tagging.[1] Subsequently, for each (word, PoS) pair, if the PoS tag corresponds to a verb, adjective or noun (except proper nouns), the word is looked up in four lexical databases to find all possible synonyms. We use WordNet, Thesaurus, paraphrase.org, and domain-specific databases[2] to ensure a comprehensive coverage. We use the PoS tag while looking up synonyms to avoid issues arising due to polysemy, words with same spelling but different meanings (consider the difference in meaning between "lead" as a verb – guide, versus "lead" as a noun – metallic element).

To preserve grammaticality, the system, then, applies morphological changes to the obtained synonyms so that the synonyms match the PoS of the original word. The changes applied include singularization or pluralization for nouns, setting superlative or comparative forms for adjectives, and tense conjugation for verbs[3].

Finally, the system selects only the synonyms which are indeed simpler than the original word. For that we apply an intuitive simplicity criterion: if the (Synonym, PoS) pair appears in a large corpus of text[4] more often than the (Word, PoS) pair, we assume that the synonym is more common and hence is a simpler alternative of the original word. By repeating the above process on all the words appearing in the text, we obtain a simpler synonyms dictionary with many possible synonyms for each word.

Lexical Substitution   In this phase, the system uses the obtained synonyms dictionary in conjunction with a language model to produce a set of candidate sentences and select the simplest among them. This process happens in an iterative greedy manner. First, the (word, Pos) pairs of the input sentence are scanned sequentially and for each pair with an entry in the synonyms dictionary, a corresponding set of sentences are produced where each sentence has the word replaced with one of the possible simpler synonyms. This set is then scored using a language model and the highest scoring sentence, based on perplexity scores, is deemed to be the simplest and hence replaces the original sentence. This process is repeated till all (word, PoS) pairs of the input sentences are scanned. The last obtained sentence is the output of the lexical simplification module.

The choice of the language model is extremely important to ensure that the sentence with the highest score is indeed the simplest. To choose a suitable language model, we ran experiments using a validation set of 2000 sentences from WikiLarge corpus. We found that the best performance with respect to simplicity metrics, was obtained using language models which had been trained on a simple English corpus. This tends to encourage output sentences which are simpler and more common. The best performance was achieved using a 5-gram language model (Brown et al. 1992) trained on the Simple Wikipedia corpus[5].

2.2 Syntactic Simplification

For the syntactic simplification, we adopted an existing open source implementation - The Multilingual Syntactic Simplification Tool (MUSST) (Scarton et al., 2017) - whereby the syntactic simplification is performed on a sentence level by applying a set of general-purpose simplification rules on its dependency parse tree. Those rules implement four operations that are arguably the most useful simplification operations.

- Splitting conjoint clauses
- Splitting relative clauses
- Splitting appositive phrases
- Changing passive-voice to active-voice

To apply the above rules, the sentence is first parsed using the Stanford dependency parser

---

[1] We use Stanford tokenizer and PoS-tagger in *NLTK* Python library

[2] An example of an automatically extracted medical dictionary is presented in section 3 of this paper

[3] We use *Pattern* Python package for morphology changes

[4] We use *News Crawl 2013* corpus in *WMT16* Task

[5] simple.wikipedia.org

(Chen & Manning, 2014) and then three main operations are performed to achieve the final output:
Analysis: where the sentence is analyzed in search for simplification clues such as discourse markers for conjoint clauses (ex: "and" or "when"), or relative pronouns for relative clauses (ex: "who", "which").
Transformation: where the core operations are applied to transform the sentence into a simplified form. It is applied in a recursive manner until the sentence has no more simplification clues.
Generation: where the simplified sentences are reconstructed ensuring proper grammatical structure.

3   Medical Domain Adaptation

With the above proposed system architecture, our simplification system was able to efficiently handle general-purpose English simplification such as simplifying news articles or Wikipedia text. However, it struggled when trying to simplify domain-specific text such as Medical text or Financial text. This is due to the limited coverage of general-purpose dictionaries (such as Wordnet and Thesaurus) to such domains. In this section, we show how our system can be adapted to address such domain-specific applications in a low-resource setting. We present an adaptation of our system to the medical domain, where the objective is to simplify medical discharge summary reports using a very small training set of parallel complex-simple sentences from the target domain.

Recalling our system architecture, the syntactic simplification module would have no issue simplifying domain-specific text as it operates on the sentences dependency parse tree and hence is domain-agnostic. This is not the case, however, for the lexical module; since the lexical module uses dictionaries to lookup simpler alternatives, it would fail to address domain-specific jargon which is non-existent in general-purpose dictionaries. To counteract this issue, we employed a data-driven approach to enrich the lexical module dictionaries and extend its coverage to domain specificities.

Medical Dataset   First, we compiled a small parallel corpus of complex-simple medical text by manually simplifying 500 sentences drawn from "General Medicine" medical summary reports.

The 500 sentences were randomly selected from a pool which included reports with the highest lexical diversity in the entire dataset. We calculate the lexical diversity as the ratio of unique word count

in a report to the total length of vocabulary. This is to ensure that the selected sentences dataset captures a diverse representation of the underlying medical reports corpus. The simplification was conducted by a medical expert and was targeted to address audience of Grade 6 level on the Flesch-Kincaid scale (Kincaid et al. 1975).

Extracting Synonyms   After compiling the medical dataset, we used Moses toolkit (Koehn et al. 2007) to train a phrase-based machine translation model using 450 parallel sentences (the remaining 50 sentences were held out to test the system). One of the outputs of the trained model is the PBMT phrase table, which depicts potential mappings between source (i.e. complex) and destination (i.e. simple) phrases accompanied with maximum likelihood alignment scores for each phrase mapping. We used the phrase table to extract a phrase-synonyms dictionary of medical jargon, by scanning through each source phrase and selecting the destination phrase with the highest PBMT alignment score as its synonym phrase. Finally, we used the extracted phrase mappings dictionary to complement the general-purpose dictionaries in the lexical module, proposed in section 2.1. This yielded a great improvement of 11 points on the simplicity scale, as will be shown in more details in section 6.

4   Neural Simplification Overview

Before we proceed with the systems comparison, we, first, briefly describe the neural-based approach for text simplification as proposed by (Zhang & Lapata, 2017) dubbed as DRESS (**D**eep **RE**inforcement Sentence Simplification).

In their method, they treat text simplification as a sequence-to-sequence modelling task. They draw inspiration from Neural Machine Translation, where they train an encoder-decoder model on a monolingual parallel corpus of complex-simple English. To further encourage a simpler output, they train their model in a reinforcement learning framework where the reward function is a weighted combination of the output sentence relevance, simplicity, and fluency. As a proxy for relevance, they use an LSTM-based sequence auto-encoder to obtain a vector representation for both the source and output sentences, the relevance reward is then defined as the cosine similarity between those two vectors. As for the fluency reward, they use an LSTM language model trained on simple sentences to obtain a normalized perplexity score for the output sentence. For the simplicity reward, they use the SARI metric (Xu et al. 2016) which measures the n-gram overlaps between source, output and reference sentences. SARI will be further elaborated in section 5. Finally, to encourage lexical simplification, they use a separate pre-trained encoder-decoder model, trained in a non-reinforced setting on a parallel corpus of complex-simple sentences, to obtain lexical substitution probabilities based on a given source sentence. Using the latter model favors lexical simplification operations but does not take into account the fluency of the overall output. Therefore, the output of their system is determined by linearly combining the two encoder-decoder models.

5 Experimental Setup

In their study, (Zhang & Lapata, 2017) have conducted an extensive comparison between multiple competitive simplification systems. We hence use a similar experimental setup to be able to directly use their results in our comparison.

Baseline   Our baseline is simply an echo system where the input complex sentence is not simplified but rather passed through as the output. This allows a first-glance evaluation of whether a comparison system has indeed yielded a simplified output.

Datasets   We perform two types of testing:
(1) General-purpose Simplification: on *WikiSmall* (Zhu et al. 2010) and *WikiLarge* (Zhang & Lapata, 2017) datasets, where the latter is a superset of the former and both are collated by automatically aligning complex and simple sentences from the ordinary and simple English Wikipedia articles. We use the same test splits used in the mentioned study (100 sentences for *WikiSmall* and 354 sentences for *WikiLarge* not containing duplicates). This enables us to use their system output directly. We don't use *Newsela* dataset (Xu et al 2015), which was used in their study, as it is not publicly available.
(2) Medical Simplification: We use the held-out test set (50 sentences) from the medical dataset mentioned in section 3 to test our system. We couldn't test the DRESS system on our medical dataset due to its extremely limited size leading to non-sensible results when used to train a neural-based architecture such as DRESS. We, therefore, only compare our results with the baseline in case of medical data.

Evaluation Metrics   We use two commonly used metrics, in the simplification literature, to evaluate the systems: (1) Flesch Kincaid Grade Level (FKGL; (Kincaid et al. 1975) which is measured on a corpus level to indicate the readability of the text as a function of number of words, sentences and syllables (lower values signifies more readable text); and (2) SARI (Xu et al. 2016) which indicates the goodness of a simplification by measuring the n-gram overlap of the System output Against References and against the Input sentence. More specifically, SARI measures the average n-gram precision and recall of addition, deletion and copying operations. It, hence, rewards deletion operations when it occurs in both the output and reference sentences. Similarly, it rewards addition/substitution where words in the output appears in the reference but not the input. This implies that producing longer output sentences doesn't necessarily lead to higher SARI scores.

6 Results

Examining the results obtained in table 1, we can see that both systems do indeed produce simpler and more readable output as opposed to the original sentences. We also see that while our non-neural system outperforms the neural system in terms of simplicity, it lags in terms of readability. This indicates that the output of our proposed system correlates better with the reference simplifications, yet it is lengthier and hence harder to read. The latter observation is attributed to the fact that our system doesn't perform deletion operations. Instead, it introduces more words during splitting and hence creates longer sentences leading to higher FKGL values (i.e. worse readability). We designed our system this way considering the task of "Medical Text Simplification". In a medical context, it is not desired to delete words but rather to elaborate on abstract terminologies and hence deletion operations were not encouraged. Incorporating further deletion rules into our syntactic module shall lead to improved readability scores.

Qualitative examination of the output of the two systems (table 2, upper) shows that the non-neural system is doing a better job in terms of both lexical and syntactic simplification. The rule-based system successfully substitutes difficult words with what seems to be reasonable and easier alternatives. It also splits composite structures into simpler form. For example, the appositive phrase in example 1 (the trickster character) and the conjoint

	WikiLarge			WikiSmall			Medical		
	FKGL	SARI	Avg. words/sent	FKGL	SARI	Avg words/sent	FKGL	SARI	Avg words/sent
No Simplification	9.2	7.2	22.61	12.1	4.5	27.8	20.13	15.7	8.4
DRESS	**6.58**	37.08	16.39	**7.48**	27.48	16.7	N/A	N/A	N/A
Rule-Based	8.37	**40.42**	20.83	9.25	**28.42**	26.29	**15.26**	**26.79**	10.2

Table 1: Evaluation results on the three datasets

Input	The tarantula, the trickster character, spun a black cord and, attaching it to the ball, crawled away fast to the east, pulling on the cord with all his strength
Reference	The **tricky** tarantula spun a black **web** and attached it to the ball. **Afterwards**, it crawled away and pulled the **web** with him
DRESS	The tarantula, the trickster character, spun a black cord and, holding it to the ball
Rule-Based	The Tarantula **turn** a black **string**. And the Tarantula **connecting** it to the ball, crawled away **soon** to the East, pulling on the **string** with all his strength. The Tarantula is the trickster character.
Input	They are culturally akin to the coastal peoples of Papua New Guinea
Reference	They are **similar** to the coastal peoples of Papua New Guinea
DRESS	They are culturally **referring** to the coastal peoples of Papua New Guinea
Rule-Based	They are culturally **similar** to the coastal peoples of Papua New Guinea
Input	It is situated at the coast of the Baltic Sea, where it encloses the city of Stralsund
Reference	It is **located** at the coast of the Baltic Sea where it **surrounds** the city of Stralsund
DRESS	It is situated at the coast of the Baltic Sea
Rule-Based	It is **located** at the coast of the Baltic Sea. It **contains** the city of Stralsund

Input	AKI secondary to heart failure medication
Reference	**Kidney injury from related** heart failure medication
Output	**Kidney damage because of** heart failure medication
Input	82F from LLC with worsening SOB and lethargy
Reference	**82 female were admitted to hospital** from **low-level care facility** with worsening **short of breath** and **tiredness**
Output	**82 female** from **low-level care facility** with worsening **breathlessness** and **tiredness**

Table 2: System output comparison from WikiLarge (upper), examples of medical reports simplifications (lower)

clause (where it encloses) in example 2 were rightfully split into separate sentences. On the other hand, the neural system seems to favor deletion operations, even when it affects the meaning. In all three examples, a chunk of the sentence was deleted despite changing the meaning.

As for the medical simplification results, our proposed system has achieved an improvement of 11 points on SARI simplicity scale and 5 grade levels on FKGL scale, when compared to the original input sentences. (two example simplifications are shown in table 2, lower). Looking at the average words per sentence, it is evident that our system tends to produce longer simplified sentences. Once again, that is due to the nature of the medical simplification task which requires elaboration rather than deletion.

7   Conclusion

We developed a non-neural approach for text simplification which implements rules for lexical and syntactic simplification. We used two common test sets to compare our system output with that of a recently proposed neural simplification approach. We showed that our system produces simpler and more meaningful output and scores higher in terms of simplicity metrics. We presented a comparison between both systems output to capture where the neural approach fails. Finally, we presented a hybrid method to enable our system to perform domain-specific text simplification, with high performance, in low-resource situations.

Acknowledgements

The authors are grateful to the reviewers for their insightful comments and feedback. This work is partly supported by the ARC Future Fellowship FT190100039 to G. H. and an MRFF TRIP Fellowship to MAR.

References

Brown, P. F., deSouza, P. V., Mercer, R. L., Pietra, V. J. D., & Lai, J. C. (1992). Class-based N-gram Models of Natural Language. *Comput. Linguist.*, *18*(4), 467–479.

Chen, D., & Manning, C. (2014). A Fast and Accurate Dependency Parser using Neural Networks. *Proceedings of the 2014 Conference on Empirical Methods in Natural Language Processing (EMNLP)*, 740–750.

Kincaid, J., Fishburne, R., Rogers, R., & Chissom, B. (1975). Derivation Of New Readability Formulas (Automated Readability Index, Fog Count And Flesch Reading Ease Formula) For Navy Enlisted Personnel. *Institute for Simulation and Training*.

Koehn, P., Hoang, H., Birch, A., Callison-Burch, C., Federico, M., Bertoldi, N., … Herbst, E. (2007). Moses: Open Source Toolkit for Statistical Machine Translation. *Proceedings of the 45th Annual Meeting of the ACL on Interactive Poster and Demonstration Sessions*, 177–180.

Kurohashi, S., & Sakai, Y. (1999). Semantic Analysis of Japanese Noun Phrases: A New Approach to Dictionary-based Understanding. *Proceedings of the 37th Annual Meeting of the Association for Computational Linguistics on Computational Linguistics*, 481–488.

Papineni, K., Roukos, S., Ward, T., & Zhu, W.-J. (2002). BLEU: A Method for Automatic Evaluation of Machine Translation. *Proceedings of the 40th Annual Meeting on Association for Computational Linguistics*, 311–318.

Scarton, C., Palmero Aprosio, A., Tonelli, S., Martín Wanton, T., & Specia, L. (2017). MUSST: A Multilingual Syntactic Simplification Tool. *Proceedings of the IJCNLP 2017, System Demonstrations*, 25–28.

Siddharthan, A. (2002). An architecture for a text simplification system. *Language Engineering Conference, 2002.* 64–71.

Siddharthan, Advaith. (2014). *A survey of research on text simplification.*

Sulem, E., Abend, O., & Rappoport, A. (2018). *BLEU is Not Suitable for the Evaluation of Text Simplification.*

Vickrey, D., & Koller, D. (2008). Sentence Simplification for Semantic Role Labeling. *Proceedings of ACL-08: HLT*, 344–352.

Xu, W., Callison-Burch, C., & Napoles, C. (2015). Problems in Current Text Simplification Research: New Data Can Help. *Transactions of the Association for Computational Linguistics*, *3*, 283–297.

Xu, W., Napoles, C., Pavlick, E., Chen, Q., & Callison-Burch, C. (2016). Optimizing Statistical Machine Translation for Text Simplification. *Transactions of the Association for Computational Linguistics*, *4*(0), 401–415.

Zhang, X., & Lapata, M. (2017). Sentence Simplification with Deep Reinforcement Learning. *ArXiv:1703.10931 [Cs].*

Zhu, Z., Bernhard, D., & Gurevych, I. (2010). A Monolingual Tree-based Translation Model for Sentence Simplification. *Proceedings of the 23rd International Conference on Computational Linguistics*, 1353–1361.

A string-to-graph constructive alignment algorithm for discrete and probabilistic language modeling

Andrei Shcherbakov   Ekaterina Vylomova
The University of Melbourne
Parkville, Victoria 3010, Australia
`andreas@softwareengineer.pro  evylomova@gmail.com`

Abstract

We propose a novel algorithm of graph-to-string alignment that constructs automata from a sample of string sequences. While being a variant of global edit distance, the algorithm also employs graph construction operations in order to form an optimal alignment. It allows dynamic insertion of edges and nodes driven by optimization of the best string-to-graph alignment score. The algorithm may be used both to derive discrete non-deterministic acceptor (or a regular expression) and to build a probabilistic generative model of an input language. An outstanding ability to produce accurate approximate models from extremely sparse training sets constitutes the main advantage of the technique.

1   Introduction

Tasks such as text generation or language modelling might require approximate string matching. Often the models are trained on a set of matching samples (sometimes augmented with mismatching, or negative, samples). In most cases, they rely on extrinsic metrics (n-gram similarity (Kondrak, 2005), perplexity (Jelinek et al., 1977), Kolmogorov (Li and Vitányi, 2013) or cognitive (Rogers et al., 2013) complexities, Levenshtein distance (Levenshtein, 1966)). An objective function may not directly correspond to any formally proven or intuitively observable reasonable goal. In current paper, we attempt to combine structure awareness of graph-based models with simplicity of similarity-based approaches. We train a graph-based model that minimizes modified recurrent edit distance[1] between each training sample and the path in the graph closest to it. As a graph-based model we propose to use a weighted non-deterministic finite state acceptor (WFSA) to

---

[1] Here "recurrent" means that a path may contain loops.

enable a compact representation of learned sequences as well as to allow alternations and repetitions of substrings. The approach we consider in the paper is essentially based on the hypothesis that sequences that are likely to appear in a language normally form dense clusters around some basic patterns. In other words, the sequences are characterized by relatively low edit distance to *some* cluster centroid. The proposed technique handles both branching and looping of subsequences in a consistent way. As a result, pattern generalization may be carried out without any extra pre- or post-processing.[2]

2   Architecture

We first provide a set of positive (and, optionally, negative) string samples in order to build a weighted acceptor (WFSA). The training procedure runs as follows. Initially, the acceptor only contains unconnected start and finish (accepting) nodes. At each training iteration we compute the best possible alignments between the acceptor and a given sample string using Smith–Waterman (Smith et al., 1981) alignment search procedure with the following major differences. First, it allows virtually any automaton edge (even non-existent ones) to be considered for alignment paths.[3] In such a way, it enables new candidate edges that should be built in order to improve fit to a given sample. Second, it speculates on prospective new states of acceptor, one per sample string character. Each string sample y is processed in the following two phases during training.

Phase 1 - counting alignment scores and building a temporary transducer. We construct a ma-

---

[2] The code is available at http://regexus.com/jumpalign , https://github.com/andreas-softwareengineer-pro/jumpalign

[3] Contrary to it, Smith–Waterman algorithm effectively considers both string operands as unmodifiable linear-shaped automata

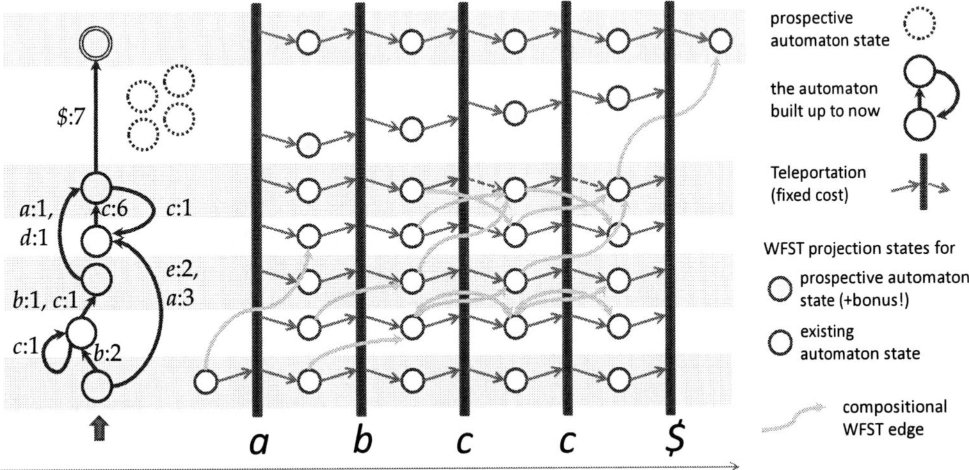

Figure 1: A single acceptor-to-string alignment step.

trix of best partial alignment scores $S_{i,j}$, where n is number of existing WFSA states, $i \in \{0..n + |y|\}$ is existing or prospective state of acceptor, and $j \in \{1..|y|\}$ is sample string position. For each j we consider all n existing automaton states augmented with one new (prospective) state "number" $n + j$. In order to assign candidate scores for $S_{i,j}$ cell, we transfer scores from $S_{*,j-1}$ cells in two ways: (1) using existing WFSA edges that match the y_j character,[4] applying respective edge weights as increments; or (2) using virtual "teleport" edges that might be added between any pair of states, with a fixed teleport penalty T:[5]

$$S_{i,j} = \max \begin{cases} \max_k S_{k,j-1} - T \\ \max_{k:\exists k \xrightarrow{y_j} i} (S_{k,j-1} + w(k \xrightarrow{y_j} i)) \end{cases}$$

(1)

where y_j is the jth character of the sample string y; $k \xrightarrow{y_j} i$ is WFSA edge from state k to state i labelled with y_j character; $w(k \xrightarrow{y_j} i)$ is its weight.

Indeed, we build a transient weighted finite-state transducer (WFST) which translates the acceptor into the sample string. Each transducer state $s_{i,j}$ maps into the respective $S_{i,j}$ score. In order to reduce complexity, we upper bound the number of incoming edges to each WFST state by a constant hyperparameter K, only creating WFST edges that yield best candidate scores to a given $S_{i,j}$ according to Eq. 1. Other potential in-

---

[4] We track a modifiable *character* $\mapsto$ *weight* map for every edge

[5] Technically, for the sake of efficiency, one may handle the matrix as a sparse one, assuming the default score of any missing (i, j) element to be $\max_k S_{k,j-1} - T$.

coming edges are ignored, if any. In Fig. 1, WFST edges that would be built at infinitely great K but rejected at $K = 2$ as not yielding competitive scores, are given in dashed line.

For each j we create a new candidate transducer state $s_{n+j,j}$ that is only "accessible" from $s_{*,j-1}$ by teleportation and apply a fixed bonus B to its score: $S_{n+j,j} = \max_k S_{k,j-1} + B$. Such a state (shown in yellow color in Fig. 1) may further be either mapped to a newly created state of the acceptor or deleted if it fails to improve the resulting alignment score. The bonus encourages initial endorsement of newly hypothesized states, which otherwise wouldn't have competitive scores.

Phase 2 - endorsement. After calculation of all $S_{i,j}$ scores, we trace paths of alignment from $S_{accepting,|y|}$ back to $S_{start,0}$. We *endorse* all WFSA edges laying at WFST-to-WFSA projections of those optimal and near-optimal paths. *Endorsement* here means increasing weight of an existing or prospective WFSA edge $k \xrightarrow{y_j} i$ by an amount of $\phi(k \xrightarrow{y_j} i)$, which is *endorsement flow* trough the WFST edge $s_{k,j} \mapsto s_{i,j-1}$ that maps back to $k \xrightarrow{y_j} i$ at some j. If multiple WFST edges map to a single $k \xrightarrow{y_j} i$ (in a case of looped path), the latter receives multiple endorsements. If an edge ought to be endorsed doesn't yet exist (which happens in case of teleportation) then we create it just in time; such a procedure lets the WFSA grow. Endorsement flow ϕ is calculated by summing outgoing edge flows at each WFST state and then distributing through the incoming edges. The final (accepting) state is assumed to receive constant endorsement flow R from outside which is then distributed to all states using a dynamic programming procedure. R plays part of learning rate. Choosing a reasonably low value for it ($0.1B$) helps one to alleviate bias caused by a particular order of sample learning.

The distribution of flow over incoming edges of a given state s is determined by the softmax:[6]

$$\phi(e) = \frac{\exp\left(-L(e)\right)}{\sum\limits_{v \in V_s} \exp\left(-L(v)\right)} \sum_{u \in U_s} \phi(u) \quad (2)$$

where $\{V_s\}$ and $\{U_s\}$ are sets of incoming and outgoing edges, respectively, for some state s; $e \in V_s$; $L(e)$ is *edge loss* which is calculated as difference between the respective $S_{i,j}$ score for s and a candidate score brought to it by e edge.

For negative training samples, we apply a similar procedure (*disendorsement*) with negative amounts of flow. The endorsement/disendorsement procedure described above keeps the sum of incoming edge weights and the sum of outgoing edge weights equal for any given WFSA state. Besides other benefits, that fact enables simple realization of unbiased sampling procedure, just as easy as random weighed selection of an edge to proceed with.

3 Experiments

3.1 Learning a WFSA from positive samples

The approach demonstrates ability to recognize basic branching and recurrent patterns in string sample sets that can be used to construct regular expressions. Fig. 2(a) illustrates an acceptor for the following set:

```
12345 , 1232345 , 123232345 ,
abfg , abcdefg , abcdecdecdefg ,
123456, 12323232323232323456
```

3.2 Contrastive learning of WFSA

We experimented with training acceptors on both positive and negative examples. At every epoch, for each sample, we applied a respective positive or negative endorsement to the edges. Although we started with a *symmetrical* approach by endorsing proportionally to the score differences, it made any graph prone to any reshaping necessary for better fitting to a training set. Therefore,

we found *asymmetrical* approach to be significantly more efficient. For false positive matches we randomly set a negative score to some of edges constituting the best path of acceptor-to-sample alignment. This leads to a permanent denial of those edges, and alternative edges will be considered in further learning process to achieve a high enough score for positive samples. Our experiments showed that the acceptor easily learns combinatorial rules like one that requires it to accept "`aaabbb, aaaccc, dddccc`" but to reject `dddbbb`". For most cases, it achieves a 100% accuracy in less than 20 epochs.

3.3 Probabilistic language modeling

We created WFSAs on the basis of small samples of vocabularies of the English (Germanic, IE) and the Kukatja (Pama-Nyungan, Australian Aboriginal) languages.[7] For the latter, we reused the linguistic resources introduced in Shcherbakov et al. (2016). We generated "novel" possible words using the acceptors and measured precision of the outputs, i.e. percentage of predicted strings that were observed in the corresponding language dictionaries. To generate a word, we traversed a path in the weighted acceptor from its accepting state back to the initial state, choosing an incoming edge and a character to generate at each state. In our experiments, the likelihood of test vocabulary word production was comparable with the one obtained in modified Kneser-Ney approach (Heafield et al., 2013) if the training corpus size is large enough. However, for very low-resource settings ($10 \ldots 500$ training words) the alignment-based approach outperforms n-gram approaches (at the best fixed n) in $\sim 1.2+$ times. Fig. 2(b) shows a graph trained for a random 300 words sampled from Kukatja dictionary. Although the automaton is quite simple, as many as 10% of its output words hit the remaining known Kukatja vocabulary that contains $\sim 9,000$ words.[8] A larger automaton may be built if we increase L hyperparameter, but this choice does not lead to precision increase. Interestingly, a model trained on the English poem "Humpty Dumpty" (only 18 words!) predicts real English words with a precision above 18% which is 1.5x greater than the best result achieved by

---

[6]Minor terms below a threshold are ignored in the implementation in order to avoid excessive growth of the WFSA and performance loss.

[7]Kukatja is an Australian Aboriginal language spoken by about 300 people in Western Desert, Australia.

[8]Since the real vocabulary size of Kukatja is not known, we may reasonably expect that the real precision is greater, even exceeding one measured for English.

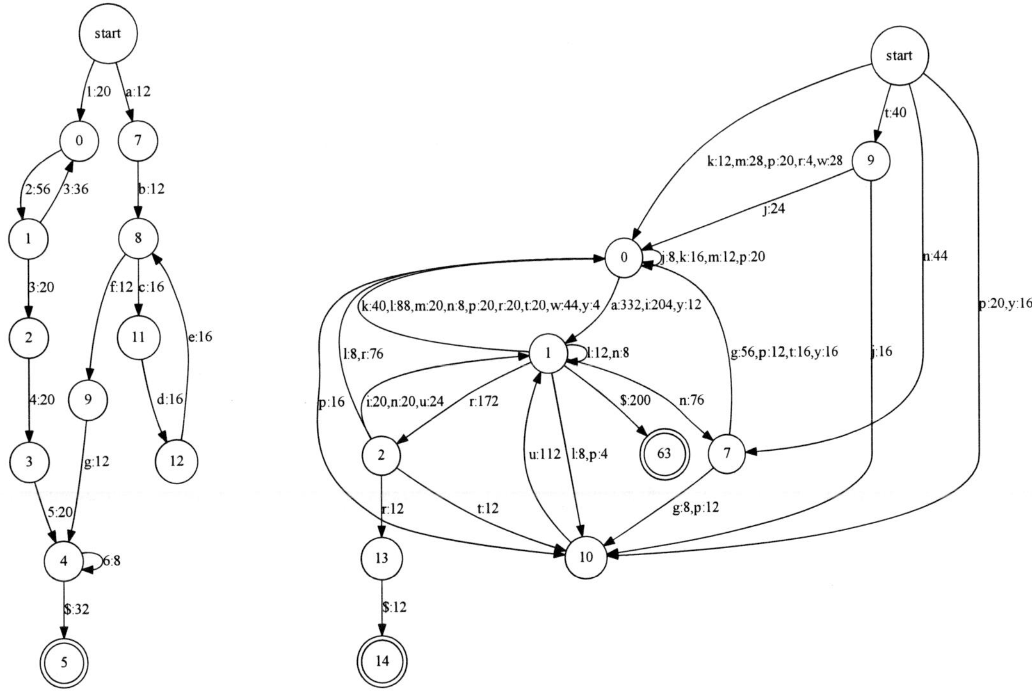

(a) Example in Subsection 3.1   (b) 90 words of Kukatja (paths with low weight edges were pruned)

Figure 2: Examples of the learned WFSA.

the modified Kneser-Ney model. Finally, since finite state machines are well-known in the domain of morphology modeling, we additionally explored this direction. We used short (100..1000 words) samples of CELEX English morphology database (Baayen et al., 1995) to train an acceptor. We observed that common prefixed and suffixes got aligned and represented compactly in a resulting automaton structure. However, overfitting to stems significantly affects its overall generalization potential that results is perplexity values comparable to ones achieved by n-gram models (Table 1).

Resource	Test set			Train set	
(language)	K=1	K=2	2gr.	K=1	2gr.
Kukatja	1.79	1.77	1.66	1.9	1.63
English	2.54	2.46	2.32	2.4	2.13
CELEX	2.69	2.66	2.55	2.28	2.18

Table 1: Per-character perplexity (natural logarithms) for acceptors trained on 300-word random subsamples at different settings of K hyperparameter. Figures for a bi-gram model ("2gr.") are given for comparison.

3.4 Learning software control flow graphs

Reverse engineering of a software control flow graph (CFG) based on samples of execution traces is another area where the proposed constructive alignment algorithm performs well. Experiments with sample programs demonstrated its ability to produce accurate estimations of CFG suitable for analysis and verification purposes.

Consider a simple abstract program example given in Figure 3. Suppose that each abstract action writes a respective character to a log upon execution. In such a way, every program run produces an execution trace string. For instance, given $num = 1, c_1 = c_2 = c_3 = false$ it will produce a `bcfefq` trace. An automaton learnt from a collection of traces obtained at different inputs is shown in Fig. 3. The result correctly back engineers the program control flow graph. It may be noted that procedure call context was properly preserved. Indeed, two different edges labelled 'f' were produced for procedure `f` calls originating from different points of code.

Speaking more generally, it may concern dis-

189

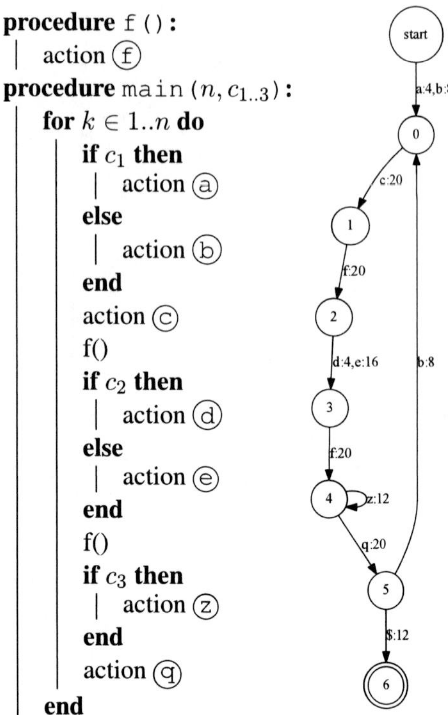

```
procedure f():
    action (f)
procedure main(n, c_{1..3}):
    for k ∈ 1..n do
        if c_1 then
            action (a)
        else
            action (b)
        end
        action (c)
        f()
        if c_2 then
            action (d)
        else
            action (e)
        end
        f()
        if c_3 then
            action (z)
        end
        action (q)
    end
```


Figure 3: A control flow graph inferred from a code sample execution traces.

covering latent states of transition graph for various natural and artificial processes (process mining).

4 Discussion

The constructive alignment algorithm demonstrated its ability to efficiently solve various kinds of tasks when training sets are too small to employ other options. This fact supports the hypothesis that most of the acceptable sequences are likely to congest within low edit distances from a relatively sparse variety of alterable common patterns.

The method also demonstrated its advantages over n-gram language modeling for "dense" training resources, still its higher complexity may challenge the advantages as a kind of "light" learning algorithms. The approach seem to be promising for regular expression construction since it addresses repetitions and branching in an intuitive, uniform way of alignment alternative trade-off.

5 Related work

Tomita (1982) made an early successful attempt to address automaton construction from sets of positive and negative samples. Their approach employs a global optimization over edge mutations. Dupont (1994) proposed a further adaptation of genetic algorithms to the task of automata creation. Formalization of a regular grammatical inference task was also a major contribution. Brauer et al. (2011) employed a feature-based approach which constructed a query answer that had the shortest possible description length. Bui and Zeng-Treitler (2014) applied the Smith–Waterman algorithm (Smith et al., 1981) over sequences of keys to align input positive samples. A dedicated "primary" sample string was aligned to all other strings and then a branching graph was produced. The authors proposed to use a machine learning classifier to derive optimally performing sequences of keys from given samples. Recently Shcherbakov (2016) proposed to build a regular expression acceptor by incrementally aligning input samples to a topologically sorted representation of the automaton. It essentially did fuzzy alignment of characters dynamically reducing character sets to character classes at corresponding score penalties.

Finally, Fernau (2009) used a simplified block-wise alignment procedure and a dedicated generalization for the loop creation. The construction process combines *generating* prospective patterns with *inferring* them from input samples.

6 Conclusion

We proposed an approach to language modeling that constructs an acceptor driven by optimization of minimum edit distance between a learning sample and a path in the automaton. We carried out a series of preliminary experiments demonstrating its effectiveness in four major areas of the algorithm's potential application, particularly, for low-resource task settings.

References

R Harald Baayen, Richard Piepenbrock, and Leon Gulikers. 1995. The celex lexical database (release 2). *Distributed by the Linguistic Data Consortium, University of Pennsylvania.*

Falk Brauer, Robert Rieger, Adrian Mocan, and Wojciech M Barczynski. 2011. Enabling information extraction by inference of regular expressions from sample entities. In *Proceedings of the 20th ACM international conference on Information and knowledge management*, pages 1285–1294. ACM.

Duy Duc An Bui and Qing Zeng-Treitler. 2014. Learning regular expressions for clinical text classification. *Journal of the American Medical Informatics Association*, 21(5):850–857.

Pierre Dupont. 1994. Regular grammatical inference from positive and negative samples by genetic search: the gig method. In *International Colloquium on Grammatical Inference*, pages 236–245. Springer.

Henning Fernau. 2009. Algorithms for learning regular expressions from positive data. *Information and Computation*, 207(4):521–541.

Kenneth Heafield, Ivan Pouzyrevsky, Jonathan H Clark, and Philipp Koehn. 2013. Scalable modified kneser-ney language model estimation. In *Proceedings of the 51st Annual Meeting of the Association for Computational Linguistics (Volume 2: Short Papers)*, volume 2, pages 690–696.

Fred Jelinek, Robert L Mercer, Lalit R Bahl, and James K Baker. 1977. Perplexitya measure of the difficulty of speech recognition tasks. *The Journal of the Acoustical Society of America*, 62(S1):S63–S63.

Grzegorz Kondrak. 2005. N-gram similarity and distance. In *International symposium on string processing and information retrieval*, pages 115–126. Springer.

Vladimir I Levenshtein. 1966. Binary codes capable of correcting deletions, insertions, and reversals. In *Soviet physics doklady*, volume 10, pages 707–710.

Ming Li and Paul Vitányi. 2013. *An introduction to Kolmogorov complexity and its applications*. Springer Science & Business Media.

James Rogers, Jeffrey Heinz, Margaret Fero, Jeremy Hurst, Dakotah Lambert, and Sean Wibel. 2013. Cognitive and sub-regular complexity. In *Formal grammar*, pages 90–108. Springer.

Andrei Shcherbakov. 2016. A branching alignment-based synthesis of regular expressions. In *AIST (Supplement)*, pages 315–328.

Andrei Shcherbakov, Ekaterina Vylomova, and Nick Thieberger. 2016. Phonotactic modeling of extremely low resource languages. In *Proceedings of the Australasian Language Technology Association Workshop 2016*, pages 84–93.

Temple F Smith, Michael S Waterman, et al. 1981. Identification of common molecular subsequences. *Journal of molecular biology*, 147(1):195–197.

Masaru Tomita. 1982. Learning of construction of finite automata from examples using hill-climbing. rr: Regular set recognizer. Technical report, Carnegie-Mellon University Pittsburgh, PA, Dept of Computer Science.

Overview of the 2019 ALTA Shared Task: Sarcasm Target Identification

Diego Mollá
Department of Computing
Macquarie University
diego.molla-aliod@mq.edu.au

Aditya Joshi
CSIRO Data61
aditya.joshi@csiro.au

Abstract

We present an overview of the 2019 ALTA shared task. This is the 10th of the series of shared tasks organised by ALTA since 2010. The task was to detect the target of sarcastic comments posted on social media. We introduce the task, describe the data and present the results of baselines and participants. This year's shared task was particularly challenging and no participating systems improved the results of our baseline.

1 Introduction

Sarcasm is a form of verbal irony that is intended to express contempt or ridicule. Sarcastic text has been understood to be a challenge to sentiment analysis because a sarcastic text may appear to be positive on the surface but is intended to be negative. Empirical results also show that sarcastic text is detrimental to sentiment analysis (Maynard and Greenwood, 2014). Applications where sentiment understanding is important are also impacted by sarcastic text. These applications include dialogue systems where the correct prediction of sentiment is important to generate appropriate responses. Towards this, computational sarcasm has gained interest in the research community.

Sentiment in a text can be understood to be composed of valence (positive/negative) and the target (Liu, 2012). The connection between sarcasm detection and sentiment analysis is the target. Sarcastic text bears a target of ridicule. It is this target that receives negative sentiment in the sarcastic sentence.

The goal of the 2019 ALTA Shared Task is the automatic detection of sarcasm targets. Section 2 describes the general aims of the ALTA shared tasks, and the specific aim of the 2019 shared task. Section 3 briefly presents related work. Section 4 describes the data. Section 5 shows the evaluation

results. Section 6 presents the results, and Section 7 concludes this paper.

2 The 2019 ALTA Shared Task

The 2019 ALTA Shared Task is the 10th of the shared tasks organised by the Australasian Language Technology Association (ALTA). Like the previous shared tasks, it targets university students with programming experience, but it is also open to graduates and professionals. The general objective of these shared tasks is to introduce interested people to the sort of problems that are the subject of active research in a field of natural language processing. Depending on the availability of data, the tasks have ranged from classic but challenging tasks to tasks linked to very hot topics of research.

There are no limitations on the size of the teams or the means that they may use to solve the problem. We provide training data but participants are free to use additional data and resources. The only constraint in the approach is that the processing must be fully automatic — there should be no human intervention.

As in past ALTA shared tasks, there are two categories: a student category and an open category.

- All the members of teams from the **student category** must be university students. The teams cannot have members that are full-time employed or that have completed a PhD.

- Any other teams fall into the **open category**.

The prize is awarded to the team that performs best on the private test set — a subset of the evaluation data for which participant scores are only revealed at the end of the evaluation period (see Section 5). The organisers reserve the right not to award the prize if no teams obtain better results than those of the published baselines.

">

Given a sarcastic text, the task of the 2019 ALTA shared task is to identify the set of words which are the target of sarcasm. The words are to be returned as a list with all words in lowercase, where all duplicates have been removed. If such set of words is not found, the system should return a fall-back label "OUTSIDE". Table 1 shows examples of sarcastic comments and the annotated targets. The assumption in each of the samples used in the shared task is that they are sarcastic.

3 Related Work

Sarcasm has been understood as a challenge for sentiment analysis (Pang et al., 2008). Over the past years, automatic detection of sarcasm gained interest. Several approaches have been reported for automatic detection of sarcasm in text, spanning rule-based approaches to deep neural architectures (Joshi et al., 2017).

Since sarcasm is a peculiar form of sentiment expression, the target of a sarcastic text bears implications on attribution of the negative sentiment to the appropriate target. For example, for an aspect-based sentiment analysis system, the sarcasm target will be the aspect towards which a negative sentiment will be assigned. Two prior papers report approaches for sarcasm target identification.

The problem of sarcasm target identification was introduced in Joshi et al. (2018). They present three kinds of methods: (a) rule-based which use heuristics to determine sarcasm targets, (b) learning-based which use a sequence labelling algorithm trained on a dataset labelled with sarcasm targets, and (c) a hybrid of the two where output of the two systems is combined to make the final predictions.

More recently, Patro et al. (2019) present a deep learning-based architecture for sarcasm target identification. The semantic representation of each word is captured in terms of its context window using a bidirectional LSTM. This semantic representation is then concatenated with features based on LIWC, NER, empathy and POS tags, to learn a classifier. They show an improvement over the prior work.

4 Data

The data used in the 2019 ALTA Shared Task consists of 950 training samples and 544 test samples. A count of the words appearing in the tar-gets of the training data (Figure 1) reveals that a large percentage of the data is labelled as OUT-SIDE, and many of the remaining words are personal and possessive pronouns, including first person "I", "we", "my". This observation led us define a baseline that focus on the presence of pronouns — see Section 6 for details of the baseline.

5 Evaluation

As in previous ALTA shared tasks, the 2019 shared task was managed and evaluated using Kaggle in Class, with the name "ALTA 2019 Challenge".[1] This allowed the participants to submit runs prior to the submission baseline for immediate feedback and compare submissions in a public leaderboard.

The test data was split into a public and a private partition. Submissions by participants were evaluated on the entire test data but only the results of the public partition were shown in the public leaderboard. Only the shared task organisers had access to the results of the private leaderboard, and these results were used for the final ranking after the submission deadline.

Each participating team was allowed to submit up to two (2) runs per day. By limiting the number of runs per day, and by not disclosing the results of the private partition, the risks of overfitting to the private test results were controlled.

The evaluation metric was the mean of the F1 score over the test samples (Formula 1),

$$
\begin{aligned}
F1 &= 2\frac{p \times r}{p+r} \\
p &= \frac{tp}{tp+fp} \\
r &= \frac{tp}{tp+fn}
\end{aligned}
\tag{1}
$$

where the true positives (tp) in a sample were the set of target words correctly identified by the system, the false positives (fp) were the set of words incorrectly identified as target, and the false negatives (fn) were the set of words from the target that were not identified by the system.

The mean F-Score is equivalent to the mean of the Sørensen-Dice coefficient (Formula 2),

$$
D(A, B) = 2\frac{|A \cap B|}{|A| + |B|}
\tag{2}
$$

where A represents the set of words of the target, and B represents the set of words of the prediction.

---

[1] https://inclass.kaggle.com/c/
alta-2019-challenge

Comment	Target
Your shirt reminds me of my 10-year-old	your shirt
This is the best film ever!	film
Oh, and I suppose the apple ate the cheese	OUTSIDE

Table 1: Examples of sarcastic comments and their targets.

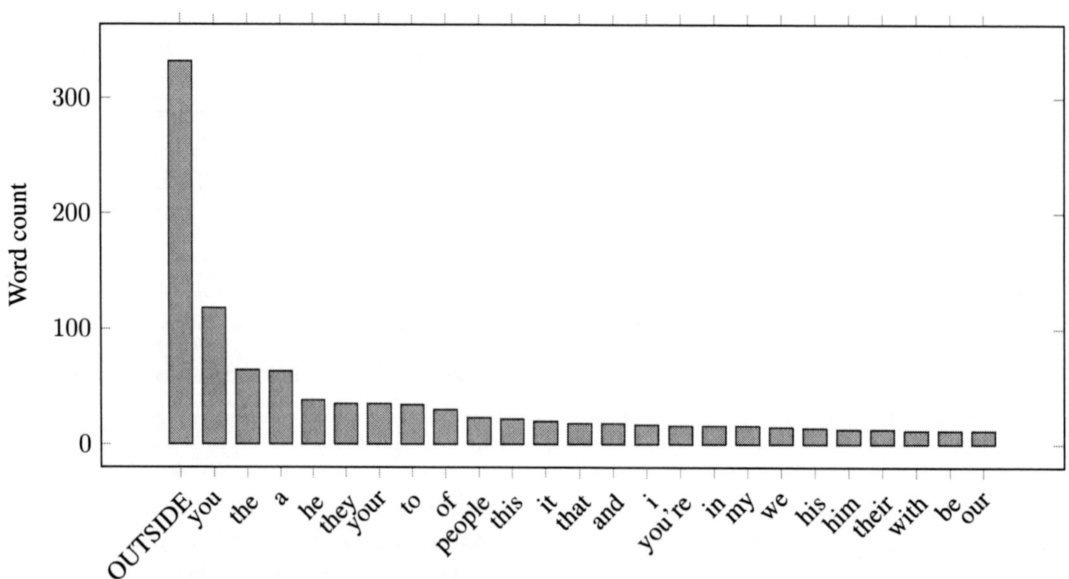

Figure 1: Most frequent words appearing in the targets of the training data.

| | | Leaderboard | |
Name	Category	Public	Private
OUTSIDE	*Baseline*	*0.36764*	***0.34926***
Powers	Student	**0.38624**	0.33311
Orangutan	Student	0.37150	0.29218
Pronouns	*Baseline*	*0.20933*	*0.22539*

Table 2: Public and private leaderboards based on runs selected for the final ranking (by default these were the runs with highest score in the public leaderboard). The figures indicate the mean F1 score.

| | | Leaderboard | |
Name	Category	Public	Private
OUTSIDE	*Baseline*	***0.36764***	*0.34926*
Powers	Student	0.34731	0.34490
Orangutan	Student	0.33242	**0.37802**
Pronouns	*Baseline*	*0.20933*	*0.22539*

Table 3: Public and private leaderboards based on runs with best scores in private leaderboard. The figures indicate the mean F1 score.

6 Results

Two baselines were made available to the participants as a Kaggle notebook.[2] The first baseline simply returned the word OUTSIDE, meaning that in all cases the target was predicted as not explicitly mentioned in the text. This baseline proved particularly hard to beat, as discussed below.

The second baseline is based on the observation that many of the target words are pronouns (Figure 1). Thus, the baseline returns all personal and possessive pronouns, and if no such pronouns are found, it returns OUTSIDE.

In total 16 teams registered for the competition — 14 in the student category and 2 in the open category. Of these, only 5 teams submitted runs, and only 2 submitted valid runs with results different from the baselines. Table 2 shows the results of the public and private leaderboard for the baselines and the 2 teams.

As Table 2 shows, no teams outperformed the OUTSIDE baseline in the private partition. A team was allowed to submit up to two runs per day, and the team received immediate feedback of the score of the public leaderboard. By default, the final submission was the one with the highest score in the public leaderboard, and the team had the option to override the default and select a different run. We observed that, even though none of the selected runs outperformed the baseline in the private leaderboard, some runs with lower scores in the public leaderboard did outperform the baseline in the private leaderboard. Table 3 shows the results of the best runs in the private leaderboard and their scores in the public leaderboard. The runs of Table 2, however, were not considered for the final ranking.

It is possible that the existence of the OUTSIDE label made the task particularly challenging. We therefore also conducted an alternative evaluation (not used for the final ranking) where we removed all samples labelled as OUTSIDE by either the annotators or the system (Table 4). The data set for this evaluation was the entire test data set combining the public and private partitions.[3] The table also includes the results of the pronoun baseline evaluated on the same data. None of the systems beat the pronoun baseline on the same test data.

The results of Table 4 use different data for each system and therefore they cannot be used for comparing the systems. Also we should note that the systems were designed assuming that some of the data would be labelled as OUTSIDE, so the results are probably not indicative of the quality of the systems.

7 Conclusions

The aim of the 2019 ALTA shared task was to detect the target of sarcastic comments. As in previous years, the task was managed as a Kaggle-in-Class competition. This year the task proved particularly challenging and none of the selected runs obtained better results than the baselines in the private leaderboard and therefore no prizes were given. The challenge will remain open in Kaggle in Class and new submissions are welcome.

Acknowledgments

The authors would like to thank Pranav Goel, University of Maryland, for his assistance with obtaining the dataset.

---

[2] https://inclass.kaggle.com/dmollaaliod/baselines-for-sarcasm-target-identification

[3] The reason behind using the combine public and private partitions was that the information about what samples belonged to each partition was not available in the Kaggle in Class platform.

Name	Category	Mean F1	*Mean F1 of Pronoun Baseline*	Test Size
Powers	Student	0.37931	*0.38152*	170
Orangutan	Student	0.35469	*0.31534*	105

Table 4: Evaluation on the test data after removing entries labelled as OUTSIDE by annotators and systems. The figures indicate the highest mean F1 score of each of the participant's submissions, which could be a different submission from the systems of Tables 2 and 3.

References

Aditya Joshi, Pushpak Bhattacharyya, and Mark J. Carman. 2017. Automatic sarcasm detection: A survey. *ACM Computing Surveys*, 50(5):73:1–73:22.

Aditya Joshi, Pranav Goel, Pushpak Bhattacharyya, and Mark J. Carman. 2018. Sarcasm target identification: Dataset and an introductory approach. In *Proceedings of the Eleventh International Conference on Language Resources and Evaluation (LREC 2018)*, Miyazaki, Japan. European Language Resources Association (ELRA).

Bing Liu. 2012. Sentiment analysis and opinion mining. *Synthesis lectures on human language technologies*, 5(1):1–167.

DG Maynard and Mark A Greenwood. 2014. Who cares about sarcastic tweets? investigating the impact of sarcasm on sentiment analysis. In *LREC 2014 Proceedings*. ELRA.

Bo Pang, Lillian Lee, et al. 2008. Opinion mining and sentiment analysis. *Foundations and Trends® in Information Retrieval*, 2(1–2):1–135.

Jasabanta Patro, Srijan Bansal, and Animesh Mukherjee. 2019. A deep-learning framework to detect sarcasm targets. In *Conference on Empirical Methods in Natural Language Processing*, Hong Kong, China. Association for Computational Linguistics.

Detecting Target of Sarcasm using Ensemble Methods

Pradeesh Parameswaran, Andrew Trotman, Veronica Liesaputra, David Eyers
Department of Computer Science
University of Otago
New Zealand
`[pradeesh,andrew,veronica,dme]@cs.otago.ac.nz`

Abstract

We describe our methods in trying to detect the target of sarcasm as part of ALTA 2019 shared task. We use combination of ensemble of classifiers and a rule-based system. Our team obtained a Dice-Sorensen Coefficient score of 0.37150, which placed 2nd in the public leaderboard. Despite no team beating the baseline score for the private dataset, we present our findings and also some of the challenges and future improvements which can be used in order to tackle the problem.

1 Introduction

We humans are complex creatures that use language as a communication tool in order to express our thoughts to one another (Sabbagh, 1999). One of the ways that we communicate with another person is through use of verbal irony. Verbal irony is defined as where the words that are being used to communicate differ from the supposed meaning (Sperber, 1984). An example of this would be from Austen (1813) Pride & Prejudice, when Darcy said to his future beloved wife, that she is *"tolerable but not handsome enough to tempt me"*.

Sarcasm is a kind of verbal irony that expresses a cynical attitude towards a person or circumstance (Gibbs, 2000). In our daily lives, sarcasm is often conveyed using the tone of our voice, and/or our facial expression, to give the signal to the other person that the person is being sarcastic (Cheang and Pell, 2008). Recently, with the growth of social media many researchers have embarked on various ways of detecting sarcasm automatically. Most of their work were focused on detecting sarcasm on Twitter and on online reviews (Bamman and Smith, 2015; Rajadesingan et al., 2015; Amir et al., 2016).

Prior works treated this problem as a binary text classification problem. To the best of our knowledge, there is little work that has been done in the realm of identifying the target of sarcasm in sarcastic text. The earliest work in this domain was (Joshi et al., 2019). Identifying the target would help in certain Natural Language Processing (NLP) tasks such as in the realm of improving cyberbully detection by helping to identify the target of ridicule (Raisi and Huang, 2016). It has also sparked the organisers at the Australasian Language Technology Association (ALTA) to organise a shared challenge task to tackle the problem.

We employed a 2-phase approach to attempt to solve this task. In our *first phase*, we employed an ensemble of classifiers along with a meta-classifier to classify sarcasm targets which are marked as *"OUTSIDE"*. First, we built a Support Vector Machine (SVM) using word embedding to classify the text, followed by the use of a Logistic Classifier. Finally, we used a Linear Classifier to combine the results of the two classifiers. In the *second phase* of our system, we used a rule-based approach to extract the target sarcasm words from text that are marked as *"NOT OUTSIDE"*. With this proposed system, we achieved 2nd place in the public leader board of the ALTA competition. We describe our method in details in the methodology section. Next, we present our results along with some of the challenges and recommendations in improving the task. We end our paper with our plans for future work.

2 Dataset

The dataset[1] provided by the organizers of the ALTA 2019 shared task consists a of collection of sarcastic texts. There are 950 sarcastic texts for training and 544 for testing. The training dataset comes with the sarcastic text (text), along with the set of words which are the target of sarcasm (tar-

---

[1] `https://www.kaggle.com/c/alta-2019-challenge/data`

Features	Values
Number of Outsides	332
Number of Inside	618
Average Sentence Length	25.3
Average Sarcasm Target Length	3.1
Number of Subreddits	123

Table 1: Distribution and Pattern of Training Data

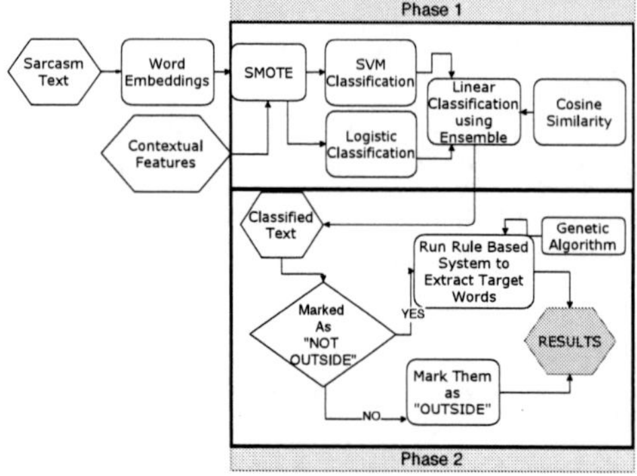

Figure 1: System Architecture

get). If the target of sarcasm is not in the text, it is marked as "*OUTSIDE*". Our task was to predict the target of the sarcasm.

We decided to analyse the training data further to understand the distribution and the pattern of the dataset. Table 1 describes the pattern. We observed that several instances of ("*NOT OUT-SIDE*") have 14–19 sarcasm targets (which is half of the sentences) and other times they only have one sarcasm target. We found there to be no correlation between the sentence length and the number of sarcasm targets.

3 Methodology

We employed a 2-phase approach to tackle this problem. In the first phase, we used a series of classifiers, followed by a rule-based system in the second phase. In this section, we describe our method in detail, along with the steps that we performed. The complete system architecture is shown in Figure 1. We have also made our system's source code publicly available on GitHub.[2]

3.1 Class Imbalance

We observed that the ratio of "*OUTSIDE*" to "*NOT OUTSIDE*" in our training data set is not balanced. In order to improve our classifier's performance, we used SMOTE (Dal Pozzolo et al., 2002) to balance our dataset. SMOTE achieves this by artificially over-sampling the dataset. This has been demonstrated to improve the performance of classifiers when the dataset is small (Luengo et al., 2011).

3.2 Word Embedding

We used pre-trained model of Universal Sentence Encoding (USE) (Cer et al., 2018) to convert the text into a high-dimensional vector representation. USE is known to work well on noisy social media data. We experimented with stemming in our data to increase its accuracy, however it negatively impacted our results.

3.3 Contextual Features

We observed that our dataset was obtained from Khodak et al. (2019)'s Reddit[3] Corpus where there were both sarcastic and non-sarcastic texts present, but there was no information about the target of sarcasm. We were inspired by Wallace et al. (2014)'s work that humans require context when it comes to understanding sarcasm. In their work, when annotators were asked to classify sarcastic comments, on average 30% of the comments required annotators to ask for additional context such as the previous comment before they were able to decide. We hypothesized that we can improve our classifier's performance by adding additional context extracted from Khodak et al. (2019)'s corpus to our original dataset.

We converted each Subreddit label found in Khodak et al. (2019)'s dataset into categorical data values using one-hot encoding. For categories that were not present in both training and testing data, we grouped them together into a category known as "Others". We have also extracted the number of likes and dislikes on each post. They are continuous features, we used Z-Score normalization to improve our classifier's performance (Jayalak-shmi and Santhakumaran, 2011)

$$x' = \frac{x_1 - \mu_1}{\sigma_1} \tag{1}$$

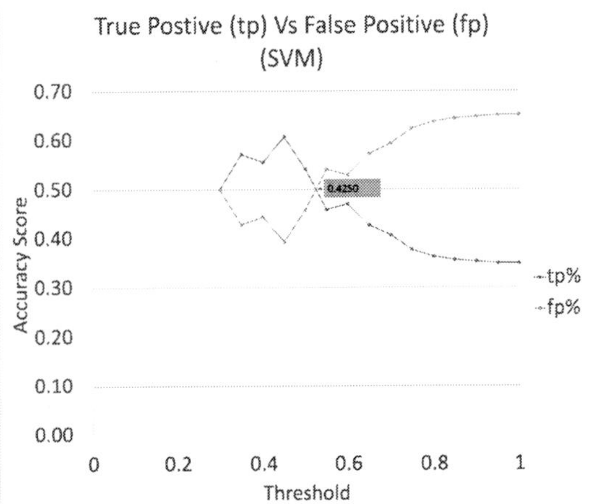

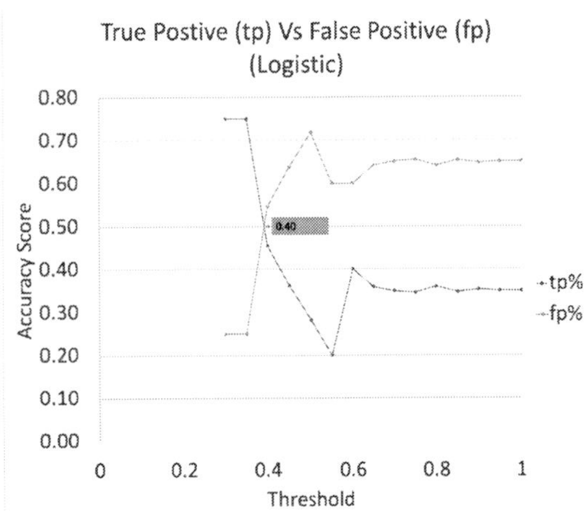

Figure 2: Recall Score against Threshold for SVM Classifier

Figure 3: Recall Score against Threshold for Logistic Classifier

where x_1 is the value of the feature, μ_1 is the mean value of the feature in training data and σ_1 is the standard deviation for the feature in the training data.

3.4 Phase 1

In our first phase, we used a Support Vector Machine (SVM) with word embedding from USE as its input for our SVM Classifier. SVM has been known to perform very well on high dimensional input vectors (Goudjil et al., 2018). We experimented with other classifiers such as Logistic Regression and Random Forest but it did not yield good results. For our SVM Classifier, we set the classification's threshold value to be 0.425 and above in order for the text to be classified as *"OUTSIDE"*. This was done to minimize the false positives. Figure 2 shows the various thresholds and the accuracy score regarding true positive (TP) and false positives (FP).

The additional data features that we have extracted from Khodak et al. (2019)'s corpus are used as input vectors for our logistic classifier. Just like our SVM Classifier, we fine-tuned our logistic classifier's threshold value to be 0.40 and above for a text to be classified as *"OUTSIDE"*. Figure 3 shows the performance of the classifier. The values for both of the classifiers were obtained by performing 3-fold cross-validation.

We introduced cosine similarity to further strengthen the meta-classifier's performance. It is calculated by using the word embedding we obtained earlier. If we obtain a similarity score of 0.70 or higher, we assign a score of 1 otherwise a

Rules	Rule No
R1	Pronouns & pronominal adjectives
R2	Named entities
R3	Object of a positive sentiment verb
R4	Phrase on negative side of verb
R5	Gerund & infinitive verb phrases
R6	Nouns after positive sentiment adjective
R7	Subject of interrogative sentences
R8	Subjects of comparisons (similes)
R9	Demonstrative adjective-noun pairs

Table 2: Definition of the Rules for the Rule-based Component within the Proposed System

score of 0.

Finally for our meta classifier, we used a Linear Classification (Džeroski and Ženko, 2004).

We used the probability scores from both of the classifiers and cosine similarity as input vectors into the classifier. We did not fine-tune the linear classifier and used the default value of 0.5 and above to classify text as *"OUTSIDE"*.

3.5 Phase 2

In our second phase, we used the rule-based system to extract the target of sarcasm from the texts. The rules that we used are described in Table 2, and adopted from (Joshi et al., 2019). We implemented the rules using NLTK Toolkit.[4]

We applied some minor adjustments to R1 and R2 that increased the performance 4.49% and 39.68% respectively, over the original rules, as described below.

For R1, we included the subject of each pronoun. For example in the training set one of the

---

[4] https://www.nltk.org/

Rules	DSC Score
R1 (Without Subject)	0.2696
R1 (With Subject)	0.2817
R2 (Without Truecase)	0.0814
R2 (With Truecase)	0.1137
R3	0.0266
R4	0.0800
R5	0.1094
R6	0.0598
R7	0.0766
R8	0.0105
R9	0.0196

Table 3: Performance of Rules Score

target of sarcasm was identified as *"you,op"*.[5] The original rule set would only identify *"you"*.

As for R2, in order to get the Named Entities (NE) recognized, we used Truecasing (Lita et al., 2003). This helped to correct the case of our noisy data which further improved NE recognition. Lowering all the cases does not work as it presents a problem in distinguishing named entities from nouns. For example, the word *"apple"* may be interpreted as the fruit and not the company. However due to time constrains, we did not take a look at other rules in-depth but intend to do so as future work.

In order to determine how effective each rule was, we ran the rules one by one over the training data after excluding all the text which were marked as *"OUTSIDE"*. We used Dice-Sorensen Coefficient (DSC) in order to measure the performance.

$$D(A, B) = 2 \times \frac{A \cap B}{|A| + |B|} \qquad (2)$$

where A are predicted words and B are actual words.

Table 3 shows the individual performance for each rule. In order to determine which rules were likely to give us the high scores, we implemented a genetic algorithm to obtain weights for each of the rules. We ran our genetic algorithm across 500 generations with 80% probability of mutation. Figure 4 shows the performance of our genetic algorithm. The algorithm assigned a good weighting scores for R1, R2, R3, and R5 respectively. For the other rules, negative weighting scores were given.

4 Results

We investigated the results and the behavior of the system by submitting our runs to the competition.

System	Public Score	Private Score
Baseline (OUTSIDE)	0.36764	**0.34926**
Baseline (Pronoun)	0.20933	0.22539
SVM (Stemming) + Rules	0.30203	0.26553
SVM + Rules	0.35983	0.30777
Logistic + Rules	0.11397	0.12867
Ensemble + Rules	0.36889	0.30027
Ensemble + Tuned Rules	**0.37150**	0.29134

Table 4: System Evaluation

Kaggle is used as the platform for submission of runs. In Kaggle, the training data provided to us by ALTA organizers is split into public (public leaderboard) and private (private leaderboard). The private portion serves as a validation portion in order for the organizers to determine the effectiveness of the system. The scores are evaluated by using DSC Score (Equation 2). We summarise and present our results in Table 4.

4.1 Discussion

The objective set by the organizers at ALTA was to beat the two baselines provided by them. The first baseline always predicted *"OUTSIDE"*. The second one always predicted the pronouns from the text as the target for the *"NOT OUTSIDE"* text. Our system beat both baselines for the public leaderboard, but we did not manage to beat the baseline for private score. In fact, no teams beat the scores in the private baseline. Prior to proposing our final system, we have built and evaluated various different systems which included just using one classifier which is either SVM or Logistic Regression and the rule-based system. Then we used the ensemble of classifiers. We believe that our ensemble classifiers performed poorly on the

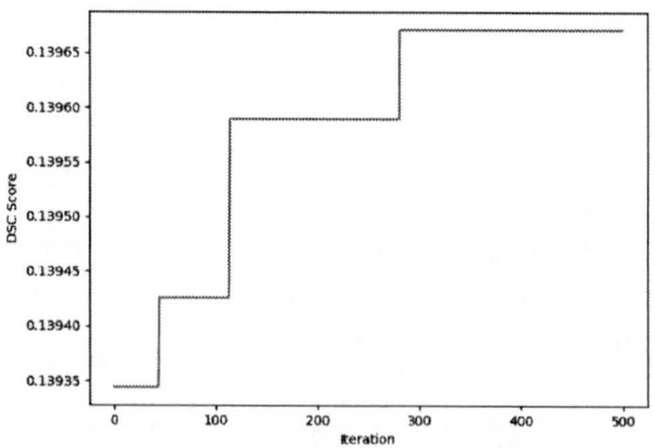

Figure 4: Performance of genetic algorithm across 500 generations

Predicted Words	DSC Score
we die out	0.5454
Entire Sentence	0.4705
sun gonna destroy us we die	0.2828
sun die	0.2000

Table 5: DSC Scores

private score as it might have been biased to the public data. On the other hand, just using the additional features alone to classify yielded poor results as our system could not identify *"OUTSIDE"* accurately.

This prompted us to look deeper into the problem and offering several ways on how it can be addressed. We discuss this in subsection 4.2 and 4.3.

4.2 Evaluation Metric

Based on equation 2, we can deduce that the score for predicting *"OUTSIDE"* would be easier to obtain compared to predicting the target of sarcasm words correctly which may be trickier. In order to demonstrate our point, let us look at the following two examples which we took from training data. The target of sarcasm given by the judges are highlighted in bold

> *"Oh man and while we are at it we can make it so when the boss dies you can hand pick the piece of gear you want!."* (*"OUTSIDE"*)

> *"The sun is gonna destroy us in a few billion years anyways, so why does it matter if* **we die out in the next few centuries?**.*"*

In the first example the target of sarcasm is outside. DSC score would yield a perfect score of 1 if it predicted properly. In the second example, it is very hard to get a perfect DSC of 1. In Table 5, we show how the score varies depending on the number of words predicted correctly, and length of the predicted words. We can clearly see that it is very challenging to get a very high score even when we can predict all of the relevant targets.

One way of addressing the performance of the system is to use accuracy score as an additional metric to determine the effectiveness of the system. This would also help to gauge the capacity of the systems identifying true positives (TP) and true negatives (TN).

4.3 Human Perspective & Relevance Judgement

In their works, (Joshi et al., 2016) have highlighted some of the difficulties that annotators face in identifying sarcasm and irony. From our failure-analysis, we have determined that humans' annotations can be inconsistent. We show two of the examples from the training dataset, with the target of sarcasm annotated by the judges in bold.

> *"OP is just some white knight who always comes to the aid of the female, if you knew her you'd know how much of a whore she is.."*

> *"$10 OP wants to do something crazy with trading cards and is just trying to get you all to sell them to **him** on the cheap"*

In the first example, we can clearly make the association that *"you"* from the first example refers to *"OP"* but only *"OP"* is identified as the target of sarcasm. However, in the second example, both the words *"OP,him"* are identified as the target of sarcasm by the judges. This shows to us that even in sentences which are constructed in a similar manner, the way judges identify the target of sarcasm differs from one person to another.

In order to address this gap, we propose that additional assessments should be conducted. For example, in the Text Retrieval Conference (TREC), participants submit their assessments and let the human annotators decide if the documents retrieved by the search engines were relevant to the given queries (Hawking et al., 1999). We believe that adopting this approach for this task instead of the current approach would help to address the shortcomings of relying entirely on human annotators.

5 Conclusion and Future Work

We presented an approach to identify the target of sarcasm. We competed in the ALTA 2019 Competition under the team name of *"orangutan"*. Our best-performing system used an ensemble of classifiers. Despite achieving a score of 0.37150 and beating the baselines in the public portion within Kaggle, we did not manage to beat the baseline in the private dataset.

We believe that there is still much work to be done in this domain. As part of future work we are planning to tackle this problem in several ways, including:

- Improving our classifier;

- Further improving the rule-based system; and

- Experimenting with deep learning models.

Acknowledgments

Many thanks to Kat Lilly, Dr.Diego Moll-Aliod for their time in proofreading this paper. We would also like to thank the ALTA organizers for their support.

References

Silvio Amir, Byron C. Wallace, Hao Lyu, Paula Carvalho, and Mario J. Silva. 2016. Modelling Context with User Embeddings for Sarcasm Detection in Social Media. In *Proceedings of the 20th SIGNLL Conference on Computational Natural Language Learning (CoNLL)*, pages 167–177.

Jane Austen. 1813. *Pride and Prejudice*. Routledge/Thoemmes, London.

David Bamman and Noah A. Smith. 2015. Contextualized sarcasm detection on twitter. *Proceedings of the 9th International Conference on Web and Social Media, ICWSM 2015*, pages 574–577.

Daniel Cer, Yinfei Yang, Sheng-yi Kong, Nan Hua, Nicole Limtiaco, Rhomni St. John, Noah Constant, Mario Guajardo-Cespedes, Steve Yuan, Chris Tar, Yun-Hsuan Sung, Brian Strope, and Ray Kurzweil. 2018. Universal Sentence Encoder. *Empirical Methods in Natural Language Processing*.

Henry S. Cheang and Marc D. Pell. 2008. The sound of sarcasm. *Speech Communication*, 50(5):366–381.

A. Dal Pozzolo, O. Caelen, and G. Bontempi. 2002. Comparison of balancing techniques for unbalanced datasets. *Journal of Artificial Intelligence Research 16*, 16(1):732–735.

Saso Džeroski and Bernard Ženko. 2004. Is combining classifiers with stacking better than selecting the best one? *Machine Learning*, 54(3):255–273.

Raymond W Gibbs. 2000. Metaphor and Symbol Irony in Talk Among Friends Irony in Talk Among Friends. *Metaphor and Symbol*, 15(2):1–2.

Mohamed Goudjil, Mouloud Koudil, Mouldi Bedda, and Noureddine Ghoggali. 2018. A Novel Active Learning Method Using SVM for Text Classification. *International Journal of Automation and Computing*, 15(3):290–298.

David Hawking, Nick Craswell, and Paul Thistlewaite. 1999. Overview of TREC-7 Very Large Collection Track. In *NIST Special Publication 500-242: The Seventh Text REtrieval Conference (TREC 7)*, pages 1–13.

T. Jayalakshmi and A. Santhakumaran. 2011. Statistical Normalization and Back Propagationfor Classification. *International Journal of Computer Theory and Engineering*, 3(1):89–93.

Aditya Joshi, Pranav Goel, Pushpak Bhattacharyya, and Mark J. Carman. 2019. Sarcasm target identification: Dataset and an introductory approach. *LREC 2018 - 11th International Conference on Language Resources and Evaluation*, (2008):2676–2683.

Aditya Joshi, Vaibhav Tripathi, Pushpak Bhattacharyya, Mark Carman, Meghna Singh, Jaya Saraswati, and Rajita Shukla. 2016. How Challenging is Sarcasm versus Irony Classification?: A Study With a Dataset from {E}nglish Literature. In *Proceedings of the Australasian Language Technology Association Workshop 2016*, pages 123–127.

Mikhail Khodak, Nikunj Saunshi, and Kiran Vodrahalli. 2019. A large self-annotated corpus for sarcasm. *LREC 2018 - 11th International Conference on Language Resources and Evaluation*, pages 641–646.

Lucian Vlad Lita, I B M T J Watson, and I B M T J Watson. 2003. tRuEcasIng. In *Proceedings of the 41st Annual Meeting on Association for Computational Linguistics - Volume 1*, pages 152–159.

Julián Luengo, Alberto Fernández, Salvador García, and Francisco Herrera. 2011. Addressing data complexity for imbalanced data sets: Analysis of SMOTE-based oversampling and evolutionary undersampling. *Soft Computing*, 15(10):1909–1936.

Elaheh Raisi and Bert Huang. 2016. Cyberbullying Identification Using Participant-Vocabulary Consistency. In *ICML Workshop on #Data4Good: Machine Learning in Social Good Applications*, pages 46–50, New York.

Ashwin Rajadesingan, Reza Zafarani, and Huan Liu. 2015. Sarcasm Detection on Twitter. In *WSDM '15: Proceedings of the Eight ACM International Conference on Web Search and Data Mining*, pages 97–106.

Mark A. Sabbagh. 1999. Communicative intentions and language: Evidence from right-hemisphere damage and autism. *Brain and Language*, 70(1):29–69.

Dan Sperber. 1984. Verbal irony: Pretense or echoic mention? *Journal of Experimental Psychology: General*, 113(1):130–136.

Byron C. Wallace, Do Kook Choe, Laura Kertz, and
Eugene Charniak. 2014. Humans require context to
infer ironic intent (so computers probably do, too).
In *52nd Annual Meeting of the Association for Computational Linguistics, ACL 2014 - Proceedings of
the Conference*, volume 2, pages 512–516.